Vanished by the Danube

Vanished by the Danube

Peace, War, Revolution, and Flight to the West

CHARLES FARKAS

Introduction by
Margaret McMullan

excelsior editions
State University of New York Press
Albany, New York

Cover image: Liberty Bridge, Budapest, 1935. Courtesy www.fortepan.hu

Published by State University of New York Press, Albany

Excelsior Editions is an imprint of State University of New York Press

For information, contact State University of New York Press, Albany, NY
www.sunypress.edu

Production by Eileen Nizer
Marketing by Kate McDonnell

Library of Congress Cataloging-in-Publication Data

Library of Congress Control Number: 2013936040

10 9 8 7 6 5 4 3 2 1

An honest tale speeds best plainly told.

—Shakespeare, *Richard II*

Contents

Prologue

During the Second World War, twentieth-century "Central European" culture, society, morality, personal integrity, wealth, traditions, and chivalry vanished. Cities such as Budapest, whose grandeur embraced, indeed spanned, the Danube River, were forever changed. *Vanished by the Danube* bears witness to historical developments from the interwar years to the Second World War and the Hungarian Revolution.

This memoir encompasses my life in Hungary from 1925 to 1956 and traces back to my ancestors, including "the first statesman" of Europe, Prince Charles de Ligne; Irish Red Hugh O'Donnell, the "Fighting Prince of Donegal"; and my great grandfather Karoly Farkas, who in 1848 served in Louis Kossuth's revolutionary cabinet.

This book describes life as it was for upper- and middle-class Hungarians during the years between the two world wars, under German occupation and Hungarian Nazi oppression. It bears witness to the wretchedness of Budapest under siege—people gathering in the streets over fresh horse carcasses, and the oppressive grind of life in basement shelters.

I recount how the Soviet Army visited its rampage upon the people—gang rapes, random abductions, enslavement, and traumas. I describe the 1948 government takeover by the Communists.

The closing chapters cover the Hungarian Revolution of 1956 and my escape to the West, ending with our disembarkation from the U.S.S.N. *Marine Carp* in Brooklyn, New York.

Vanished by the Danube is a string of reminiscences about growing up, falling in love, and fighting for survival. It describes life during the turbulence of the last century. It is intended to serve as a kind of cultural anthropological study, capturing a time, a place, a way of life along one strip of the Danube that might have vanished from the historical record, if not for accounts like this one.

Charles Farkas
Chappaqua, New York, 2013

Introduction

I first met Charles Farkas in New York at my cousin Peter de Jánosi's memorial service at The New School. Peter was originally from Pécs, Hungary, and lived in New York near his friend Charles Farkas. Both men were involved in Hungarian American organizations, among their many other interests. Charles and I were both there to say a few words about Peter, and, in this way, Charles and I found out about each other. I learned from Charles that he and Peter had coffee at least once a week to talk about retirement, the old days, the old ways, and their writing projects. Charles learned about me when I spoke about my time in Hungary on a Fulbright, teaching students at the University of Pécs about creative writing and literature from the American South. I was also there to research my mother's Hungarian family, many of whom died in the Hungarian Holocaust at the end of the Second World War.

I was born in Newton, Mississippi, and I have discovered that Hungarians are very much like us from the American South. When Southerners find other Southerners, we feel a kinship, especially when we are in the North. More likely than not, we probably *are* kin. Likewise, Hungarians in America are magnetically inclined to find one another, perhaps because they are away from "home." I consider myself an adopted Hungarian now, and even if we Hungarian Americans are not exactly kin, then at least the stories we tell and retell about our time in Hungary or our family in "the old country" find parallel lines. In addition, like American Southerners, Hungarians have experience with occupiers and with loss.

Mississippians merely lost to the North. Hungarians lost to the Turks, to the Hapsburgs, to the Germans, and to the Russians.

Most Hungarians, at some time, have lost homes, land, cherished heirlooms, and loved ones. Some have lost their country, for they feel they neither could nor would ever go back to a country that betrayed them.

Charles Farkas has written his life story not as a Hungarian, but as a Hungarian American, which is to say that his memoir *Vanished by the Danube* is a kind of farewell to all that he and his family lost, but he is neither bitter nor mournful. In the end, Farkas looks ahead to his new world and to his new American future.

In many ways the immigration story is the most American story because we see the narrator struggling against all odds to overcome his terrible, undemocratic situation, only to have to start all over again in a new land with a new language. He has only the clothes on his back, his strength, his wits, his know-how, and his can-do attitude. This is Charles Farkas's story.

We tour through Farkas's childhood memories and stories—growing up in Hungary, visiting towns and relatives along the Danube, playing cowboys and Indians, and always, lurking in the background, is the inevitable violence of history headed their way. It's difficult not to linger in this time, on these pages, before occupations and wars, in remote castles in the Hungarian countryside in a world when the solution to a band of robbers is simply to welcome them into your castle and serve them dinner.

Vanished by the Danube reads like a novel as we get more and more acquainted with Charles Farkas's father, who works at the Hungarian Broadcasting Corporation, his mother, a talented and energetic painter, Uncle Rory, who runs the family estate and vineyard, the grandmother, Countess Eveline O'Donnell, the last of the Hungarian O'Donnells, their cooks Rózsi and Ilonka, and the Mardi Gras–like parade of artistic friends, famous writers, journalists, scholars, and painters.

Farkas has wonderful stories and anecdotes such as one about the "spiritualists" coming to the family's country estate to exorcise an apparent ghost out of the house, conducting their séance only after they've had their fill of goulash. In fact, most of the real magic takes place at Uncle Rory's house and vineyard at Veresegyház.

The food alone—the iced coffee and sherbet, the dumplings stuffed with plums or cottage cheese, *krumplinudli*, gooseberry soup, his beloved noodles with poppy seeds—bookends Farkas's idyllic childhood memories both in the country and in the city of Budapest.

Even when World War II breaks out in September 1939, the Farkas world does not yet crumble, not altogether. They are Christian after all, and still relatively safe. Hungary at this point has been able to keep the war at arm's length.

Just out of high school, Charles and his friend Gyuri bicycle from Budapest to Transylvania, and then Charles is recruited to work in a Labor Battalion. In 1943, he enrolls in law school at Péter Pázmány University in Budapest. Eventually, his university suspends classes because of the encroaching war, and on March 19, 1944, when Hitler and Nazi Germany occupy Hungary their lives change. The betrayals and horrors only just begin to circle the family. Charles learns that the Arrow Cross murdered his former teacher, a Jew, because his other teachers acted as Nazi informers.

And there is the summer before the siege. Every Hungarian has this last gasp of a memory, right before everything changed. Charles is nineteen years old, studying for exams, and his world continues to remain small and enchanting. We get one last lovely glimpse of a postcard reality that would soon be over: grandmothers sitting under olive trees crocheting, a cook picking cabbages and tomatoes, an aunt sitting at a table writing letters, the beautiful peasant girls with their lovely bare arms and their many-colored skirts.

That March and April, the last Jews in German-occupied Europe are obliged to sew the yellow Star of David onto their clothing, marking them, of course, for possible extinction. Interactions with non-Jews are restricted, if allowed at all. The Farkas family does its part to protect their Jewish friends and employees: they hide a Jewish man in their apiary; his Aunt Blanka shelters three Jewish girlfriends in her apartment on Böszörményi Avenue in Budapest; the father keeps two dozen Jewish employees on the Radio Broadcasting Corporation payroll for as long as he is able. But in May 1944, the deportation of the Jews begins. More than 450,000 Jews, 70 percent of the Jews of greater Hungary are deported, murdered, or die under German occupation. More than half the Jews are annihilated.

In the early summer of 1944, Charles is conscripted and sent to Transylvania for manual labor. On his way there, at the train station, Charles sees a train wagon packed with between seven and eight thousand people, "either Russian prisoners of war or Jewish deportees." There are three to four times more people on this cattle car than the train Charles is on. The other train wagons are locked up, the people inside half-naked in order to relieve themselves of the stifling heat. Unspoken and unbidden, Farkas and his friends throw them loaves of bread, which are able to fall into the openings between the barbed wires on top of the wagons. I would like to think that one of those loaves of bread fell into the hands of one of my family members.

Everyone who survived this horrific time in our world history has a story. This doesn't make their stories less important, but more so. Such eyewitness accounts are ever more important as this generation of survivors disappears, and, frankly, these painful snapshots bear further witness and serve as proof against any Holocaust deniers.

Farkas is unsparing in his memories. During these harsh winters of the war years, schools close because there is no fuel to heat them. Most of the food and manufactured goods in Hungary are shipped to Germany. There is flooding in parts of the country. Clothing and footwear are rationed. We learn the tricks some use to stay alive: one of Charles's friends, for instance, lives on smoked horse tongues and a jar of candied cherries. There is one heartbreaking letter, which Charles Farkas includes here, from Artúr Elek, a Jewish friend of the family, forced to remain hidden in a one-room apartment on Mátrai Street before the siege in Budapest. He writes, "Life is beautiful, regardless of one's destiny. Now that I have re-read your letters, I have re-lived your experiences: the pleasures of meadows and villages alike. I am glad that you are well, and I hope that you will stay well forever, never falling into despair or brooding."

Books, especially memoirs, need not have a message, but if this one did, it would mirror Artúr Elek's thoughts in his letter to the Farkas family. *Vanished by the Danube* is Charles Farkas's letter to us. Never fall into despair or brooding. We relive Charles Farkas's experiences, both good and horrific. During the siege he digs graves for two young girls, one decapitated, while a carpenter builds coffins out of dresser drawers. He comes upon a pile of uniforms only to discover they are infested with lice. In this nightmare landscape, where everywhere the Russians are raping and pillaging, where the streets of Budapest are littered with the corpses of horses, overturned automobiles, bombshell craters, crumbling walls, and dead civilians, Farkas never despairs, not completely—even during the most horrendous circumstances. So, it follows that if he does not, we cannot allow ourselves to do so either.

The Charles Farkas of today can take comfort in the fact that he belonged to a family who never compromised themselves. Even under the very worst circumstances, his father remains heroic, his mother saintly, and the young Charles Farkas is ever the dutiful, game, loyal son and friend.

Reading this memoir, I couldn't help but feel closer to my cousin Peter, to Hungary, and to all our lost ancestors. In *Vanished by the Danube*, Charles Farkas opens the windows and doors of his life, invites us in, gives us a tour, and allows us to walk freely among his rooms.

One of my favorite moments in these pages is when Charles and his best friend are on the boat headed toward the United States. A military orchestra strikes up to play the Hungarian anthem. The musicians are black, a novelty for the Hungarians. They play the anthem in a bluesy way. Charles regrets that no one took a picture.

But of course he did, for the scene is perfectly photographed here in these pages.

Statisticians write that this Hungarian exodus surpassed any other which came before. Never in the history of the United States have so many people from one ethnic group arrived at the same time, with such high intellectual status and education.

Most of them had had to leave. Charles's presence at the 1956 storming of the Radio in Budapest made remaining in Hungary impossible. If he had stayed, Farkas would have almost certainly been one of those imprisoned, or worse, one of those who disappeared.

This is the story of a lost world, but this is also a story about survival. This is the story of a boy who dressed up with a cowboy hat and a Smith & Wesson hoisted into his belt, a boy who dreamed of becoming a cowboy, and whose dreams came true, for this boy became a young man, and this young man did go west—as far west as Brooklyn, New York.

Margaret McMullan
Melvin M. Peterson Endowed Chair in Literature and Writing
University of Evansville, Evansville, Indiana
Fulbright Professor, University of Pécs, Pécs, Hungary, 2010

1

Social Life in the Budapest Cafés
in the 1920s and the Farkas Family Line

In 1925, winter arrived early in Budapest. At the end of November the snow fell briskly in large flakes, making the sidewalks slippery. My father and my mother were heading home from the hospital. My father held my mother's arm firmly; walking ahead of them was our young maid with a small bundle in her arms. My father worried that the maid would slip and fall on the frosty pavement, but my mother reassured him, "She's doing just fine." The bundle the maid was carrying was me, and my parents were on their way home from the Baross Street Hospital where I had been born only a few days earlier, on November 26. That's how my life began—with some anxiety on my father's part.

On the day we left the hospital, my parents, perpetually short on money, were unable to afford a cab. They had a tendency to overspend, so they usually ended up taking a streetcar or a bus.

My mother was an artist and a journalist. When she was about twenty years old, she met the preeminent painter Béla Iványi-Grünwald and ended up working as his apprentice, eventually becoming his friend and associate. My mother's creativity was not limited to painting. During a journalistic career spanning two decades she contributed to several daily papers. She was a reporter for *Ujság* (*The News*), and later had regular columns in *Esti Ujság* (*The Evening News*) and *Függetlenség* (*Independence*), writing narratives on everyday topics, humorous anecdotes, or informative commentaries on women's fashion. She covered parliamentary proceedings as a reporter for *Ujság* and her sketches of members of parliament accompanied her

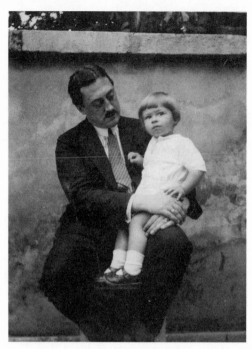

My father and me

articles. Mother had a phenomenal memory, she fought against injustices, and as a proud daughter of a chief justice she never told a lie.

My father was a professional writer and the editor of the Hungarian Radio's flagship magazine, *Rádió Élet* (*Radio Life*).

During their courtship, before I was born, my parents lived a very nocturnal Budapest lifestyle, spending much of it in cafés. Half of Budapest's artists and creative types spent most of their time there. The writers, the painters, the actors had their breakfasts, and their dinners, in coffeehouses. They read the newspapers there and when they couldn't pay the check, borrowed money from the headwaiter. They used each other as sounding boards, cross-fertilizing minds.

Sometime in 1935, Hally Huberman, the Dutch violinist, came to visit my parents and they asked him what attraction he would like to see. He chose the *Café Ostende* because it was there that an orchestra of one hundred fifteen-year-old gypsy boys played violins in bright red uniforms.

Rádió Élet visiting Béla Iványi-Grünwald on December 17, 1928

My mother, Rózsi Dabis, in her studio

Composer Béla Bartók lecturing in the Radio's new studio on January 15, 1934

My parents' wedding photo

Even after my parents got married, they kept frequenting the coffee houses.

They came home late every night, which was an embarrassment to them because they had to wake the concierge up to get in. This cost them an added expense, since he expected to be tipped for this service. One night, after leaving the coffee house, they realized that they had no money for the superintendent to let them in. Along their way on the long walk home, they went into each telephone booth looking for coins that had fallen to the ground through the wooden grates that served as floor mats and separated slush and rainwater from shoes. What most people did not realize was that the grate could be lifted and fallen coins retrieved from under it. Their resourcefulness paid off so well that by the time my parents reached their building they had more than enough coins to tip the concierge.

Farkas family, 1926

Portrait of my grandmother, Eveline O'Donnell

Portrait of my mother, Rózsi Dabis (self-portrait)

Portrait of my father, Jenő Farkas

My mother, who wrote a short sketch each week for the daily paper, once asked "Why do people from Pest go to cafés?" in one of her columns. Her answer was:

The stress of life, the noise, the lost connection to nature makes the city dweller touchy and nervous. Some of those urban illnesses, eccentricities, are the spleen and the melancholy mood. From time to time the educated city dweller is captive to gloom. Whether someone becomes a target of this doom is a very individual thing. In a general sense everyone is influenced by the weather. Fewer people go to the theatre in the rain and the jokes of the actors generate less hilarity. If the sky is overcast it is mostly depressing; similarly most people admit that between four and five on a Sunday afternoon they experience attacks of sadness. There are also some who have especially sensitive nervous

My parents at the Budapest International Fair, 1937

systems and whose hearts are anxious for some hardly recognizable reason. Some people are rather sad in the morning, others in the evening. One person feels suffocated in an apartment furnished with tacky items—perhaps just the sight of a kitschy pillowcase or a lattice tablecloth is sufficient—while another experiences mild sorrow when the shadow of a tree is projected onto a yellow wall.

"L'heure bleu," the blue hour, is in Paris the time of a milk-like foggy blue when people go to the corner of Place Vendôme to chase away their sadness. In London, the five o'clock tea was allegedly invented because the majority of the Brits are downcast in the afternoon and they are able to overcome it at their cozy communal tea times.

Most people in Pest feel their anxiety in the afternoon; thus they grab their hats and head toward the café. A café frequently bears the name of an exotic city or beautiful sea resort. Already at the revolving door the pleasant whiff of the coffee hits one's nose. When the head waiter notices one's entrance he will exclaim in a military order: "Filtered café au lait, no whipped cream, to Table Two." The illustrated monthlies will rock one into the dream world of unknown territories in this smoke-filled, lukewarm locality.

At times like this, in the cloudy, chilly weather, the café is a sanatorium for the man or woman of Pest.

∿

The first Farkas in the family line that we know of is György, an eighteenth-century landowner in Feldebrő, which is in northeastern Hungary. That's all we know about him; we know more about his son Mihály. Mihály was an attorney, working and living in Huszt and Munkács, towns in northern Hungary and present-day Ukraine, and he was the bailiff of the estate and legal council to Prince Schön-born-Buchheim. Judging from Mihály's correspondence, he had a very busy practice with a large clientele. His wife, born Cecilia Troll, was an attractive young lass.

My great-grandfather, Károly Farkas (1805–1868)

Mihály's son, my great-grandfather, was Károly Farkas. A contemporary photo of him (the fashion in those days was to give people you met small photographs that were used like business cards) shows a somewhat balding, round-faced, middle-aged man with a small mustache.

He wears the attire and boots of a Hungarian nobleman, giving an impression more of a gentleman farmer than of the attorney and judge that he was.

But Károly Farkas was in fact also a gentleman farmer. He wrote a number of articles on the economy and during the revolution of 1848–49 he was a member of the new Hungarian parliament, which held its sessions in the town of Debrecen. In March 1848, Lajos Kossuth named Károly Farkas first secretary in the Ministry of Finance, an appointment that lasted one year—as long as Kossuth's government. After the revolution was crushed, he became sub-prefect of the County of Pest, then chief prosecutor of Buda, and served as a judge in several county courts. Károly Farkas's marriage to a noblewoman, Elsa Bakody, produced four children: two girls—Josephine, whom we called Aunt Zefin, and Aliz, who died in early childhood—and two boys. The older

Portrait of my grandfather, Miklós Farkas

My grandmother, Eveline O'Donnell, as a young woman

son was Róbert. The other son was Miklós, my grandfather. Miklós had a commanding appearance and a strong presence. He was tall and thin and, after getting married, sported a well-trimmed beard. He eventually became president of the Land Credit Institute, a position he retained until he retired.

My grandfather married late. He was thirty-eight years old when, according to the family history, he attended a ball where he asked Countess Eveline O'Donnell to dance. They ended up dancing together most of the night, but dancing more than two dances with the same partner was strictly against the unwritten rules. At the end of the night, my grandfather felt that he had compromised the young lady by spending so much time with her; he was thus obliged to ask for her hand in marriage, which he consequently did. If Eveline had thanked her partner after a couple of rounds of dances and returned to the table where her parents were sitting, this marriage might not have come about. Maybe shrewdness kept Eveline dancing with my grandfather, or simply her ignorance of the breach of etiquette. Wittingly or not, she was in command. My grandfather could not thank her for the dance and escort her back to her table without her explicit request; that would have been interpreted as an insult to the young lady. My Grandmother Eveline was fourteen years younger than her soon-to-be husband, but at twenty-four she qualified as a spinster.

Around the time that I was born, when Grandmother Eveline was about fifty-five years old, she had a serious thyroid operation, after which her doctors suggested that she spend as much time in the countryside as possible. Thus began her life in the country. Her parents had already passed away, leaving her a vineyard at Őrszentmiklós, where she now began spending her springs, summers, and falls. She would supervise work in the vineyard, discuss life with the local people, and sell wine to workers returning from the factories at the end of the day. This lifestyle was quite unusual for a countess.

My grandfather was ill at ease in Őrszentmiklós, because there were few amenities and no cultural diversions. There was no run-

Prince Charles de Ligne (1766–1814)

My grandparents, Eveline and Miklós, playing chess as I watch

ning water; one had to draw water from a well and carry the pail into the house. The only brick oven was in the yard and it was used for baking big round loaves of bread. The range in the kitchen was fueled by a large pile of vine shoots. Lacking electricity, my grandparents used candles and kerosene lamps (interestingly, called *petróleum lámpa* in Hungarian).

Lounging at Őrszentmiklós: Grandmother Eveline, Grandfather Miklós, my father, and I

The image of Grandfather Miklós with a walking stick is etched in my memory, since he was frequently photographed holding one. Some of these, with their finely carved ebony handles, looked like ordinary walking canes, but in fact contained daggers, stilettos with blades made of the finest Spanish Toledo steel, that could be rapidly unsheathed. In those days, such armaments were a part of a gentleman's attire, just as brass knuckles were in the lower segments of society.

At bedtime, my grandfather would sit by my bedside and ask me which story I wanted to hear. My request would inevitably be for a story about his travels in Italy. One evening he told me about a night at a little tavern by a roadside. Just as he was about to blow out the candle to go to sleep, grandfather took one more glance at a portrait hanging on the wall opposite his bed. Scrutinizing it more closely, he noticed that one of the painting's eyes had a hole in it, through which a real eye was watching him. He suspected that a

Grandfather Miklós with a walking cane sitting on a bench with Grandmother Eveline and my father

My father and Grandmother Eveline

gang of robbers had set a trap for him. He quickly dressed, pushed a chair under the doorknob of the entrance to his room, and sat in front of the painting in an armchair staring into the eyes of the portrait. (In Hungarian, when you look straight on, defiantly at someone, it is called a "wolf stare." The fact that my grandfather's name was Farkas, Hungarian for "wolf," was quite apropos.) All night long, until dawn, he kept this vigil, his revolver on a table at his side. I haven't the slightest idea whether this farfetched-sounding little story ever really took place, or whether it was only a figment of his imagination for the benefit of my entertainment. Either way, I never tired of hearing it.

My grandfather loved my mother very much, and the feeling was mutual. One summer night, my parents and Grandfather Miklós were sitting on the long vine-covered porch of the house at

Őrszentmiklós. As they were tippling and chatting my grandfather noticed that my mother's wine glass was frequently empty. He was so amused at the speed of my mother's consumption that he secretly nudged my father to keep on refilling her glass. Mother was oblivious to the secret cabal between them, but in spite of it she held her liquor and stayed self-possessed.

A few months before Grandfather died, he had dinner with my parents in the city center, as they often did. As they parted, my parents looked back in amazement at this dashing figure, my grandfather, in his eighty-third year, walking on foot toward his home on Rökk Szilárd Street without even the help of his ubiquitous cane.

This cane, while not necessarily functional, served on at least one occasion to make a point. In March 1919, a short-lived communist "Dictatorship of the Proletariat" or "Commune" seized power in Hungary and faced an attempted counterrevolution, which became known as the "Revolution of the Ludovica." It was instigated and organized by the cadets at the Ludovica Military Academy. By this time, my father, who was about twenty-three years old, had been discharged from the army, but as a student and reserve officer he

My father in the trenches on the Russian front during the First World War

was recruited by his former army comrades and other university students to participate in the uprising. Ultimately, their uprising was crushed and those arrested, including my father, were called before a Bolshevik revolutionary court.

Following his military trial, my father disappeared. His parents checked all the prisons of the capital to no avail. In desperation they presented themselves at the headquarters of Ottó Korvin, the head commissar, to get information on their son's whereabouts. Somehow, they succeeded in getting in to see the commissar himself. Korvin must have tried to make up some excuse to cut the visit short, whereupon my grandfather slammed his walking cane down on the commissar's desk, which was an incredible, if not an insanely mad, insult to the commissar. My grandfather got away with it, although he failed to learn where his son was.

My father was in prison in Vác, awaiting his execution. One of the prison guards had in fact already showed him which of the gallows in the courtyard would be his: "The third gallow in that row is yours, Farkas."

Thanks to the intervention of Italian Colonel Guido Romanelli, a member of the Allied military mission, the Communist Commissariat cancelled the execution of my father and of the other prisoners. By the time the train returned with my father from Vác to Budapest, the Romanian army had occupied the city. The Reds had been beaten by the Romanians, and that was the end of the 1919 communist regime.

On his way home to Pál Street, my father ran into his good friend Ottó Táborszky. By the time my grandparents came home from their futile search for their son, they found the two friends seated at the dining room table. Standing empty before them was a long line of fruit compote jars, the only edible items in the whole apartment.

∾

The life of a child is full of mysteries and misconceptions. One of mine involved a mythical character "Quasi." I kept hearing Quasi this or Quasi that. During heated disputes in the Farkas family sentences would often start with "Quasi." "Quasi insinuated that I lied." "Quasi pretended that he couldn't hear me." From these statements my mind conjured a mythic personality, one who constantly interfered with the life and the peace of my family. It was a great relief

My father, in uniform, with his mother, Eveline O'Donnell

when I learned that this Quasi was just a Latin expression meaning "as if," "as it were," or "just as," and was used in hypothetical comparisons.

In another instance, when I was six or seven years old I was reading Gyula Pekár's book about the history of Hungary, specifically about the death of King András II, when I came upon an illustration of the king lying on his deathbed. Below it was an inscription that read: "King András returned his spirit to the Lord." This sentence gave me considerable consternation: Why did King András return his spirit, what was this "spirit" that he returned, and who was this mysterious Lord?

∾

My mother's grandfather Károly Ecker lived in Kőszeg, next to the Catholic church. One part of the house was occupied by his hardware store and its enormous basement served as the store's stockroom. My great-grandfather would go on various business trips, on one occasion venturing as far as the United States to procure items for his store. Among the objects he returned with was a Smith & Wesson six-shooter that I inherited in my early teens. I cherished this revolver, especially for the carved notches in its handle.

Of course, most of the time Great-Grandfather Károly's business trips were more local in nature, primarily to Austria. He was still single when once, on his way back from Austria, he ran into a blizzard. With visibility close to zero and the road impassable, he sought refuge in a mill. The miller helped him tow in his sled and put his horses in a stable. He was invited to join the family for dinner. At the table he met Anna Kindl, the sixteen year-old daughter of the miller. After dinner, the family gave lodging to their weary traveler. The following morning, after the storm had passed, he thanked his

My mother and I on the Castle promenade

host for the shelter and the hospitality—which had been generous, for leaving with him on his sleigh was Anna, the miller's daughter. The couple arrived in Kőszeg at noon and went directly to the parish priest, who performed the marriage ceremony immediately, despite the canonic requirement for three marriage ban announcements. This prerequisite, which should have taken place over three consecutive weeks, is intended to give an opportunity for outside objection or decrying of relevant information about prospective spouses.

Anna Kindl, now Mrs. Károly Ecker, gave birth to two children, one of whom was my Grandmother Róza. Kőszeg is a small Hungarian town on the Austrian border that stays cool even in the summer, likely due to its proximity to the Austrian Alps. Kőszeg serves as a transition between Austria and Hungary—in its flora and fauna, its architecture, and its populace. I have a vivid recollection of one summer vacation there with Grandmother Róza when I was five years old. Grandmother would take me down to the town swimming pool in the wee hours of the morning when the water was still so cold that not a soul was around. It made me miserable.

On one of my visits to Kőszeg, Grandmother Róza took me to a nearby forest where a unique tree and its setting had become a tourist attraction. The tree's trunk was so enormous that it took about twenty adults to form a chain around it. The surrounding ground was covered with wild strawberries and colorful cyclamens. We gathered some strawberries and in the woods we searched for various edible mushrooms. On our way back, we passed small fords and rivulets that ran between the hillsides.

I have very little recollection of my grandfather Antal Dabis, aside from the fact that he had a mustache, like most men in those days. At mealtimes a glass of water was always at his side. He drank it at the end of his meal, and it served him well as a mouth rinse. When I was five years old, Grandfather Antal had a gallbladder operation. I saw a small jar containing his gallstones; they were all yellow and the size of hazelnuts. Shortly after that operation, he passed away. The greasy diet back then made some people walking gallstone factories.

My parents and I once took a journey to Zebegény and Dömös, two small villages nestled just before the bend in the Danube. Zebegény is on the northern shore while Dömös is on its southern side. At Zebegény we visited Baroness Vilmos Dőry, whose maiden name was Elizabeth Karácsonyi and whom we referred to as Aunt Erzsi. Her villa in Zebegény had its own story.

After Aunt Erzsi became a widow, she took to traveling. On one of her jaunts on the Danube, as she was returning from Austria on a steam cruiser and delighting in the scenery, she noticed a unique bend into a horseshoe-like projection in the river at the point where Nagymaros and then Zebegény came into her sight. She made a mental note of a spot on a hill that she deemed the most romantic. Afterward she went to the village of Zebegény and had a villa built on the land she had selected.

I was about eight years old when we visited Aunt Erzsi. From Aunt Erzsi's villa a steep path led down to the shores of the Danube. After lunch my father's cousin Julia Aggházy and I descended the steep slope. From the shore, we were able to see a group of people camping Indian-style on a small island. These people called themselves the Indians on the Hungarian Danube. Their organizer was Ervin Baktay, a writer along the lines of Paul Brunton. Baktay wrote about Tibet, India, astrology, and the mysticism of the Far East. The small group of nature lovers surrounding him would spend their vacations together on this little island playing Indians. They wore moccasins and feathered headwear and rode in canoes.

Around the age of seven or so, I became hooked on stories about North American Indians. I was eight years old when I stepped into the wondrous world of Karl May, whose books sold over seventy million copies in twenty-two languages. He wrote of the most incredible adventures of the North American Indians in the wilderness, including an Indian chief called "Winnetou." In Zebegény, I couldn't help but think of those Indian stories I had been reading about. I was thrilled by the sight of the war-painted natives in their canoes.

2

Strange Happenings

When I was about eleven years old, one afternoon as we were sitting around the dining room table, my father brought over Andres's *Hand Atlas* to show me the land of which I had been reading with such enthusiasm—namely, the Wild West and its Indians. The so-called hand atlas was surely a misnomer, or else the Germans would have had to have had quite large hands to hold it, since it covered a big portion of our dining room table. As my father began to show me the land across the ocean, the United States, I was seized by something of a supernatural premonition. A shiver went through me and I felt almost dizzy. I looked at the vast country lying between two oceans whose map filled up two pages of the atlas with its colorful rectangles and strangely named cities and states.

An odd feeling came over me, as if my subconscious was telling me that someday that land would be my home. Today, as I am writing these lines, it is January 15, 1997, the fortieth anniversary of my arrival to the United States. January 16, 1957, was the day on which the fourteen thousand registered ton U.S.N.S. *Marine Carp* docked in Brooklyn with 1,725 Hungarian refugees on board. By now I have already lived longer in my adopted country than in Hungary. Looking back, I can make sense of the feelings that came over me so many years ago, when as a child I first laid my eyes on that map.

According to occultism, all events happen at once. There is no past and future; only the present, which encompasses the past and future. And space does not exist. Space and time are only construed for us human beings so that we can create order in our lives. If time did exist, there would have to be a beginning. Without a beginning, there can hardly be an end. But once you stipulate a beginning you have an unsolvable and inexplicable problem. Suppose that there was a beginning. Then what existed before that? A vacuum is not an explanation, because it is impossible for something to appear out of nothing. The question of space is likewise troubling. If the universe has concrete measurable boundaries, where are those boundaries and what exists beyond them? If only vacuums and voids exist beyond the borders of the world, then the same question presents itself— what does this nihility consist of and where are its boundaries? With this riddle we can go on and on. We may also posit that the human spirit is an incredible, inexplicable instrument, and that each person's fate perhaps because of his character, is preprogrammed and its fine vibrations can adumbrate something to someone, something that will take place only in the future.

So perhaps at that time, for a fragment of a fleeting moment I was in the United States, which might have been a premonition or a lightning-like regression into a previous lifetime.

3

Jaunts into the Countryside

My parents felt that as an only child I needed to be exposed to my peers, but they made sure that they vetted all my future playmates. I can remember the last little peasant girl with whom I played at Őrszentmiklós: her name was Margit Lehotzky. Her parents András and Juli worked for my Grandmother Eveline and later for my parents.

When my wife Edit and I first revisited Hungary after years of living in America, I took her to Őrszentmiklós to show her Grandmother Eveline's house. Edit was not terribly impressed with Eveline's cottage, but she very much liked the sight of the little peasant houses in a row with their red brick walls and red tile roofs. As we passed by the houses, Juli Lehotzky stood before her house as if she was waiting for me, knowing exactly when I was coming. She may have heard that we were at Veresegyház—where my mother lived at the time—and hers was the next town over. In that neighborhood the news spread from person to person, and by the time we arrived people frequently greeted us saying that they had heard that we were in town.

Juli Lehotzky stood before her house like her own statue, a peasant woman carved into stone by the Yugoslav sculptor Ivan Mestrovic or the Hungarian Pál Pátzay. She still wore the old peasant attire, even though it was no longer in fashion in Hungary in 1969 and generally only worn on the weekends or on holidays. She stood there shielding her eyes against the setting sun. She told me that her husband András, Grandmother's favorite worker, had passed away. Their children, Andris and Margit, who had been my playmates, were starting families of their own. She had become a grandmother, but she still wanted to live in the same small red brick building that

25

she and András had built. When it was time for us to say goodbye, she did not tell me that we must see one another again before I go back to America, as Hungarians traditionally do. She embraced me and kissed me on my cheek. Both of us wanted to banish from our minds the thought that we would never see one another again.

~

Around 1938, when I was in my fourth year of high school (equivalent to the eighth grade in the United States), it dawned on me that I was no longer a child and that my toys did not appeal to me in the same way anymore. As a result of my feelings, coupled with the pressure of outside interests, my mother and I decided to pack up my toys. Into the boxes went my tin soldiers, my papier-mâché soldiers, and my little mortar and cannon. The tin soldiers were Americans with stars and stripes, the gray papier-mâché soldiers were Germans, and the khaki-colored papier-mâché ones British. My playthings were packed into a trunk and landed in the attic of our house at Veresegyház, presumably awaiting my offspring.

During the siege the trunk, with its many cherished toys, disappeared without a trace. At that time the local peasants and the vagrants from Erdőváros grabbed anything movable. The toys, I'm sure, made some children very happy.

With the passing of time, all toys become simple objects of nostalgia or of archival quality. Toys become the objects of admiration or curiosity, something a person might see at an autumn fair or in an antique shop in Budapest's inner city. Toys have their fate, their lives, as well. They are born and live and die with the passing of childhood. We want to safeguard our toys for our children, but it rarely ever works out that way. People move, leave things behind, and new generations of girls and boys have other toys that interest them. The time of Raggedy Ann and Andy gave way to Barbie dolls, which were in turn taken over briefly by Cabbage Patch Kids; while blocks gave way to Legos, and finally computers and video games like Atari and Nintendo took over for both girls and boys. Thus, with the passing of time, the toys which my generation called toys may have no meaning or interest for new generations. As a child I had the joy of running around in the yard or on the road, chasing an iron hoop with a forked rod. It was such a simple toy, yet it gave me and many other children so much joy. As a teenager I took delight in collecting stamps, which also enhanced my knowledge of geography and history. I also played chess, which improved my strategic thinking.

~

In 1937, with the arrival of summer, I was taken down to Aunt Margit's farmhouse at Fegyvernek, 145 km east of Budapest, for two weeks. I was twelve and did not relish being sent away into an unfamiliar environment to be with a cousin who was my age but had quite a different personality. Of course, my parents thought it was a splendid solution for me to go to Fegyvernek. It gave them a vacation.

Aunt Margit, my mother's half-sister, was an exemplary housewife. She kept the house and the family in order. One day I sent a postcard home that had a succinct summary of our daily life. It was mailed from the Fegyvernek post office by my Aunt Margit. The laconic message said that I was well and playing a lot with my cousin Iván, but at the end of the card I scribbled, "Please come and rescue me at once!" It was like a message in a bottle at sea, and the likelihood of an eventual escape was somewhat similar to the chances of that bottle being found. Aunt Margit either did not notice the cryptic message or let it slide.

Perhaps thanks to this SOS message, my Aunt Blanka arrived shortly thereafter. There was some similarity in her mission to the British Lord Runciman's, who in 1938 was sent to Czechoslovakia as a diplomat to prevent the outbreak of war. His mission failed, however, while Blanka's was a success, because she brought with her a small old-fashioned English woman's bike. It was not a free-wheeler, it did not have a ratchet, only a fixed cogwheel gear where the wheels moved in sync with the crank arm and pedals. One had to be careful not to bruise one's shin with the crank arm as it went on turning. This type of fixed-wheel bike is still in use on the bicycle racetracks. This little bike was the embodiment of my dreams. When the sun went down and the heat was less oppressive, we rode out and biked on the concrete highway.

Aunt Blanka stayed with me for my remaining days there and elevated my mood considerably. I loved Blanka dearly. We had nice chats, and our judgment in general was quite similar. Having her around gave me a feeling of security. She was around twenty-six years old, and thus a young lady. I was only disappointed with her once, when I asked her what the word *romanticism* meant. Her terse answer was that it is a "strange bug." For quite a few years I was truly under the impression that there was an insect named romanticism.

At the end of the two weeks at Fegyvernek, I went back to Őrszentmiklós. My life there in Grandmother Eveline's vineyard left behind the memory of a bittersweet childhood.

4

Malvina Tarnóczy

M y great-grandmother on my father's side was Malvina Tarnóczy.
For official purposes and for the *Almanac of Gotha,* Malvina gave
her birthday as July 7, 1843.

Malvina was the firstborn of eight children of Kázmér Tarnóczy.
She was unwilling to disclose her actual year of birth (1831), but
toward the end of their lives she admitted to her husband Count

A young Malvina Tarnóczy

The Tarnóczy Castle at Laszkár

Henrik O'Donnell that she was in fact fourteen years his elder. During her marriage ceremony to Henrik O'Donnell at the town hall, she used her elbow to knock over the inkwell, blotting out the date on her birth certificate. A historical event seems to validate her belated confession about her age—she participated in an important episode during Hungary's 1848 revolution against the Habsburg emperor of Austria. In February 1849, during the last phase of Hungarian commander Artúr Görgey's retreat from Northern Hungary, a struggle began for the mountain pass of Branyiszkó in the Carpathian Mountains. The battle opened with an attack by the Austrian General Kiesewetter, commandant of the town of Lőcse to the west of Branyiszkó. The attack was repelled by the British general Richard Guyon, a volunteer for the Hungarian revolutionary forces, but Kiesewetter escaped to the Branyiszkó mountain pass. There he was joined by another Austrian general named Deym. Guyon found himself outmaneuvered and in danger of encirclement. The only way to capture the pass was to go straight through the Austrian-occupied town.

At this point Guyon sent a messenger to Lőcse, asking the Tarnóczy family for assistance. Amália Tarnóczy and her daughter Malvina immediately set about organizing a Shrovetide Ball to celebrate the end of the Mardis Gras season. Malvina invited all of her beautiful young friends and all the ladies from the town. She also invited all of the Austrian officers; since the Hungarian men were away serving in the Hungarian Army, the Austrians would have their pick of the young ladies of society. The whole town participated, making certain that there was enough to eat and plenty to drink. One barrel of wine after another rolled into the town hall, where the ball was being held.

Malvina sent a note to General Guyon, telling him to watch the top window of the town hall that night. If a candle appeared, it would mean that all of the Austrian staff officers were completely drunk. After midnight, the candle was lit, signaling to Guyon, whose troops then swept through the town and over the Branyiszkó pass. Guyon's surprise attack on February 5, 1849, encircled the Austrians and stunned the commandants of the Austrian Army. At the time of this victorious "Breakthrough at Branyiszkó" Malvina was still very young.

Seven years later, in 1856, Malvina married Count István Niczky. A year later, the childless marriage abruptly ended with Niczky's suicide. Niczky left his castle at Csapi and his wealth to Malvina. After a widowhood of fourteen years, Malvina met Count Henrik O'Donnell at a Viennese ball. They fell in love and were married on February 21, 1870. By this time the young count had retired from the Austro-Hungarian Army, and the couple moved to Budapest, but they spent much of their time at Malvina's parents' castle in Csernek in Croatia-Slavonia. Malvina and Henrik had two children, Eveline and Rory. Malvina was a gifted woman recognized for her literary talents and musical compositions. One of her operettas was performed in Vienna.

Both my great-grandmother Malvina and my grandmother Eveline had some memorable experiences living in remote castles in the Hungarian countryside. When my Grandmother Eveline was about twelve years old and living in her grandfather's castle at Csernek she went with her governess for a visit. On their way home, through the forest, their coach was suddenly surrounded by a group of highwaymen. The hooligans asked them where they were headed. When they found out that the two ladies lived in Tarnóczy Castle they offered to escort them home to ensure their safe arrival. The outlaws warned Eveline and her governess about the dangers of traveling by themselves through the woods, which were filled with hooligans and robbers. They were made to feel fortunate that they had them as escorts. Upon their safe arrival, the castle's servants rolled out a barrel of wine for the ruffians. The outlaws made a bonfire in the park, roasted some bacon, drank the wine, and departed peacefully.

Many years earlier, when Malvina was a widow living at the Niczky Castle in Csapi, in the middle of the Bakony wilderness, highwaymen came to attack the castle. The servants ran to Malvina bewildered, saying, "Twenty-five armed robbers have surrounded the castle." Malvina quickly changed into an evening gown and went out to greet the robbers. "Gentlemen," she said, "You are all welcome here. Please honor me by joining us for dinner."

The rascals were suspicious, afraid of being trapped. Nevertheless, they accepted the invitation. Splendid dishes were served, and it was all washed down with champagne. Malvina, the hostess, sat at the head of the table and had a lively conversation with her unusual guests. She was as animated as if she were at the Hofsburg palace. At the end of the feast, the robbers departed as gentlemen. On their way out, Malvina called out to them extending them a welcome for whenever they might next be in the neighborhood. From then on, they came by once in a while, but never to rob the castle. Malvina later said that she had had such a good time during these robbers' visits, which chased away the monotony of her country life, that she had almost regretted not seeing them more often.

Malvina was quite the social dame in her time, and was well known for her great sense of humor. Even after her death she managed to pull a trick on us. Four of us witnessed it: my mother, my good friend Albert (Berti) Roediger, Berti's wife Zsuzskó, and me. It happened in 1955, shortly after the new government of Imre Nagy had introduced a somewhat more liberal form of communism. Among other liberalizing measures the regime returned freedom of movement to those who had been forcibly deported from the cities to the countryside. Thus, my friend Berti, his wife Zsuzskó, and their five-year-old son Niki had been able to leave Hunya in eastern Hungary and move into my mother's house at Veresegyház. They stayed with us there from 1954 until 1956.

It was a Sunday evening in the winter of 1955 when Malvina tricked us. We had just said goodbye to our group of weekend visitors, who were heading back to the city. Zsuzskó, Berti, my mother, and I stayed behind. The four of us were warming ourselves by the tile stove in the library. The night was dreary, with snow showers and howling winds. My mother and I were seated side by side on a settee covered with an oriental rug under a portrait of Grandmother Eveline. Zsuzskó and Berti were standing with their backs against the tile stove. Many of our jackets had brownish spots on their backs testifying to close encounters with the hot maroon-colored tiles.

As we discussed the weekend's events our conversation somehow turned to Malvina Tarnóczy. My friend Berti made an irreverent comment about her. The very next second the miniature four-inch by

Oval-framed lithograph of Malvina Tarnóczy

seven-inch oval portrait of Malvina that hung near the door jumped off the wall, flew across the full length of the room—about twenty feet—face down at a constant level of four feet off the ground and then drop-landed before the window with a thud, its oak frame broken in half.

This event was so unique and supernatural that Berti still reminisced about it in one of his letters to me in 1984.

5

The Vineyard at Veresegyház

Grandmother Eveline's father was Count Henrik O'Donnell, the son of Moritz O'Donnell and Helene Cantacuzene. He served as a lancer officer in the Austro-Hungarian Army and in 1870 married Malvina Tarnóczy, a Hungarian lady of noble birth. They had two children: Eveline, born on November 11, 1870, and Rory, born on October 20, 1871. Although Rory was baptized as Roderich, we all called him Uncle Rory. He served in the Austrian Army, retiring in 1905 with the rank of "Rittenmeister," which was roughly equivalent to the level of a captain. He married Johanna Bauer, an actress from Brunn, who was called "Hansi." Eveline, in 1894, married Miklós Farkas. Henrik died in 1907, and Malvina died in 1917.

Uncle Rory inherited the family vineyard at Veresegyház, which at that time comprised nearly one hundred acres surrounding a manor house. There was a kitchen garden, and a few acres of arable land by the main road connecting Veresegyház to the village of Őrszentmiklós, which was some distance from the vineyard.

Uncle Rory also inherited the family house in Buda, located in Vizivaros (Watertown District), along with portraits of the O'Donnell ancestors, family jewelry, and furniture. Grandmother Eveline's inheritance consisted of approximately two acres of vineyard in Őrszentmiklós, and a peasant house, a typical farmhouse for that region. She also inherited a few family paintings and some family jewelry.

While Uncle Rory was educated by the Jesuits in Kalksburg, Austria, Grandmother Eveline did not have any formal schooling at all. In those days education for women was very limited and its emphasis was on learning to converse fluently in the major languages. Grandmother Eveline had governesses who taught her German, French, and English. She was also tutored in basic mathematics and reading. This rudimentary math came in handy in her later years when she had to sell her own wine. Grandmother Eveline had a natural intelligence, paired with a great sense of humor, but also a good deal of naïveté that she managed to retain until the end of her life.

Grandmother Eveline was a devoted, loyal wife and was more understanding of her son, my father, than my grandfather, who had a rather short fuse. Grandmother loved her brother Uncle Rory dearly as well, but sometimes had difficulty getting along with her sister-in-law Hansi. This was mainly due to Eveline's possibly overprotective concern for her brother's physical and psychological well-being.

When my great-grandparents Henrik O'Donnell and Malvina Tarnóczy moved from Csernek in Croatia-Slavonia to Budapest, they decided to also settle down in Veresegyház in the County of Pest. There were a number of good reasons to choose this location. In the eighteenth century the phylloxera bug had destroyed the vineyards of Europe. One way to renew the plants was to graft old vines onto new roots, utilizing the roots of North American wild grapes that phylloxera bugs abhorred. The other method was to plant vines in sandy soil, where it was discovered that phylloxera bugs could not survive. Veresegyház, known for its sandy earth, became the right choice for my great-grandparents. The location also suited them because the newly built railroad from Budapest to the town of Vác passed through Veresegyház. With the railroad in place, the area became more sought after—especially after the line was electrified. The local station was called Vicziántelep. It took an hour and a half to reach it from the Budapest Nyugati (Western) Railroad Station.

From the train station, a road led directly into the courtyard. Just before arriving there a traveler would come to a crossroads. Turning to the right, the road passed by the kitchen garden fence, went south toward the town of Veresegyház, and from there headed on to Erdőváros (Forest City). Turning to the left, the road led to Őrszentmiklós-Vácbottyán, also known as Nyires. In those days these sandy roads served horse-drawn carriages and carts, as well as pedestrians.

The locality was unofficially called Nyires (Birchgrove) on account of small groves of silver-barked birch trees, some of which had been planted by my great-grandparents. The flora also included trembling poplar or aspen (*populus tremolantis*) and the green and tall Lombardi poplars (*populus canadensis*) recognizable by their slender columnar shapes. We were proud of these scenic, forever shimmering, swaying trees, which together with weeping willows and acacia trees served as guideposts for approaching travelers. The roads were bordered by white flowers. White carnations, which according to my mother had come from Siberia, sprinkled the meadows. Red poppies livened up the sandbanks.

At night, dogs barked at the moon, which lacquered the land with its lemonade-like hue. Around the wetlands of the Kigyóstó Dűlő (Snake Pond Ridge) in the Revetek district, frogs croaked incessantly. A fine veil of mist covered the land. The air at Veresegyház was in constant movement; a cavalcade of fragrances released by the orchard, the acacia and linden trees, and gilly flowers permeated the air. The only audible intrusion of man into this natural panorama was the shrill whistle of the midnight train.

The lake at Veresegyház was refreshingly cool in the summertime and offered splendid possibilities for vacationers fleeing the heat of the city. Cabins were built around the lake, and a restaurant perched above it. There, a gypsy orchestra played and giant glasses of dark pink *málnaszörp*, or *himbersaft* (raspberry syrup mixed with carbonated water), were served. The lake had two docks, with diving towers.

It was a beautiful landscape—nothing spectacular, but enchanting nonetheless. My mother called our little paradise "typical French countryside." It was a place where Monet, Pisarro, or Sisley would have felt quite at home and easily been seduced into picking up their paintbrushes.

While Hungarians in the past built their houses, especially ranches and farmhouses, mostly in a crescent shape, Henrik's house had a U shape—allegedly a favorite Irish design. The local peasants referred to the house as the "castle," which had more to do with the fact that the owners were aristocrats than with the actual design of the building. It would have been more fitting to call it a "*kuria*," the Hungarian term for a manor house, usually denoting a more modest dwelling of nobility.

My great-grandfather Henrik hired gypsies to build his house. They were the cheapest labor available and they knew how to build adobe walls extremely well. They poured clay and straw into vats and mixed the two together with water. They built a frame for the walls out of planks and poured the clay and straw mixture between them. After pouring the mud in, they trampled on it and squeezed it in tight, mostly by dancing on top of the slowly widening wall. Once the walls had sufficiently dried, the planks were removed. These adobe walls were fortress-like in their thickness. But they had to be in order to support gigantic crossbeams, rafters, and heavy roof tiles. These tiles were called beaver-tailed, or round-end, tiles. Over the years, the walls became so hard that it took a sizable effort to carve out a new door or install a window.

In the center of the courtyard was a draw-well. A little farther away from the house were some wetlands, where my great-grandparents put their vegetable garden. A long wine cellar connected the two wings of the house. It contained huge Slovenian oak barrels and other wine-making equipment. In addition to the vineyard there was an orchard, pigsties, chicken coops, horse stables, and a shed for carts and wagons. All of the carriages, harnesses, and saddles were decorated with the silver monogram of the O'Donnells beneath their nine-pointed crowns.

My great-grandfather Henrik had a knack for farming. The design of the living quarters and of the areas devoted to agricultural activities was based on very sound principles. For instance, water could be pumped out of the well by manually turning a wheel that would cause pistons to pump water up through a pipe and into a pail. Any water that overflowed would land in a basin and from there trickle down across the courtyard, via underground clay irrigating pipes, into a pile of manure that would thus be kept wet. Great-grandfather Henrik also had a manual cutting machine that was used every year to chop up pruned pieces of vine stock. These cuttings were dispersed in the vineyard and left to decompose, which took five years. The land thus got back what it had given away.

By the turn of the century approximately one thousand hectoliters of wine were housed in the Slovenian oak barrels. There was Pozsonyi; Ezerjó, a strong and sweet white wine with great body and bouquet; a Burgundy, Kadarka; Aramond; and Merlot (in those days Merlot was not cultivated for its own sake, but rather used to lend red wine an exquisitely beautiful color).

My great-grandfather's house at Veresegyház was painted yellow. Its exact shade was referred to as "Schönbrunn yellow" after the color of the Hapsburgs' Schönbrunn Palace. The roof tiles at Veresegyház were beige, the chimney bricks pale red. The chimneys were very tall, supported on all sides by long iron rods embedded in the rafters of the roof. On top of the chimneys were weathercocks. With the passage of time they became rusty, their creaking noise creating an eerie sound. The attic on the right wing of the house had a few vents that were made of crescent-shaped tin plates.

The house in its simplicity served my ancestors well. Aesthetically, it became an integral part of the landscape, going through some big changes over the span of several decades. One photograph taken at the turn of the twentieth century and another taken around 1935 illustrate well the passage of time. The first one shows the house surrounded by the vineyard without trees, shrubbery, or any evergreens. The later picture shows the new veranda with its white columns, flower beds in front of the house, hemlocks on both sides of the stairs, and somewhat farther away oleaster trees. When we moved to Veresegyház from Őrszentmiklós in 1941, my father took another picture of the house. This one he took from a distance, with a landscape view that lent the house a whole other character, a romantic one with a movie-like ambiance.

O'Donnell Manor House, courtyard view

As time passed, the house became more beautiful. From a distance, its yellow walls merged into lush green environs. The trees around it grew to great heights. The entranceway to the stairs in the inner courtyard was thickly covered with the intertwined vines of the Rose of Jericho, also known as honeysuckle or woodbine.

The farm structures at Veresegyhaz comprised pigsties, a henhouse, stables, an outhouse, a cart shed, an apiary, and a small house by the entrance to the courtyard that served as a home for the vintner. These were all built in my great-grandfather Henrik's time. In the attic above the stable was a hayloft. In the left wing of the main building was a carriage house and the coachman's flat. Next to the latter was a separate room for the washhouse with a three-hundred-liter copper cauldron, mangle, or rolling calender, and a sitting bathtub for the servants that looked like a huge armchair. Before the entrance to the washhouse was a stand that served as a carpet hanger. There, a person could beat the sand and dirt out of a carpet with a *pracker,* a carpet beater. Later, after the war, we used to lay the carpets down on the snow and beat them there, the snow acting as a magnet for

O'Donnell Manor House, garden-side view

the dust. Beyond the washhouse were two rooms used by Uncle Rory and Aunt Hansi's son Henry. In the corner was a bathroom and a toilet with running water.

The right-side wing of the U-shaped manor house served as the living quarters for my great-grandparents Malvina and Henrik. In front of this side of the building stretched a long front porch with three exits. Sectioned off at one end of the porch was a woodshed, next to which was a double door leading into a library. This double door had the same thickness as the adobe walls of the house. Iron push bolts were installed on its upper and lower ends. From here, one room opened into another until finally off the third room a small door led into the entrance hall. The entrance hall also had a double door that opened directly onto the center of the porch; the outer of the two doors was solid oak and the inner one had glass windows. One more door off of the lefthand side of the entrance hall led into a storage room of sorts. That room held objects that had been saved for every kind of unforeseen eventuality that of course never happened. All of the doors were massive, soundproof, and painted dark green or maroon.

Stepping from the entrance hall out onto the porch, on one's righthand side was the outside wall to a small outdoor pantry. The pantry had one tiny window and retained a cool temperature even in summer. The scents, the fragrances, of that chamber of "culinary delights" were such that they wrote epistles in one's memory. Each distinct smell converged into a delightful orgy of smells: flour, smoked sausages, wurst, ham, fruit, dilled pickles, and vegetables (those not stored in the vegetable cellar). Even the eggs in a basket had their own exquisite scent. The pantry's sentry was a padlock that hung on the green door.

To access the porch beyond the pantry, one had to step down onto the ground, bypass the pantry, and then step back onto the porch again. There, one once again faced two doors. The first, very massive door led directly into the attic. Farther on, in the corner, was another double door that led into the kitchen. This large kitchen had a concrete floor and was adjoined by a large pantry. From the kitchen, one could descend through a double trapdoor and down a solid wood staircase into the vegetable cellar.

A small family photo album has preserved the sights of my great-grandfather's world. One can see the manor house from the courtyard, the poultry farm, a little peasant girl and boy sitting on a farm cart, a hand cart on the road with a barrel containing liquid copper sulfate used to spray the vine stalks, geese in the courtyard, and a huge Mangalica hog elbowing on the edge of her sty. Others depict the coachman leading a horse out of the stable and workers hoeing in the vineyard. One of the workers wears long white shepherd trousers, notwithstanding the heat, as was customary in those days. Another photo shows my great-grandfather sitting on the porch with his bull terrier in his lap, a cigar in his mouth, and a Girardi straw hat on his head.

Two photographs preserve the memory of the kitchen garden. In one Aunt Hansi and her sister are holding onto a wooden pail they are balancing on the edge of a large vat of water. In the second, the two sisters are standing among giant cabbages. They wear city attire—Aunt Hansi has her hair up in a bun and carries a parasol;

Henry O'Donnell sitting on the porch with his bull terrier

Coachman leading a horse out of the stable

her sister wears long white gloves and a white hat. They definitely don't resemble housewives collecting a few heads of cabbage for lunch. Photography was still in its infancy then; one can only imagine the crisp fresh background and the vivid colors of the lush garden. The scene would have befitted Renoir's or Monet's paint brush—or perhaps, by virtue of its subjects, Berthe Morrisot's or Mary Cassatt's. As a matter of fact, it would have been a perfect scene for my mother to paint. Had destiny permitted, my mother could have painted the kitchen garden, the trembling poplars, the haystacks à la Monet, with little channels and Japanese-style bridges above them. She would often mention to me the enchantment of this landscape.

After Uncle Rory retired from the army in 1900, he built an addition onto the house. The two wings of the building that my great-grandfather Henrik had built were now connected by a third section above the wine cellar. At one end of this section was added on a press house, which contained four wine presses, grinders, vats,

Aunt Hansi and her sister in the kitchen garden

and a wine pump. To reach it one had to climb a few stairs and cross a small terrace. Here the newly pressed juice of the grapes flowed into vats. From the vats the juice was pumped through rubber hoses down into barrels in the cellar.

The new addition on top of the wine cellar was built of brick and became the center of the U-shaped building. It made a complete connection between the two wings and it was this section of the house that became Aunt Hansi and Uncle Rory's residence. This part of the building had an entry hall at its center with openings onto the courtyard on one side and onto the garden on the other side. The hall was furnished with peasant furniture painted with a colorful red-tulip motif.

On the left side of the entry hall was Uncle Rory's study. He had a sizable desk, on top of which sat a postal scale, magnifying glasses, a paperweight, and a pile of *Pester Lloyds* (*Lloyds of Pest*, the

Studio photo of Aunt Hansi and Uncle Rory

leading German-language daily in Budapest). On the wall behind his desk was a set of shelves in three rows that were attached to the wall by stirrups. Various O'Donnell portraits hung on the walls as well as hunting scenes and paintings of famous horses. Uncle Rory also had a battery-operated radio. It was on this radio in 1936 that we listened to the Olympic Games held in Berlin that year. Hungary excelled in the medal counts at the time and placed third overall behind the United States and Germany. Even though Uncle Rory had a radio, he still had no telephone since there were no telephone lines in Nyires. From Uncle Rory's study a door opened onto his and Aunt Hansi's bedroom. From there another door led downstairs to a bathroom and toilet.

Entering the house from the courtyard, the first room to the right of the entry hall was the salon. Glass-enclosed bookcases and family portraits covered the main walls. The books included the collective works of Karl May, favorite readings of Uncle Rory's son Henry. They were my favorites as well, but this set was in German and I could only read them in Hungarian. There was also a complete set of Géza Gárdonyi, in Hungarian, which of course I thoroughly enjoyed. I am convinced that that set was a testament to Uncle Rory's low sales resistance. It was very likely that an itinerant salesman stopped by and sold it to him. It is likely that his set of Russian classics (from Chekhov to Tolstoy) translated into German had been acquired in a similar fashion.

From this salon one could enter the dining room. A small sliding window in the far corner of this room served as a dumbwaiter between the dining room and the kitchen. In the kitchen, the cook would step up onto a platform, slide open a window, and place dishes into the opening. The chambermaid would then slide open her window in the dining room, take out the dishes, and serve the meal. In this way, servants didn't have to trudge through the open courtyard and reenter the upper section of the house with all the dishes.

Wine was always served with meals. Uncle Rory kept his wine in tall so-called "Rhineland" bottles and used alpaca coasters beneath the wine glasses. A glass urn on the table was used to wash grapes, and another one to cool off hot corn on the cob. A glass bowl of water was also passed around for diners to rinse their fingers. Silverware was put beside each place setting on silver stands that looked like miniature sawbucks.

After my great-grandfather Henrik died in 1907, Uncle Rory took over the management of the vineyard. Gradually, he made improvements. The well that had been turned by a wheel could now be switched to a water pump that would pump water up into the attic to fill a tank. On the side of the house facing the courtyard was a red arrow that reflected the water level. The arrow was connected to a bobbing buoy inside the water tank, and a scale mounted on the courtyard wall indicated the water level. Gravity did the rest of the job, sending the water from the container to the kitchen, bathroom, and washhouse.

Uncle Rory installed running water for the bathroom, washhouse, and kitchen. When it came to lighting, the household had to resort to kerosene lamps. Their light was warm and friendly and since Uncle Rory had enough domestic help, the cleaning and cutting of wicks was not a problem for him.

Whenever a guest expressed his or her admiration for culinary delights, exclaiming that something was *prachtvoll* (wonderful), Uncle Rory's standard reply was, "*Wie alles in diesem Haus*," translated as, "As is everything in this house." Of course, as the war went on and especially during the siege, these complimentary remarks faded and then disappeared altogether.

From the dining room, two winged solid oak doors opened into the guestroom, which had a magnificent bed with a copper frame and a delightful horsehair-filled mattress. There was a washstand with a washbasin and water pitcher, a mirror above it, and towels on both sides.

Opening the shutters of the guestroom window, one could experience the breathtaking view toward the village of Veresegyház; the meadows, the weeping willows, the interplay of sun and moon, and the "plain air" scenery were captivating. In the early morning hours a fine silvery mist would envelop the low-lying land. Above this room was the attic, where one could behold through a small round window an even more enchanting, more encompassing scene. My secret hope was that one day we could install an "atelier" up there and replace part of the roof with glass tiles (a forerunner of the modern-day skylight). There my mother would have had an ideal art studio in which to create her beautiful paintings and immerse herself in artistic reverie and solitude.

From spring until fall Aunt Hansi and Uncle Rory lived in their comfortable home at Veresegyház. At the vineyard they had a coachman and a vintner whose family helped with a multitude of chores. They also had someone who was in charge of the kitchen garden and greenhouse. For a while they even had someone to handle the apiary, until all the bees died. During the winter months they would return to their home in the city with their cook Lenka and their chambermaid Terka.

It was a nice life while it lasted.

6

The Tragic Death of Henry O'Donnell

Uncle Rory and Aunt Hansi had a son named Henry who was born on October 23, 1908. Henry began his short and adventurous life in a brougham carriage on the way to the hospital. When he was a teenager, his favorite books were Karl May's stories about American Indians and the Wild West. At the age of twelve, one day on the spur of the moment Henry decided to leave home and go to America to see the Wild West. For days, his parents were beside themselves, with no idea where their son was. Finally, on the tenth day of his disappearance, they received word that he had been found in a small town in Austria, whence the gendarmes brought him back to his parents.

Henry O'Donnell

Henry O'Donnell sitting in a wicker chair

I remember seeing Henry once when I was about four years old. He had come on horseback to pay my grandmother, his aunt, a visit. His horse clearly needed a good run since it was acting skittish and rearing to throw him off. He held his turf and stayed in the saddle.

It was around this time that my mother and I paid a visit to Uncle Rory. My mother told me that my father was spending a few nights in the side wing of the house to give Henry succor. I was somewhat surprised, but I didn't ask any questions. Today I am convinced that Henry was badly in need of a sober evaluation of his life and that Uncle Rory must have asked my father—someone closer to Henry's age—to have a heart-to-heart discussion with his son.

Even to this day, Henry's life is a great puzzle to me. One story my mother once told me may have had a bearing on later events. At one time Henry was courting Mariette Bolza, a marriageable young lady three years younger than he from a family of great wealth. Had she consented to marriage it would have been quite a feat for Henry.

Allegedly, at the beginning of the courtship the interest was mutual, but since an incredible fortune was at stake, a small crowd of young men was vying for Mariette's hand. Mariette's social circle encompassed a viper's nest of intrigue and false innuendos, and eventually someone started a rumor that Henry, who was a card player, was an inveterate gambler. With Henry's reputation now in question, the Bolza family pressured Mariette to break off contact with him.

It seems that Henry was constantly short of money. There was a gap between his pocket money and his lifestyle. He would save up his allowance in a little box and from time to time would venture out to play cards. Between gambling stints Veresegyház served him well; it was a place where he lived like a recluse—a frugal, quiet life. It was also conducive to studying for his law exams. Henry's living quarters were two bright sunny rooms in one corner of the house with a separate entry off the courtyard.

One of the last people to see Henry alive was Ágota Kállay, a friend who on May 12, 1932, had left her dog in Henry's care while she went away for a few days. That night Henry had yet one more visitor, Baroness Vera Hatvany, who drove out from the city in the evening and left the following morning at dawn. She had come to say goodbye to Henry, since she was leaving for Rome on the following day. The baroness was very attractive, an exotic beauty who was also very rich.

In the early hours that morning, Ruttkay the vintner woke up to the barking of Ágota's little dachshund outside Henry's door. Going to investigate, he looked through the window and saw Henry lying on his bed and the wall behind him sprinkled with blood. Horrified, he ran up to Őrszentmiklós to alert my Grandmother Eveline, who in turn rushed down to the manor house. Even after having shot himself, Henry had washed up, donned a clean white shirt and put a cross on his chest, and was lying on the bed. When Grandmother Eveline got down to the house and rushed in, a still-conscious Henry said to her: "Aunt Eveline, I don't regret it. I don't regret it."

Blood was splattered everywhere—on the wall, on the floor, and on the Japanese vieux-lacquer writing desk. Someone went for an ambulance (there was no phone in the manor house nor in the near vicinity) and Henry died in it on the way to the hospital. Aunt Hansi once remarked to my mother that her son had died in an ambulance at just about the same spot in the road where he was born in a brougham carriage.

Since Henry couldn't be buried in Veresegyház's cemetery (the Catholic Church deemed suicide a sin), his parents chose a spot in their garden surrounded by the pine trees that had been Henry's favorite place to play as a child.

On May 13 a lengthy article was published in *Ujság* under the byline of Elemér Oszmann. The headline read: "The Young Count Henry O'Donell Shot Himself at His Father's Vineyard in Veresegyház."

By and large *Ujság* served the sensation-hungry public. The style of the article reveals the paper's desire to accomplish this. The version of this sad event that I heard from my mother doesn't quite jibe with the published account, which mentioned two suicide notes, one to the parents and one to an unnamed woman. My mother never mentioned any suicide notes, though it is conceivable that Uncle Rory destroyed them. I heard from my mother that Henry had been

Grave of Henry O'Donnell

in love with Baroness Hatvany. A supposition was made that Henry was short of money, couldn't afford to escort the beautiful rich baroness to Rome, and that this inability to accompany her drove him to suicide—at least this was the theory that was kept alive for the family's internal consumption.

An article also appeared in *Nemzeti Ujság* (*National News*), written by Baroness Lily Doblhoff, a friend of Aunt Hansi and Uncle Rory who also knew Henry quite well. The headline reads: "The Twenty-Three-Year-Old Henry O'Donell Was Buried amid Daffodils, Lilacs, Tulips, and Lilies of the Valley."

I remember the stories my mother told about Henry's gambling habits. I don't believe that he was an unscrupulous sharpie, since no one in a casino would have sat down to play with him if that were the case. My theory is that Henry might have incurred a tremendous loss at the card table and since he didn't have enough cash he must have left behind an IOU that was supposed to be paid out in a set time period, such as forty-eight or seventy-two hours. As soon as he left the casino he must have tried to find someone from whom he could borrow the money. As time ran out, he probably decided to kill himself, since he knew that his parents didn't have the money either.

Thus, there was no one left in Hungary to carry on the O'Donnell name. A few days after Henry's suicide, my parents set out from Grandmother's house in Őrszentmiklós to visit Aunt Hansi and Uncle Rory, a walk of approximately twenty minutes. As my parents were nearing the vintner's cottage the vintner and his wife ran out and kissed my mother's and father's hands. They had never made this gesture before and my parents realized that the vintner and his wife were paying homage to the future squire and his wife.

7

The World of Grandmother Eveline

In the early 1920s, Grandmother Eveline developed hyperthyroidism, which in those days was treated by a thyroidectomy, a far more serious operation at that time than it is today. Following the operation, Grandmother's doctors suggested that she spend more of her time in the countryside, where she could rest and get fresh air. Grandmother Eveline was self-conscious of the scar that the operation left on her neck and tried to hide it with a large pearl necklace.

From this point on, my grandmother would hire a coach every spring to take her necessities out to Őrszentmiklós and every fall, after the harvesting of the grapes, to bring her back into the city. From the age of about five I vividly remember the summers that I spent with Grandmother Eveline in her vineyard. She was one of those people whom I dearly loved, and we understood each other extremely well. She was incredibly modest, accommodating, and a loving wife to my Grandfather Miklós.

Grandfather Miklós had a strong, well-balanced, cheerful personality but was a typical city dweller. He never felt entirely at ease in the vineyard and spent his time there only because of my grandmother. Their son, my father, meanwhile, was a writer whose métier didn't have agriculture in it and he himself didn't like the lack of comfort at Őrszentmiklós. Nevertheless, with the passage of time, my father too discovered some great advantages of our bucolic lifestyle—including the ability to raise livestock and preserve fruit during wartime.

My mother grew up in an artistic millieu. Her life centered on drawing parliamentary portraits, writing weekly newspaper columns, and going to the printing shop and to the atelier to paint. But her inner nature resonated with the land. Somewhere inside her was a hidden peasant. Around the time I turned twelve years old, a half-acre of vineyard and orchard went up for sale in close proximity to my grandmother's vineyard. My parents scraped together 1,700 pengő and with 135 pengő that I lent them, bought that piece of land. From then on, my mother became an avid farmer. She learned how to prune peach trees and vines and to replace missing grape stalks. She got hooked on country life. Being an artist helped her immerse in nature; she looked at Őrszentmiklós and Veresegyház with the eyes of a French painter. The traits of the two, the artist and the peasant, amplified one another.

It was a much easier task to manage the household in the city than the one in the vineyard at Őrszentmiklós, where water had to be drawn from a well and an outhouse in the proximity of the chicken coop served as the toilet. Instead of a bathroom, Grandmother had a Japanese vieux-lacquer chest that held a washbasin, water pitcher, towels, as well as a water glass, toothbrush, and soap. While she washed, a paravan, or folding screen, assured her privacy. It could only be an enterprising and resourceful personality who would willingly forsake the amenities of technological civilization from spring until fall. However, one constant for my grandparents was that they always had a cook or some household help in the city or at the vineyard.

Our sources of light were a kerosene lamp, candles, flashlights, lanterns with candles, a miner's lamp (it dripped water on calcium carbide crystals, generating gas that could then be lit), and finally the "Hurricane Lamp." It was a candle of adjustable height sheltered in a glass ball. As the candle burned and its light sank, one could raise the candlestick. Because of its glass protection, it could be used outside regardless of wind or breeze, which is how it derived its name.

All of these light fixtures emitted smoke and stench. They needed to be cleaned frequently, to be filled with kerosene from time to time, and to have their wicks trimmed.

Out in the countryside, we had three options for grocery shopping. In the village of Őrszentmiklós there were two grocery stores, one belonging to Mr. Spitzer and one to the Hangya Consortium (Ant Consortium). The third option was Mrs. Hübner's store at the Őrszentmiklós railroad station. Going into the village was an excursion. Going to Mrs. Hübner's was considerably quicker. As I became older, starting around the age of twelve, I was often sent to Mrs. Hübner's, mostly for cigarettes or other small items. These errands generated mixed feelings in me. On the one hand, I was scared of the dogs, grown-ups, and strange children I would encounter along the way. On the other hand, I was somewhat compensated for my fears in that Mrs. Hübner invariably gave me a Stollwerk (caramel-like toffee) at the end of our transaction. As I entered the store, a little bell would ring and an incredible orgy of scents, a mixture of spices and tobacco, would hit my nose. Her store carried sundry merchandise, raffia (palms used to tie vine stalks), carved wooden handles for various tools, and of course there was always some rock candy around.

In order to reach this magical place, I had to cross the railroad tracks by the station. There, in the bright, enveloping sunshine, I would pass the villa of Mrs. Szitányi, a widow who played the piano. The sound of piano music would burst forth through the open window, the music mixing with the sunshine. I vaguely recall some of the grownups criticizing her repertoire; she probably played Debussy or Ravel, considered by some in those days to be revolutionary.

As spring neared, Grandmother grew anxious waiting for the warmer weather to arrive so that she could go out to the vineyard. There was no fireplace in the house at Őrszentmiklós, only a kitchen stove. We would use the previous year's vine stalks as kindling wood in the stove for cooking or for boiling water for tea. Each spring, after Grandmother watched the dray leave with her household items, she would board the train and arrive at the vineyard much sooner than the coach. After settling in she would collect her animals, which had been left in the village for the winter. During the summer, the livestock would create a hubbub in the yard. The rooster exercised his voice and our dog returned to his favorite spot on the porch. Our maid set the brick oven in the yard to work again, and baked bread the size of a coach wheel.

When school let out, my whole life changed and I would enter Grandmother's world. Grandmother Eveline and her brother, Uncle Rory, notwithstanding their aristocratic backgrounds, were simple, modest, and unpretentious people. In their personalities they combined the aristocrat with the peasant. From spring until the fall harvest, they spent more time in the company of peasants, railroad workers, cooks, coaches, innkeepers, and factory hands than they did with members of their own class. Nowhere was this simplicity of character more apparent than in their diet. For Uncle Rory, *Grenadirmarsch* (pasta with potatoes) was a heavenly delight; likewise *Zwekkerl* noodles with sautéed cabbage; stuffed cabbage; noodles with poppy seeds nuts, or cottage cheese and sour cream; potato pancakes; *Schmarn*, a type of semolina omelet with a preserve topping; and caraway seed soup. He was also fond of dumplings—plum-filled, cheese-filled, liver-filled—*Knödels* in any imaginable form.

Grandmother's favorites were similarly simple, as was her life-style. She dressed simply. She was not a fan of opera or theatre, but sometimes she and Grandfather went to the movies. She didn't drink, she didn't smoke, and she didn't frequent restaurants. Most likely she read literature in French since she had a fondness for the language. She conversed with her husband in French and they regularly took French lessons.

Grandfather was a nocturnal bird. Whether at the vineyard or in the city, he always turned in very late. He initialed the daily paper with a blue marker after he had finished reading it to indicate that it could now be used in the stove for kindling. He liked to write with red- or green-colored ink and would write down long lines of numbers—making calculations and notes. When the washerwomen came to return the freshly laundered linen, he would pull out a list to check what had been sent out against the newly arrived bundles. That he was a banker was undeniable.

Grandmother's house was an elongated peasant house with a good-sized porch with green pillars. There were trellises on the front side of the porch on which climbing vines shaded us from the sun. Occasionally, my parents and my grandfather would sit on the porch chatting over a glass of wine.

During the summers that I spent at Grandmother's house, she always had a cook. One season we had a male cook whose last name was Szakács, a fitting name since it means "cook."

The grapes in Grandmother's vineyard were mostly red and green Veltliners—a sweet grape that one could also eat as a table grape. Her other varieties of wines were Ottonel (a corruption of O'Donnell) Muscadet, Riesling, Oporto, and Burgundy.

Grandmother's fruit trees were mostly apricot, though she also had peach and plum trees, one almond tree, and one large walnut tree by the corner of the house. Next to it was a large wild olive tree. In front of the house stood a wild apricot tree that would have split into two if not for a wide iron ring that held it together. This was my favorite place to camp out. I would put a plank on top of the iron ring. The space there was wide enough for me to sit and

My mother and I by the apricot tree

read. The small fruits on the wild apricot tree were not suitable for the market, but made first-class fruit preserves.

The vine stalks were collected in a pile to dry and utilized as firewood. Out of them I made an imaginary French Foreign Legion fortress in which to hide from the Bedouins.

Two sandy roads framed Grandmother's land at Őrszentmiklós, one to the right and one to the left. Her house, which was situated at the center of the vineyard, had a walking path behind it connecting the two public roads. My parents often took strolls by moonlight on this private lane. As I lay in my bed at the rear of the house preparing to fall asleep, I would hear my parents' voices from a distance. As they approached their conversation would seep through the window. Then it would fade out as they passed on in the other direction.

On the opposite side of the house, at the far end of the court-yard, was the chicken farm. Grandmother Eveline had a rooster,

My parents walking down the lane behind Grandmother Eveline's house

which, with his shrill "kee-kee-ree-kees," greatly contributed to the character of the place. Due to her many hens, not only were we well stocked with eggs, but little fluffy yellow chicks also livened up the courtyard.

Every spring or early summer the chicken coops would be washed with lime by peasant girls. The young maids would carefully tie up their hair with a kerchief before entering the poultry farm. As a young boy I was intrigued by this lime-whitening activity. One year, oblivious to the lurking menace, I curiously stepped into the coop. My head uncovered, the poultry lice promptly arranged a convention in my hair. My parents did not want to shave off my brown hair, so instead, they washed it with kerosene, causing my skull to itch dreadfully. My grandmother, however, remained concerned, and as a precautionary measure, a few days later when our itinerant barber showed up and my parents were no longer there, ordered that my head be shaved. Having undoubtedly been given the appearance of a convict in a chain gang, I sank into utter despair and went into exile in the farthest corner of the vineyard. To make matters worse, it was a Saturday, my parents were due out from the city in a short time, and I couldn't bear the thought of having them see me like this. When my parents found me they were shocked by my new look. I suspect that my grandmother was given strict instructions never to do this again.

The young girls who lime-washed the chicken coops wore old-fashioned peasant attire. One afternoon, I observed one of these girls as she put the kitchen in order. When she had finished her task, she disappeared into the cook's room and then reappeared with a host of colorful skirts on her arm, which she proceeded to put on one after another. In all there were about twelve of them. This enormous bundle of skirts was her normal daily attire. These skirts may have served one other purpose: helping to disguise a pregnancy. A woman could shed one skirt layer after another as she became larger.

After a new veranda was built at Őrszentmiklós we were able to elevate our breakfast to its proper festive importance. Early in the morning the sun would shine onto the veranda as we drank our ritual tea. My father was a connoisseur in everything. Whether food, drink, or cigarettes he would have only the best; expense was no concern. His cigarettes were handmade. Every month, Mrs. Sárási, who worked in a cigarette factory, would come over to my parents on her day off to make my father's cigarettes.

My father was also a tea connoisseur. His favorites were Orange Pekoe, Darjeeling, Prince Edward, and Ceylon. Gradually, I became a tea drinker too, and by the time I entered the fifth grade I had joined my father in his daily tea ritual, only I drank it with sugar and milk. For breakfast I frequently had *kifli*, a crescent-shaped hard roll. I would split the *kifli* in half, butter it, and then submerge it into the tea. The butter from the *kifli* would partially melt into the tea, lending the tea a special, exquisite taste.

About a decade later, when I was twenty-two or so, I read about a custom in Tibetan monasteries of serving tea to guests with small cubes of butter attached to the inside of the cup. The number of cubes would vary between one and four, based on the importance of the guest. Intrigued, I tried putting small cubes of butter in my next few cups of tea. The taste of the buttery tea brought back childhood memories—a Proustian experience. When I mentioned my déjà

Family portrait in front of the new veranda

vu–like delight to my mother, her laconic response was, "Well, that is all very nice, but I'm fairly certain it wasn't the mothers of the monks who washed their dishes." By this point, the war had ended and we didn't have domestic help anymore.

When school let out in June, it was time for me to go to Grandmother's vineyard. The first few days at Grandmother's were usually spent visiting and greeting the local *dramatis personae*, who would remark, "Oh, little Károly," or, "Young Master, you have arrived, haven't you?" These banal comments, combined with small talk about school and vacation, irritated me endlessly. Most of the time, I hadn't the slightest idea how to respond. As a child of around twelve, I lacked self-confidence. To a certain extent, these scenes repeated themselves when I returned to the city.

In June, life in the vineyard entered full swing. Spring had passed and summer beckoned. One by one, the familiar faces appeared on the scene. First, I would usually see Mr. Cinkota, Grandmother's righthand man. Cinkota had a nice wife and two pretty girls, Zsuzsi and Bözsi. Grandmother would have been hard-pressed to run her vineyard without her trusted Cinkota. She never contracted out any of the work. She paid for labor with hard cash, and she tried to cover her costs and then some by selling her wine.

My great-grandfather Henrik was the first to hire a Lehotzky lad, in the late 1800s. He became the vintner—a steward for the vineyard, which at that time spread out over close to one hundred acres. I met this Lehotzky when he was in his seventies. He recounted stories for me, including one about hunting hares during the wintertime. He would set up traps between the rows of vines, and he also carried a hunting rifle. When the whole landscape was covered in snow it was easy to spot the brownish-grayish rabbits as they scurried about.

Mr. Lehotzky had two sons, András and József, who in turn had one son—László, or Laci. Laci was the same age as me. After the war he became our foreman, and we spent years working together. He was a source of constant surprise to me, with his wide range of knowledge about the vineyard, the orchard, masonry, or carpentry, and great practical skill. He must have learned it all from his grandfather, my great-grandfather Henrik's vintner. Laci was incredibly thorough. He was also an extremely slow worker, but he worked steadily and without interruption.

Mr. and Mrs. Cinkota harvesting the grapes at Grandmother Eveline's vineyard

A few years after the war, in 1949, Laci married Mari Gast, the daughter of a poor widow. We were invited to Laci and Mari's wedding ceremony, which took place in the Calvinist Church down in the valley in Őrszentmiklós. Afterward, everyone was invited to Laci's parents' house for a festive dinner, and all of us escorted the newlyweds there on foot. It was a long walk from the center of the village up a steep road and we advanced at a leisurely pace. On both sides of the road were neatly kept peasant houses and in front of the houses stood elderly women, looking a little bit like old hags and shouting incredible obscenities at the young couple. This was the first time I had encountered this folk custom, which must have been the rural version of sex education.

Laci's parents' house was overcrowded with people and food. After the soup, my father gave a speech at the dinner table, speaking warmly, simply, and to the point. He quoted from the biblical verse that says that everything has its time. This was the time to celebrate cheerfully the communion of two young people at the beginning of their married life. The food was delicious and the quantities mind-boggling. It was a hard task to keep up with the drinking. Everyone wanted to clink glasses with us, and the expectation was that one would regularly empty his or her glass. Gradually, the wine began to make me wobbly. My father, on the other hand, was a master diplomat. He always had a full glass from which he just sipped. Should one of the guests or the hosts egg him on with a "bottoms up," he would tactfully respond with a wink, "Thank you very much, but I don't wish to go home so soon."

While staying at Őrszentmiklós, I came to know quite a few of the local personalities. Among them was Mrs. Schmidt, our mail carrier with a shirt as voluminous as a sail and a giant leather mail pouch hanging over her shoulder. Another unique character was Mr. Csonka, who was a field guard, or ranger, and constantly on the move. He was a small, jovial person with reddish cheeks. He carried a leather satchel and a gigantic six-shooter, and made a big impression on me.

One morning, Mrs. Schmidt, who was a conveyer of gossip and news as well as the mail, arrived with the sad news that the engineer Mr. Rados had committed suicide. He had taken a lengthy piece of wire, attached one end of it to a stone, and thrown the stone over the high-voltage electric line above the railroad tracks while he held on to the other end of the wire. He died instantly. We heard that a widow had been left behind with two small children, a girl and a boy. Years later, we would spend many evocative and enchanting hours on the veranda of the Rados family's house. That I would be passionately attracted to Judit Rados, and remain her friend to this very day, was all yet to come.

Grandmother hired various artisans for their services. She had a cooper, Mr. Printz, who for many years was indispensable to the vineyard. Later, József Boldizsár became our cooper; our cook Rózsi was Mr. Boldizsár's girlfriend.

From time to time, the Kaltenbach family coach came by the vineyard. It was driven by a peasant woman who sold produce, chiefly dairy products. The Kaltenbachs sent their coach out daily laden with milk, cottage cheese, and sour cream, all of which Grandmother would often purchase since she did not have an icebox, and her cool pantry was only suitable in the heat of the summer for smoked meat products. Whenever it came by Grandmother's, my lunch would be cottage cheese mixed with sour cream, which I enjoyed tremendously.

When I was around ten years old I was given a little red racing car, a child-sized Bugatti imitation. I would sit in it and try to pedal it, but its thin tires, its large chain wheel, and its small cog wheel rendered it impossible to move on the sandy road. The chain would also constantly fall off. Luckily, I was able to persuade a couple of pals to push me in it while I steered across the sandy paths. One of these boys, Sanyi Hayek, became a regular playmate. He would come over during the day and leave only around sundown, when the cows were being milked and he had to pick up milk from the farmer.

Sanyi's father was a worker in the Viczián brick factory. I went to their home once, an apartment in the factory tenement that consisted of one living room and a kitchen. One other instance where I encountered living conditions similar to this was in the city, at the home of a playmate named Laci Gangler. Laci's father was a waiter and they also lived in a sort of tenement house in a flat that had only one room and a kitchen.

On each of these occasions, I was puzzled. I would automatically compare our apartment and the apartments of relatives or other friends' homes with these families' dwellings. Up to that point, I had only seen the apartments of writers, artists, painters, and country gentry. It boggled my mind that people could live without decent furniture, paintings on the wall, carpets on a shiny parquet floor, or bookshelves filled with books in colorful bindings. These visits remained etched in my mind forever.

In 1935, after my lamentable fifth-grade performance at the Református Gimnázium (the high school of the Reformed Church), my parents took me out to Grandmother's vineyard in Őrszentmiklós. Upon my arrival, I was told that my father had found a young man who lived close to Grandmother and was willing to tutor me in math. He had dropped out of high school in the eighth grade but allegedly had an excellent command of math at my grade level. He knew fractions in and out and was happy to prepare me for my make-up exam in September. This young man, Rezső Nagy, was a customer of my grandmother's; he bought wine from her.

Thus I became acquainted with the Nagy family. They lived on another strip of land not too far from Grandmother. Rezső's mother was a very small, quiet, and humble woman. She was always in the background, shadowed by a little maidservant. There were three sons in the family. The oldest was called Béla. He had good bearing and manners, and he tried to teach me how to play soccer. We went out to the plowed field to practice, but after a couple of sessions I lost interest. The second son's name was Tibor. He had finished high school and was working for the Hungarian railroad like his father. The youngest son was Rezső, my appointed math coach.

The Nagy family house stood in the center of an extinct vineyard, on a small sloping piece of land. The entrance to the house was a tall, carved so-called Székely gateway, the likes of which can be seen in Transylvania. A few strips of wire dangled in the air on both sides of the gate but there was no trace of a fence. Nevertheless, there it was—this impressive carved wooden gate painted in gaudy colors standing all by itself.

The house was rather small. It is a mystery how it sheltered so many young boys, parents, and guests, though they did utilize the attic. I most remember the house for its lack of amenities. Perhaps it was only meant as a summer cottage.

The first time I visited the Nagys, Rezső, my future math tutor, was making lunch. He was cooking *lecsó*, a stew of green peppers, tomatoes, and rice. I passed up an invitation to join him. The skins of the tomatoes had rolled up and looked like small sharp lances. I got the impression that those tiny spears would puncture my stomach from the inside out.

During my frequent visits to Rezső's home I met a close friend of the boys named Kvaccs. He was a guest of the Nagy family when he was not working—which seemed to be the case that summer. He was the one they sent to Grandmother's to buy wine. Kvaccs walked around barefoot and naked, but for a pair of brown sweatpants that only his hipbones prevented from falling down. It was a bit of a touch-and-go situation, though had they fallen down it wouldn't have mattered much, since Kvaccs and the Nagy boys all wore white swimming trunks (their whiteness was questionable), in order to be ready to plunge into the lake at a moment's notice.

Kvaccs's real name was Károly Füredi, but nobody called him that. He had gotten his nickname during a camping trip with friends in the Mátra mountain range in northern Hungary. As he climbed the mountain, he found a gigantic rock at the edge of a cliff. He rolled the rock to the ledge and then sent it over the side, into the abyss below. When the rock landed, it made a crashing sound, at which he elatedly shouted, "Kvaccs!" From then on, his friends had referred to him by that name. Kvaccs wore a yarmulke on his head, which was somewhat surprising, or rather puzzling, since all of the pipes he smoked had swastikas carved into them. Even though I was still very young at the time, the sight of the swastikas repulsed me. I was well aware of the antipathy my parents held against everything that Hitler stood for, yet I instinctively felt that Kvaccs was not necessarily a bad person. Over time my instincts proved me right.

I learned that Kvaccs had two occupations. He was a boxer and also a sailor in the Hungarian Merchant Marine, whose small ships of one thousand registered tons cruised down the Danube to the sea and from there on hugged the shoreline. I was delighted by this friendship—what could have been more fun for a boy than to spend time with someone who was both a boxer and a sailor!

Thus, Béla Nagy, after giving up all hope of teaching me soccer, handed me over to Kvaccs. My boxing lessons were followed by swimming lessons and diving into the lake. Although boxing was an entirely new field for me, I also did not yet know how to do the crawl stroke or dive. It was Kvaccs who helped fill in the gaps.

Another time Kvaccs scored really big in my book was when I learned that he played the harmonica. He played "Red Sails in the Sunset" and other popular tunes of the 1930s, and my admiration for him grew further still. The following weekend, my father presented me with a little "Hohner" mouth organ in C major. It had cost him five pengő (about a dollar). From then on, Kvaccs also taught me how to play the harmonica. It took quite a while for me to learn where to put my tongue, how to take breaths, and how to use the palm of my hand to regulate the airflow. Nonetheless, after two weeks I was able to perform, and soon I was entertaining my parents and grandparents. One song that I played was a popular hit of the day and now reminds me of Sinatra. The words to the song went, "Never mind how old you are, as long as you are young at heart."

Regrettably, summer passed and fall made its presence felt. The day for my math make-up exam was threateningly at hand. My father discovered that Rezső, the boys, and I were having a wonderful time together, except that I wasn't learning any math. Thus, for the five days remaining Rezső had to come over to our house, where we feverishly crammed for the exam while sitting in our vine-covered bower, in the shade of the trellises. Due to the shortage of time, this was a daunting task. When it came time to take the makeup oral exam, my father, Rezső, and I went to the Calvinist High School, where the teacher, Béla Kolozsváry, quizzed me about fractions. Interestingly, I was able to solve the problems and Mr. Kolozsváry let me pass. Yet he was not entirely satisfied with my performance. He said that my way of solving the problems exposed the fact that I was not solving them the way he had taught us to and that this was a shortcoming that would very likely haunt me for the rest of my life. He was right about my having lifelong problems with math, but not because of fractions. He had no idea that all summer long instead of practicing his particular methods of problem solving, I had been practicing the arts of diving into a lake and playing the harmonica.

The passing of time disrupted my friendships with my funny bohemian friends in Őrszentmiklós. I only saw Kvaccs once more. Then the Second World War broke out, though Hungary was not yet a belligerent. Kvaccs was serving on a small, seaworthy merchant ship. In those months, which were referred to as "The Phony War," even though Hungary and Great Britain still had diplomatic relations, Kvaccs's ship was taken into custody, or a kind of internment, by the British. Kvaccs and his shipmates spent a few days in a British port, possibly in Gibraltar. There, Kvaccs had a revelation. He saw the incredible power of the British fleet and the dignity, self-confidence, and bearing of the British sailors, and became totally disillusioned with the Germans. Once his ship was released, he threw all his pipes with their swastika carvings into the sea.

I never saw him again.

Starting in my mid-teens, the lore of the sea, ships, and sailing greatly intrigued me. My father's cousin Béla Hilberth was a chief executive of the Hangya consortium, a company involved in international trade, and I heard stories from him about the audacious small ships of the Hungarian Merchant Marine. In the first phase of "The Phony War" the Hangya consortium received an assignment to fill a seaworthy ship with green peas. It was to sail from Budapest to a neutral country, Spain or Portugal. There, the small Hungarian ship anchored between a large British ship on its left and a large German ship on its right. The Hungarian sailors proceeded to transport the green peas in wheelbarrows from the Hungarian ship to the British ship in exchange for leather shoe soles. Once they had made it back to the Hungarian ship, they proceeded on to the German one with their wheelbarrows full of leather soles.

At the center of another amusing story was Mr. Dobozi, captain of the steamship *Budapest*. He was the father of the attractive Melinda Dobozi, with whom we boys were infatuated; we took dancing lessons with her. Mr. Dobozi's ship was referred to as a *tengerjáró*, which means ocean liner. As opposed to the many ships of the Danube that did not go out to sea, these small ocean liners were able to navigate the sea, albeit only by hugging the shoreline.

One time, when Captain Dobozi was returning from abroad, he was stopped by the Hungarian customs officers. His boat reeked of rose oil, a fine essence produced in Bulgaria. The customs officers demanded that Captain Dobozi disclose the location of his contraband and how much of it he had. Dobozi in turn denied any breach of the law and insisted that he had no contraband. The customs people became furious. They quarantined the ship and began a search. Soon the ship looked like a skeleton, as if piranhas had consumed the planks, the sides of the ship, and everything else that was movable. They couldn't find anything, yet a strong scent remained. After a while, the customs officers, in their rage and desperation, made an offer to the captain. The deal was that if he told them where the oil was hidden, he could leave scot-free and keep his oil as well. Captain Dobozi thereupon took his pipe out of his mouth and nonchalantly pointed up at the pale light of a kerosene lamp hanging high above his head. As it turned out, all of the kerosene lamps on the ship had been filled with rose oil essence. Some of these lamps were burning; most of them were not, since burning the oil was a costly disguise.

A far more dramatic episode took place on the Danube in 1938. An article about this event by Zalán Petneházy, a retired sea captain, was published in the daily newspaper *Magyar Nemzet* on November 28, 1987. Petneházy described how he and his Hungarian sailors had transported persecuted Jews from all over Europe via the Danube. These passenger cruisers were deemed the safest traveling modes for Jewish refugees gathered from Czechoslovakia, northern Hungary, Carpatho-Ukraine, Poland, and Germany. They used the *Pentcho*, the *Erzsébet Királyné* (*Queen Elizabeth*), the *Car Dusan*, and the *Noémi Julia*, and sailed as far as Constanta, Romania.

Two good friends of Uncle Rory participated in this rescue mission: Herbert Thierry and Miklós Roediger. Thierry, who was at the time counselor to the Hungarian ambassador in Ankara, made the preparations for the secret journey on the diplomatic front. The execution of the mission, on the other hand, emphasizing the "extra-sensitive and confidential nature" of it, was placed in the hands of Roediger, commercial director of the Danube Shipping Company, who was a retired frigate captain from the Austro-Hungarian Navy during the First World War. József Antal, a high-level employee in the Ministry of the Interior (and father of Prime Minister József Antal, 1990–93) also had a role. He breached the existing regulations and gave instructions to the captain of the *Pentcho*, the last steamer to slip out of the Nazi encirclement. Years passed before news of the success of this rescue mission reached Budapest. This was a rare instance of a kept secret, a hush-hush operation that was not supposed to be disclosed to the German Nazis, the Hungarian Nazis, or the British. The *Pentcho*'s arrival at Constanta was reported by Bratislava's Swedish councilor in February 1945.

When Grandmother Eveline began selling wine independent from Uncle Rory, she had a new addition built onto the house in Őrszentmiklós. A deep wine cellar was built into the ground and above it was a small entrance hall where the wine press, the grinder, and a vat stood. Grandmother's other appliances—rubber hoses, suckers, plunging siphons, demijohns, bottles, glasses, funnels, and pails—were kept down in the cellar or in her kitchen. From the entry area a door opened onto another room whose two windows faced the vineyard. This room became my safe haven, my secret hideout, which I called the "Sheriff's Office."

This little enclave fueled my imagination and meant new adventures for me. I decorated the Sheriff's Office in accordance with my admiration for the Wild West. As always, I submerged my entire being into fantasy. I had an interest in history, and particularly in war, and now my imagination was fired up by the Wild West. I clipped photographs from *Rádió Élet*, the weekly magazine of the Hungarian Radio Broadcasting Corporation, whose publisher happened to be my father. I framed photos of Jeanette MacDonald, Nelson Eddy, Olivia de Havilland, and Errol Flynn and hung them on my walls. In those days children of my generation were infatuated with Westerns. *Dodge City*, starring Errol Flynn and Olivia de Havilland, was our favorite; next was *Gold Is Where You Find It*, also starring de Havilland. Other favorites included *Stagecoach*, with John Wayne, and *Rose Marie* and *Girl of the Golden West*, with Jeanette McDonald and Nelson Eddy. There were innumerable other great

Grandmother Eveline's House. My "sheriff's office" was on the right-hand side of the building where two windows are visible.

features of that golden era of film and popular music; we would have liked to see all of them. I developed a crush on Olivia de Havilland. Unfortunately, *Gone with the Wind*, with de Havilland in the role of Melanie, was banned twice in Hungary: first, when the United States and Hungary became belligerents; next, when the communists took over the government. I, along with my fellow Hungarian refugees, was able to see it for the first time only in Vienna in 1956. As the theatre darkened and the film began, a woman's voice could be heard saying in Hungarian, "I have been waiting for this moment for twenty years."

In my sheriff's office I also had a poster on the wall offering a $100 reward for the capture of a certain bandit. I had a couple of hunting rifles and a Smith & Wesson six-shooter befitting a sheriff. To top it all off, I also had a couple of Rastgasser revolvers. Fortunately, my supply of ammunition was meager, and I used it sparingly. Adding to my accessories, my Boy Scout hat served as a cowboy hat. My father's leather leggings from the First World War and a red checkered shirt completed my attire. I also had a mandolin, in case I had a fancy to transform myself into a singing cowboy.

Once, I went to visit the Vicziáns' farm and their Aunt Linzi happened to be there. When she saw me, she clapped her hands together and exclaimed in a high-decibel voice, "Here is the little *kovboy*, the little *kovboy*!" From then on, this became my nickname.

Me, as a singing cowboy, with Aunt Blanka

Me in my cowboy attire

Returning to my sheriff's office, on the bookshelves in my little refuge stood my favorite readings. There was a series published in paperback, called *Uj Élet* (*New Life*). On its covers were illustrations and photos from my favorite movies. One of the covers was taken from *Test Pilot*, starring Myrna Loy, Clark Gable, and Spencer Tracy. These exciting stories were geared toward providing my young generation with better literary nourishment. Another set of cheap paperback thrillers, Westerns, and mysteries referred to as "yellow novels" were published by the daily paper *Pesti Hirlap* (*Pest News*). These little yellow books, considered to be "trash literature" by my father, were the cause of my downfall. My grandmother's cook Rózsi and her boyfriend, our cooper, Józsi were avid readers of these thick, square, yellow paperback books. Many of them were translations from English and they were inexpensive. As I learned from my father, these books were being printed during slack time in the middle of the night, when the rotary presses were not printing the daily papers. They contained relatively decent, light literature by authors like P. G. Wodehouse and Max Brand. They were filled with great adventure, mystery, and suspense, and since they were affordable books they became the favored literature of people of modest means. This was how Rózsi and Mr. Boldizsár got hooked on them.

One day, I was out in the vineyard reading one of these books, a Western by Max Brand called *A Halálfejes Bika* (*Bull Hunter*). Afraid that my father might discover my newfound interest, I had dug a hole in the sand, inserted a few planks, and neatly shelved the paperbacks that Rózsi and Mr. Boldizsár had already read, constructing a small library in the sand. Luckily, there was no rain for those few days.

Dusk had fallen, yet I kept on reading *Bull Hunter*. I couldn't stop reading it; it was not "down-puttable," as Churchill once said. Finally, I drifted into the kitchen with the book in tow and continued reading it there by the light of the kerosene lamp. Grandmother Eveline asked me if it was a book that my father would approve of me reading. Based on my reaction, she took the book away and later showed it to my father. When he found out that not only was I reading this particular book but also that I had a little library collection in the sand dunes, he ordered me to speedily return all of the books to Rózsi and Józsi. I was terribly embarrassed, so much so that it was Mr. Boldizsár who had to finally go out into the vineyard and repossess the little yellow books himself.

I could never understand why my father held such antagonism for Max Brand. His reasoning was that one's time shouldn't be wasted reading *"Lekturs,"* light literature for entertainment, when there were lots of good books and life was not long enough for all of them. With regard to Zane Grey, I tried to point out to him that these novels were filled with vivid descriptions of the West, beautiful canyons, mysterious thick forests, wilderness, ice-covered lakes, and wild horses. This alone made the novels worth reading and the cliché-like love stories in Grey's books tolerable.

The truth is that I was irritated by my father's literary snobbishness, and since I was unable to convince him to be more open-minded, I devised a trap. One day in the early summer of 1944 I was not staying at Veresegyház but at Logodi Street, from where I was departing for a bicycle race. Before I left the vineyard, I placed *Texasi Lovas* (*Lone Star Ranger*) by Zane Grey on my father's nightstand. This was the story of Buck Duane, an honest outlaw. On its cover was a nice photo of the West. That night my father picked the book up, and since he didn't want to disturb my mother he went into my room with a kerosene lamp, and lying on my bed decided to have a glance at the story, just to skim over a few pages. As my mother later told me, she woke up early in the morning to the stench and the smoke of the kerosene lamp irritating her nostrils. Upon entering my room, she found my father on my bed reading *Lone Star Ranger*, his eyes red and the lamp still smoking but with little kerosene left in it. On seeing my mother, he remarked, "That rascally kid of yours made me stay up all night." By then it was five o'clock in the morning. I had had my sweet revenge.

All those summers that I spent out in the vineyard, my father would give me books, many of which were somewhat boring. Such was the case with Charles Dickens and Sir Walter Scott. It wasn't that the ambiance of the age of Dickens didn't hold my interest, since I greatly enjoyed Arthur Conan Doyle's stories about Sherlock Holmes, which were written during the same time period, and I also enjoyed Robert Louis Stevenson's novels. It was more that they were a little bit over my head.

My sheriff's office, which served me well as a hideaway when I felt like reading, over time became the source of a different delight, which was music. In 1938, when I was twelve years old, despite my father's employment at the Radio Broadcasting Corporation, we still had no radio. Learning from friends how to make one, I collected the various items needed and got to work on it. Although the sound was not loud, it was audible; Guglielmo Marconi would have been proud.

Despite the amateurishness of the contraption, this little set worked well and gave me great delight, particularly since it was my own unique device. My introduction to music started with Irving Berlin's "Blue Skies" and his theme song for the movie *Alexander's Ragtime Band*. In those days, in the late 1930s, Budapest Radio played a variety of popular hits, Hungarian and American. Katalin Karády was at that time the most popular singer and movie actress in Hungary. One of her films, *Halálos Tavasz* ("Mortal Spring"), was an overwhelming success. Its music was composed by a colleague of my father's, Tibor Polgár, the conductor of the radio orchestra, who presented me with the musical score of the song and a humorous written dedication to go along with it. This was the same year that we took a class trip, a cruise on the Danube to Esztergom. We brought along a hand-cranked gramophone and for the entire trip our Italian language teacher Elemér Virányi sat by the gramophone and played "Mortal Spring" over and over again. We young boys didn't realize yet that grownups could sometimes act crazy as well.

I would lie in bed with my faithful radio as the moon shone through the windows and listen to the music until I fell asleep. Sometimes I would wake up to the unpleasant pressure of hard Bakelite earphones against my ears.

At the same time that I became a music lover, I also became interested in girls. Since I didn't have a Chinaman's chance of talking to Lilly Alberti otherwise, I asked my mother to organize a children's party. My mother, being a good sport, went along with it. The three Alberti kids, Lilly, my friend Franci, and Annie Róza, took the train down from Szada to Veresegyház, where they switched trains for Vicziántelep. In addition to them, we invited the Viczián cousins; Tóni the eldest and his brother Szabolcs, János Brencsán, and the two Kenderesy brothers. Then, in order to guarantee the success of our afternoon garden party, my mother bought the finest cookies a mother could get. During the party we played various games. One of these was "*Nemzetesdi*" ("Nationalities"), in which each player represented a different nation. We also played "*Adj, Király, Katonát*" ("King, Give Me a Soldier") and another game in which one player had to pick up a small ball and hit another player with it while everyone else tried to run away.

After a while, all of the fine cookies were gone. I hadn't even had a chance to taste one. Lilly, on whom I had a crush, was openly flirting with Tóni Viczián. It was Tóni who over lengthy sessions

Horseback riding on the Viczians' farm during winter break

Me with my suitcase

had previously taught her how to swim in the lake, holding her up on the palm of his hand while she learned the breast stroke. Lilly didn't look at me once. All in all it seemed everyone had had an excellent time except for me. Soon, our guests from Szada got ready to go back to the train station. Even though the Viczián boys didn't need to take the train to get home, they also left in order to escort the Alberti kids to the station. There I was, without my friends and with only an empty plate of china staring me in the face. I felt terrifically let down.

At my grandparents' vineyard in Őrszentmiklós in the 1930s, faces of various children, boys and girls, would appear on the scene at different times, as if in a film, only to fade out after Saint Stephen's Day on August 20. "September in the Rain" arrived. The sand beneath my feet felt wet and I walked about in damp shoes and damp socks. The days passed by in a quiet, grey mood. It must have been gloomy for Grandmother Eveline as well, since she didn't put her usual cards out on the table, stopped playing solitaire. Her only amusement was small talk, chatting with the mail carrier Mrs. Schmidt, with the field guard Mr. Csonka, with customers who came to buy wine, and with other local characters. She was entertained by them; perhaps she was a simple soul herself.

The weather would turn even more rainy as my vacation slowly came to a close. The landscape grew gloomy and the unheated house cold. We used the kitchen "sparherd" stove for warmth sparingly, saving the vine stalks for cooking. There was no sense in going to the lake anymore; it had become deserted. Guests stopped coming. The familiar faces went back to their fall routines, to school and to work. I became imbued with fright, knowing that another school year beckoned. Soon I would have to switch to my other life—friends in the city, old teachers and new ones.

8

The World of the Viczians

Although I had my own enclave in my grandmother's house where I could listen to music and read, what I missed most in those days were playmates. Even more, I missed having someone I could call a friend. At this time there was scarcely anything I could offer to another boy in the way of amusements to strike up a friendship with me. Gradually, though, things changed. Of all the Viczián boys, including their cousins, the Kenderesy boys and János Brencsán, it was Szabolcs (Szabi) who from time to time came to visit me in my sheriff's office. Yet even he suggested that I should instead visit his family's grange, since there were always five boys there with whom to chase away the time. Szabi and the other boys were always busy with various activities, were never bored, and would always welcome me into their group. Szabi also never failed to point out to me that his bicycle tires were worn down to a mirror-like state, putting him in constant danger of getting a flat when he came to visit me on a road bordered by acacia trees with their hard bristles. It was a well-known fact that the mechanic Mr. Dulkai charged a liter of wine to repair a flat tire. Nonetheless, with some cajoling, Szabi did come visit me from time to time. I took a real liking to him, as a friend and as a role model, someone who could do everything far better than I. He was a better swimmer, runner, target shooter, horse rider, archer, table tennis player, polo player, and card player. In a way our friendship became a continuation of that of our fathers. For my father and Szabolcs's father Toni had struck up a friendship when the two of them were around five years old. Back then the Viczians also had landholdings in the village of Vácbottyán. As boys our fathers would ride there together on horseback to watch the laborers tend the land.

The Viczián household was not an ordinary one, and it was fun to be around. Not once did I see the family eat at a normal time or on a regular schedule. We youngsters could always go and join them after we had already had our lunch or dinner. The Viczians would invariably be getting ready for their meal just as we arrived.

The Viczian family lived in an incredible mess. Hidden in one wing of their house was the so-called storage room. The cave of Ali Baba and the forty thieves wouldn't have held a candle to the Vicziáns' storage chamber. There was so much junk piled up in it, some of which dated back to the First World War or beyond. They saved everything—"Perhaps someday it will come in handy." It was the triumph of General Clutter. We kids were delighted by the chaos of the old objects. We dressed up in old costumes, hats, and uniforms, and held impromptu theatrical performances. When I ran out of reading material I would go see the Viczián boys and borrow their books. I read *Tom Sawyer* and *Huckleberry Finn,* in translation.

The last summer I spent at Grandmother's vineyard was the summer of 1939. I was fourteen years old at the time. Grandmother Eveline couldn't come out to Örszentmiklós that summer because Grandfather was not well. My parents didn't come out either, and I was left in the custody of our cook Rózsi. Every morning she would ask me what the daily menu should be. One day we would have pork chops, the next day noodles with poppy seeds, and the following day crêpes suzettes with apricot jam. Then we would repeat the same order all over again. Rózsi didn't mind the lack of variety in our diet; as long as she got her daily quota of wine, she happily went along with my requests. In those weeks at Örszentmiklós I had a most carefree and leisurely life. I didn't have to account for my activities or whereabouts to anyone. I got up when I wanted and went to bed as late as I wanted. Every night I would go to bed listening to music and fall asleep with the hard earphones pressed against my ears. I enjoyed the beauty of the waxing and waning moon and the setting sun.

Unfortunately, over the course of the summer Grandfather Miklós's health deteriorated. I saw him only once after I returned from my vacation. He was lying in bed with his torso and head propped up by pillows to ease his breathing. The sun was shining and the room was bright, and my grandmother and parents stood at the far end of his bed. Grandfather was in his eighty-third year then. By early autumn he had passed away, his death coming as a great loss, especially to Grandmother Eveline.

During those long summer months, my parents and my grandmother must have gotten used to the idea that Grandfather was not well and that it was time for him to go. It was a rainy fall day when we went to the cemetery. A great crowd had assembled and there was a beautiful collection of flowers. The funeral was somber, not ostentatious. It was not very emotional, as it was not customary in our family to show our innermost feelings in public. In those days mortality didn't yet have a place in my mind. The grown-ups, on the other hand, seemed to regard death as part of the human experience, an unavoidable occurrence. With Grandfather's death in September, an era came to an end. He died and the Second World War began.

9

The World of the Child and the Servants

By the time children grow up, they have forgotten most of what happened during their childhood. The remaining memories assume a grayish hue, and some of them become more beautiful in a nostalgic way. Although adults look upon childhood as a most carefree experience, with honest scrutiny they must admit that it is a difficult time. Even the concept of time is different from a child's perspective. Dezső Kosztolányi wrote a beautiful collection of sad poems about the childhood, entitled *A Szegény Kisgyermek Panaszai* (*Sorrows of a Poor Little Child*).

Children lack the usual armaments of grownups. Adults can consult or ask for advice from a spouse, relative, or friend. Children engage in rivalry more than adults, and have a more limited base of support.

Childhood is basically a learning and waiting experience concentrated into one. It is filled with anxious waiting to be able to join adult society while being busy with studying, practicing, and experiencing life according to one's surroundings and possibilities. A child spends much time observing the details of his or her environment. Feelings are more acute and expressions more direct and natural. Yet, there is no sense of urgency—at least that was the case for me. I had the leisure of watching clouds form in the sky. Since nothing was urgent, time had less meaning. I felt joys and sorrows intensely. Experiences were vivid, whether joyous or painful. Events excitedly anticipated were frequently followed by disappointing letdowns. With age these exaggerated contrasts ameliorated, as I was able to remain on a more even keel in spite of surrounding turmoil.

When I had my small mishaps, my little traumas, as a child, the role of the grownups around me was that of bystanders. They couldn't quite understand why things that seemed minor to them made me so upset. This only made me feel lonelier and more isolated. At times like this my parents would try to console me, yet I could feel that they didn't quite understand my misery. (Conversely, my parents were likely pained as much as I by my not being able to fully convey my feelings to them.)

When I was very small, I spent a great deal of time in my mother's company. I would be at her side while she worked on her newspaper articles, colored Béla Iványi-Grünwald etchings, or did some oil painting in the atelier. Later on, I was taken care of by live-in domestic helpers. Once, when I was around three or four years old, I was playing on the terrace of the apartment on Ráth György Street where two maids were in charge of watching me. On a whim, they decided to try to scare me by lifting me up and dangling me over the wall of the terrace, holding me up in the air as if they were going to drop me four floors down into the street. Needless to say, I was scared to death and squealed like a piglet in protest.

We tend to recollect our childhood traumas more than our everyday experiences. On one occasion the suffering party was not me, however, but my mother. I was in the New School in Budapest at the time, a first grader, when my classmate Dezső Kemény proposed that we escort another boy home. Dezső knew that the boy possessed a beautiful papier maché castle that just had to be seen. The temptation was strong, so I went along. Indeed, the large fortress was mesmerizing. I just sat there before it, probably looking like the little boy in the famous Maxfield Parrish painting, wearing his large straw hat with a ribbon and staring up at the beautiful castle on the hill.

Dezső took his leave shortly, but I just couldn't tear myself away. After a while, my classmate's mother asked me whether my parents knew my whereabouts. Since my parents of course had no idea where I was, she quickly placed a couple of phone calls. Shortly thereafter our maid arrived and I had to say goodbye to the castle. At home, our maid led me into my mother's bedroom. There, looking like T. H. Lawrence, with a white turban on her head, my mother lay on her bed with the shutters rolled down. Acknowledging my entrance, which I made with my usual flair, with the wave of her hand she graciously ended the audience. Poor mother, this time it was she who had had a traumatic experience. She had managed to equate my absence with the kidnapping of the Lindbergh baby—the downside of reading the daily paper.

My next mishap took place in Uncle Rory's garden at Veresegyház when I was six years old. My parents and I were invited for Easter lunch at Uncle Rory and Aunt Hansi's. The burial and the funeral ceremony for their son Henry had taken place the prior week. When we arrived my parents went straight into the house. I made my polite greetings and was permitted to go outside to play until lunch was ready. In the course of roaming around, I made my way into the kitchen garden. Passing over the little bridges—I adored those wooden contraptions—I looked into the water vat and saw my mirror image. Out of curiosity, I touched the sweep-pole of the well, and before I knew it a large wooden pail on its other end jumped up before my nose. This small incident frightened me. From there I walked into the greenhouse. It was full of beauty, warmth, and pleasant fragrances. After a while I grew bored and drifted back to the garden to await my parents' call. As I walked around I discovered a large wooden framework lying on the ground, a construction of white planks. It looked like a door with its face down. Of course I stepped onto the frame and walked across the planks, where a surprise awaited me. As I reached the edge of the frame and took a step, there was a loud plopping sound. The next thing I knew, I found myself submerged in a pit of some strange liquid. It turned out to be liquid lime, used to whitewash the walls. The pit was deep enough that even my head went under. I climbed out of the pit and presented myself to my surprised family. Until I opened my mouth to speak I must have looked like an enormous white mouse. Once my identity had been verified, I was transferred into the hands of the vintner's wife, who washed me down from head to toe and put my wet clothes out to dry. All cleaned up, I joined the group for lunch as planned, and sat through the rather solemn occasion bundled up in Uncle Rory's oversized white bathrobe.

A few weeks later, my mother and I visited the half-acre vineyard that my parents had recently purchased. There, my mother spent some time on springtime preparations, pruning the peach trees and vines. Since there was nothing for me to do, I decided to climb a peach tree. It all felt like so much fun until I lost my footing and fell. As it happened, a vine prop was right below the tree and my rear end landed on top of it. I was in such pain that I just lay on the ground motionless, moaning and groaning for a few minutes while my mother stood by totally shocked. Luckily, in a few minutes the pain left me. I stopped moaning and groaning and was able to walk again. Some years later when I read in school that the Turks frequently impaled their prisoners, I had some idea of what that must have felt like.

Another source of agony related to the way my parents dressed me. Like so many other upper-middle-class or aristocratic couples my parents were anglophiles, Anglo-maniacs in fact. Their role models were the Brits. Anglo-Saxon mores dictated that one should always be a gentleman and always play fair. One should be understated, rather than brag. My upbringing was in line with the British way, which meant that it also dictated how I dressed.

The first photographs of me after baby shots were taken by Margó Hajagos and Ada Marsovszky, friends of my mother who were among the top photographers in Hungary. In my first photo shoot, I was clad as a Russian muzhik. I wore a shirt, tied around my waist with a string, that had a high collar and buttons right up to my chin. My hair was rather long for a boy and I had a pageboy cut like the child stars in early silent films. It wouldn't have been so bad if I had only looked this way for the photograph. But I sported the pageboy hairstyle, and my clothes resembled those worn by Christopher Robin in Winnie the Pooh stories. I had a small checkered raincoat with a hood like his, and most of the time I walked around in shorts like he did. At times, I wore a navy blue sailor suit. My parents' goal was to make me look like a child of the British upper class. The more I resembled an English boy, the better. What this aim of theirs created, however, was a little boy who stood out like a sore thumb in the company of his peers. Fortunately, before I started school my hair was cut short.

An exception to my formal garderobe was my Boy Scout uniform, which fortunately conformed with the attire worn by the other boys. A drawback was that the uniform consisted of shorts, a chilly outfit in wintertime. I was about fourteen or fifteen years old when I started skiing and received my father's gray field artillery officer's riding breeches for the occasion. Earlier I had also received his leather leggings but those were reserved for my Western outfit. My father had looked very elegant in these clothes during the First World War. Of course, by the time I became their owner the old glory had somewhat faded. At least knickerbockers, or knee breeches, were de rigeur again in high school so no one frowned on them. In my parents' view, it was beneath me to wear regular pants or trousers. When I found a volume of Mark Twain in which Tom Sawyer and Huckleberry Finn were depicted escaping together in long pants, I tried to make a case, but to no avail. The Prince of Wales, as well as F. Scott Fitzgerald, both wore knickers or breeches, and so I had to do the same, according to my parents. This I endured until I graduated from high school.

In September 1939, the Second World War broke out, and by 1941 Hungary had become a belligerent—first against the Soviet Union, later against Great Britain, and finally against the United States. One consequence was scarcity. Resoling a pair of worn-out shoes, not to mention buying a new pair, posed serious problems. Textiles were also rationed, although my parents were already of the view that it was not worth having more than one set of clothes for a child, since children outgrow their clothing so quickly. Since I was still growing, this served as a splendid excuse for them to not buy me anything. Nonetheless, one Sunday afternoon my father and I went to the Reisz Department Store at Kálvin Square. (Interestingly it was open, which was not normally the case on a Sunday at the time in Hungary.) The salesperson showed me a business suit and a sports jacket. They both looked good on me. Father and I calculated the number of textile ration points we had remaining. Based on that, my father told me I could have one or the other but not both. It was an utterly painful choice. The dove gray business suit fit me well, almost as if it had been tailor made. The tweed sport jacket was a bit large but I had become completely enamored by it, with its rust color that was favored by Englishmen, aristocrats, foxhunters, and the like. My father asked me, "Which one will it be?" Feeling as if I had to make a near-biblical decision, I sized up the situation and with a deep sigh chose the gray suit. Practicality won out. My heart bled as we left the store and the rust-colored sports jacket behind. It was a jacket just like one my schoolmate Lala Szabó wore, and I had been pining for it ever since the first time I saw him wear it.

The issue of footwear may well deserve a separate chapter. When I was four or five years old I wore buttoned boots that required the use of a buttonhook. This was a small chromium rod with a hook on its end (like the artificial hand of a pirate in one of the old Hollywood pirate movies), the likes of which exists now only in museums. I was little in those days, but even so I realized the dreadfulness of this footwear. Shortly thereafter, I received my first pair of sports shoes, with orthopedic inserts. It took a lot of practice before I could tie the shoelaces.

As summer approached the season for sneakers took hold and it was time for me to get a pair of tennis shoes for everyday use. Of course, in those days these shoes weren't as high-tech and ventilated as they are today, and the smell that emanated from them could have annihilated an entire army division. The smelliness of these shoes was made more pronounced by the fact that hygiene and cleanliness took a backseat in Hungary in those days. The idea of wearing deodorant had not yet been conceived. Women never shaved their underarms nor their legs, and on overcrowded streetcars, and especially buses, the wafting stench of body odor could almost cause one to faint.

The turn for the better in my shoe situation came in 1942. That winter I joined the Ferencváros (Ferenc District) Sports Club—in those days a rival in fame to England's Wolverhampton Wanderers—as a member of its cycling division. At its annual meeting, we had a sumptuous dinner of breaded veal cutlets or pork chops and I had the occasion to meet the great bicycle champions of the day. Here, I became acquainted with a Mr. Eigner, who in addition to his role as sports manager was also a shoemaker. I bought some leather on the black market and he made a pair of buckled shoes for me styled after a U.S. military officer's shoes.

As far as shirts were concerned, I had detachable collars and cuffs on my white shirts, the practicality of which was obvious when it came to extending the life of the shirt between launderings. My sweater was reversible; one side was blue and the other red. On even-numbered days I wore the blue side out and on odd days the red. On occasion I wore a tie; for instance, when we went for a visit or posed for a photograph.

The worlds of the countryside at Őrszentmiklós/Veresegyház and of Logodi Street in Budapest orbited side by side like two planets on concentric lines. At times they intersected, but these orbiting celestial bodies were quite different from one another. In the autumn when we moved back into the city, our life acquired a different style and by and large we were surrounded by a new group of people. And when spring arrived, we moved out into the vineyard and again our surroundings and our lifestyle changed. At the vineyard, I had several playmates, boys and girls, whom I would never see in the city and vice versa.

In the fall, I kept busy with school and I joined the Boy Scouts. In the city, I spent most of my time with my parents, and my social life intertwined with theirs. When I was in the eighth grade, my good friend Szabi Viczián from Veresegyház moved in with us on Logodi Street. Szabi became the only friend to bridge the two worlds; we not only spent our time together in the vineyard, but in the city as well. There is a saying: "He is a good man to go down to the well with." Szabi was definitely that kind of a friend.

When I entered the ninth grade, Gyuri Sághy joined our class and I soon became best friends with him. He, Szabi, and I ended up as lifelong friends. Gyuri also felt equally at ease in Veresegyház and on Logodi Street.

My parents were always surrounded by a whirling group of friends. Due to their vocations and personalities, they came to know a wide variety of people, and they cultivated their friendships by inviting people over often. When we lived on Ráday Street in Pest, we were in the center of the city, so people would often drop in. Our cook Rózsi would only be surprised if there weren't any guests

Me in my Boy Scout uniform at 6 Logodi Street

for lunch. Among the visitors at lunchtime were my mother's cousin János Lauringer (we called him Janika, or Little John), my mother's sister Blanka; and László Korvin, the print shop owner, who delivered my mother's print orders. (He once joked that he was the only Jewish printer in history to go bankrupt.) From time to time, the "master" Béla Iványi-Grünwald, the great painter to whom my mother was an apprentice, came by to talk shop. He never forgot to give me a silver pengő when he stopped by (in 1935, a value equivalent to twenty U.S. cents).

When we moved into Uncle Rory's house on Logodi Street in Buda, we went from Pest, a pulsating lively city, to Buda, a sleepy and conservative backwater town (my Grandfather Miklós often despairingly said that Buda was many degrees colder than Pest). The writer Sándor Márai had said of Buda: "To live in Buda is to have a 'Weltanschauung' unto itself." From then on we had fewer visitors. When people came to visit now, they came with a purpose; not just because they happened to be nearby.

Even though the Radio Broadcasting Corporation was a publicly owned consortium and working for it should have required long hours, I could always hear my father clearing his throat around three o'clock as he came home from work and climbed the stairs from the Tunnel up to Logodi Street. He would have a late lunch and take a nap. This would be followed by the sacred ritual of teatime, after which he would sit down to write. He would stop writing for dinner, but resume after dinner and keep at it late into the night.

10

Uncle Rory and My Father
Make a Deal

A couple of years passed by, and the reverberations of Henry's death faded out in the light of other historical events. After his son's death Uncle Rory had drawn up a new will and named my father as his heir. Aunt Hansi would inherit the villa on Logodi Street, while my father would inherit the Veresegyház house and vineyard.

One afternoon in 1940, when we were already living as Uncle Rory's tenants on Logodi Street, my father went downstairs to visit Uncle Rory and Aunt Hansi. When he came back, he was upset. He told my mother that Uncle Rory was planning to sell the vineyard, as he felt that it was too much of a burden for him. My mother urged my father to go back downstairs and stand up for his rights—and for us, who were to be the heirs of the vineyard, Uncle Rory's decision mattered a great deal. My father thereupon went back down to Uncle Rory and tried to dissuade him from selling the vineyard. My father had several strong arguments against the sale. Namely, that during wartime, money has no value and whatever money Uncle Rory might receive for the property he wouldn't be able to invest, not to mention that at that time he would only be able to sell it at a considerable loss. Finally, he said that he would drop the idea of selling the vineyard, provided that my mother was willing to go out and take charge of it. In that case, he would draw up a legal agreement with my father, giving the title of the estate to him with the proviso that he, Uncle Rory, would receive any income from the estate. We could, of course, live there, keep livestock, and take whatever fruits and vegetables we needed for our own household.

My father reported back to my mother with this proposal. In those days my mother was a freelancer and not committed to a full-time job. She therefore gave an emphatic yes to Uncle Rory's offer.

11

New Dwellers in the
Old Manor House

So it was that 1941 became a turning point in our lives. In May of that year we moved into one side of the manor house.

Shortly thereafter, in order to strengthen the crew in the vineyard, my father sent our cook, Miss Juszti, and our concierge, Mr. Böttkös, from 6 Logodi Street out to Veresegyház. Mr. Böttkös, in addition to being the janitor and superintendent on Logodi Street, was a jack of all trades. Miss Juszti couldn't have arrived at a better time for my mother.

With Aunt Hansi and Uncle Rory still in the city, the courtyard looked forlorn. The manor house was enshrouded in a profound stillness and silence. Only the weathervanes grated on the tops of the chimneys.

One evening a couple of days after my mother, Miss Juszti, and Mr. Böttkös had settled in at Veresegyház, the peaceful night was disturbed by a sudden noise. Doors slammed and windows trembled. There was trampling, stomping, and thudding, with no apparent cause. The noises were independent of physical reality. Although the doors could be heard slamming, they never moved. My mother's first thought was that a poltergeist, a mischievous spirit, might be making the ruckus. Her second thought was that the spirit of Henry might be trying to call attention to something. The next night, when the last candle was blown out, the rattling resumed. My mother was exasperated. She left the house hurriedly in her nightgown and went to spend the night at the home of the Vicziáns, approximately a fifteen-minute walk away.

Mr. Böttkös had been a sailor during the First World War and, like all seamen, was superstitious. He was so scared of the noises that he left his nighttime abode, the vintner's cottage, and paced up and down in our courtyard until daybreak.

The following night, my mother again woke up to the noises. The door between her room and Miss Juszti's was open, and she could hear as Miss Juszti scraped a matchbox to light a candle. My mother could also hear, with a slight bit of amusement, as Juszti repeated, *"Beruhige dich, beruhige dich"*—"Calm down, calm down." Juszti thus gave her support to the idea that the noises originated with some restless soul.

By the end of the week my father had arrived. He was a man of action and solutions, and, with my mother urging him to do something, he decided to get to the bottom of the matter. He alerted Uncle Rory, who in turn contacted a group of spiritists (people who believe that the dead communicate with the living). My parents had a wonderful sense of humor and were quite thrilled with Uncle Rory's intervention.

Uncle Rory had in the past dabbled in the occult, and so now, thanks to his connections, a group of spiritists materialized from the unknown. Since I was not present on this occasion my mother recounted the events for me later. The "people of the spirit" arrived on the afternoon train—a mixed group of nearly a dozen men and women from all different strata of society. Among them were a streetcar conductor, a university professor, and various other characters. The only link connecting the members was their interest in the occult and in spiritist practices. It was a rather large and hungry crew, so my mother prepared for the evening meal, assigning various tasks to the spiritists. One woman descended with my mother into the vegetable cellar, from which they brought up onions, carrots, potatoes, and parsley. Another busily cut up meat. Yet another peeled potatoes. My father and a gentleman of scholarly mien went into the wine cellar and filled a demijohn with our excellent Riesling. In no time flat, my mother was serving a sumptuous, ghoulish goulash.

Once the spiritists had had their fill and darkness had descended, they went into my room and settled around the huge dining table in it. My parents told the group about Henry's suicide and suggested that the members ask the spirits some questions related to this tragedy. The spiritists told my parents that they would communicate with the spirits using rapping and tapping sounds, and suggested that my parents retire for the night. So my parents left, but the door between my room and theirs remained open.

My mother and father put their pajamas on and went to bed. But the whole scene was so strangely funny that they couldn't fall asleep. They kept on laughing quietly, so much that the big gothic bed shook beneath them.

In the meantime, the spiritists sat around the table and formed a circle. They connected with one another by touching each other's pinkies. As it turned out, based on various information gained from the other world, Henry's role as a possible cause of the nocturnal ruckus was excluded almost at once.

As the séance drew to a close, one of the members knocked on my parent's door and asked whether my parents would like to join in and sit in the circle around the table. So my parents also sat in, connecting their fingers with those of their neighbors. My mother described the strange sensation they experienced. As soon as they had been seated and were touching fingers on either side it was as if a low electric current coursed through their bodies. When the spiritists finally ran out of questions and were overcome with fatigue and sleepiness, the leader exclaimed: "Spirit, show us your strength!" At the verbalization of this request, everyone pushed his or her chair back as close to the wall as possible, leaving the center of the room free of obstacles. Immediately our massive dining room table lifted itself up off the floor approximately five inches into the air and then with a dignified slowness hovered its way over to the wall by the window and plunked itself down. With this, the séance ended. The members of the small gathering said farewell and departed on the early morning train.

This *Nachtlager* at Veresegyház didn't make my parents any wiser when it came to nighttime rattling and other disturbances, but the midnight pandemonium did in fact come to an end.

Around this time, my father stopped screening my reading. Although he was far from happy with my choices, he tolerated my reading Zane Grey. One of Grey's novels that had been translated into Hungarian entitled *Uj Lakók a Régi Házban*—that is, *New Dwellers in the Old House*—was a timely read for me. Today I recall only one of the book's episodes, in which the homesteaders warmed bricks in the cooking stove and placed them in their beds at night to keep them warm. This practice was followed by my family as well on shivering nights.

Uncle Rory had made a good deal for himself. Not only did he get a free estate manager, or vintner, in my mother, but in my father he also got an accountant, business manager, and purchasing agent. Granted, vineyards are not generally handed over as freebies either.

～

After having stayed at Őrszentmiklós from about five years of age to about sixteen years of age, I said goodbye to my sheriff's office at Grandmother Eveline's and transferred the seat of my operations to Veresegyház.

Although I had now settled in, I didn't burn my bridges at Grandmother's either. From time to time I would visit Grandmother and cajole her cook Rózsi into preparing me some noodles with poppy seeds. Grandmother was an early luncher, so I had time to get back to Veresegyház for lunch there too, where Miss Juszti would await me with noodles with poppy seeds as well. Uncle Rory, on the other hand, took his lunch late. This gave me a chance to negotiate with his maid Terka for a final portion of noodles with poppy seeds. I didn't consume this with the old gentleman, however, but, rather, in his spacious kitchen, where I received an enhanced version topped with melted butter and honey. These lunch jaunts were not the routine, however, but rather a Lucullus-like splurging, something that made for a good story later.

My parents and I began our life at Veresegyház as pioneers, starting from scratch. Lighting there was like something out of the Middle Ages. Every room had a candleholder, spare candles and matches, snuffers, and wick trimmers. The trimmers were needed to discipline the unruly candles, which from time to time began to smoke or drip, drip, drip their wax all around. Decorative candles had not yet been invented. I greatly enhanced my reputation when I demonstrated my method of removing wax from a tablecloth by placing a paper napkin over the wax and pressing a hot knife on top of the paper. My other accomplishment was collecting two or three decrepit Zippo cigarette lighters and cannibalizing them to create one functional one. My parents, the artists, lacked practicality. They couldn't get over the fact that their son lacked their artistic talent, while at the same time he was able to think up various practical ingenuities.

When elderly ladies came to visit us and were ready to go home they would pick up their little candle lanterns, sheltered on each side by glass windows, and use them to guide their way home. Our main source of light was kerosene lamps. The *"flach brenner"* had a flat wick, the *"rund brenner"* a round one. Aunt Hansi led a crusade against the use of *rund brenners* because they used more kerosene, though of course they gave off a far nicer light. In the beginning, the kerosene lamps were made of metal, but with the passing of time a glass kerosene lamp was invented that allowed you to see the level of kerosene in the lamp. The carbide lamps we had were very smelly. Their mechanism was simple: as water dripped on the carbide crystals, gas was generated. That gas was then lit with a match; it gave off a sharp bluish light. In another sign of progress, so-called Aladdin gas lamps made their debut. In this case, a pump gasified kerosene, which then burned in a small silk socket. The little socket sizzled with a powerful, bright white light that lit up the room.

We had flashlights at our disposal as well. These had served my father well during the First World War when he was out on the front line. Getting batteries for the flashlights, however, had become a difficult undertaking, since the army coveted the supply. In the Boy Scouts, we had a flashlight with an elongated pipe form whose light could be focused.

My father and I had lengthy discussions on the usage of flashlights. My father frequently made remarks like, "There is no need for a flashlight right now since it is practically daylight," or, "There is no need for a flashlight right now since the moon is shining so brightly." Or he would say, "Just go on outside and your eyes will adjust to the darkness." I, on the other hand, felt the need for a flashlight to chase away my fears, when shrubs, bushes, and trees could transform themselves in my mind's eye into frightening, hostile beings. On bicycles in those days it was mandatory to have a lamp that was either a flashlight or a dynamo. The dynamo led to the invention of the so-called *csipogó* (chirping) flashlight, which was activated by constant pumping in one's hand. The faster one pumped, the brighter the light became—but it became noisier as well. Even though the *csipogó* didn't need a battery, I disliked it because I thought that it gave away my position to the imaginary lurking enemy.

When, in May 1941, my parents and I moved into the curia at Veresegyház, we received the rooms on the righthand side of the house—the right wing. Since my great-great-grandparents used to live there, it was furnished and even had some paintings on the walls. Its entrance hall became our kitchen. From there a room opened to the right that became Juszti's dwelling. From Juszti's room opened another room, which became my parent's bedroom. Their room on one side had a gothic bed, a king-size bed of yore. On the other side was a washbasin stand and its paraphernalia—basin, paravan, water pitcher, and mug. The credenza containing the washbasin was topped with a slab of pink marble. One of the corners of the room held a maroon-colored tile fireplace. The floor was a jointed deal floor in a natural unvarnished color.

Entering from my parent's room into my room, on the lefthand side was an iron stove. It had a quadrangle opening on its front, which we could use to warm coffee pots and iron skillets. Since my room had another exit on its righthand side—a double door shrouded in heavy curtains that opened onto the porch and courtyard—the door of my parent's bedroom could be closed at any time. The beauty of this extra entrance was that I could come and go at any time of the night without disturbing anyone. Parallel to my room was the enclosed porch that served as a woodshed.

In my room, opposite the windows stood a couple of gigantic wooden bookcases with elaborate, heavily ornamented carved mythological motifs. In the center of the room was a large dining room table. A couch in the lefthand corner of the room as you entered was covered with an oriental rug. Next to it was a large walnut cabinet, which was soon filled with Western novels, revolvers, and paraphernalia related to my bicycle racing hobby.

The thin batten strips of the flooring in Uncle Rory's half of the house had been painted in light pastel colors. Some of our heavy oak doors were painted in forest green and others in a deep burgundy red. The windows were protected by iron bars, and folding shutters on the inside were used to retain the heat in the winter and the cold in the summer. In the blackout period during the war it was obligatory for these shutters to be closed at night. When we moved in, in 1941, the air raid instructions had just begun to be given, but we preferred the windows to be open even at night, when we could see the silvery shine of the moon and smell the sweet fragrance of the jasmine and lilac bushes whose branches nearly intruded through the windows.

A short distance from the house was a small wooden structure—an outhouse, or, as it was called in Hungarian, a "shadow chair" or "plopping toilet." In our case it held two seats, one of which was locked from the outside and reserved for my family's use. Although a plank wall separating the two seats made some attempt at privacy, sounds and smells from the two cubicles would amicably intermingle. We nicknamed the structure "the twin doo-doo nook."

The attic above our section of the house was utilized for various purposes. In one corner, nuts and almonds were laid out in their hulls on the floor to dry. After grape harvest, some of the table varieties were strung on stretched twine from end to end of the attic crossbeams. By the attic's entrance door was a smoking chimney with a tin-plate opening. Sausages, wursts, and kielbasas would be hung inside it on rods. The tin plate would then be closed and billowing smoke sent up from a small fire made of select wood burning in the ground floor kitchen.

This is how the old manor house awaited us, the new pioneers, who faced it as if we were entering a time capsule. We began our new life in the old manor house filled with hope and anticipation, amazed by our new surroundings and its ambiance. We didn't know how long we would live there nor under what circumstances. When the Chinese want to curse someone, they wish that person an interesting life in historic times. Very soon, historic times arrived, and from that point on we didn't have a dull moment.

~

Once my mother had taken over the management of Veresegyház, it was no longer necessary for Uncle Rory to constantly check on the vineyard; he could now come and go as he pleased. From time to time, he would venture forth from his study to inspect the vines, the kitchen garden, and the orchard. In the process, with his nonstop criticism, he would make a nervous wreck out of my mother. After these encounters with Uncle Rory, my mother felt much closer to obtaining sainthood. One of the times when she and Uncle Rory headed out on an inspection tour, my father, like a puckish little goblin, followed them and took a few snapshots with his camera. The pictures show in dramatic black and white how Uncle Rory in his wide-brimmed hat and walking stick towered over my diminutive mother, pointing out mistakes and failures as they walked through the garden and the vineyard. My mother can be seen sheepishly following Uncle Rory, as if trying to explain her shortcomings.

Even as late as the summer of 1944 when I was away in Transylvania, I remember reading a letter from my Aunt Blanka in which she described Uncle Rory's continued meddling in the management of the estate. She wrote, "When the laborers were hoeing, he would ask Mother why they weren't spraying instead. Then, when they were tying up vine stalks, he would ask why they weren't hoeing, and so forth." In the grand scheme, all of this was irrelevant since Uncle Rory knew that he had transferred the management of Veresegyház into the very able hands of my mother. And in spite of these little skirmishes, they had a harmonious relationship. It also helped that my mother felt a great deal of appreciation and love for Uncle Rory. My father, for his part, refused to be intimidated by Uncle Rory and physically was just as towering a presence as his uncle.

At my mother's request, Uncle Rory dismissed Vendrey, the vintner. My mother didn't want to compete with another manager

Uncle Rory scolding my mother

and it would have been costly to retain him, but because she still needed someone to help she hired Jani Nagy as a foreman. Now the keys to the manor house were firmly in my mother's possession.

Jani moved into the coachman's apartment, and the vintner's cottage was left vacant. Jani Nagy had a large family with many small children. He was skilled at pruning the vine stalks and apple trees, but he was a drunkard and when he drank he abused his wife. On one occasion, when Jani was drunk once again and hitting his wife Juli, calling her a whore, my mother had finally had enough. She marched over to the Nagys' living quarters and gave Jani a tremendous slap on his face. This must have at least temporarily caused him to sober up, for he sheepishly said with a wimper, "If only it hadn't been milady who had slapped me." My mother had chosen Jani as her foreman not only because of his skill, but also because she took a liking to his wife Juli and to all those little children. Their lifestyle was squalid, but it couldn't be helped because of Jani's constant drunkenness.

During the summer of 1941, Grandmother Eveline rented out her house in Őrszentmiklós. The following winter, while it stood vacant it was burglarized. When Grandmother came out in the spring, she was shocked at the sight. The physical upheaval surpassed the loss. As it was, there was no jewelry or money in the house, but drawers had been emptied and their contents strewn across the floors. Flour, sugar, and spices that had been in the cupboard were scattered all around. Since the house lay uninhabited during the long winter months, it was not entirely surprising that it had become the target of some wandering hoodlum or local bum. Some shady characters lived in the nearby shantytown of Erdőv-áros; in all likelihood the burglars had come from there. Before that, we had never experienced a burglary.

Stealing, of course, was a different matter. Once, when I was about eight years old, we were at my grandmother's house preparing to celebrate Easter. My parents had brought over a beautiful ham to share with Grandmother Eveline, our friends Uncle János and his wife Ancsurka, and Aunt Blanka. In the midst of the festive preparations, my dog Mackó (Little Bear) snuck into the kitchen, snatched the ham from the table, and took off with it. As soon as we saw him running off, we started after him, but we were unable to catch him. We ended up running past Uncle Rory's vineyard all the way to the outskirts of Erdőv-áros. By this time, we were in the midst of sand dunes, surrounded by huts, shacks, and a veritable shantytown of A-frame dwellings dug into pits in the sand. Finally, there was Mackó, sitting still on his haunches with no ham in sight. Nearby stood Illés Hamar, a despicable vagabond. When we asked him about the ham, he feigned ignorance.

The burglary at Grandmother's house, of course, was a far more serious matter than the ham. Grandmother was a determined Scorpio who stuck with her decisions once she had made up her mind. As soon as she had regained her composure, she walked down to Veresegyház looking for my mother, who was already busy with the springtime yard work. She handed the keys to her house over to my mother and said that she was *degutant*, fed up with taking care of the vineyard all by herself—without Grandfather, my parents, or even me. She told my mother that this was now all ours to deal with. With that, she turned around and returned to the city on the very next train. From then on, she would only come out to Veresegyház to visit Uncle Rory during the summertime, when Aunt Hansi was away at her sister's in Salzburg.

Since my mother had pledged to Uncle Rory that she would manage the estate, she paid close attention to the vineyard, the orchard, the arable land, the greenhouse, and all aspects of the enterprise. This included overseeing the laborers and dealing with the market women as well. The only thing that my mother didn't do was sell wine at a retail level, as Grandmother Eveline and Uncle Rory's vintner had done.

In the kitchen garden, water flowed in small irrigation channels. Bailed out in pails or shovels, the water was sprinkled onto the vegetable beds on either side of the channels. Water was also drawn for this purpose from the sweep-pole wells. One day, while in the garden, my mother noticed oily spots floating on top of the water in the channels. Intrigued, she took a closer look. It looked as if someone had spilled an oily liquid on the surface of the water. She went to Uncle Rory to tell him what she had seen. Uncle Rory replied, "About this we are going to stay mum." Had someone found out that we had oil on our land, we could have been ruined. Uncle Rory had obviously already seen the same thing in the past, thought carefully about it, and reached the conclusion that we would never have enough money for drilling and for the license fee. Whether a consortium could be created was also questionable. The most likely outcome would be the expropriation of our land by the state at an artificially low price. That would mean that we would lose our property, would have to move, and with the money we received from the state we would never be able to buy another property or home of equal value, not to mention one with such an enchanting life and neighborhood.

Travelers who came on foot toward the house from Veresegyház could see the house's yellow gable and the round opening in the attic from afar. I often went up into the attic to look out the window and take in the landscape. For years after the war, on our frequent walks to and from the village of Veresegyház the sight of the façade was like a beacon. Even today it remains vivid in my mind's eye. Uncle Rory used this image on his letterhead with an inscription beneath it that read *O'Donelisches Weingartentum* (O'Donnell Vineyard). A visitor arriving by coach or automobile would pass by the side of the house, continue on the *Auffahrt*, and stop in front of the terrace at the main entrance to the house. This was in the days when people of high society came to visit. Then Terka the chambermaid would go out onto the terrace and serve ice coffee or sherbet.

Leading from the terrace down to the quarter-acre park-like gardens below were stairs framed on both sides by Thuja shrubs and great hemlocks. In equal proximity to the left and the right of the bottom of the stairway were green and white benches. Paths in front of the terrace and the house were paved by crushed white stones and on the opposite side of the walkway from the stairs a round flower bed was planted with flowers of various colors. There were phlox, petunias, asters, geraniums, carnations, and various others. Beyond the flower bed, olive trees stood in a group, creating a border between the garden and the vineyard. These were barren oleasters, beautiful trees with small silvery inedible fruits. Nevertheless, they were a practical choice, as they thrived in the sandy ground.

Every Christmas for as long as Henry was alive, Uncle Rory would buy a pine tree, and every January, after the holiday season had ended, he would have the tree transported from Logodi Street to Veresegyház and replanted. As the years passed the pine trees' numbers increased and by the time my parents and I moved out to Veresegyház seventeen of them were thriving there in a little grove. After we moved in, we enjoyed the sight of the tall pines.

I especially liked the side of the vineyard that had a view of the hills of Mogyoród and St. Jakab in the vicinity of Gödöllő. Most of the time there was a steady breeze that gently swayed the shrubs and the trees as if they were dancing. Carried on the breeze, the sweet smell of the blooming linden tree would waft into the house. The heavenly fragrance of the flowering vines was so subtle we could only smell them for perhaps a day or so, and even then only when the wind brought it straight into our noses.

On the other side of the house were the courtyard and well. Between the right wing of the courtyard and the kitchen garden stood large weeping willows (which our gardener Mr. Cinkota strongly disliked because of the shadow they cast on the vegetable garden). Seen from afar, these trees added character to the landscape and served as a point of reference for travelers.

A path leading down from the courtyard to the kitchen garden was bordered by lilac bushes on both sides. Their higher branches intertwined, creating an allée that protected household members from the scorching sun as they ventured down to fetch something from the kitchen garden for the cook. The vineyard, the orchard, and the kitchen garden reached their peak of beauty, maturity, and development in the 1920s and '30s.

While my mother was doing less and less artwork and thereby foregoing some of her income, it was worth it, because she was able to do more and more work at Veresegyház. Although the income still went into Uncle Rory's pockets, he was generous; he told us that we were welcome to everything, whatever the estate could provide. From the garden, we accordingly enjoyed vegetables, such as peas, beans, tomatoes, and peppers, and from the field potatoes and corn. We ate fresh fruit all summer long. By the end of the year we were able to fatten up a hog so that we had an ample supply of ham, sausages, and wurst for the coming year. We stored the lard from it in large firkins. We also made head cheese, pork scraps, and smoked bacon. We gathered potatoes and beans, and stored them along with other vegetables in the cellar. We had a poultry farm that provided us with eggs, which we stored for the winter in grain or in water mixed with lime.

During the summer, we canned preserves and dried fruits. In the fall, it was time to make plum preserve—*lekvár*. Young peasant girls, their hair covered in red kerchiefs, stood before a huge cauldron stirring the bubbling hot, dark-blue substance. We harvested rye, ground it up into flour, and on occasion baked our own bread. At other times we exchanged our wine or brandy for flour. With my grandmother's grapes, we had our own supply of Oporto, Veltliner and Riesling wines as well. We piled up the unsalable fruit—cherries, apricots, plums—and fermented them in large vats, after which we sent them to a local distillery. In January, we made brandy from the husks of pressed grapes.

Our living standard improved. Our diet was simple but varied. My father made a list of one hundred different soups and argued that if we only had each soup three times a year this menu would cover the better part of a year. His favorite soup was made with caraway seeds and endowed with croutons floating on top. Split pea soup was another top choice. These soups were frequently followed by an entrée of crêpes, which also served as dessert. Bread toasted on the stovetop and then rubbed with garlic cloves was another delicacy, as was toast spread with bone marrow harvested from the shinbone of a calf.

Dumplings stuffed with plums or cottage cheese were a common treat. Plum dumplings were made by encasing a plum inside dough after having substituted a cube of sugar for the plum's pit. Potato noodles (krumplinudli) were another choice item. Potatoes were served in various other forms as well: sliced and fried in lard, or baked in their skins in the oven. Fresh beans and asparagus were usually prepared casserole-style with a topping made of sour cream mixed with bread crumbs that had been toasted in butter. We would also eat noodles with poppy seeds or walnuts, drizzled with honey. Our meals were often finished off with freshly picked corn on the cob. We especially liked black corn, which was the sweetest but was hard to come by, since invariably after a while the black corn would degenerate into white. For dessert, we ate raspberries or red currants sprinkled with powdered sugar. Gooseberries were made into a delicious soup, while quinces were turned into jelly after they had been nipped by the first frost.

My great regret was that we hadn't planted any watermelons or cantaloupe; in order to savor those we would visit Aunt Bözsi at the upper Viczián grange. Fortunately, whenever we felt like it, we could easily show up at the Viczián's for a meal since they were customarily late with every meal. If we went over in the early evening they were usually about to sit down for lunch. If we showed up late, then perhaps at around ten o'clock we could participate in dinner. Aunt Bözsi had a large cauldron where the servant girls boiled water for one hundred cobs of corn. She was well prepared for her large family and unannounced visitors at any time of the day.

My mother once said that our family could best be described by a poem out of a J. B. Priestley novel called Let the People Sing:

My mother is always thirsty
My father is always hungry
My auntie is a sweetie who is always thirsty and hungry.

The original English version that Priestly wrote:

You can't give Father any cockles;
You can't give Mother any gin;
Auntie's a sport,
But don't giver her port,
You never know what she'll begin . . .

When war broke out we were in an enviable situation compared to the city folks, who were reduced to living on ration coupons. We could also exchange our wine or brandy for foodstuffs. The income from my grandmother's vineyard went to her, but the income from my mother's small orchard went to Mother. When my father was promoted, his salary increased. In addition, he was selling freelance writings to the Radio. Ironically, as the country became mired deeper and deeper in war, and as every day brought us closer to the final catastrophe, my family was enjoying a better life.

The time for slaughtering a hog arrived in January. This was an opportunity for my father to invite his closest friends over for a tasty meal. Needless to say, they would happily accept the invitation. Alongside the sumptuous dinner we would serve our precious Riesling or Kadarka. Our guests were the illustrious representatives of Hungary's intellectual life. Among them was Albert Gyergyai. He had translated Proust, Gide, Giraudoux, and other notable French writers into Hungarian, and as a result received the *Légion d'honneur* (a meritorious order) from the president of the French Republic. Another frequent guest was Artúr Elek, a contributor to the literary journal *Nyugat* (*The West*). Elek was an aesthete, an art critic with an encyclopedic knowledge of Italian art who could describe from memory a random sculpture, altarpiece, or painting from a secluded little church in a hidden Italian village. At times he helped me with my Italian language studies.

Other guests included László Cs. Szabó and Gyula Ortutay from the Broadcasting Corporation. Cs. Szabó was the head of the Belles Lettres section of the Radio. He was a highly esteemed author of books on contemporary social issues. His assistant was Ortutay, who made a name for himself writing about Hungarian folklore and customs.

Another of our guests, the youngest member of this distinguished group, was Emil Kolozsváry-Grandpierre. He was a prolific writer who, by 1942, when we were having our literary feasts, had already published his sixth book, the semi-autobiographical novel *Tegnap* (*Yesterday*), which made waves with its unconventional views and courageous social criticism.

During these dinner table conversations, I sat like Jacques, the young apprentice in Anatole France's *At the Sign of the Reine Pedauque*, and listened silently, awed by solemn words. Of course, not just the words were solemn, but also the intellectual exchange. Each word had meaning, had substance. There was no room for small talk. In this literary circle, everyone knew one another's merit and values and tried to compel the other's admiration. There was no excess drinking, only enough to bring a bit more humor and levity into the conversation and leave a good taste in our mouths. One of the stories from these evenings remains vivid in my mind. A guest related an episode that took place at an international convention of writers. Apparently, at the end of the conference, the master of ceremonies suggested that for their parting words every writer express the words "I love you" in his or her mother tongue. The delegate from Hungary made a quick decision. Instead of saying "*Szeretlek,*" which he feared would sound like the bleating of a sheep to the other delegates, he picked a combination of two words that he felt had a far more romantic ring to them and exclaimed, "*Dio olaj!*" Nobody knew that he had just proclaimed, "Walnut oil!"

On another occasion, between a bit of lemon-spiced wurst and a sip of Riesling, we heard Cs. Szabó quote Goethe:

> *Über allen Gipfeln*
> *Ist ruh*
> *In allen Wipfeln*
> *spürest du*
> *kaum einen Hauch*
> *die Vögelein schweigen im Walde*
> *warte nur, balde*
> *ruhest du auch*

Hearing Uncle László recite the poem in German increased my admiration for him. One English translation reads:

WAYFARER'S NIGHT SONG II

Over all the hilltops
is calm.
In all the treetops
you feel
hardly a breath of air.
The little birds fall silent in the woods.
Just wait . . . soon
you'll also be at rest.

Goethe, in a melancholy mood in his twenties, etched this poem on a plate of glass with a diamond. For him, the *"ruhe,"* the rest, came only when he was eighty-five years old.

12

My School Life

You are told a lot about your education, but some beautiful sacred memory, preserved since childhood, is perhaps the best education of all. If a man carries many such memories into life with him, he is saved for the rest of his days. And even if only one good memory is left in our hearts, it may be the instrument of our salvation one day.

—Fyodor Dostoyevsky

Before the Second World War, the Hungarian school system had three options for study at a level equivalent to that of middle schools in the United States. The first option was to continue elementary school up to the sixth grade. The second was to leave elementary school after the fourth grade and enter trade school. The third was to leave elementary school after the fourth grade and enter high school.

In the decades since my grandfather had attended high school (*gimnázium* in Hungarian; gymnasium in English), curricula and grade structure had changed constantly. In my grandfather's day, in the 1870s, Greek and Latin were mandatory languages. By the time my father entered gymnasium, in the 1910s, Greek was an elective subject, and by the time I entered high school, in the late 1930s, Greek wasn't even offered anymore. Then the majority of the high schools were operated by religious denominations or the state, but there were a few accredited private high schools as well. These private schools were of the extreme kind—either extremely good or extremely bad. My Grandfather Miklós attended Rösler High School, which belonged to the latter category (in fact the worst of its kind).

The religious high schools were run by the Catholic monastic orders, the Protestant denominations, and the Jewish community. The monastic orders included the Benedictine Fathers, Cistercians, Piarists, Franciscans, and Premonstratensians. Religious high schools for girls were run by various nunneries, the most noted of these being Sacré Coeur (Sacred Heart). The Protestant high schools were the Fasori Evangélikus Gimnázium (Tree Line Evangelical High School) and the Református Gimnázium (Calvinist High School). Jewish rabbis, meanwhile, ran the Zsidó Gimnázium (Jewish High School). The high schools of the religious denominations were known for their high standards. The Piarist High School enjoyed a reputation similar to an Ivy League college in the United States. There were also several well-known boarding schools such as the College of Sárospatak. Before the Second World War there were no coeducational high schools.

In general, the municipal or state-run high schools had lower standards and it was easier to be admitted to them—or at least that was my impression. In the Calvinist High School, behaving well was not of paramount importance; the emphasis was on academic achievement. On the other hand, in the state-run István Verbőczy High School students' scholastic achievements needed not to be so high as long as one was well behaved. In the denominational high schools, students had to say a short prayer before classes began. In the state schools, the class stood at attention while a student leader reported the number of students present, sick, and absent without notice.

During the Second World War, about a half-dozen Hungarian scientists were involved in the United States' Manhattan Project, including Leo Szilard, Eugene Wigner, Edward Teller, and John Von Neumann. A number of them were graduates of the Evangelical Lutheran High School, located on Queen Wilhelmina Allée in Budapest (under communism renamed Gorkij Allée). At the first meeting of the project, its director, Enrico Fermi, stepping into the conference room, is said to have remarked, "As I look around here, we might as well hold the meeting in Hungarian."

After my father flunked six of his subjects at Piarist High School his father sent him into exile in Kaposvár. There, he boarded with a local family called the Mackós (little bears), a family of pharmacists, and became a student at the municipal high school. He was only allowed to return to Budapest for his last four years of high school, which he attended at Calvinist High School on Lónyay Street.

When it was time for me to enter high school, I went with my father to various schools, only to find out that I was not on the list of accepted students anywhere. I had not been accepted by the Benedictine Fathers, or the Piarist Fathers, or the so-called Minta Gimnázium (Model High School). Finally, my father and I went over to the Calvinist High School on Lónyay Street, my father's alma mater, where he approached the director, János Samu, and in the end I was admitted.

The classrooms at Calvinist High School were crowded, with sixty-three students per class. Béla Kolozsváry was the headmaster of the class. He was a math teacher and leader of the Boy Scouts. Our gym teacher, Kálmán Jakus, taught us archery after school. Discipline was not a primary concern of the school. We were a rowdy bunch of boys. One day, the class decided to pile up all our heavy wooden benches against the entrance to the classroom, to prevent our teacher from entering. We were promptly ordered to dismantle the barricade, but no disciplinary action followed.

As I was about to enter the sixth grade, Uncle Rory enticed my parents to leave our apartment on Ráday Street and rent the top floor of his building on Logodi Street. This required me to change high schools. Uncle Rory visited Ferenc Korpás, director of the nearby István Verbőczy High School, and arranged for my enrollment there in September 1939. Uncle Rory's son Henry had graduated from Verbőczy, and Uncle Rory was well known to its administrators.

When I entered Verbőczy High School, my new homeroom teacher Kálmán Miklóssy's first words for me were, "Where did you escape from?" When I told him that I was coming from Calvinist High School, he remarked, "Then you will be an outstanding student here." Verbőczy High School was known to be slightly less competitive than the Calvinist High School. Of course, his prophecy was completely amiss. I managed to stay a rather mediocre student with the exception of the eighth grade, when I excelled in every subject.

As I entered middle school, a critical phase of my life began to unfold. My school and playmates discovered a very entertaining pastime that happened to be at my expense. They became aware of my sensitivity to their playfulness, so much so that after a while they made a sport of competing to see which one of them could arouse in me the greatest demonstrations of jumpiness. They did this to a point where I would get red in the face and at times even become teary-eyed.

They teased me over things like my attire or my parents' jobs. My father was the editor and publisher of *Rádió Élet* (official weekly of the Hungarian Radio Corporation). Dénes Csongrády once made up a tongue-in-cheek story about *Rádió Élet*. He said that he had been reading it at home, when his father noticed and snatched it out of his hands. Replacing it with a most outrageous pornographic magazine, he said, "My dear boy, you should rather read this than that scandalous tabloid."

Taunting me became a daily sport, played just to make me defensive and resentful. I bore my suffering without telling my parents. I thought that even if I had mentioned it to them, they would have just brushed it off as being a natural part of growing up.

I concluded that I would have to change my attitude. I would become indifferent to their teasing. I would tell myself not to get worked up over their pulling my leg no matter how hard they tried. Should I have needed to, I was prepared to defend myself, even physically, but I was no match for some of the boys.

Turning over a new leaf in my attitude brought about its reward. Seeing that no amount of pulling my leg would make me jump, the boys gave up trying. They threw in the towel and acknowledged that I was on even footing with them. From then on, my relationships with them were in equilibrium, something I also needed in order to be accepted as a full-fledged Boy Scout. Members of the faculty were a fascinating congregation of eccentrics, splendid pedagogues, total shipwrecks, and outright sadists. My favorite teacher was our headmaster, Kálmán Miklóssy. He taught us Latin, Hungarian, and Antiquities. He was short in stature, had dark black hair, and was a decorated veteran of the First World War. He carried a couple of bullets in his flesh, and when the weather changed he would suffer from acute pain. During class intermissions his favorite pastime was puffing on his short pipe and playing chess. We nicknamed him "Pipás" ("Pipe Smoker"). He was the head of the chess club, where players played against the clock. He also taught an after-school target shooting class, which I joined.

He was a man of intellect, very low key, and an enlightened liberal humanist. He also had a good sense of humor. He had no patience for people who were pompous, conceited, or presumptuous. He had a tendency to degrade even those who might have had some reason to be conceited. During one of his Latin classes he talked about

Cicero's case against Catilina. In his view, Cicero's charges against Catilina were exaggerated. Catilina couldn't have been characterized as a great public danger, but rather as a sort of playboy. He may not have been a man of great character, but he was far from the villain Cicero depicted him to be. Thus, Pipás put even Cicero in his place.

When Pipás expressed his views about us he was not exactly complimentary either. He once noted, "Scipio was fifteen years old when he destroyed the fleet of Hamilcar. Now, can you imagine what would have happened if Hennefeld had been in charge of the Roman Fleet?" The class roared. Our classmate Gyuri Hennefeld, son of the famous refrigerator manufacturer of the time, was a chubby, clumsy boy, who during gym class would knock down the bar in the pole jump and fall off the horse vault. He was, undeniably, fifteen years old, however—just like the Roman Scipio.

Miklóssy was well liked by everyone. We students admired him for his knowledge; he had our respect, so the class was always disciplined without any special effort on his part. Once, during our Hungarian literature class, he gave us an assignment to write about Mihály Vörösmarthy, a great Hungarian writer of the eighteenth century. We were to describe the writer in the present day, what he would be like and how he would have lived if he were alive today. I wrote that Vörösmarthy would have been meeting with other writers at places like Café Philadelphia and eating his lunch at Krisztina Beerhouse and so forth and so on. Finally, he would go for a stroll and muse about the kind of life he would have had if he had happened to have been born one hundred years earlier. After a while, he would poke his walking stick into a pile of fallen leaves and exclaim to himself, "Mihály, Mihály, what kind of silly thoughts do you harbor in your head, just for the sake of chasing away your time?" Miklóssy let my literary snippiness pass and gave me a good grade.

The years that I spent at Verbőczy High School passed in harmony. These were the years that I spent slowly growing up. Just as one cannot nudge the cherry tree to bear fruit sooner than it's ready to, one must patiently wait for adulthood to arrive. Some credit is due to Pipás, our homeroom teacher, for the peaceful environment in the high school, and also to the fact that our class as a whole was a well-balanced group of boys with a very good sense of humor. We didn't bully anybody. When somebody did something that called for retribution, we did it in a joking manner. On occasion we resorted to throwing an overcoat over the culprit, forcing him to the ground and then piling on top of him. If there was a more serious breach of camaraderie-etiquette, we would drag the perpetrator out into the corridor and to the water fountain, where we lifted his shirt and poured cold water on his stomach. This type of punishment, however. was rarely necessary.

Even though Verbőczy was a state school, religious instruction was obligatory in Hungary throughout all eight years of high school. Depending on the students' denominations, at the beginning of each school year, every student would either go to church for a "Veni Sancte" (where they played Bach's Toccata and Fugue) or would attend another similar religious service. Likewise, at the end of the school year there was a "Te Deum" and other religious services for non-Catholic denominations. Jewish boys went to the synagogue.

It was well known that Miklóssy was a liberal. Jewish parents therefore preferred to have their sons get into Class A, which was his class. Miklóssy influenced the class's spirit. We never engaged in heated political or religious debates. Neither those who were rooting for a German victory in the war nor those of us who were Anglophiles were looking for a verbal clash. During my seven years at Verbőczy from 1936 to 1943, I never once heard the word *Jew*. In our yearbook, the denominations of the students were noted next to their names—Catholic, Protestant, Israelite.

We all had our hobbies, and in this respect each one of us kept to our own trade. Pali Hunfalusy saw the movie *Strike up the Band,* starring Mickey Rooney and Judy Garland, with Paul Whiteman's Orchestra. It made such a big impression on him that he purchased a drum set. From then on, all Hunfalusy cared about was drumming. Jumbó Csongrády sat behind me and kept himself busy during class drawing sketches in his notebooks. One of his drawings was of the three little pigs, another a sketch of Pluto the dog, and yet another Donald Duck and the three little ducks Huey, Louie, and Dewey. This was later followed by Danny the singing cowboy and other outstanding personalities of American popular culture.

Tomi Szentgyörgyi compiled a list of all of the battleships in the Royal Navy: the *Romney,* the *Hood,* the *Nelson,* and others. Then came all the ships whose names began with "In": *Indomitable, Invincible, Inflexible,* and so on. The sounds of all those names made his heart flutter. The boys who harbored sentiments strongly in favor of England created an informal circle called the Hoboes. The leader of this little gathering, with his highly colorful personality, was Gyuri Sághy.

This atmosphere of liberal tolerance stayed with us throughout our eight years of high school. Even though the teachers didn't talk to us about politics, we boys somehow knew their true feelings and sympathies. In our senior year of high school, our history book started out rather up-to-date, covering all of the most notable events up to its publication. It dealt with the German victories up to then in the war. It described the German victory in the Caucasus, where the swastika was displayed on the highest peak of the Elbrus Mountain, and in the Port of Sevastopol on the Crimean Peninsula. But by the time we began to prepare for graduation in June 1943, the book had become dated, as the Germans were already withdrawing from these territories. The German occupation of Hungary took place on March 19, 1944. By then, we had left the benches of high school behind and were dispersed among different colleges and universities.

In 1945, during the first week of the Russian occupation, Gyuri Sághy came to visit us on Logodi Street. It was from him that we learned the terrible fate of our former teacher Kálmán Miklóssy and his wife. In January 1945 a detachment from the Arrow Cross, the Hungarian Nazi party, came to the house where the Miklóssys lived. The superintendent let them into the building and they went straight to the Miklóssy's flat, where they informed the Miklóssys that they had come to escort them to the headquarters of the Arrow Cross. Miklóssy excused himself to get their overcoats and went into the rear room of the apartment. When one of the members of the Arrow Cross grew suspicious and followed after the teacher, he found Miklóssy in the act of pulling his hunting rifle out of the coat closet. The Arrow Cross man shot Miklóssy on the spot, and then shot his wife. Somehow, the Arrow Cross had discovered that Miklóssy's wife was Jewish. The Catholic Church had attempted to ensure an exceptional status for those who lived in mixed marriages, but the Arrow Cross was not abiding by the latest government edicts.

This Arrow Cross group had a command post at the Ravasz Tea Room on Krisztina Boulevard. One of their leaders was a so-called Catholic priest, Pater Kun, who was insane. He wore a cassock decorated with an Arrow Cross armband. Most of the time, the Arrow Cross collected their information through denunciations. Once, they descended on an air raid shelter near their headquarters after they learned that a soldier was staying in one of the cellars there. They shouted into the cellar that the soldier should come out. The sergeant quickly obliged, running up the stairs. There, he faced Pater Kun's "Archers," who wasted no time asking questions, instead riddling him with bullets. Pater Kun forbade the removal of the dead soldier's body. It was left on the sidewalk to serve as a deterrent to any others who were considering deserting.

Following this incident, Pater Kun presented a basket of apples to the children living in the shelter, declaring, "The good Pater not only punishes, but rewards as well."

The Miklóssys' bodies were placed on a door to be carried down to a mass grave at the aptly named Vérmező (Blood Meadow). The Miklóssys' son Gábor returned after the war and searched for his parents' bodies in vain. However, his investigations did lead him to the documents detailing the denunciations that had led to his parents' demise. One informer was Dr. Kornél Rédey. A second was Dr. Pál Jablonkay. They were both teachers at our high school and ardent Nazis. They knew of Miklóssy's political views and also of his wife's Jewish ancestry. After the war, they both joined the Communist Party and became untouchable. Gábor Miklóssy was never able to bring them to justice.

Our most colorful and eccentric teacher was Gyula Grexa. In his lifetime he was a legend, and in death he became even more legendary. The headline of his obituary read, "The Teacher Who Never Had a Bad Student Has Gone Away." In 1986, his biography, written by Dr. Zoltán Kovács and Béla Palotay and entitled *Grexa Tanár Úr* (*Mr. Grexa the Teacher*), was published by Budapest Tankönyvkiadó (Budapest Textbook Publishing Company). The book did him credit; he was a great Hungarian polyhistor.

Gyula Grexa was born on January 2, 1891. His mother was Boriska Tarnóczy, a distant relative through my great-grandmother Malvina Tarnóczy. Every year on December 6, St. Nicholas Day and the name day for Nicholas, or Miklós in Hungarian, friends and relatives would come to congratulate Grandfather Miklós (in Hungary name days are celebrated as much as birthdays, the difference between the two in the old days being that birthdays were occasions for a more intimate celebration, while on name days people would drop by without a formal invitation). On one of these occasions, Mr. Grexa came by to visit my grandparents. He knew that Miklós's wife Eveline's mother was also a Tarnóczy and he wanted to revitalize the kinship.

Grexa, like my father, served on the front lines during the First World War. When the 1918 revolution broke out and the Austro-Hungarian Monarchy collapsed, Grexa became an assistant to Count Mihály Károlyi, the first prime minister of the Hungarian Republic, and an advisor to Oszkár Jászi, the Minister of Minorities. After this government fell and was succeeded by the Bolsheviks and then later by the Horthy government, his political background became an albatross around his neck. Anyone who had been involved in the 1918 revolutionary government was stigmatized.

Grexa's first post-government job was as a librarian at the Hungarian National Museum. Then, in 1927, he became a teacher at Verbőczy, where he stayed until he retired in 1951. He taught Hungarian literature, geography, and Hungarian and world history. What he didn't know in the field of humanities was not worth knowing. His library consisted of 4,000 volumes. He had 1,400 archival records of museum quality and 1,300 modern phonograph records. He also had a photograph collection that included photos of the Tabán in Krisztina District, preserving the special features of those little old houses that were later bulldozed to make way for a park. These photographs became irreplaceable. Film studios often borrowed furniture and household objects from him that could not be found elsewhere.

Grexa visited all the countries of Europe, with the exception of England and Switzerland. He was familiar with the art treasures of the continent. Every summer he took his students on a trip abroad, where they traveled during the night and carried canned food with them to save on the expense of hotels and restaurants. When he traveled on his own, he often slept in waiting rooms. Once, when he arrived at a town at an ungodly hour, he went to the main square and positioned himself in the center of a group of sculptures, and spent the night there as just another fellow statue. At another time, during a museum tour he overheard a guide making an incorrect statement. Thereupon he went up to the guide and politely suggested a correction. The guide was so impressed that he asked Mr. Grexa to take over the group as their new guide. This he willingly did, and commented on the sites in German, French, and Italian.

As smart and worldly as Uncle Grexa was, his appearance belied this. He paid little attention to how he dressed and looked, and after nine years spent fruitlessly struggling to change his ways, his wife divorced him. After the siege of Budapest, he looked up an old flame of his, the actress Elma Haynal. Twenty years earlier, he had proposed to her and was turned down. Now, after hearing that she had been widowed during the siege, the old flame in him relit. The actress's apartment had been heavily damaged during the siege; even her toilet had been demolished. Uncle Grexa had an idea, however. He knew of a small apartment complex on Palota Square that had served as barracks for the Palace Guards and that had also been badly damaged. He climbed through its various floors, and, lo and behold, on the top floor he came upon an intact toilet bowl and tank. He dismantled the two items, lowered them to the ground on a rope, and transported them on a hand cart to his beloved's apartment. He set up the toilet, which worked, and eventually he renovated her whole apartment. After this valiant effort, he fell on his knees in front of Elma and asked for her hand once more. She couldn't say no this time. They were married in 1946, and had a happy marriage that lasted for thirty-one years to the time of his death. His wife followed him two and a half years later.

Mr. Grexa was my geography teacher. His quizzes were few and far between. He never gave a bad mark to any of his students, but by the same token, in order to get a good grade one had to have outstanding knowledge of the subject. During the graduation exams, Grexa was the supervisor for the German finals. After the exam Gyula Trombitás, the German teacher, said pointedly to Grexa, "These essays clearly show your handiwork. I keep running into these archaic German words all the time. The kids cannot know these expressions. Only you, the culprit, know them." Grexa justified his leniency by asserting that a teacher cannot tell at the young age of his students which ones will perform well in life; therefore he was unwilling to raise the bar too high, and thereby inadvertently deprive students from progressing to the next grade.

At the end of the school day, a flock of students would follow Grexa around like the Pied Piper of Hamelin. Grexa would speak nonstop and the students would listen to him with awe. Some of his students even visited him at home, and many of his students kept up the friendship for decades.

At the outset of the war, members of the class of 1939–1940 persuaded Grexa to go along with them to the Academy of Music, where one particular night a poetry session was being held by György Faludy. Faludy, an immensely popular poet among the younger generation, loosely translated or rewrote the vagabond French minstrel Villon's ballades into Hungarian. Villon had been an irreverent revolutionary who disrespected and derided all authority, and in his translations Faludy accentuated those traits. Faludy himself played the old washed-up wandering troubadour, attacking reactionary Hungarian society, authority, pomposity, and arrogance. Erudite intellectuals like the great Hungarian poet Lőrinc Szabó entered the fray, and a cultural feud broke out. Grexa and his students wrote their own parodies of Villon, which were also parodies of Faludy. Their published anthology of these pieces included some rewriting and spoofs. One of Grexa's ballads also demonstrated his courage, written as it was when Hitler was at his apogee. The original ballad was written by poor Villon in his despair and disgust at witnessing the population of Paris as wildly mad with furor for the Prince of Burgundy. Grexa's poem described a Prince of Burgundy with a cropped mustache driving the people insane. His farsighted prophecy was that the foot of the tyrant would eventually step on the people's necks. His only error was that his Prince of Burgundy made it to the gates of the City of London.

Grexa never idled, even after the German occupation of Hungary on March 19, 1944. He sat down in front of his typewriter and typed flyers for the resistance movement day and night. At the end of every flyer he urged, "Join the internal resistance movement."

Faludy himself was somewhat more subtle. He could have written, "God cursed these people with blindness," but he wouldn't have dared publish a poem like that. After the war, Faludy still wrote poetry for a short while, until he was arrested by the communists and taken to the Recsk Concentration Camp. One of his poems from 1945 appeared in the weekly satirical magazine *Ludas Matyi* (the name of a folklore figure; a young lad with a goose who was a prankster vexed by a pompous and unjust landowner). I memorized one verse from that poem:

If we Germans had conquered at the meadow of Marne
there would be a parade every noontime
the Negroes would shout Heil!
and in their nuptial bed
the Gretchens would be lying with steel helmets
If we Germans had conquered at the meadow of Marne

SZABAD SZÓ

Kiadja a
Nemzeti Ellenállási Mozgalom
/.../
Budapest, 1944 szeptember   I.évfolyam 1.szám

A magyar néphez!

Egymás után eszmélnek fel az európai nemzetek! Románia csatlakozott a szövetségesekhez, Bulgária kilépett a háborúból, Franciaország felszabadult. Belgium és Hollandia a felszabadítás előtt állnak, ... belátta, hogy a Németország oldalán foly- tatott ... csak a pusztulásba kergetheti. A szövetségesek győ- zelmes ... teszi lábukat és ebben a pillanatban a magyar ... hogy szenvedő népünk számára kiutat ke- ressen a ..., "fel a Kárpátok bérceire" küldi harcolni és hi- ába ... ifjúságát!

... minden magyar embernek, hogy Magyarország a győztes ... elkerülje és a pusztító náci haddal és quis- ling ... a harcot felvegye és a békés viszonyokat egy fel- szabadult Magyarországon mielőbb igyekezzék helyreállítani. Méltó- nak kell ... a többi európai népek szabadságharcához, a francia ..., a Balkán hős partizánjaihoz és mindenek fe- lett népünk történelméhez, 1848-hoz, a magyar szabadság eszményéhez!

Lapunk közvetlen célja az, hogy a Gömbös-korszak által kezdeményezett aljas, népbutító sajtópolitika következtében a vi- lág hírforrásaitól elzárt és most szabadságáért küzdő magyar népet a valódi helyzetéről és eseményéről tájékoztassa, a szabadságharc módszereiről, lehetőségeiről és eseményeiről hírt adjon azok számá- ra, akik elegendő erkölcsi bátorságot éreznek a cselekvésre.
Éljen a szabad Magyarország!
Éljen a győzelmes nép!

- -

Dal a hazugságházról
        De egyszer csak meging a palota
        Földindulóban, minél jobban késik
        És ... hallhatja a közönyös világ
        Halottaknak hitt ... ébredésit!
Összedől a náci hazugságház...   Ady

s ma nyugodtan, vagyis inkább vészes nyugtalansággal mondhatjuk, hogy a nácik egyetlen szövetségese immár csak Magyarország! Megint mi vagyunk Európa jó bolondja, aki még akkor is elhiszi a náci bar- bárok otromba hazugságait, mikor azokon az összes európai népek, sőt maguk a németek is átlátnak? Lovagiasság, hűség, becsület és egyéb jelszavakkal visszaélve tegyük tönkre hazánk és nemzetünk jövőjét beláthatatlan időre? A felelet megától adódik.

A magyar közvélemény sokat remélt a kormányváltozástól, de az uj kormány minden intézkedéséből azt láthatjuk, hogy tovább akarja folytatni az esztelen és kilátástalan küzdelmet.

Mit képzel ez a kormány? A magyar honvédség felszerelé- sével akarja feltartóztatni az orosz seregeket? Hiszen erre még a németek sem voltak képesek! Azt akarja-e, hogy a magyar falvak és városok az OKW jólismert rugalmas védekezésének és célszerű elsza- kadó mozdulatainak essenek áldozatul? Vegye tudomásul ez a kormány, hogy a magyar nép nem ül már fel semmiféle német maszlagnak és nem hajlandó vállalni, hogy a nácik hazugságházánál düledező épitménye

Front of a Resistance leaflet dropped into my father's mailbox

Maradványul a gyáva szavunra, dalom
Viharodnak előjele, forradalom!
                              Petőfi

_____

TUDJA-E, HOGY ...
    napi 3 millió pengőnkbe kerül
a német megszállás? Szivesen adó-
zik erre a célra?
    Németország élelmiszer- és egyéb
szállitmányokért közel 4 milliárd
márkával adósunk? Vajjon mikor fi-
zeti vissza?
    augusztusban azért nem kaptunk
hust, mert a németek a nekik "já-
ró" menyiségen felül többezer
marhát hajtottak el? Csak Sztójay-
t és a többi kétlábu marhát fe-
lejtették itt.
    a cukorjegyek lebélyegzése
csak komédia? Az egészet azért
csináltak, mert pillanatnyilag
nem tudtak cukrot kiosztani. A
németek ugyanis nem szállitották
le azt a cukrot, amire kötelezve
voltak.
    a magyar kormány nem tudja be-
hivni az idei ujoncsorványt, mert
feltöltözteti sem tudná őket?

_____

MIT ÉRDEMELNEK A NÉMETEK?
    Megmondta már Petőfi!

Fegyverre nem is méltatunk,
Mint a kut-át, kibotozunk,
Ugy kiverünk, hogy jobb se kell,
Még apánk sem iszik el!

_____

QUISLINGEK EGYMÁSKÖZT

    Az egyik dicső quisling már el-
szelelt. Endre-András menti László,
nászutazás ürügye alatt Ausztriába
mentette bőrét. S majd onnan hová?
    A finomszimatu Antal István is-
mét "orientálódik". Azt mondja, hogy
ellenállást szervez. Rajniss ugyan-
csak "revideál" és azt hirdeti magá-
ról, hogy ő mindig kommunista volt.
Na de kérem ...

_____

PETŐFI A ZSARNOKOKROL:
A hollók gyomra lesz majd sirotok,
És szemfedőtök a népeknek átka!

_____

összedől a hazugságháza ... folyt./
őt is a romok alá temesse.
Aki a mai helyzetben tovább té-
továzik, az vagy szamaloura méltó
bolond, vagy lelkiismeretlen gaz-
ember.
    Az uj kormányfő kijelentette,
hogy nem bizalmat kér, hanem fe-
gyelmet követel. Bizalmunkat meg-
tagadjuk tőle, fegyelemmel pedig
nem tartozunk neki! Mi már csak
lelkiismeretünk szavát követjük!
Követeljük a céltalan és aljas
háboru azonnali befejezését! Követeljük a békét és a magyar
szabadságot!

_____

AZ ELLENÁLLÁSI FRONT.

    Tito tábornagy csapatai a bol-
gárok által kiüritett területe-
ket megszállják és Belgréd felé
törnek előre.- Görög partizánok
a görög szigetvilágból vissza-
vonuló német csapatokat megti-
zedelik.- A szlovák hadsereg
partizánná átszerogéé alakult át,
és Besztercebányán ideiglenes
kormány alakult. A magyar quisling
kormány Kelet-Szolen volt a határvé-
delmi készültséget elrendelni.-
A francia belső front győzelmes
csapatai most végrehajtják az
áruló quislingeken a népitéletet.-
Román megszálló csapatok Kréta
szigetén rátámadták a némete-
ket.- Dán szabotőrök 3 hónapra
teljesen leállitották a legna-
gyobb dán fegyvergyárat.- A norvég ifjuság tömegesen szökik Ang-
liába, hogy beálljon a szövet-
séges norvég hadseregbe.- A cse-
peli munéziumraktár robbandsá-
nak Budapest egész lakossága ta-
nuja volt.- A Titonak szállitó
titobuszunk utat jeleznek jelző-
tüz gyujtásával a román hősvi
passzorok.

KI HOL TÁRGYAL?
    A románok Moszkvában,
    a bolgárok Kairóban,
    a finnek Stockholmban,
    a szlovákok nem is tárgyalnak,
hanem cselekszenek.
    És mi?

_____

ADJA TOVÁBB BARÁTAINAK!

Of course, it was easy to write something like that after the war.

Between the conclusion of the school year and the holding of the graduation examinations came a couple of weeks of vacation. I left Logodi Street and traveled out to Veresegyház. The spring was warm and beautiful. The light breeze carried the scent of the flowering linden and acacia trees. Cloud configurations chased each other in the sky. The birds were singing; the clanking of the hoe could be heard in the vineyard. I went out into the garden, placed my history books under my head, and immediately fell asleep. My mother was greatly amused at my method of study.

But I was not alone slumbering on top of my textbooks and drooling on the pages. Szabi Viczián also complained about the difficulties of studying in nature, saying, "Puckish spirits arise from the bosom of the earth and whisper in one's ear." He was just not an outright academic type. Nor was I.

The written exams were held on the first day of the examination period; orals followed them on the next. The school was a short five-minute walk from our house, and my father came with me for both exams. He sat them out from morning to afternoon, and in the intervals between subjects he handed me a pack of soul food: sugar cubes, walnuts, hazelnuts, and raisins. All the while, he had lively conversations with my teachers and classmates. I am sure he was the only parent in the whole country who accompanied his son and sat there like a coach at the U.S. Open. On those two days he didn't even go to work at the studio.

After the written examinations and before the orals, Miklóssy stopped me in the hall. "What types of questions are you expecting in Hungarian literature?" he asked. I mentioned a relatively easy topic to which he objected: "After the essay you just wrote about the Hungarian poet Vörösmarthy, I cannot give you an easy topic. Go and look over Zrinyi!" "But sir," I protested, "Zrinyi is three topics, not one. What should I study—his epics, his lyrics, or his prose?" "All three!" responded Miklóssy. I ran home and in a state of maximum excitement conveyed the news to my father. This had been a noble gesture on the part of Miklóssy toward me. It was a godsend; instead of having to study eighty or one hundred writers, I could concentrate on just one. Not to mention the fact that in addition to the Hungarian literature exam, I still had to prepare for history, math, German, and Latin oral examinations.

As soon as my father heard this inside scoop, he took down three gigantic volumes on Hungarian literature from his bookshelf and began cramming with me. That night my father made me learn as much about the great statesman, writer, and warrior Zrinyi as could fit into one night. Thus, it seemed that the danger of not being prepared for the Hungarian literature oral exam had passed, but there was still the Latin oral exam to worry about.

Although I had memorized many Latin idioms (with which I would try to show off later in life), my knowledge of Latin was very shaky. My problems lay with the grammar, and of course I needed to know the various Latin verb forms, since at the oral exam I was to translate an unfamiliar Latin text into Hungarian. This appeared to be quite a daunting task. Here, however, I had another pleasant surprise. Miklóssy ended up randomly selecting one volume out of a pile of books and announced that I had to translate a few paragraphs out of Ovid or Virgil. When he handed me the open book I could hardly believe my eyes. The Hungarian text was written in the book between the lines in tiny, barely recognizable script.

Now I had a new problem. I had to be careful neither to read too fast nor to be too exact in my translation, all of which would have been a dead giveaway—especially since my earlier grades in Latin had been pretty mediocre. I imagined that Gyula Ember, the professor at Eötvös College and supervisor delegated by the Ministry of Education, might have found it softly strange that this relatively poor student was translating from Latin like someone who was reading the daily paper. I therefore read carefully. At times I paused, wrinkled my forehead, and let out a few deep sighs. A couple of times I also managed to mistranslate a word, but all in all I did a respectable job. If Gyula Ember had asked for my copy of the Latin text, both Miklóssy and I would have gotten into hot water. Miklóssy could have been suspended from his job and I could have been given another topic to translate, one that might have caused me to fail.

The next oral exam was in Hungarian literature. One thing I was sure of was that it would not be on Zrinyi, since that topic was to be used in my written exam. Luckily, Hungarian literature was a territory where I felt more at home. During the oral exam I managed to steer the discussion to the autobiographical novel of Emil Kolozsváry-Grandpierre entitled *Tegnap* (*Yesterday*). This book had been published one year before my graduation and Kolozsváry-Grandpierre had dedicated a copy of it to my father as a gift. Naturally, I had read the book. Despite the fact that the author had been only thirty-five years old at the time he wrote the book, he came across as far older. He described the time he had spent at various colleges during his formative years, writing about the educational system, members of the faculty, and the greenhorn immaturity of his peers. In the last chapter of his book there is a revealing passage: "We came to the college unprepared. We were not taught to be eloquent or to compose in high school. Therefore, the foundation upon which one could build was missing. The first two years of college therefore are basically spent patching the gaps in our middle-school studies" (Emil Kolozsváry-Grandpierre, *Tegnap*, Révai, 1942, p. 274).

Kolozsváry-Grandpierre's writing was a harsh criticism of the high school curriculum. I decided to take a risk and elaborate on the subject. I could have collided with an old reactionary, rigid educational satrap, but my hunches were right. I presumed that Gyula Ember might belong to the circle at Eötvös College that subscribed to Kolozsváry's revolutionary criticism. (Eötvös College was progressive and under the circumstances a well-nigh revolutionary institution where free-spirited discussions were a normal way of life. It was, of course, hated by the dogmatic reactionary educational establishment.) As I discussed Kolozsváry's book *Tegnap*, I even ended up criticizing the high school graduation exams! Luckily, it went over well.

All of this was followed by our graduation dinner party, where I saw some of our high school teachers for the last time. After the dinner, some of the boys went to visit a house of "ill repute" to lose their virginity and step into manhood (I wonder if there was any similar ritual in the girls' high school). I was too conservative myself to engage in such sexual initiations. Many of us also had a deadly fear of venereal diseases, since the sulfa drugs used to treat them, deseptyl and ultraseptyl, weren't very effective.

After I said farewell to Verbőczy High School I lost touch with most of my former teachers and schoolmates. Gyula Grexa was one exception. After the war, he would from time to time rent an empty store or a vacant movie theatre and play records from his collection for his young admirers for a small fee. With this tiny income he supplemented his meager pension. Around 1953, he had an afternoon matinee where he played Gershwin's opera *Porgy and Bess* for a small group of young people. His comments made it even more enjoyable. He explained to us that Gershwin had based his opera on DuBose Heyward's novel titled *Porgy*, which was published in 1925.

On another occasion, he played the records of Yma Sumac, the Peruvian wonder woman, again accompanied by his interpretations. These were rare events, glimpses into the outside world. In those days, foreign movies were rarely shown—with the exception of Russian communist propaganda movies of course, which were snubbed by the public. At one point, three Russian flicks were being shown simultaneously in three different movie houses. Their titles were: *We Want to Live, Under the Shadows of Skyscrapers*, and *Far from Moscow*. The authorities didn't notice the hilarity of this combination. But it depicted just what we desired. For some of us, our wish came true in 1956.

To preserve Uncle Gyula's memory, a plaque in the entry hall of the then-renamed Petőfi High School was dedicated to him on January 8, 1979.

I still have my yearbook from István Verbőczy High School from 1942–43. This was the fifty-first anniversary of the school and my senior year. The yearbook brings back memories of various teachers. Ottó Szentirmay was our eighth grade physics teacher. After the first day of school, my father quizzed me about how it went and asked whether I had any homework. My response was to throw down my bookbag with a sigh, as if happy that the day was over. To my surprise, however, my father—who until then had never wanted to be involved in my schoolwork—suddenly showed an interest. Not only that, but he persisted in interrogating me about the homework. Finally I gave in and told him that we were supposed to learn about the workings of the six simple machines—such as the lever, the fixed or movable pulley, etc. That night, my father made certain that I understood and memorized the workings of all six of them, from A to Z.

The next day, as luck would have it, I was the first student on whom Szentirmay called to elaborate on the workings of the six elementary machines. As I recited the principles of them, the entire class listened astounded. My performance (on only the second day of the school year) was breathtaking, and Szentirmay must have concluded that he was facing a brilliant student. Needless to say, I received an A-plus for this performance and Szentirmay didn't bother calling on me for the rest of the year. I, in turn, didn't bother studying or doing my physics homework for the rest of the year. As luck would have it, at the end of the school year, for my final exam he again called on me to recite the workings of the elementary machines. Perhaps he remembered my splendid performance at the beginning of the year. Thus, based on these two, similar exercises I managed to get an A-plus in physics for the year. The others, meanwhile, sweated it out just to get an acceptable grade.

As we approached the end of the school year in 1943 and finals loomed, for a couple of warm spring days I came under a cloud. I became constipated, and one day I turned to Agar emulsion for relief. This white milky liquid had its effect on me during class. I suddenly felt as if an explosion were taking place within my gut. Then came the relief. The class became restless. The warm spring air wafted the gas from the first bench where I sat back through the classroom and violent war cries erupted. "Skunk, skunk, your guts are rotting!" my classmates kept yelling, shaking their fists at me. I had succeeded in gassing the whole class. Finally, the boys opened the windows and covered their noses with handkerchiefs. Even my best friends were unwilling to acknowledge or talk to me. I was a complete pariah.

Soon after, our math teacher Milinkovich walked into the room. Usually upon his appearance the class would become quiet, but not on this day. Now, instead, the class erupted into quiet grumbling, subdued shouts of "Farkas, get out," "Farkas, move." Mr. Milinkovich, hearing the commotion, walked to the edge of the podium, pulled himself up to his full height, and with his horrendous accent (likely Italian; he taught us Italian and was from an Italian locality of the Austro-Hungarian Empire such as Trieste) started shouting at us to be quiet: "What is this? What's going on? What is the meaning of all this?" At this point I lost my nerve, stepped forward, and in a whispering voice asked Milinkovich if I could step outside for some fresh air because I didn't feel well. He benevolently waved me off and as I left the classroom tranquility and order returned. I would never touch the Agar laxative again, but the "skunk" epithet stuck with me for a long time.

Our music teacher was Sándor Pusztay. As Mr. Pusztay entered the class at the beginning of one school year, we committed some mischief, of which I was the instigator. Mr. Pusztay stepped onto the teacher's platform and asked, "Who did it?" I stood up and said in a resonating melodious voice, "I did." "You are the first to be admitted into the choir," he replied, pleasantly impressed.

After the siege of Budapest, my father reminisced in his diary about childhood, education, and maturity. He had just finished reading the autobiographical novel of Gottfried Keller, the famous Swiss author whose novel *Henry Green* is one of the so-called *Entwicklungsroman*—coming-of-age novels.

My father wrote:

"In the afternoon I read more Gottfried Keller. It's very interesting and penetrates deeply into the soul of a child just as it does into the era, not to mention the eternal mistakes of educators. Hopefully the children can survive schooling without it causing them great harm. It has many negative effects, and if someone takes all he has learned to heart too seriously, that could be catastrophic. All that is regurgitated to death in school is made colorless and cliché-like; enthusiasm is lost for a lifetime. The schools are incapable of generating interest and keeping things fresh. They regard the banal clichés as if they were catechisms and rip everything out of context. Henry Green's fate illustrates this quite well. The situation has not changed since then either. It's interesting that the new, experimental schools can't improve on this. It seems that schools have to be such—that is to say, bad. But the French school in Kolozsváry-Grandpierre's book is entirely different. There they teach and at a terrific pace. It seems that the German schools are the bad ones.

How many people, how many millions of people, suffered for a lifetime because of bad schooling and the education system? Moreover, it wasn't those who took it easy who suffered but those who were the most diligent and ambitious. One would be hard pressed to find a person who had never had a conflict with, or a crisis in, school. Growing children are difficult to understand. It's hard for grownups to see the child's way of thinking, especially the more gifted ones, so the simple-minded educators don't even know where to begin. They are only concerned with the curriculum and not the individual student's maturation and benefit.

At school the children mostly rear each other. Maybe that's the best and most useful thing to come from it. The first encounters with society, the first bitter experiences, will

Me, György (Gyuri) Sághy, and Dénes (Jumbó) Csongrády on bicycles before graduation

prepare them for life. Everyone who makes it out of school feels some great sense of relief. Károly was that way too. He loathed school immeasurably and yet he didn't even have it that tough." (Károly is my name in Hungarian.)

Class photograph in 1941. Front row, left to right: Tibor Karsay, Dénes (Jumbó) Csongrády, Károly Farkas, György (Gyuri) Sághy, Péter Zimmer. Center: homeroom teacher Kálmán Miklóssy

13

Gyuri Sághy Appears on the Scene

In the fall of 1940, my whole class went to the church on Krisztina
Square to celebrate the onset of a new school year. As we stood in
rows and sang I noticed that the boy in front of me was a newcomer.
He wore a "Bocskay uniform," a blue suit with braid trim and buttons that were made of the same silky cord as the trim. As I took a
closer look, it became apparent that the suit was an imitation of the
Hungarian gala dress, with braided embellishments. This was the
mandatory attire at some schools, though fortunately not at ours.
The newcomer had blond hair and blue eyes and was taller than
me—though that wasn't saying much. Soon we became the best of
friends. His name was Gyuri Sághy and our friendship would last
for a lifetime, notwithstanding even the ocean that at times separated
us. Soon, Gyuri invited me to his home in the Hűvösvölgy district
of Budapest at 5 Vadorzó Street (Poacher Street), and let me in on
his family's financial situation. He told me that his father's mon-
etary affairs were somewhat volatile. "When his situation is better,
we expand and rent more rooms in the house for ourselves. When
things are tight, we squeeze together, on account of giving up a
room or two."

This introduction to his family affairs struck me as a bit strange,
but in the Sághy family nothing was traditional or bourgeois. When I
first visited him, Gyuri had his own room, his sister Zsuzsi likewise,
while the two younger boys Miklós and Lajos shared a room. I also
spotted a young maid stoking coals in the small iron stoves. Gyuri's
mother ran a tobacco shop nearby. His father worked in the Ministry
of Public Food Supplies.

From time to time, Gyuri would borrow his father's foulard silk
ties and Eau de Cologne or his lavender aftershave and his hat. The

hat was brown with a wide green band. When Gyuri asked his mother the proper way to wear it, she said, "When you are in the city turn the brim up, when in the woods turn it down." Mrs. Sághy had a tendency to philosophize. One of her famous sayings was, "If we do not have it, then we do not need it." Her maiden name was Dalma Földesy and the Földesy coat of arms hung in the family's entry hall.

Gyuri had an uncle in the United States, an attorney in St. Louis named Fisher. He once sent a ten dollar bill to Gyuri. On that occasion Gyuri invited a few of us boys to escort him to the local bank, located on Krisztina Square, where he exchanged the bill for Hungarian pengős. Gyuri was always a bit of a poseur.

Gyuri and I soon discovered each other's interests and hobbies. He took lessons in piloting a glider plane that was catapulted up into the air with the help of a large rubber slingshot. He was also an amateur radio buff. He joined our Boy Scout troop, Gusztáv Erős Troop Number 7, and from that moment forward he and I stuck together during camping excursions and hikes. With time we both became river scouts too, which we enjoyed immensely.

When Gyuri arrived at our school, Hungary was slowly drifting toward war. In those days, it seemed as if there was hardly a thing that the Germans couldn't achieve. But influenced by our parents Gyuri and I became spirited anglophiles, and therefore German-phobes. We were kindred spirits, political sympathizers on the same wavelength. We despised the Germans, their Nazi ideology, the influence that they showered on us. The latter impregnated every corner of Hungarian culture, technology, and civilization. Many newspaper columns were dripping with adulation toward the Germans and their accomplishments. But there were intelligent level-headed people in school, and grownups too, who didn't let themselves be swayed by the new political fad. As a result, our society became polarized.

Gyuri was congenial, cheerful, and bohemian. He was sloppy, partly because he was careless, and he liked to flaunt his eccentricity. He used to forget his gym shorts and shoes at home. On those days he showed up for gym class in his undershorts and socks. The amazing part was that it didn't bother him in the least. He was an extroverted individual, phlegmatic, with a good sense of humor. As a result, he was well liked by his peers. His opinions counted, and to a certain extent he became one of our class leaders without ever aspiring for the post.

When the school year came to a close, we boys dispersed in all directions. Now that school was over, and because his grades were quite good, Gyuri was ready to take it easy. Before he could begin his summer fun, however, his father Lajos called him into his study for a talk. Not being used to such formality, Gyuri was apprehensive. Mr. Sághy asked Gyuri whether he was aware of the seriousness of the food shortage in Ruthenia—people were starving. Naturally, until then Gyuri had no idea about this, and he was puzzled that his father would quiz him on such a serious subject. At last his father let on to what he was driving at. He proposed that his sixteen-year-old son take on a dangerous assignment.

Shortly thereafter, Gyuri traveled to the Port of Zenta in southern Hungary on the Tisza River. There, he met up with the captain of a long convoy of barges anchored in the harbor. The barges were filled with foodstuffs, grain, lard, sugar, and canned products. As soon as Gyuri arrived they pulled up the anchors and proceeded northward on the Tisza River to make the journey across the German blockade. The ships were stopped at the old Trianon border between Hungary and Yugoslavia, where German officers boarded to inspect the convoy. Gyuri greeted the group in fluent German. He spoke in *Hoch Deutsch*, the most elegant literary German, and made sure that his attire matched the occasion. He wore a sort of pseudo–*Hitler Jugend* uniform consisting of a Boy Scout shirt and shorts along with white knee socks, complemented by his blond hair and blue eyes. His aim was to make the Germans feel at ease and gain their trust. The German officers were quite amused to see this sixteen-year-old boy in charge of the convoy. Gyuri invited them for a meal in the skipper's room. There a table had been set with smoked sausages, salami, head cheese, ham, and liverwurst, along with dilled pickles, peppers stuffed with sauerkraut, and a bowl of cherries. There were bottles of wine, Slivovitz, and Cognac. The Germans, accustomed to their bland Wehrmacht food, felt as if they were in the midst of an earthly paradise. The officers didn't need any prodding, and as the spirits flowed the mood elevated.

At the height of the merriment, the ship's captain poked his head in and asked for permission to raise the anchors and leave the harbor. This was Gyuri's cue to present each of the officers with a gift package of precious goodies: coffee, tea, liver paté, chocolate, salami, and cognac. When Gyuri asked them whether they would like to go on an inspection tour, the officers slapped him on his back and said good-humoredly, *"Georg ist ein hubscher Bursch, ein feiner Junge"* ("Gyuri is a handsome lad, a fine youth"). Then they departed amid great merriment. This major coup of Gyuri's reminded me of my great-grandmother Malvina Tarnóczy's similar ploy to get the Austrian officers drunk in order to deceive them. The Germans liked to drink, but they could not hold their liquor very well.

Shortly after the barges passed the German blockade, Gyuri disembarked and returned to Budapest. He reported back to his father, assuring him that the convoy was on its way, and his father was greatly pleased. In reward for his services, Gyuri got a new Durkopp-Diamant bike with balloon tires (the precursor of a modern mountain bike), a Velta camera, a windbreaker, and a pair of new sunglasses. With his new bike, Gyuri slid down the side of János Hegy (Mount John). In those days trail biking was not yet in vogue. In this way too, he was ahead of his time—a trailblazer. With his new camera, he took a picture of me as I rode my racing bike on

György (Gyuri) Sághy on his bicycle

Me on my bicycle

Zuhatag Sor (Cascades Allée). It was a colored sepia photo, a forerunner already of modern color photography, which at that time was still in its infancy. That picture was also made into a slide that withstood the war, withstood the revolution, and is still with me.

Around the time when the picture was taken, Gyuri and I had just signed up for our first bicycle race. My group was made up of beginners. We used regular bikes with clinchers instead of ultralight racing bikes with ultralight tires. Gyuri went in a separate group with his touring bike. The course was flat and my group started out first. As we were heading back to the finish line I met up with Gyuri face to face. He was leading his group valiantly, even though his bike didn't even have a derailleur to shift gears and alleviate some exertion. It helped that he was in superb physical shape, but he was not really into bicycle racing and this was his first and only encounter with that sport.

While bicycling ultimately didn't interest him much, Gyuri was a passionate skier. He skied cross country and downhill, and became a good jumper as well. During Christmas vacation one year he went to Rahó, in those days a fashionable ski resort in the northern Carpathian Mountains. He was accompanied by the charming Flóri Kluge and one other ski buddy. The three rascals came up with all kinds of pranks just to shock the other patrons and staff at the local hotel, like piling up all of the furniture in the restaurant to barricade its entrance. Flóri was picture pretty, a blond starlet and the grand-daughter of Ferenc Harrer, former mayor of Budapest. Gyuri fell in love with her. He had a long line of conquests during his life, begin-ning with Mária Csongrády, our friend Jumbó's sister. One would be hard put to add up the number of broken hearts Gyuri left in his wake, but Flóri stayed in his heart forever, an unrequited love.

In Gyuri's company one was never bored. He befriended peo-ple easily, and since he was fluent in German, Italian, and English, his friends were of various nationalities. When the Nazis invaded Poland in 1939, a flood of Polish refugees crossed over the Carpathian Mountains, which was then a border between Poland and Hungary. Some of these escapees were military personnel; others were Jewish or political refugees. Many used Hungary as a way station en route to their final destination in the near east, where they joined the Pol-ish army of General Wladyslaw Anders. Others settled in Hungary. Some found occupations while others went to school. Gyuri struck up friendships with a couple of Polish boys and a girl and gave them temporary shelter in his room. It didn't take long for his father to learn of these youngsters, and since Gyuri's room faced the entry-way and was on the ground floor, with windows looking out onto the street, he suggested Gyuri find better accommodations for them. From then on, Gyuri became the benefactor of these three Polish students. There were some mysterious relationships among them. One was never certain which one was in love with the girl, Dusa, and which was just her brother. At times, Gyuri could be spotted in Dusa's company. I met her in 1943 at a performance of *Our Town*, by Thornton Wilder (Artúr Somlay played the role of the stage man-ager), at the Vigszinház. My date was Minci Alemann. Gyuri arrived with Dusa, a ravishing beauty in her cyclamen-colored evening dress. As I looked on, there seemed to be something more than a platonic friendship between Dusa and Gyuri.

As far as our adventures with the "weaker" sex (weaker, since when?!) were concerned, in his adventures and experiences Gyuri left me standing in the dust. In 1943, he casually told me that he got a Russian woman out of a concentration camp at Sátoraljaujhely.

Then, just in passing, he mentioned that she was young and very good-looking. After a while, I became accustomed to his brief and fantastic encounters. He would refer to his adventures nonchalantly, as if it were nothing more than the most mundane affair. He wouldn't go into details about any of his escapades, so I would just let him disclose whatever he wanted to. I would never try to pry information out of him if I suspected the subject might make him uncomfortable. I found that generally this worked best, since it didn't force him to cover up or embellish by lying when he was not prepared for full disclosure. Gyuri's modus operandi was to portray himself as an eccentric young man—doing a great number of things that an average middle-class young man would never contemplate doing. But of course he was not an average young man by any means. After a while these sequences of fantastic adventures didn't surprise me anymore, but Gyuri's personality and deeds were a puzzle to me, the pieces of which it took me decades to put together.

Gyuri was such a colorful character that my father even wrote a humorous piece about him that he read and broadcast over the Hungarian Radio in one of his regular short entertainment programs. The title of the sketch was "Vághy Gyuri, a Balszerencsés Madár" ("Gyuri Vághy, The Unlucky Bird"). In the skit, he narrated Gyuri's outstanding feats and adventures in the most humorous way, omitting of course the Polish refugees and the pretty young Russian woman, likely an undercover agent.

In the early summer of 1943, after our graduation from high school, Gyuri and I decided to bike down to Transylvania, where our Boy Scout troop was camping. The scouts of Verbőczy High School, otherwise known as the Number 7 Gusztáv Erős Boy Scout Troop, had set up a summer camp at Komandó. The locality was known for its logging camp, situated at the farthest nook of the southern Carpathian Mountains, bordering the Szekler counties and on top of a mountain. The only approach to the camp was by way of a small mountain train. Our friends were already at the camp, including Jumbó Csongrády, whose sister Mária was at that time the object of Gyuri's affection. Árpád Göncz, who about sixty years later became the president of Hungary, was also there as group leader. Szabi Viczián, my other devoted pal, who bridged my country and city life, was likewise a member of this distinguished group.

Our plan was to reach Komandó in one week's time, assuming we were able to bike on average 140 kilometers daily. We planned to stay there with the boys for a week, and then return by train, checking our bikes into the luggage car.

In those days very few people would have considered setting out on such a long, perilous bike ride—especially without any preparation. We should have thought of taking a couple of spare tires, a decent patch kit with some glue, a first aid kit, and more money, but of course we had none of this. Unfortunately, Gyuri was just as impractical and inexperienced as me. I had a small suitcase sitting on my rear rack that contained a sweat shirt and sweat pants that served as pajamas as well, but I didn't have a raincoat. Luckily, it never rained. I took my touring bike, leaving my racing bike behind. Gyuri hung an attaché case filled with canned food on the frame of his Dürkopp-Diamant. At least he had thought of this, though he hadn't thought of much else—not even a can opener. Looking back, it is hard to believe that our parents let us leave so unprepared. But my mother at that time was out in the vineyard, and my father gave us only a perfunctory glance when we said goodbye early in the morning. He wasn't too practical a person either. Besides, he must have thought: Here go two healthy eighteen-year-olds, strong, muscular boys with enterprising spirits. Let them have their fun and learn how to handle any eventualities. He also trusted Gyuri, who seemed mature for his age, and the type that could cope well with any emergency. By and large, my father was right. I am sure that Gyuri's parents didn't have an elaborate discussion with him before the trip either.

It was a beautiful morning when we set out in high spirits on our adventure. To reach Szolnok, we pedaled one hundred kilometers on a first-rate road. There were no hills, so we got there by noon. Gyuri, however, began to calculate that hanging onto and being towed by a moving object—being "schlepped" here and there—would save some precious time and energy.

As we neared Szolnok, we encountered a military truck that was moving slowly as it passed us. Gyuri told me to grab the rear end of the truck. I immediately grabbed it on the left side while he did the same on the right. The truck driver was not enthused about being transformed into a tow-truck service, however, so he sped up and drove in a zigzag motion, causing us to swing wildly back and forth. Gyuri yelled at me to let go of the truck as he had already done, but I had become somehow magnetized—like one of the sailors in that famous newsreel who wouldn't let go of the dirigible's rope as it rose ever higher and consequently fell to their death. My grip eventually gave way too, and I crashed with such force that I wiped up the road for a long stretch. My front wheel went flat and I was bruised and bloodied.

The first thing Gyuri tried to do was to repair my tire. He removed the inner tube, cut out the piece with the hole in it, and tried to glue the two ends together. Unfortunately, the tube was too short. Finally, I suggested that we continue our travel with both of us on his bike to my mother's half-sister Aunt Margit's grange in the town of Fegyvernek, only thirty-five kilometers from Szolnok. There I figured we could get some help. I thereupon sat on the crossbar of Gyuri's bike. He pedaled and steered while I kept one hand on his handlebar and lifted the front wheel of my bike with the other. My poor bike was thus able to roll at our side on its back wheel. In this fashion we made the thirty-five kilometer trip, limping up to Aunt Margit's farm. There my aunt cleaned my wounds and put some kind of green petroleum jelly on my leg and thigh. My cousin Iván entertained us by telling us about trains and locomotives; from then on, Gyuri would refer to him as the railroad boy.

The next day Mr. Bordás, Aunt Margit's renter, loaned me an inner tube with the promise that I send it back, under threat of capital punishment. A war was going on, after all, and people weren't inclined to just lend out rubber tires.

The green gooey stuff on my leg, the petroleum jelly, got stuck to the sweatpants that I was using in lieu of pajamas and after I woke up I accidentally ripped open my wounds. In spite of that we decided to continue our trip. Never again were we tempted to seek to be towed, but we encountered other problems. Just as bicycle racers try to follow one another and slipstream—or, in German, gain *Anschluss*—I would cling to Gyuri's rear wheel. Unfortunately, as I became more tired and my attention lagged, my front wheel and Gyuri's rear would end up parallel to one another. Then when Gyuri made a quick move, his wheel would hit mine and I again found myself in the dust. This happened a couple of times, none of which aided my cuts and bruises in their healing process.

From Fegyvernek we proceeded on to Nagyvárad (Oradea in today's Romania). The city's dusty main square was crammed with Italian soldiers speeding up and down on their Benelli and Motoguzzi motorcycles. Gyuri had me wait for him at a small pastry shop while he went to find us a meal. As it turned out, the owner of the little conditorei was an old man who was more interested in selling his daughter, or rather his granddaughter, than his ice cream. From behind a curtain, a very good-looking girl appeared with an intelligent expression. I couldn't understand why on earth she had to cooperate with this old ogre. The girl approached me, took a look at my Boy Scout attire (my bruises were healing), and smilingly invited me into a small enclave behind a flimsy curtain. This odd couple seemed all the stranger to me because they didn't speak proper Hungarian. I was still at an age where I was quite inexperienced with women and I dreaded any diseases, so I was unresponsive. Shortly thereafter, Gyuri returned, and I assured our speedy departure before he got any ideas.

After Nagyvárad we reached Királyhágó (King's Passageway). This road linked the great Hungarian plain with Transylvania. We passed up sightseeing, since we still wanted to complete our journey within one week's time. From there we encountered an incredibly steep and long serpentine road with about seven spirals. Gyuri soon passed me by and I could see him always one serpentine spiral above me until I caught up with him at the top of the mountain, which also served as a watershed. Rough as this mountain climb was, it was the only way for us to get into Transylvania.

Our first night after Fegyvernek was spent with a young couple in their tiny cottage. We met the husband, a fellow cyclist, on the road and struck up a conversation. He offered to share his cottage with us for the night. He was an elementary school teacher. The couple offered their bed to us—despite our protestations—and they ended up spending the night sitting on chairs in their kitchen. Such occurrences are the best illustrations of my theory that the people most likely to offer one love and help are those who themselves are in the greatest need of the same.

Our next stop was Palota-Ilva, near Bánffyhunyad, where our accommodations were a smaller version of the Bánffy Castle. We got the impression that the place where we stayed was specially equipped for travelers, since we were ushered into an empty ranch-style guesthouse. Here, we were finally able to get a good night's rest without having to worry about inconveniencing our hosts. In the morning we awoke to the scent of cooking food wafting into our room, but it became torture for us, because we weren't offered to join in the meal. I urged Gyuri to go and say profuse thanks for the accommodations, which he did, but sadly no one offered us any breakfast. Thus, we departed.

The next phase of our journey took us across Kolozsvár (Cluj in today's Romania), across Dés, and up to Bethlen. Being incurable optimists, we didn't look for night lodging until it was too late. In those days, since tourism was not one of Hungary's developing industries, one could only find travel lodging at a country inn. We didn't want to spend any money, though, and anyway the inns were few and far between. Thus, we intended to find lodging again with the locals.

In Bethlen, Gyuri left me resting on the roadside once again while he went to look for the mayor of the village to inquire about a night retreat. The mayor gave Gyuri an address. As Gyuri was walking up to the building, he noticed a group of giggling girls sitting on top of a stone wall. He asked them about the availability of two cots for the night. The girls began to laugh and informed him that they do indeed have beds but not for the purpose of sleeping. It seemed that the Saxon mayor, perhaps out of contempt for a couple of Hungarians, had sent him to the local brothel. Gyuri returned annoyed but, despite the mayor's prank and the tight spot we were in, we had a good laugh about it. We finally decided to randomly knock on the door of a peasant house on the other side of the village. It turned out that a lonely woman lived there. I noticed a photograph on the wall of a young man in uniform, perhaps her son, who might have been conscripted into the army, and thought that perhaps that was why she was so kind to us. She made a bed for the two of us and in the morning gave us a big jar of milk and large slices of white bread. Again, it was a person of modest means who shared with us the little that she had. To top it off, we couldn't even communicate with this poor woman since we didn't speak Romanian.

After Bethlen, we arrived in the land of the Saxons (ethnic Germans, called *Szász* in Hungarian), Szászrégen and Szászlekence. We rode into Szászlekence on a Sunday morning, when the local peasants were just coming out of church and sitting down for their usual beer. The scenery reminded us of our German reading assignment in high school: *Tyl Uilenspiegel in Köln*. The red-faced peasants were far from sympathetic personalities to us, but what really outraged us was the swastika flag flapping in the wind on a flagpole in the center of the village square.

Leaving the land of the Saxons behind, we arrived at the Maros River. From there the meandering road led us down toward the farthest corner of the Székler counties, to Kovászna. At this point we still had a good stretch of biking ahead of us. Our expected daily pedaling of 140 kilometers now seemed longer.

On our way toward the banks of the Maros, where the road was close to the Romanian border, we ran into gendarmes and were asked for identification papers. My papers were in order, proving my residency, which in those days was mandatory, but this was not the case with Gyuri. He didn't have his residency or identification papers. He didn't have a lamp on his bike; he had no proof of its ownership either, no nameplate, no horn. The gendarmes wrote up a long report and mercifully waved us on.

As we continued our journey along the Maros River I got a flat tire (my only one that was not accident-related during the entire trip) and in my anger at Gyuri for not noticing, I didn't call out to him to alert him. Thus, while I felt the air quietly whooshing out of my tire, he merrily rolled away. I thereupon sat down in the grass and enjoyed the evening breeze. Nearby, two pretty young Romanian girls were sitting on the shore in picturesque peasant dress shouting for the ferry. Their words sounded like *"Danyjama Lutrema,"* which they kept repeating. After a while Gyuri realized that I was no longer following him and circled back. We managed to patch the tube.

The distance between Budapest and Komandó by how the crow flies is approximately 575 kilometers, but the winding roads greatly increased the distance. We could not head south, our desired direction, all the time. Sometimes we had to pedal north, until finally the road would turn south again.

Toward the end of our journey we were both worn out and irritable. I began blaming Gyuri for hitting my front wheel and causing me to wipe out, while he accused me of negligence for allowing his sunglasses to break in my suitcase. By the end of the trip, we were no longer on speaking terms.

At last we arrived at Komandó, where a meandering little choo-choo train took us up to the logging area and the Boy Scout camp, where the other boys were elated to see us. For a short time we enjoyed celebrity status. And since we were only guests, instead of campers, we didn't have to be on night watch or kitchen duty peeling potatoes. My good friend Szabi was there and I entertained him with our adventures while he was fly-fishing. Szabi said proudly, "I only catch trout that have red dots on a silver body." I suspected there wasn't any other type of trout. Once he caught the fish, he rolled them into newspapers and fried them barbeque-style on embers. He shared this sumptuous meal with his friends. Szabi was what the Germans called a *Naturbursch,* "a nature boy." He knew all the secrets of rural life.

After passing a week in the wilderness, Gyuri, I, and our bikes boarded the train to go home. The train ride back was fast and comfortable, in great contrast to our trip out there. Finally, I arrived at Logodi Street, and after a short rest there I biked merrily out to Veresegyház.

At summer's end, I received a summons in the mail requesting me to present myself at the local police station with one of my parents. The summons reported a traffic violation for which I was either to pay twenty pengő (roughly the price of ten movie tickets in those days) or to serve time in jail, from 8 in the morning to 2 in the afternoon. I figured that this charge—which was not laid out in any detail—must have had something to do with my disregarding the rules of the road while biking, so I didn't pay much attention to it. I decided I would rather sit in the slammer than pay. God forbid that I pay twenty pengő to these despicable characters, not to mention that I somewhat eagerly looked forward to my incarceration as an exciting Jack London–like adventure. The following day, after asking my father to come for me when my time was up, I presented myself at the Pauler Street police station, where I was led into a cell with a wooden bench. There were about ten of us boys sitting in there and chatting (all of us were there for bicycling infractions), so time passed by pleasantly and quickly. In the afternoon, my father showed up and checked me out. I was terribly proud of my criminal record. Since my father abhorred any authority, any red tape or bureaucracy, I didn't receive a hard time from him for my little misadventure either.

Sometime later, when Gyuri and I met again, it struck me as strange that he didn't mention anything about his being incarcerated for the same infraction, especially since he had always had far more clashes with the police than me. At times he had been under house arrest on Sunday afternoons; his mother would have to make sure he stayed home and a police officer would come by to verify his presence. Thus, it baffled me how the gendarmes could have overlooked him. To Gyuri's great delight, we eventually concluded that the authorities mixed up our identities, with the end result that I served a jail sentence on his behalf.

14

Romantic Encounters

There were a couple of peasant girls whose beauty stunned me. One meeting with these girls happened shortly after we had moved from Grandmother's vineyard at Őrszentmiklós to Uncle Rory's house at Veresegyház. I was around seventeen years old at the time. There was some transaction between my parents and a farmer, and I was sent down to the village with an urgent message. The trip to the village of Veresegyház itself was nothing new to me, as the village and the lake were only about four kilometers away from Uncle Rory's vineyard and I frequently went there on my bike. For the first half of the ride, I followed a path running by the railroad tracks. On some days there, biking parallel to the train, passengers would cheer me on to pass them by. With the electric train as my competitor, this required some speed.

Once I reached the village and found my destination, I leaned my bike on the fence, opened the gate, and stepped into the courtyard. There in the center of the courtyard was a stool with a washtub on top of it, next to it stood a young girl. Her head was covered with a red kerchief and she wore the customary multiple peasant skirts. I didn't pay much attention to her attire and I could barely see any of her hair because of the kerchief, but the little that showed was brown. I took note of her brown eyes. Her arms were bare—the sleeves of her blouse were rolled up. We were about the same height. I judged her age as less than mine, but since peasant girls bloom early she looked my age. Girls like her, when they reached their eighteenth birthday, were considered marriageable in the interwar years. As I passed the message to her, I was mesmerized by her beauty. She was striking in the peasant environment—a girl who had a distinguished aura, like an exquisite, disguised movie star or a princess, waiting to be snatched from the hut and carried away in a coach.

At that time I was a teen and an inexperienced one. I didn't know how to flirt yet. For years I was infatuated with Olivia de Havilland. Now I found myself strongly attracted to this girl, but not so strongly that it would have led me to action. I didn't even attempt friendly banter. As soon as I had conveyed the required message, I left the courtyard in a daze.

The above excursion etched itself into my memory. I often wondered what became of this girl. Whom did she marry and what did her voice sound like? (She didn't speak to me, but only nodded while I was there.) The thought flashed through my mind: Could I have lived with her, or she with me? But marriages like that in those days were the exceptions.

It is conceivable that I impressed a few girls in the village, but I had a problem connecting with them. Small talk was not my forte. I didn't know how to start up a conversation, and I preferred to speak when a conversation had meaning and was progressing in a certain direction. I belonged to a family of landowners. My grandmother's and Uncle Rory's vineyards were well known. I was different from the village boys, who were relatively rough and unpolished. My mustache had been growing since I was fifteen or sixteen. I was also athletic—another reason that I might have caught the eyes of the maidens.

On one occasion, I experienced proof-positive that I wasn't short on sex appeal. It happened in the summer of 1941 when I became acquainted with the Rados children. I was fifteen years old at the time, Judit Rados was thirteen, and her brother László was around eleven. I had become a regular visitor at their house. We kids referred to their vineyard as the Gunda farm, after their grandfather's name on their mother's side. The three of us struck up a good friendship, and on my part it became a strong sentiment.

When we kids didn't go to the lake or visit another villa at Nyires, we gathered on the terrace of the Rados villa, dancing, chatting, churning the ice cream maker, or sipping wine. Our parents didn't interfere much with our drinking habits. Since we all grew up on vineyards, the wine bottle had been ever-present on the table, whether during meals or at social gatherings. When I was still very young, my parents had given me a glass of wine diluted with water. Thus, I was gradually introduced to alcohol in a way that I could learn how to handle it.

In those days I wasn't a bicycle racer yet, but I adored cycling and the bicycle was my constant commuting device. To visit Nyires, the district where the Radoses lived, I would hop on my bike, the "Blue Arrow." It had a padded cover on the saddle to make it more comfortable, since its springs were rather worn.

Once the summer had ended, for some reason I removed the cover of my saddle. A piece of paper fell out from underneath it. Two words appeared, in somewhat childish handwriting: *Nagyon szeretlek* ("I love you very much"). I knew immediately that this note did not originate from Judit or from any of her girlfriends. The handwriting was a dead giveaway, and the only person who would have had the occasion to touch my bike was the Rados family's kitchen maid—a peasant girl about the same age as Judit, but to whom I had never paid any attention.

I looked at the note and I was touched by its content, but I knew that I would never respond to it. What made that scribbled note even more meaningful was that the little servant girl who wrote it must have known that her case was hopeless, that my main interest was in her young mistress. Yet she ventured to write me the note, knowing that I might never even find it. I was deeply touched and saddened at the same time.

In the book of destiny, a romance with this girl was not meant to be. So this furtive gesture remained unanswered, like a tiny pebble thrown into a lake, leaving no ripples behind. But for me it was beautiful and touching. Should I meet this girl in the afterlife I would tell her that her note did not get lost, and that writing it was not a waste of time.

My last encounter with the maidens in the countryside took place in the summer of 1943. In those days telephones were nonexistent outside of the cities. The custom then was to communicate by messenger or visit people haphazardly, regardless of whether it might be convenient or not. Even for a more formal occasion, such as a weekend bridge gathering or a birthday party, messages would usually be sent verbally and only once in a while through the mail.

In our case, my parents would send me as their messenger to neighboring villas. One particular afternoon, I walked over to the

Arcfalvy estate and came upon a group of men and the owner of the vineyard, Aunt Boriska, an attractive widow, cheerfully tippling on the terrace. Aunt Boriska was the object of Uncle Tóni Viczián's admiration. These gentlemen, who were around my father's age, were drinking out of small wine glasses that they frequently emptied. I was offered a seat and a glass of tart white wine. A young peasant girl walked around the table and kept on refilling the glasses. Her height was about the same as mine, her figure was well proportioned. Her hair was light brown and her eyes were a greenish-grey color. She wore a simple peasant skirt and a white canvas blouse. She walked around without saying a word or smiling; her only care was not to let the glasses go empty.

When I caught sight of her, it was breathtaking. I might have fancied in my mind that I would kidnap her, lean a ladder beneath her window on a moonlit night and then place her in a car or a carriage and elope with her. This girl exuded sexuality. Out of her skin, her hair, her body a current was flowing, a mysterious alluring spell mixed with the flood of a silent cry. From her demeanor, gestures, and how she carried herself, I interpreted her body language as, "Here I am, use my womanly being. You may have me if you wish. I don't care if I don't see you again, just let me be yours."

As I headed home from the neighbor's villa, I couldn't get this peasant girl out of my mind. To have seen her, to have observed her, was an adventure. She must have been a phenomenal lover. What would her fate be in this peasant environment? Would she only experience work, childbirth, and the poverty of the village life? Would there be a man who would appreciate her? Would she find a responsive love?

15

Magnolias in the Moonlight and September in the Rain

Why is it that the divinest of the arts—music—is nevertheless the most evanescent of the arts?

—Paul Brunton

Shortly before Grandfather Miklós died in 1939, my father bought us our first radio. I remember the radio well, because the day after Grandfather's burial my father turned it on, and I was taken aback, feeling that it was an act of disrespect.

A couple of years later, my father came back from work carrying a "Radiola" phonograph, a hand-cranked machine called a "gramophone," and a few records. By then, there were some radios with built-in turntables, but since we didn't have electricity at Veresegyház we had to use the manual version. Among the records that my father had bought was "Song of the Island," which was the background music for a broadcast of a play of his on the Hungarian Radio. The protagonist of the play was a young bachelor who lived on an island in the middle of the Danube. The play begins with him saving the life of an attractive young lady whose motorboat has overturned. I trust the lively imagination of the reader to fathom the conclusion.

Other recordings my father purchased included "Magnolias in the Moonlight," "September in the Rain," "Auf Wiedersehn, My Dear" with Russ Columbo, and a Richard Tauber song. He liked to use Tauber records for his broadcast series "The History of the Operetta." We had an exclusive selection, with no gypsy music or German popular songs, with the exception of Willie Frost and Zarah Leander.

We could listen endlessly to Leander singing *"Kann die Liebe Sünde Sein?"* ("Can Love Be a Sin?") and we could never get enough of *"Ich Stehe im Regen Warte an Dich"* ("I'm Standing in the Rain Waiting for You"). But we still wouldn't buy these records. We were adamantly against purchasing anything German.

My first great interest was reading, then came music. I began to enjoy music through my first audio contraption, the tiny crystal radio set at my grandmother's house at Őrszentmiklós. With it, I would listen to *"Kék Ég"* ("Blue Skies") and other hits of the day, Hungarian or foreign. The productivity of the musical world during those years was formidable. Hit songs of the 1930s from Irving Berlin, Cole Porter, George Gershwin, and Jerome Kern, just to mention a few, are still a joy to listen to. These were the forerunners to the age of Frank Sinatra, whose trailblazing predecessor was Bing Crosby. The songs of the Crosby era withstood the test of time through Sinatra's modernizing and enhancing interpretation. Sinatra preserved the crop of the previous decades' musical output for posterity. If there was an "Aspirin Age" in the 1920s, there must have been an "Age of Sinatra" as well.

That is how my enthusiasm for music began—with the small crystal set in my sheriff's office, where the moon shone through the windows. In the mornings, I would wake up with those hard Bakelite earphones on my ears and to aching earlobes. In our apartment at 6 Logodi Street we didn't need earphones to listen to the radio, and there I enjoyed the music even more. One episode, when I was about thirteen and my listening pleasure was in jeopardy remained with me. On this particular day, my father had asked me to fetch some beer in a pitcher from a nearby pub. It is likely that our dinner was going to be knockwurst or the like with sliced onions in vinegar, for which a beer is a must. In the city, we drank mostly beer, not wine. Wine, we would have had to carry in from Veresegyház in a large demijohn, all the while slithering between the Scylla and Charybdis of revenue officers.

My father handed me the money and the pitcher, but I didn't budge. I stood there motionless. I was never quick to carry out a task. My father had made an inside joke out of this, calling me "Little Turtle." He liked to tell a joke in which Mama and Papa Turtle send their son Little Turtle to the city to buy some chocolate. Fifteen years later, Papa Turtle remarks, "By now Sonny must have reached the city." Another fifteen years pass by again when Mama Turtle speaks up, "By now Sonny must have bought the chocolate." Suddenly, Little Turtle calls out from behind a bush in an irritated voice, "If you're going to rush me like that, I'm not going to go at all!" At other times my father would put a twist on this joke, asking me to do something and then after a while he'd turn around and casually remark, "Oh, I didn't realize you had come back already." Then, if I chanced to protest that I hadn't even left yet, my father would say, "That's impossible. It couldn't take that long. You must be kidding!"

On this evening, however, I was purposely dragging my feet. I wasn't about to budge. At last my father's patience wore out, and he howled at me, "Why aren't you moving? Dinner is almost ready!" I stood there for another minute speechless, and then quietly began to cry. Now it was my father's turn to be stunned. "What did I do? What did I say?" he asked. "Why are you crying?" At this I blurted out, "If I leave now, I'll miss 'Indian Love Call' with Nelson Eddy and Jeanette MacDonald!" Since my father was great at child psychology he immediately responded, "Alright, alright. Let's listen to Nelson and Jeanette first, but right after that you must go to fetch the beer." It helped that my father also enjoyed listening to Nelson Eddy and Jeanette MacDonald programs. I never went for beer as fast as I did after the program that evening.

Youngsters of today would marvel at the musical appliances of those days. Our fellow Hungarian Péter Károly Goldmark hadn't yet dreamed up the long-playing record (his technology made possible the 33 1/3 long-playing record produced by Columbia in 1948). Our records in the 1930s were the 78 rpms with a maximum playing time of five minutes, which had been the case for decades. My father once bought a recording of Beethoven's Kreutzer Sonata, which came in a little pile of records. Each side of a record had three minutes of play time. Thus, the thirty-minute sonata required five records.

When we were dancing and the three minutes were about to expire, we would extend the time by placing the needle back at the beginning with a nimble movement of the wrist. But you couldn't use this shortcut for long, since the gramophone needed to be rewound. If it were not, an extended whine would signal the end of its strength. And after a few drinks the nimble movement might no longer be an option.

Also, the needle was only optimal for the first four or five plays before it wore out and had to be replaced. Originally, there were two types of needles—a fatter, louder kind for partying and a slimmer, quieter kind for listening. Later bamboo needles came into vogue. At a party in Szada at the Hajós villa someone conscientiously kept replacing the needle in the membrane, only to find out at the end of the party that the whole time he had been inserting needles from the used box!

The 78 rpms were pressed out of hard Bakelite plastic. They were thick (relative to later versions) and heavy. When they fell, they cracked and broke into pieces. I bought my records at the Láng family store on Rákóczy Avenue. There, one could sit in a booth and sample the available records. This method didn't do any good to the record, of course, but every record eventually found a buyer. At parties, the records scratched easily, especially when they were handled by a tipsy member of a gathering. The needles would speedily run over the surface of the record and leave behind a permanent scar. In a worst-case scenario, a band would get scratched and the needle would get stuck endlessly in the same groove. This must be how the expression "sounds like a broken record" originated.

All of my friends collected records, and out in the vineyards, in Nyires, where there was no electricity, the gramophone was the instrument that made dancing possible. We grew up mostly in the Bing Crosby era; Glenn Miller entered our lives toward the end of the war. Some afficionados listened to U.S. Armed Forces Radio and learned to play "In the Mood."

Occasionally, we borrowed or exchanged records. One summer afternoon, on the sandy path on my way home to Veresegyház I exchanged two of my records with Dudi Luttor, the pretty, blond, blue-eyed, plump daughter of Dr. Luttor. I gave her "If You Knew Suzie" and "Some of These Days," and she gave me "Will You Remember?" and "Sweetheart," by Nelson Eddy and Jeannette Mac-Donald. What I gave her was a sacrifice on my part, but the emphasis was not on the songs but rather on the barter. It was a simple way to establish amicable relations, and Dudi was probably well aware of my ruse. Unfortunately, our mutual interest didn't extend any further than these hits.

It was interesting that, almost without exception, members of our little gang all bought different recordings. As I perused my compiled discography I could hardly find one record that a friend of mine also had—the one exception being Charlie Kunz, who was everyone's favorite piano player. Kunz, who was American, played in London.

Playing records in the garden: Genovéva (Móki) Marosszéki, Pötyi, Balázs Kenderesy, me, and Dénes (Jumbó) Csongrády

His records were pressed by Brunswick Records, with its beautiful gold and black label. In those years, under the oppressive influence of Germany, Charlie Kunz became extremely popular. It might have helped that the songs he played were British and American tunes. Kunz became so popular in Hungary (and quite possibly in other German-occupied territories) that charges were brought up against him, accusing him of spying for the Nazis and conveying secret messages through his works. Later, the charges brought against him were dropped, since they were utter nonsense.

As September came, with its rainy days, my parents and I would settle down in the manor house with teakettle and cooked sliced pumpkin on the stove, somewhat depressed in the dim light of the kerosene lamp. Our only consolation was to play and replay "Auf Wiedersehn, My Dear" and "September in the Rain" on the gramophone.

16

My First Visit to the Gunda Farm

In May 1941, when we moved into Uncle Rory's house at Veres-egyház, I was still in school. In June, I left for a tour of the Danube with the water scouts. Upon my return, I was assigned the room at the end of the right wing of the house. This room had a double door that opened onto the porch facing the courtyard. I had my own entrance and was free to come and go without disturbing the privacy of my parents. Since my father worked in the city and was reluctant to commute, he came out to Veresegyház only on the weekends or for vacation. My mother meanwhile kept the household going with her usual auxiliary forces—our cook and the new vintner, Jani Nagy, who with his family had moved into the coachman's apartment. The small vintner cottage, which had one multipurpose room, a kitchen, a pantry, and a porch, was left unoccupied. My mother had it cleaned and whitewashed and hung up some curtains.

Shortly thereafter, a couple moved into this little bungalow. The man, Béla Kovács, was an engineer who allegedly worked in the city—as did his wife Aline, who was French. She was extremely shy and afraid of practically everything. After finding out about Aline's phobias, my mother had to laugh because, prior to the Kovácses moving in, she had left a somewhat tacky ashtray in the cottage that depicted Death with his scythe. "That is the last thing poor Aline needs on her nightstand," said my mother.

How and why the Kovácses came to live in our vintner house, I hadn't the slightest notion at the time. In those days before 1944, the Allies hadn't yet bombed Hungary. So the couple would not have been bombed out of their home or have moved out of a fear of bombing. Only much later did it occur to me that the Kovácses

Vintner house

might have been endangered when the Germans occupied France. The Germans didn't respect the citizenship of Hungarians who lived in France if they were Jewish or had emigrated to France for political reasons. Therefore, it seemed that coming back to Hungary was a sort of reverse escape for the Kovácses. In Hungary their status was also shaky, however, which may be why they landed at Veresegyház hidden away from the authorities. After a while, they left our bungalow.

Once we had settled in at Veresegyház it was inevitable that we would become acquainted with the people who literally crossed our paths daily. Some of these acquaintances matured into lifelong friendships.

One day, Judit Rados was crossing our property on bicycle on her way home from the train station. As kismet or destiny would have it, as she turned into Almafasor (Apple Allée) her bike got a flat tire. I almost bumped into her and came to a sudden halt. I jumped off my bike, introduced myself, and offered to help. I told her that I would come by her family's home later in the afternoon to patch her tire. Upon my arrival, and after meeting her grandparents, Mr. And Mrs. Gunda, and her mother, I did as I said. I repaired the tire, and from then on I became a regular visitor at the Gunda Farm.

Judit was one of two Rados children. At the time of our chance encounter she was thirteen years old and her brother Laci was twelve. About six years earlier, at Grandmother's vineyard in Őrszentmiklós, we had heard of the suicide of Mr. Rados and that two small children had been left behind.

Judit and Laci's maternal grandfather Lajos Gunda had retired from the position of chief comptroller in the Ministry of Agriculture. He stayed true to his calling, and every time produce was taken from the family garden or orchard he would have it weighed and track its market value with pedantic bookkeeping. His wife Izabella came from a rich patrician family that owned an apartment house on the corner of Gisella and Thököly Avenues in Budapest. She had a cousin Antal Zahár Jr., who had an estate and country home nearby in a village called Zsidó (Jew) whose name was changed to Vácegres (Vác Gooseberry) when the Germans occupied Hungary.

The second time that I visited, Aunt Iza handed me an ice-cream maker. This contraption consisted of a wooden pail filled with crushed ice and a center piece that held the sugar and various fruits—usually cherries, strawberries, or apricots. The ice was salted

Apple Allée

and I had to crank it with some speed and strength in order for the fruity substance to solidify. As luck would have it, I arrived just in time to rescue Aunt Iza from this strenuous churning.

I introduced my parents to the Gundas and a warm friendship ensued between our families. Visits to neighbors had been carried over as a tradition, starting with my great-grandfather Henry O'Donnell and continued by his son, Uncle Rory. Now we added the home of Iza *néni* (Aunt Iza) and Lajos *bácsi* (Uncle Lajos), and their daughter Izabella (Judit's mother) to our list of possible destinations. Judit had also been baptized Izabella, but three Izabellas would have been too much, so they called her Judit.

We, the youngsters of Nyires, would go up to the Gunda house and sit on the terrace for hours, sipping wine and cranking the gramophone, playing our favorite numbers over and over again. I would do the same thing at home. My mother told me that I repeated the same records so many times that she would hear the songs in her sleep.

After the war Aunt Iza nostalgically recalled these pleasant afternoons, moonlit nights, and flirtations. She told us how she had gone out of her way to buy these records, knowing that hearing those songs and dancing to them would bring us much pleasure. She said that as the war was nearing, "I felt that money shouldn't be an issue. You kids should enjoy yourselves while you were young. That's why I bought those records in heaps and carried them out to Nyires. I was afraid that the type of life we had would vanish with the war." How right she was.

Presumably Aunt Iza was also driven by a desire to have her little girl in the company of a nice circle of well-groomed handsome boys; and this way she could have a close look at potential suitors. She may have been trying to protect her daughter from experiencing a tragedy similar to the one she had suffered when her husband committed suicide.

Judit was a brunette or medium blonde. At the lake at Veresegyház she would get a nice suntan without ever burning. In her bathing suit she evoked a Roman or Greek goddess—with perfect proportions and a finely chiseled, dainty nose. She was around my height, her face symmetrical, her lips full, and her eyes hazel or bluish-green. With her light-colored hair, blown by the breeze, she was enchanting. She caught people's attention when she entered a room.

Judit Rados

Over the years, she impressed me with her repose, her demeanor, her sense of humor, and her dignity.

As a young girl, Judit often helped her mother in the vineyard. I once stopped by when she was dangling on a branch at the top of a cherry tree, picking the fruit and gathering it in her apron. I remember she was wearing a light blue summer dress, a kind of Dirndl (a short Tyrolean skirt). She was like a beautiful fruit of nature, a peach or apricot, tanned, blossoming, and fresh either from swimming in the lake or bicycle riding.

While I was in Transylvania in the summer of 1944, working in a student labor battalion, Judit and I maintained a lively correspondence. I wrote to her a great deal and she responded in kind, keeping me up to date on life at Veresegyház. I received letters from others as well. In one of Aunt Blanka's letters, she described an afternoon when she and her cousin Janika went down to the lake for a dip. They surreptitiously surveyed a group of young maidens (Blanka was thirty-four at the time and Janika thirty) and made observations, registering their favorites among the girls. According to Blanka, Janika found the most strikingly beautiful one—not surprisingly—to be Eszter Hajós, while Blanka remarked, "To me Juci Rados is still the most attractive." This didn't surprise me.

When I was fifteen, I felt that Judit and I might be a good match, but at that time my experience with girls didn't go further than dancing school. It is conceivable that Aunt Iza viewed me as a potential suitor for her daughter, but she didn't demonstrate that in any way. In those days, in matters of feelings, of sentiments, both the young and the old were reserved. My parents' main fear was that I would be ensnared or enmeshed by the wrong girl; their concern was unfounded. Most of the time I was the hunter. And if my quarry showed signs of interest, I tended to beat a rapid retreat.

Our adolescence was carefree and beautiful. In those days in Hungary, students didn't work during the summertime. After school was let out and Boy Scout camping was over, everybody showed up on the scene: the lake at Veresegyház. Our main occupation was swimming. The Viczián cousins played tennis on the courts by the train station, followed by billiards at Gyula Kemény's pub. Eszter and Menyus Hajós would visit their aunt, Edit, at the Viczián's manor house.

On the weekends, the grownups usually played bridge. At one point my two grandmothers, Eveline and Róza, took a vacation together to Várgede. There, they took a dip in the local hot spring thermal pool, which was well known for its miraculous rejuvenating power, and drank Csevicze, a famous sparkling spring water. My father would come out from the city whenever he could. In retrospect, we led a charmed life, an idyllic one, in our small paradise. Of course, with hindsight it's easy to discard any unpleasantness and reminisce fondly.

I can recall only one incident at Veresegyház where I got into a bind. That took place in the early summer of 1942. As a rule, when I went into the village I would cycle on the sidewalk. Unlike the dusty, dirty public road, the path for the pedestrians was hard and clean.

When I was given an errand, I would swoosh across the village, through the marketplace, and head for the lake. One morning as I rode by the village office, two men suddenly jumped out in front of me, one from the right and one from the left, and dragged me off my bike. I recognized one of them as the village manager, Ghéczy; the other was his office messenger. Ghéczy was known for his brutality and coarseness. As it turned out, they had pulled me off the bike because biking on the sidewalk was allegedly not permitted. They took my bike and turned it over to the gendarmerie. By this time I was too old for crying, so I just slogged home dejectedly.

At home, wheels began to turn. My mother visited our neighbor Béla László, a retired gendarmerie officer, and asked him to intervene. Mr. László was very well respected. He also happened to have a telephone (rare in our neighborhood at the time), so he was able to call the station right away and instruct the gendarmes to return my bicycle. Mr. László had an enormous red nose, the likes of which one could see only on old hags in children's picture books. His wife Irén escorted me to the station. On the return trip, she sat on my crossbars. She was quite slender, so this was no hardship for me, but I was terribly embarrassed because it seemed like a flirtatious thing for her to do.

Ghéczy, my new ferocious enemy, was generally disliked. In those days, we Boy Scout "hoboes," as our nickname was, sported small skull caps (yarmulke-like). Ghéczy was an Arrow Cross supporter. Fascists like him regarded the scouts as reactionary, and not pro-German. The sight of me riding around in a skull cap must have generated a response like a bull seeing red. But Ghéczy was also rude to poor farmers. He would go out at night when a partial blackout order was in effect and kick off the kerosene lamps that hung beneath the farmers' passing drays. Cars, incidentally, were only required to dim their headlights (the face of the headlights would be covered with paint, with just a small sliver remaining open). His actions were mean and sadistic.

When I biked from Buda to Veresegyház I usually chose to take the turnpike that ran through the villages of Gödöllő and Szada. The road to Gödöllő was much better than the one that ran across Fót, and a road across Ujpest required enduring a belt of disgusting stench emanating from the zone of leather tanning factories. Heading toward Gödöllő, on the other hand, I got excellent training on hill climbing, while the surface of the road was first class. I enjoyed going out to the vineyard on bike since it meant door-to-door transportation. I abhorred the train and the streetcars, not to mention the extra time they took. Riding my bike, I felt free and I enjoyed the scenery. It's true that I couldn't carry much, but this was probably a blessing since nobody could ask me to transport anything out to Veresegyház. Once in a blue moon, my friend János's father, Károly Brencsán, would give me a ride from the country into the city in his elegant Austin automobile, but he would drop me off on the city's outskirts and I would still have to take the electric tram to reach Logodi Street.

One early summer morning, as I was swooshing down the road across Szada toward Veresegyház, I crashed into a group of geese crossing the main road. The geese made an infernal noise, but they were unharmed. I wiped out on the dusty gravel road, but, my bike was intact. Since I was bruised and bleeding profusely I biked to Uncle Ernő's apothecary for first aid. He mobilized the blond, blue-eyed Dudi Luttor, who was planning to go to medical school like her father Dr. Luttor. This became my first acquaintance with Dudi, who cleaned me up, bandaged my wounds, and sent me on my way. From the apothecary I still had to ride another three miles to get home.

On that particular evening, I joined my pals amid the crowd at the Keménys' restaurant. They bragged to me that they had consumed a great quantity of Napoleons (cream-filled pastries) without paying. They dared me to do the same, and it didn't take much prodding for me to give in to the temptation. Consequently, I also gobbled up a few of them. The following day, when I gave an account of the previous night's caper to my father, he took out his wallet and gave me the amount for the Napoleons I had consumed. He made me hop on my bike and go into Veresegyház to pay for them.

At the restaurant, my reception was not exactly as I had hoped. I didn't even receive a handshake for my honesty. Instead, I felt like Ronald Colman, in the movie *The Prisoner of Zenda*, because the headwaiter wanted to put me in handcuffs and keep me there until all of the other culprits showed up and made their amends. Only with the greatest of difficulty was I able to extricate myself from his deadly embrace. Needless to say, none of the other boys suffered from any pang of guilt or outburst of honesty. By the next day they were all out there again, playing billiards.

On occasion, Genovéva Marosszéki, aka Móki, would cycle down to our house in the morning. She would lean her bike on the porch, come into my room, and while I was finishing my slumber, sit on the edge of my bed for a chat. My parents viewed her visits with some concern, but these tête-à-têtes were innocent encounters. While she was prepared to turn them into flirtations, I was still firmly lodged in my cocoon. Gyuri's encouragement to try out my charm notwithstanding, I was still far from ready. This is not to say that Móki was not pleasing to the eyes. She was taller than me, had a slender figure, an oval well-shaped face, medium-blonde hair, and eyes like Judit's. But her interior was in need of some improvement. In character she lagged far behind Judit.

The next chapter of my life involving Judit took place in the wintertime. Our Boy Scout troop, the Balassa (named after the national hero, warrior and poet Baron Bálint Balassa), organized an afternoon tea dance. We were in the tenth or eleventh grade and our dancing partners came from the Erzsébet Szilágyi Girls High School. We knew most of them already from our dance classes. In dancing school, Mrs. Elekes taught us six dances: Hungarian Csárdás, Viennese Waltz, English Waltz, Tango, Fox Trot, and Slow Fox. In the classes we formed two circles, according to our age. When Mrs. Elekes struck a castanet, the boys would take one step forward to the next dancing partner; every boy thus had the chance to dance with every girl, and vice versa.

An exam was held, where each boy had a booklet listing the dances. We had to ask six different girls to be our partner for each of the six dances. They would sign their names by the particular dance that they completed with us. After we had danced the obligatory pieces, our teacher would put on a medley of dance music and we were free to ask any of the girls to dance. This would be followed by the closing dance of the evening, the so-called "lady's choice," when the girls got to choose their partners.

Since I still had feelings for Judit, I invited Judit to the Balassa tea dance. At the dance, a number of other girls were present with whom I was already on friendly footing. Among them was Mária Csongrády, Jumbó's sister and the object of Gyuri's affection. All of these young ladies were dressed in their prettiest outfits and exuded social grace. We boys, on the other hand, were still clumsy teenagers, notwithstanding our formal attire.

In addition to Judit I also invited Menyus Hajós. Despite the fact that he was three years older than me, he graciously consented. This greatly raised my social standing since Menyus arrived elegantly dressed, was tall and dashing, and danced very well. He knew some quite unusual, exotic dance steps, which he tried out on the prettiest girl there (Brigitta Kaposy). As he was dancing with his partner, all of the sudden he would take fake steps as if he was about to fall on them. Before the young lady even realized what was about to happen he had already adroitly moved on to the next phase of the dance, smoothly following the rhythm of the music.

When I asked Judit to come to the tea dance with me, Aunt Iza was initially reluctant and declined to give her approval. She might have been concerned that Judit was too young to participate in a dance. I don't know how Judit felt at that point; I only know that I completely collapsed under this seemingly negative response. What followed was a rollercoaster of emotions. All the while, my parents quietly observed my agony and empathized.

A few days later, Aunt Iza's hesitancy dissipated, and I received a call from Judit telling me that she and Aunt Iza accepted my invitation to the tea dance. But when they appeared, I had to disguise my disappointment.

Aunt Iza had dressed her daughter as if Judit had just stepped out of a boarding school run by a convent. Judit's hair style was nice, but she didn't have any makeup on—not that she really needed it. But then, she wore high-laced black boots, black wool stockings, and a black velvet school uniform with white frilled jabot on her blouse. If there was ever a test of mythological proportions for a sixteen-year-old boy, this was it! I had been expecting a little Roman Goddess, the one I pictured at the lake shore in her swimsuit with her adorable figure nicely tanned, or else in her blue dirndl perched up in a cherry tree. There was nothing doing—I was obliged to dance with her; after all that's why I had invited her in the first place. At the first opportunity I stepped down and ran around to get hold of my friends. After much persuasion, begging, threatening, and cajoling, I was able to line up Jumbó, Gyuri, and Tibor Karsay to ask Judit for a dance, since I was too bewildered to dance with her exclusively.

I don't recall where Aunt Iza was all the while, but I could hardly wait for the end of the evening so that she could depart with Judit and I could leave with a loud sigh of relief. Of course, there were other young maidens with whom I would have enjoyed a dance, but by then that was out of the question. At the tea dances,

Bandi Dékány would play the piano and Gyuri Szőlősy was the drummer. On some occasions, Gyuri would graciously let me take his place at the drums, but on this night all my energy was taken up with strategizing my retreat. Judit enjoyed the fray immensely; she was exhausted from so much dancing. I managed to hide my disappointment quite well, and I believe she was oblivious. This had been an opportunity to carve myself into her heart, especially since at that time I didn't have any rivals. She may have sensed my reticence, but she didn't give any sign of it. Had I cared to nurture our relationship, it might have blossomed. But after the Balassa dance I concluded that I shouldn't covet her favor while she was still a little girl in a boarding school. So even though there may have been some interest on her part, I took safety in flight, and the winter passed by.

As summer returned, the lively social hubbub of Nyires reemerged as well. The regular members of our gang gathered, plus one, Dezső Kemény, my former playmate and schoolmate. Hermina "Minci" Alemann from Őrszentmiklós made her debut as well. She went to Sophianum Women's High School. The Alemann villa was in the neighborhood of my grandmother's vineyard at Őrszentmiklós. Móki had Lajos Kenderesy as her indentured servant, but let other boys sit in her circle as well. Over the course of the summer, we all repeatedly visited the Gunda-Rados family, one cozy afternoon following another. We wound up the phonograph, put on the records with the red label in the center, and played and replayed "Blue Skies" and "Solitude" by Anita Best.

Seeing Judit again in the countryside I realized my feelings had changed again. From then on I approached our relationship with some trepidation. She was a well-rounded personality in body and in spirit. Her blond hair was just the right length—not too long, not too short. Her alto voice was pleasing; her eyes had a beautiful hazel hue. Her mouth was faultless. It is a rarity when a human being has such a balance of beauty. She was not the giggly type, but smiled frequently, warmly, and always apropos. I had mixed feelings. I didn't want to put myself or her on an emotional roller coaster, but since she kept showing me kindness and openness I was unable to get out from under her magic radiation. At the same time, Dezső Kemény began to pay attention to Judit, trying his best to woo her.

Once, when the former vintner's bungalow at the entrance to our courtyard was vacant, we decided to utilize it for a party. It was a foregone conclusion that Dezső would bring a few of his favorite records, including "By the Waterfall" and "Shanghai Lil." We decorated the place with colored garlands, which along with lampions, candles, and kerosene lamps lent the place an enchanting ambiance. The small cottage's intimacy further enhanced the cheerfulness and romping around of our little group.

My father joined us. He was young in spirit and he hit it off well with my pals. As a writer he also took mental notes, memorizing our discussions, our adventures, and our silliness. He could mentally replicate our conversations. He became especially fond of Gyuri Sághy; a friendship between them evolved.

Father also liked Balázs Kenderesy, a puckish, small, blond, somewhat saucy kid. Once when we were preparing our red wine in the press house Balázs offered up his little white cap to dunk in the juice and dye it red. In the end, the cap didn't turn red but became a lilac color instead, nevertheless we had great fun in the process. Szabi Viczián was as much a member of my family as his own. Among my female acquaintances, my parents strongly favored Judit and very likely secretly hoped that our relationship would turn out to be everlasting.

My father's impression of the vintner's house was of a "sailor's pub in an exotic port." We danced, flirted, and enjoyed ourselves to the fullest. Our love affairs in those days were still going andante. Laci, Judit's brother, lured Móki out into the garden, where he asked her to lay down and then tried to lie on top of her. When they returned, Laci complained to his inner circle that Móki had thrown him off. Such were the first wingbeats of youth.

The only person who smoked was my father. We drank in moderation, my father being an expert at that. He would have a small glass filled with wine and stretch it out for a long time. When the grownups played bridge, they would drink from small glasses. At an afternoon party at the Kenderesy's, Aunt Erzsike hung small numbers on the sides of the glasses for identification. During the course of the evening, János Brencsán rushed into the room bewildered and explained to his mother Aunt Iduska, that he had just swallowed his number with its fishhook attachment. Aunt Iduska calmly suggested that he take several bites of the inside of a slice of bread. This would presumably envelop the fishhook.

As summer turned into fall, I consulted with Balázs about my new romantic interest—Minci Alemann. At his urging, I targeted Minci for conquest. What really prodded me on was the fear that time would pass me by, that all my friends, chief among them Gyuri, would surpass me massively and I wouldn't have the trophy of possessing even one girl's heart. I wasn't aiming for any sexual entanglement, since I was greatly concerned about an out-of-wedlock pregnancy and I knew tradition would dictate that it result in marriage. Nonetheless, I set out on this adventure without any consideration for potential repercussions.

The Alemanns' villa was close to my grandmother's house at Őrszentmiklós. It was built in a Swiss chalet style in the middle of their vineyard. Mrs. Alemann, Minci's mother, was divorced. She had raised three children, two boys and a daughter, there: Guszti, Fritzi, and Minci. She was from an Austrian family, a fine lady who had endured much hardship in her life.

After every harvest, the family would move back to their apartment on Baross Street in the city. The Alemann children were brought up extremely well; they had good manners and fit into Nyires society. Fritzi and Minci were my age. Guszti was older, and was soon called up for military duty.

In the fall of 1943, I enrolled in law school at Péter Pázmány University. Minci was in her last year of high school at Sophianum High School, an elite girls' school. The fall and winter of 1943 became earmarked for wooing her. She was slender, athletic (she biked and swam), and had a well-proportioned body with somewhat strong calves. She was blond, blue-eyed, light-skinned—a typical Austrian girl. Her face was oval, and her jaw suggested a strong personality. Her voice at times was slightly hoarse. In five words: she was a pretty girl.

Slowly but surely, I vanquished my competitors. The boys saw that I had the inside track and one by one fell by the wayside.

Before we all moved back to the city that fall, we had a farewell party at the Alemann villa where we introduced a new game. We lay down in a circle on our stomachs, put our hands behind our backs, and drank our wine with no hands, just by lifting the glass with our lips. We laughed a lot and became tipsy. In the meantime, Minci's German Shepherd ran around us sniffing, somewhat bewildered by the crazy gang. From time to time, Szabi would wind up the gramophone and play his favorite record "I'm Sorry for Myself." As a rule, the Viczián boys could hold their liquor very well, but on this occasion they were slightly drunk. István Kormos, meanwhile, a

Group photo: Genovéva (Móki) Marosszéki, László (Laci) Rados, Balázs Kenderesy, myself, and Gyuri Sághy

newcomer to our group, stayed sober at Judit's side. We also played "Amapola," "Honolulu," "Thanks for Everything," "Deep Purple," and "That's a Plenty."

After the party I became a daily visitor to Baross Street. Minci seemed to like my personality, and small signs told me she was doing everything to get into my good graces. When I suggested she wear flat shoes (she was taller than me and her legs were muscular), she wore them the very next day. She had bought herself a pair of flats even though a new pair of shoes was hard to come by. Once, she broke one of my records (featuring a Swedish piano player, Borge Friis). By the very next day she had managed to replace it with a new one.

My parents were concerned about my fickleness and inconsistency in my relationships with girls. I kept desiring the unobtainable, the unrequited, and if I was about to achieve it, I would run away. When I aimed for a young lady's heart it was a game and a challenge, but once it turned in my favor, I realized that if I continued in my pursuit it would cost me my independence, and I was not ready to sacrifice it. In each of the endgames over those years, I couldn't find a mutual love, a meeting of souls that could have led me into marriage. When I reflect on the various possibilities that I relinquished, each would have resulted in an entirely different life than the one that I eventually led. But at the age of eighteen I still yearned for a few feathers in my manly cap. I suspected that my friends were all ahead of me, and when it came to Gyuri it was not a suspicion, but a fact. Gyuri was head over heels in love with Dusa, the Polish lassie, and then much later with the young Russian woman whom he had helped escape from an internment camp (who was allegedly a spy).

17

Champion du Mond

I had a chance to judge my athletic prowess by competing with the neighboring Viczián boys, who were all-around athletes. In my sheriff's office at my grandmother's vineyard, the walls were decorated with swords and helmets. Once, when Szabi Viczián came to see me, I handed him a sword and asked him to fence. As it turned out, he was an accomplished fencing champ, and he hit my head forcefully and frequently. He was also considerably taller than me, and when we ran he left me in the dust from the start. I learned to swim, but unlike him I didn't dive.

One winter, I started to ski. To take up skiing I needed skis, shoes, and suitable clothing. Fortunately, Aunt Blanka came to my rescue. As a teenager, Blanka had become acquainted in Austria with an old man who had served as a sharpshooter in the Austro-Hungarian Army's Imperial Rifle Corps. He was a member of an Alpine unit. These soldiers were the best skiers ever; they spent half their lifetimes on skis. He once found himself transported by an avalanche, landing in a valley with most of his bones broken. Miraculously, he healed and never lost his zest for skiing. He taught my aunt how to ski and presented her with a pair of his old skis, which later became mine. These skis were short and heavy. Their bindings consisted of a metal plate pivoting on a hinge. The toe caps of the shoes were belted onto the ski with a wide leather strap, while another leather strap fastened the heel of the shoe to the metal plate. The bindings were so rigid that you could navigate with them only by moving your feet up and down, not sideways. You had to be quite skillful to avoid a sprained ankle or broken bone. My skiing attire consisted of my father's field-grey breeches from the First World War and my

Boy Scout windbreaker and cap. My aunt presented me with ski boots and poles.

At this point I need to mention Herta Obstgarten, a girl I met at dancing school when I was around fourteen. She came over for lessons from the Erzsébet Szilágyi Girls' High School. The Obstgartens lived nearby on Atilla Street. Herta's father Gyula had also been a mountain trooper during the First World War. He had been wounded and as a consequence could only use one of his arms when skiing. His other arm was retained in a Napoleon-like pose, folded across his torso. Nonetheless, this didn't handicap him in his skiing in the least. He and his daughter skied so incredibly well it was outright scary. Herta was blond with blue eyes. She was a prototypical Austrian girl, and I developed a huge crush on her, adorable in her red windbreaker and perky little red cap. When Uncle Rory heard of my interest in Herta—especially of her last name—he, the gentleman farmer, was elated. He remarked, "Nomen est omen"—that is, name foreshadows destiny. For *Obstgarten* means orchard.

Out of the blue Herta suggested that we go skiing together. When I met her and her father in the Buda mountains at the top of the Swabian Berg slopes, the first words out of Mr. Obstgarten's mouth, as he looked down at my cherished skis, were, "Where did you get those bed planks?" With that one remark, I was psychologically eviscerated.

We were standing at the edge of the Nagy Egyetemi (Great University Slope) slope by Normafa (Norma Tree). As I looked down the steep mountainside, I could see that it was covered in ice. In the blink of an eye, I saw Herta, the owner of the red vest and cap, swoosh over the rim of the slope and disappear like a phantom into the misty wintry landscape. One second she was standing next to me. In the next she was deep in the valley, in the shadow of the mountain. She was followed by her father, with his poles neatly tucked under his arms. I was scared to death. I had never skied before in my life. I didn't have the slightest idea how to slalom, brake, or come to a stop. I knew only that I must follow Herta or I would lose this charming maiden forever. In addition, I would be the laughing stock of the entire Erzsébet Szilágyi High School. Enough said! All day long I followed the little wizard, tumbling down the slopes while she gracefully skied past me and left me behind. I went down those slopes in an incredible manner, just like the old trooper in the avalanche—minus the avalanche. Luckily for me, I didn't break any bones, but I did end up with plenty of bruises, physical and mental. At least I had saved my honor. All day long, whenever and wherever Herta and her father slid down I rolled after them. Alas, this skiing excursion put an end to my romance. There was never such a dramatic end to a romance in a Jack London novel on the snow-covered Klondike as I had that day. Never again did I want to ski with a female companion.

Instead, I teamed up with Jumbó Csongrády, Gyuri, and the Karsay brothers. We kept away from the Svabian Berg Slope of my Obstgarten adventure, and leisurely skied down from atop and across the meandering Farkasvölgy (Wolf Valley) valley to Lejtő (Slope) Street. At the bottom of the valley stood the Karsay house, where we would warm up with a cup of tea with rum. At these afternoon teas I would wind up the phonograph and repeatedly play Duke Ellington's "Caravan" by the Bar Trio or Mihály Tabányi on accordion. My ski attire remained rather shabby, although I did manage to buy Gyuri's old skis of questionable quality before the siege. After the siege, I didn't ski for about five decades. When I put my new fancy skis on at the ripe old age of seventy, my family and friends were apprehensive, but there was no need for that. I did fairly well, all things considered. But I still don't ski with women.

My chance to show off my skills came when we became river scouts and went out on the Danube to build up our rowing strength and ability. There were docks in Óbuda that we visited as soon as the spring weather turned balmy. I sniffed the invigorating smell of the river and the intriguing smell of the tar that was used to make the bottom of the boats waterproof.

We took our first baby steps under direction of the sappers, soldiers who built bridges and handled barges and boats. They handed over to us the clumsy boats, the large poles, the steering oars, the skulls, or sweeps, for paddling. There were two-man crews in each boat. One rowed while the skipper with the oar navigated and contributed power to the propulsion. At times we set our oars aside, stuck our long poles in at an angle, and started pulling our hands up the pole until we reached the top. We would then remove the pole and re-entrench it, only to repeat the process. These maneuvers required great effort, whether we used our poles or our oars. And whether one rowed or steered, both jobs were equally demanding. To cross the Danube we had no choice but to row. Boats were good body builders.

In those days, we Boy Scouts participated in paramilitary training, a necessary adjunct of Boy Scout life since the nation was at war. After the sapper training, we changed conveyances. Our next boat looked exactly like a galleon and we looked like a chain gang. Only the lash was missing from the hand of our skipper. We sat in rows of two and the skipper steered our terribly heavy teaching boat. It took the greatest of effort from all of us to move the boat forward but it also made us stronger and prepared us for the next phase. We graduated to the patrol boat, the double scull, where three boys rowed on each side while the skipper sat in the rear of the boat facing the direction the boat was going. In the front of the boat sat a so-called *Spitz*, a boy who would jump into the water and tie the boat to the shore. This, of course, was the coveted position, which I was frequently able to finagle, making it more or less a pleasurable ride.

During the wintertime we participated in war games at the Boy Scout Park. Cadets from the Ludovica Military Academy would instruct us. They came carrying their machine guns, making our exercises all the more realistic. On one occasion, when our task was to climb a very steep and tall wall of rocks, I had made it halfway up when I glanced down. At the sight of the abyss below me I was filled with horror and I froze. I was now blocking the path of the boys behind me on the wall. At the same time all of the boys ahead of me had disappeared. In the end, a rescue squad reached down for me from above. Somehow I was pried off of the rock, and dragged up to the top of the hill.

Parallel with river scouting, I became an avid cyclist. Although my parents didn't buy me a bike, I had a piggybank in which I had saved all of the silver pengős from Béla Iványi Grünwald, as well as gifts from various relatives and friends.

Fortunately, we had a superintendent at 6 Logodi Street, Lajos Böttkös, who was a telephone lineman and a technical wizard. With him, I made my first visit to Teleki Square, a steady conglomerate of stalls and booths, an all-weather flea market on the outskirts of the city. With my meager savings, this was an ideal place to buy a secondhand bike. Thus, as Mr. Böttkös's tow, I bought my first marvelous steel steed. It was a worn out, decrepit bike that I named "The Blue Arrow." Since something was constantly wrong with it, it made a mechanic out of me. Then again, I only paid fifty-eight pengős for it, approximately twelve dollars in those days. Eventually

I traded it in for a lightweight sport bike made by Rendessy, but I stuck with the color blue.

My love affair with bicycling led to my acquaintance with Menyhért (or Menyus) Hajós, who opened up new vistas to me. The very first time that Menyus saw me with my bike at the Veresegyház Lake, he pulled a wrench out of his pocket and adjusted my brake pads. That was the beginning of a beautiful friendship. He also invited me over to Szada to meet his family. His sister Eszter was a stunning beauty, and there were hardly any young men who would not have had a crush on her; I, of course, was no exception.

Menyus was two years my senior. At the time we met he was attending Cistercian High School on St. Imre Avenue. He was good-looking, tall, with a somewhat ski slope–like nose. After we met at the lake, I invited him to visit us at Uncle Rory's, where we became absorbed in discussing the mysteries of bicycling. He had a lightweight custom-made bike by Biró; it was black and yellow and had regular handlebars and clincher tires. It was a three-speed (in those days that was the top of the line) equipped with a French Champion derailleur. Menyus went into great detail explaining how he utilized his three speeds. He would start out from the lake with cogwheel number sixteen, using it until he reached the railroad tracks. After the crossing, he would change into gear number eighteen, and for the last leg of his trip home he would switch over to gear number twenty.

In the fall, Menyus took me to Népliget (Peoples Park) to see a bicycle race. He taught me the trade secrets of bicycle racing. The race course was a flat, elongated ellipse on which the racers made laps. Feri Éles, a crack racer of the FTC (Francistown Gymnastic Club), who had a good shot at winning the race got a flat tire and fell behind the peloton. Two of his club mates, who had also fallen behind, then went ahead of him to reduce the air resistance and give him some slipstream. This helped him close the gap and rejoin the group of racers.

The ambiance of the race, the colorful spectacle of the racing bikes and spectators, filled me with enthusiasm. I looked down at my legs. They were somewhat chubbier than those of my peers, but I judged them powerful enough and therefore decided to become a bicycle racer. This decision was easy for me to make, but executing it was more problematic. I needed a real racing bike and I had to become a member of a club.

I began collecting parts for a lightweight racing bike while I continued to train on heavy, so-called iron wheels, or clinchers, and I decided to join the Francistown club. It was a well-known sports club and a shade classier than the Póstás (Mailmans Club) or the Bszkrt, the trolley and streetcar employees' club. Most of the bicycle racers didn't exactly come from the House of Lords, which prejudiced my father slightly against the sport. In those days gentlemen were horseback riding, playing tennis, fencing, or sailing yachts. But his snobbery was unjust, since some of the bicycle racers were college graduates and skating champions.

The first time I went out for a group training run was in March 1943. By then, the frigid winter had yielded to a pleasant, balmy spring. Everyone in the FTC went to train on the turnpike toward Gödöllő. My fellow club members were riding their lightweight racing bikes with sew-up tires on wooden rims (aluminum rims were not yet in vogue). I was the only one with clinchers, a regular handlebar, and no derailleur. At St. Ilona's Slope I dropped behind. I was embarrassed, but through superhuman effort, I caught up with them well before Gödöllő. One member of the group, Károly Szenes, took note of my effort. He was an excellent racer from among the Category 1 first-class racers—those who had already placed at three races—and he had just recently returned from France. During a race there he had taken unfair advantage by following an automobile, whereupon the French Cycling Association barred him from any further racing in France. At Gödöllő, we turned and headed back toward our starting point, a restaurant by the beginning of the Kerepes Turnpike.

Here, I received an energetic dressing down from my club mates. Since it was the first time I had ridden a bicycle in a pack, surrounded by other cyclists, I had been scared to death of crashing. Consequently I had zig-zagged right and left in the middle of the pack. The end result was that I created a hazard for the others. It was a near miracle that we avoided a mass pileup. Thus, my next task became getting used to being crowded in by other cyclists. I had to learn how to change positions in a cramped situation without endangering my fellow cyclists and myself.

Károly Szenes had been impressed that I was able to catch up with the group on my outdated bike. On another training run, on our way back from Gödöllő, Károly and I had been riding side by side, but when we came to the Patkó (Horseshoe) curve on the uphill serpentine I dropped behind. In spite of Károly's energetic encouragement, I couldn't hold onto his rear wheel and catch up with him. I was in the dark as to how much and how I should train on the bike or via other activities, such as running up stairs. I was left to my own amateurish self-coaching. The other riders were careful not to share trade secrets with an eventual competitor—even in the same club.

During the winter of 1943, I began to collect parts in earnest for a real racing bike. I bought a pair of Swiss brakes, a German Lohman saddle, a pair of French pedals, and an Italian three-cogwheel Regina sprocket. By now I had become friendly with the Vass mechanics, Ernő Halász and József Vass. I ordered a frame from them that was made of Mannesman Steel and weighed 3.65 dekagrams. These two men had their shop at Szerdahelyi Street in Józsefváros (Joseph Town District). Their specialty was motorcycles, but they also manufactured lightweight bikes.

Over the years, I became their regular "tormentor." At the beginning of our acquaintance, I would park my old bike on the sidewalk by leaning it against a sickly looking acacia tree and go into the store to borrow their tools. I would fix my minor problems with their tools and avoid paying the mechanics. By then, I had outgrown Mr. Böttkös's tutelage. Mr. Halász and Mr. Vass were far from enthusiastic about my pestering them for tools and tinkering with my bike on their sidewalk under the shade of the tree, but somehow they tolerated my youthful enterprising spirit.

On January 16, 1944, an awards ceremony was held for the members of our bicycle club. Several trophies were given to the winners of the prior season's races. During the presentation, we had a sumptuous dinner of Wienerschnitzl and beer. The topnotch racers received precious racing tires. I was given bicycle shorts, a token of confidence in my future racing achievements. The celebration heightened my desire to become a racer myself.

By the spring of 1944, my new blue racing bike with its Vass decal was finally ready. Menyus surveyed its beautiful workmanship and sang its praises to my father, who was worried about its thin, flimsy-looking tires and wooden rims. I was looking forward to racing with it, but the war double-crossed my plans. Racing tires were unavailable, and I had no black market connections.

Spring turned into early summer, when I signed up for the first road race of the season, a one hundred–kilometer one. At the start, Kornél Pajor, a well-known skating champion, and another racer, who was right in front of me, bumped into each other and crashed.

Luckily, I was able to skirt around them and avoid a major pileup, but shortly thereafter I got a flat tire. Since there weren't any motorcyclists around to help and I didn't have a spare tire, I had to slog back to the starting line.

Mr. Halász repaired my tubular tire, patching it and sewing it up. My next race began on the outskirts of Budapest on the turnpike toward Székesfehérvár. It started at the twelve-kilometer marker and went through the sixty-two-kilometer sign, where we turned and headed back to the starting line. All in all, it covered a one hundred–kilometer stretch. Up until the turn-around point I was doing great. But as I took the turn I also had to hand over my number. At this movement my rear wheel slid sideways, rubbing the frame. I had to dismount to adjust my wheel and fasten the winged screws. The pack was elated to see one of their members in trouble and began to pedal more furiously. It took me a considerable amount of time to catch up with them, but I did. I could barely catch my breath at the base of the hill of Baracska with its short but famously steep slope. My fellow racers all rode like madmen and zinged by me. I had a three-cogwheel ratchet and couldn't change gears since I lacked a derailleur. Most of the race took place on a flat road, so I used the smallest cogwheel, which took the most effort. Consequently, by the time I was able to reach the top of the hill my strength was gone. A few other boys who had likewise fallen out of the peloton were nearby and I tried to join them. One rider behind me was unwilling to share the work by going in front of me from time to time. By getting into my slipstream he took it easy, and I didn't have the energy to speed up and get rid of him. Even more galling, my sandwich was poking out of my jersey pocket and he began begging and cajoling me for it until I finally got fed up and handed it over to him. This proved to be a monumental mistake. The sandwich gave him enough strength to open up a furious attack and pass me like lightning at the finish line. When I complained to my club members afterward, they wisely remarked that if I was willing to donate my sandwich to another racer I should have done it after the race.

There was one more race during the war at which I tried my luck. This race took place at Székesfehérvár. Our club members decided to ride down the previous night. We stayed at a school. There was no food, no cots, no blankets, only empty classrooms with study carrels. My teeth chattered and I could barely sleep from the cold. Yet at that time of year the weather should have been warm.

In the morning, we set out for the race, which was called "around the block." It was indeed a square-shaped route with four sharp corners. At the start I was at the head of the pack. For the first few laps we sprinted on and off, but no one attempted to break away. As the race went on, the clouds dissolved and the sun began to shine in earnest. I was sweating profusely and was making another turn around a corner when a young woman stepped forward and, out of the goodness of her heart, flung a bucketful of water at me. The water hit my stomach smack in the center, my chest began to ache, and suddenly I lost my strength. Thus, I gave up the race. I waited for my fellow cyclists to finish, and we all cycled back to the city together.

Then in June, a few days after the race around the block, I read an announcement that said that I, like so many other college students, was to present myself to a labor battalion. Thus, my racing career was cut short.

By the time I returned from Transylvania, the summer was over and races were suspended. Harvest was approaching, and the war threw a shadow over our daily life. Menyus Hajós was called up for military service and joined an artillery cavalry unit. He asked me to bring his bike into the city from Szada. I made the journey from Szada to Buda with two bikes, riding and steering my bike with my left hand while guiding Menyus's bike along next to me with my right hand. At the end of the war Menyus left Hungary, never to see his bicycle again. He emigrated to the United States and worked for IBM. After fourteen years we finally met again in New York City in 1958. A few weeks later, we both went to the Piarist Charity Ball, where we were joined by another good friend from Veresegyház Tóni Viczián.

I believe that bicycling has added years, if not decades, to my life. Not for nothing do the French say that cycling is "cardiovascular par excellence."

18

Illusion, Emotions, and the Coming of the Whirlwind

Shortly after I graduated, my father came into my room and began: "Since you have no idea what you would like to do, your best bet is to enroll in law school. Then you have four years to think about it, and with a law degree you could get a job in the Hungarian National Bank, the Bank of Commerce, or the Ministry of Agriculture, to name a few possibilities. They are all decent places to work." He went on: "Or, if you wish, I could even bring you into the broadcasting corporation. Then, there are, of course, the cushy positions as a university professor or a judge. These people have the charmed life, but I doubt that you have the inclination to become a judge or a university professor. We also have to keep in mind that you have to serve a year in the military."

When I later recalled what he told me on that day, I had to laugh. How little did we know! Nevertheless, in 1943 I enrolled in law school at Péter Pázmány University in Budapest. The majority of the students didn't attend classes and would show up only for exams. Some professors had attendance requirements, but missing a class was not an obstacle to taking the exams. I chose to attend the lectures instead of having a job. My father was concerned only that I should pass my exams. Should I fail, I was to get a job.

At the age of eighteen, I yearned increasingly to find a girl with whom I could spend my spare time. I frequently went to visit Minci on Baross Street and soon these visits became an obsession. Minci and I went to root for Balázs Kenderesy at his ice hockey matches in the City Garden, we went to the movies, and we celebrated birthdays with our friends. In the meantime, Minci was busy preparing for graduation. Neither of us knew what the other was feeling, at least not until January of the following year. From then on, it was clear that our love was mutual, but then a new question arose: What's next? I was not convinced that she would be a suitable partner for me in the long run. I judged every woman in comparison to my mother, and according to that criterion, she was not up to par. Consciously—or, rather, subconsciously—I knew that, but I didn't want to break off a pleasant relationship with a nice girl, especially without any real reason to do so. Thus we navigated into the uncharted waters of the spring of 1944.

19

The Last Summer before the Siege

A s a nineteen-year-old, my world was small. My perspective was narrow and egocentric. I moved around in a small circle of friends, preoccupied with daily affairs. My problems included where I should train for the bicycle races, what records I should buy, how I would pass my final examinations, and where my infatuation with Minci would lead me. I didn't listen to the radio or read the daily papers. My father, on the other hand, was a passionate news reader, nearly obsessed with the military columns of Pál Szvatkó in *Magyar Nemzet* (*Hungarian Nation*). "I cannot fall asleep without my daily dose of Szvatkó," he would say.

Nyires and Vicziántelep were an enchanted land. The old Viczián manor house, with its thick yellow columns, had a historic ambiance. The Italianate villa of Károly Brencsán, looking down into the valley toward the Egérvári Water Mill, was exquisitely elegant. The Gunda-Rados family villa and its surrounding garden and vineyard had its unique lively staccato life. We youngsters hardly ever saw the inside of the house. Our territory was the terrace, with a pile of phonograph records and an abundance of food and drink.

My father and his friends were gentlemen farmers. They had office jobs, while their wives were busy with the household and children. Although the womenfolk had plenty of help, my mother, Aunt Iza, and Aunt Bözsi all worked from daybreak until dusk. Grandmothers helped with the canning of fruits and vegetables, and they sat under the olive trees in the garden plying their knitting needles. Ilonka, our cook, would go down through the lilac allée into the cabbage patch or into the kitchen garden to pick some tomatoes.

In the evenings, provided the women were not too tired, they turned to letter writing or reading their mail or fashionable novels of the day. My mother had a straw hat like a Chinese coolie's. At one point she stood on the top of a ladder picking apples while my father took a snapshot of her. That moment said it all: while my mother was working, my father was taking pictures.

My father was not a commuter type. He liked his comfort and was unwilling to forsake it for the daily drudgery of getting up early and going home late. He also couldn't give up his radio and the daily papers. He felt the need to be informed about the war on an ongoing basis. All of this meant that he would spend the week in the city, even in the summertime when my mother and I were out at Veresegyház. From time to time, our cook Ilonka would go in from Veresegyház to do some shopping for my father and prepare a meal for him. Occasionally, my mother also managed to get away from the vineyard. She would go into the city to get a permanent wave (a popular hairstyle of the 1930s), a good bath, and a manicure.

On the weekends, when social life in the vineyard perked up, my father would come out to Veresegyház. One of our favorite songs then was "Csak Egy Nap a Világ" ("The World Is Only One Day"). It mirrored our mood, reflecting the sense that catastrophe was near and unavoidable. We concluded, therefore, that it was best to drink and be merry for as long as we could. As the battleship gray–colored storm clouds gathered, our awareness of the demise of the world as we knew it amplified our pleasure seeking and diversion from everyday life. We youngsters tried not to think about what was to come.

War would soon engulf us, but for now Veresegyház and our vineyard were beautiful. The newspapers were censored but, *durch die Blume* ("in the guise of flowery language"), as the Germans say, one could make one's own deductions. As Churchill put it, "Facts are stubborn things." Thus, my father could see that the Russians were at Warsaw or at Moldavia and not at Karkhov or in the Caucasus, as the authorities would have liked us to believe. Everyone, except the fanatics, could grasp where the front line was. Invasion by the Allies was a foregone conclusion. Only the place and the timing was a secret. The Red Army piled up one success after the other on the eastern front while the Americans were engaged in Africa, Sicily, Italy, and the Far East. Slowly, they made progress, engaged in a gigantic fight on the sea, on land, and in the air. But for now we were still some way from the coming siege—the battle between the Allies and Germans for Budapest.

Around us, everything was in bloom, the air felt fresh, the vegetation was lush. The fruit trees bordering the roads were laden with cherries, apples, pears, and plums. The grass and weeds were mowed by scythe. As a traveler or visitor neared our property, the yellow walls of the manor house peeked out from behind the trees and bushes. Woodbines cascaded down the roof above the entrance to Uncle Rory's tract. Their blossoms were white, with green leaves peeking out from beneath them. Specks of green moss settled on the biscuit-colored roof tiles. Aunt Ancsurka, the wife of my father's good friend János, went to pick asparagus and in the process lost her wedding ring. In desperation, she prayed to Saint Anthony, the saint of lost items. She beseeched him for help. After an arduous hour of shifting the sand around she got her reward. It was a miracle.

In those days we didn't have horses anymore (they had long been taken by the army), but there were plenty of other livestock around. Crickets chirped, frogs croaked at the edge of the meadow. Roosters crowed in the early morning, dogs yelped and barked at all hours of the day, and ducks and chickens created their own cacophony. The linden trees permeated the air with their sweet smell, announcing that their flowers were ready to be picked. The flowers would be made into a fine scented tea and in the wintertime offered as a cure to cold sufferers. Throughout my mother's life, she adored Nyíres, Veresegyház, and our vineyard. She reminded me of Van Gogh's saying: "Painters understand nature and love her and teach us to see her." This was my mother's *Weltanschauung*. A small poem by Duvernois, from his novel *Edgar*, expresses well how I felt in the early summer of 1941:

> *Gyermekkorunknak hajnalától*
> *Egy volt a vágyunk minden álmunk*
> *Szivünk repes a hír szavától*
> *Hogy soha többé el nem válunk*
> *E kertek, e virágok, e rétek,*
> *E csönd, e harmat, e zene,*
> *E játékok, s e sok szerelmi ének,*
> *Mind érte él, miatta, ővele.*

> From the dawn of our childhood,
> Our desires and our dreams were one.

And now our hearts leapt for joy at the news
That never again shall we part.
These gardens, these flowers, these meadows,
This silence, this dew, this music,
These games, and these many songs of love
All live for her, because of her, with her.

Not only was our landscape beautiful, but all around it each of the surrounding parcels of land and houses created a serene environment. At night the moon cast a silvery shine across the land, causing the endless railroad tracks to glitter as they disappeared into the distance.

During the summer of 1944, István Kormos became a regular part of our circle. He was a neighbor of Anti Zahár, Aunt Iza's cousin and Judit's uncle. István looked up to Anti as his role model. Anti had an excellent sense of humor and appealed to the girls. István spent his summers in his uncle Dr. Lala Ziehrer's vineyard. He wore riding boots and britches, in imitation of Anti; thus he gave the impression of a landed gentry. His great skill was his ability to impersonate. He was a standup comedian by nature and could tell stories for hours on end. On the train ride out to Veresegyház or back to the city he would entertain his companions the whole way. He graduated a couple of years ahead of me and was already holding down a job at the Hunnia Film Factory as an apprentice to a director, waiting for a break. For some reason, he didn't like his first name; he wanted us to call him Gyula, but we never quite gave in.

István could come up with the most amusing stories. One was a story that had been told in the cafeteria of the film studio where he worked. At lunchtime, all the people working in the studio—the stars, the understudies, the extras, the stage electricians, the directors, etc—would gather around a long table and eat communal style. One day, László Szilassy, the young movie hero, joined them and with his customary flair began to relate a story to the surrounding audience. "You will never believe what happened to me a half an hour ago! One of the most beautiful women in the world was in bed with me. The sun was shining into the apartment, the window was open, the breeze was tossing her blond hair into her face. It was like heaven. One moment she was in my arms, writhing with pleasure. The next moment a bumblebee landed on her butt and stung her!" Everyone at the table roared with laughter.

Shortly thereafter, barely finishing his lunch, Szilassy left. No sooner had he gone than Erzsi Simor arrived and took a place at the table. In those days, she was the most beautiful actress in Hungary, idolized by the moviegoing public. She was a slender blond with green eyes. She sat down, fidgeted a bit, and with a wry face began to talk. She said, "You won't believe what happened to me a half an hour ago! I was lying in bed, the sun was shining, when all of the sudden a bumblebee flew in my open window, landed on my butt, and stung me!" Her audience broke out in uproarious laughter. Some hit their drinking glasses with their knives; others slapped their knees. Poor Erzsi Simor sat bewildered by the uproar.

István's repertoire was inexhaustible. And as he told stories, he impersonated his subjects. One story took place at a buffet. Customers were standing by tall oval tables laden with food. One bought himself a stein of beer and placed it on a tall table. Then he left to buy himself a plate of spinach soufflé. While he was away, a shaggy, unshaven bum discovered the forlorn stein of beer and proceeded to gulp it down with great delight. Just as he had placed it down, its owner returned to witness his empty stein, whereupon he made a tremendous ruckus. The bum, looking surprised, released an enormous belch, and then shuffled off, remarking loudly, "Fölháborító!" ("Outrageous!").

Another of István's stories was also about two movie personages, Mici Erdélyi, the actress, and her husband, Imre Ráday. The couple had a small Scottish terrier that died one day. The heartbroken owners decided that the nicest way to bid farewell to their pet would be to dig a small grave for it in a wooded area. They put the dog into a suitcase, boarded the electric tram, pushed the suitcase under their seats, and laid the spade next to the cabin door. As they headed out of the city, more and more people got on the trolley. Before long, a couple with three unruly children made themselves comfortable in the Ráday's compartment. After the approximately two-hour train ride, Mr. Ráday picked up the suitcase and the spade and, smiling benevolently, he and his wife waved goodbye to the family.

Out in the woods of the Royal Park in Gödöllő, they found a nice clearing away from the tourist paths. Mr. Ráday started to dig the little grave while Mrs. Ráday opened up the suitcase. Lo and behold, their beloved pet was nowhere in sight. Instead there were all kinds of goodies for a picnic: a thermos full of coffee, ham and cheese sandwiches, breaded drumsticks, apples, and slices of Linzer

Torte. Fate and a little dog served them this unforeseen nice lunch at others' expense. One can only imagine the scene at the other picnic table.

It didn't take long for István, with his debonair ways and witty personality, to encroach on Dezső's romantic turf. He became a daily visitor to the Gunda farm and while Dezső took Judit's goodwill and naïveté for granted, István smuggled his way into Judit's heart. Ultimately, Dezső navigated over to Móki's more friendly waters.

Due to the encroaching war, the university suspended classes. I was now in danger of being called up for labor duty or being inducted into the army. To fend off these threats I sought a job at the Hangya Consortium, where my father's cousin, Uncle Béla, was chief executive officer. Hangya was categorized as a Class-Two company— not as important to war production as an ammunition factory, but not as dangerous either. For the time being, this employment saved me from having to join a labor battalion headed who knows where.

When I was hired, my father warned me, "Never be late on your first day of a job. Later, it is not as critical." The following Monday morning, on what was to be my first day at work, I woke with a jolt, frightened that I was already late. I threw my clothes on and left the house in a panic. When I was just exiting our gate, I could hear the whistle of the train as it was leaving Őrszentmiklós and nearing our station, Vicziántelep. I ran like a maniac. I was still on the steep embankment, on the opposite side of the tracks from the platform, when the train slowly began to move away from the station. With my last ounce of strength, I jumped onto the railroad tracks and ran after the last wagon. The conductor noticed me, and as I ran up parallel to the car's steps, he grabbed my arm and pulled me up. Once I had caught my breath, I learned from the conductor that I had made it onto an earlier train than the one I had intended.

Around five in the afternoon, we, the commuting toilers, boarded the smoky train at Budapest Nyugati Pályaudvar (Western Railroad Station). In 1944, a coal-burning locomotive was introduced. Its biting sulfuric stench stung our eyes, and it spit red sparks out of its chimney. It was not the Orient Express, but at least it was a direct route to Vicziántelep. The train had comfortable seating compartments and on the windows a sign in several languages told the traveler that leaning out the window was dangerous and forbidden. Among the various languages posted was Croatian: "*Opazno je van se nagnuti."* These signs were relics of the Austro-Hungarian Empire, illustrations of one of the more enlightened minority policies of the day. Halfway home, as we neared the hills of Csomád, this coal-driven, smoke-belching, antediluvian monster would become sluggish, to the point where one was inclined to believe that it would never make it up the hill. Indeed, it often would slide backward as it tried to generate more steam and gather strength. István Kormos would sometimes jump down from the train, collect a bouquet of wild flowers, and then jump back onto the train, where with a mock courtesy he would present this makeshift bouquet to a girl on the train. This was a feat—a competition between man and train—fit to be entered into *The Guinness Book of World Records.*

Anti Zahár, who was in the Army Reserves but hadn't been called up yet, was instrumental in the recruitment of two other young ladies for our coterie. He had met Éva Szinyei Merse at a party in the city. Éva came from a well-known family. One of her uncles was minister of education. Another was Pál Szinyei Merse, an outstanding painter whose best known work, *Majális*, is a cherished treasure of the Hungarian National Gallery. Éva worked in the city for a company called Viscosa that manufactured artificial textiles for export. Éva had complained to Anti that the aerial bombardments were interrupting her life and preventing her from getting any sleep. The nightly raids frazzled her nerves and she detested the time she had to spend in the air raid shelter. Up until the Nazi takeover in March 1944, the Allied Air Force had given Hungary special treatment. From then on, however, air raids became a common occurrence; the Americans bombed during the day and the British bombed at night.

Anti promptly invited Éva to stay at his manor house, from where she could commute into the city to work during the day and enjoy a restful sleep at night. Éva jumped at the opportunity and accepted the invitation, thereby setting in motion a series of events. Éva made her entry into Anti's estate, but she did not do so alone. She brought along her younger sister Sisi, who had just graduated from high school.

Soon after his guests had settled in, Anti introduced the two Szinyei girls to the gang at the Gunda-Rados vineyard. The girls brought a bunch of records with them. With the arrival of Éva and Sisi, the spirit of our little group was rejuvenated. The female old-timers of our circle—Judit, Móki, Minci—had become a bit "shopworn" by then. Though we boys loved them, the arrival of new blood was more than welcome. István Kormos was the exception; he already knew the girls, and his attention was directed toward Judit and Móki.

As soon as the balmy weather arrived, we began to go out to the lake at Veresegyház. Our whole gang would bike down in a colorful procession, but since we had one bike fewer than we had people, Szabi would give Sisi a ride on his crossbar. This feat was a testimony to Szabi's strength and skill, and the excellence of his Győrffy bicycle.

Both of the Szinyei girls were pretty, polished showstoppers, with elegance and social skills, and they danced extremely well. Compared to them, the girls in our triumvirate were provincial country lassies. The first time I set my eyes on Éva, she swept me off my feet. In details she had imperfection after imperfection, but when all of her parts were put together, she was beautiful (a beauty similar to that of Audrey Hepburn). She had a beguiling deep alto voice, was five feet tall, had red fingernails, and smoked Chesterfields. She was four years older than me, which filled my parents, Aunt Blanka, and Uncle János with fear. This woman was like something from another planet. She was not a petit bourgeois girl of the Krisztina District in Buda, nor a celebrity of Veresegyház. She had a rarified, refined air about her, and a puckish pixie quality. I, on the other hand, was a country noodle, an immature young lad. If I had been a couple of years older and possessed a debonair style or flair, I might have had a better chance with her. My skills at wooing women were still rather elementary. At this point, I hadn't even given a bouquet of flowers yet to any girl. Surprisingly, my parents never pointed out to me the importance of such niceties. The only time I ever gave a present to Judit was during the siege.

My parents didn't emphasize chivalry in my upbringing, but they expected that I would know how to accommodate or show concern for people. One hot summer day, Judit, Móki, and I were coming home from the train station when, right as we were about to say goodbye at the crossroad of Apple Allée, a thunderstorm broke out. I ran to our house for cover while the girls continued on their way home. At the house, I offhandedly mentioned to my father that these poor girls would get soaked. No sooner had I informed my father of the girls' fate than he gave me a dressing down. He told me that I was by no means a gentleman. I should have either invited them in to wait in our house until the storm ended or else ran after them with an umbrella and escorted them home. My father's lecture remained with me for a lifetime. At one point its consequences would be seriously felt (more about that later). All in all, the arrival of the two Szinyei girls considerably stirred up the still waters of Nyires.

During this short spell of time, a period of enchantment followed, but I still felt like I was under a cloud. Before meeting Éva, I had spent all of my time with Minci. Now, I abruptly terminated our friendship and vanished from Minci's life. She commuted on the same train as me, but I purposely sought another compartment where I could enjoy Éva's companionship. Minci must have been aware that we were riding the same train, but if I didn't offer her any explanation for my abrupt disappearance, she wasn't going to come after me; she was too proud for that. At this time, I didn't know how to take cordial leave of a relationship. I wondered whether Éva knew about Minci. Most likely she did, since at Nyires there were hardly any secrets. I put my head in the sand, while Minci must have been heartbroken and confused.

I became Éva's constant traveling companion. I knew that she had to be somewhat older than me, since her younger sister Sisi had just graduated from high school, but I didn't know just how much older. In retrospect, it's no wonder that my family regarded my infatuation with the greatest concern. I was like little *Hans Gluck in die Luft*, constantly looking up into the sky, instead of watching his step, until the day he falls into a canal; I, likewise, strolled toward an abyss.

The concern of the elders was not entirely without cause. Éva was elegant, with those manicured crimson red nails, and always impeccably dressed. She was slender and small, with big brown eyes. She had a beguiling smile and freckles around her nose. Her hair was short and brown. Sometimes we would go to the movies, mostly to a movie theatre owned by her family in Buda. Even as the war went on,we could still occasionally see a good foreign flick.

Éva accepted my company, so we became traveling partners. On a Saturday at noon, with our workdays over, we arranged a rendezvous at the Ilkovics buffet, opposite the Budapest Nyugati Pályaudvar (Western Railroad Station). This meeting was the start of an avalanche in my life. It became crystal clear to me that I was head over heels in love with Éva.

At the buffet we ate crêpes suzettes filled with apricot jam. I took care of the bill and used up all of my ration coupons to cover her lunch as well. As we stood by one of the tall tables eating, a ray of sunlight enveloped us. A German soldier approached the table and addressed Éva. He was a young corporal and his intentions were quite obvious. Éva didn't pay any attention to the guy, but I felt that the time had come for me to lower the visor on my helmet and enter the fray in defense of my adored damsel. To the extent that a nineteen-year-old boy can metamorphose himself into Errol Flynn in a second, I did just that. My face darkened, I racked my brain for the proper German words, and then I informed him that his company was unwanted. Besides, I told him, it was not befitting a young Wehrmacht officer to be acting as he was. The young corporal—he must have been around twenty-six—promptly changed his tune and profusely apologized, explaining that he didn't see rings on our fingers; therefore, he didn't know that we were engaged or married. He wished us good luck and smilingly disappeared. Éva didn't negate the soldier's statement. She enjoyed the scene and from then on, with a prankster's nod and a wink, willingly played along with me in my game.

I promptly invited Éva over for tea, and instead of getting off at Erdőváros she continued her journey with me to Vicziántelep. We strolled home from the station and I introduced Éva to everyone present, first and foremost to my parents. My father graciously extended an invitation for tea to Éva. We made ourselves cozy in my corner room and had a nice conversation. I presume that she was impressed by the old manor house with its Schönbrunn yellow color, the nicely arranged flower beds, the long porch, and the cool rooms with antique furniture and portraits of ancestors hanging on the walls. We were used to our surroundings but she, with her discriminating eye, must have noticed that she had walked into an enchanted world. I learned later that my father and Uncle János were secretly worried when they saw Éva's fingernails. Perhaps Mata Hari or Marlene Dietrich came to their minds. I was blissfully unaware of the grownups' panic.

Éva, with her colorful personality, good looks, and deep, beguiling voice, monopolized my attention. With each passing day, her appeal grew. She was worldly, intelligent, had an excellent sense of humor, and never said or did anything that created a negative effect. She liked my companionship and enjoyed our conversations. We discussed Somerset Maugham's outstanding talent, we shared our political views. Like my family, she was also completely on the British side of the war; both of our record collections reflected that quite well.

In the ensuing days, Éva and I frequently took the train out of the city together and she came home with me. We would stroll in and sit down for tea beneath a portrait of Prince Charles De Ligne. I nicknamed Éva Evelyn, thinking it sounded more elegant. Following afternoon tea with my father, we would trudge across the orchard and pick sour cherries. Then we would go to the Gunda Farm, where we would play Éva's and her sister Sisi's records. In the evenings, Éva taught us a couple of dance steps that she had learned from Fred Astaire and Ginger Rogers movies. But there were shadows around, and many dark clouds on our horizon.

My idyll with Éva was disrupted by the war. Even though the Hangya Consortium was categorized as engaged in war production, it was in the second class; therefore, I couldn't avoid being called up for labor service much longer. One morning, those of us who studied law, engineering, and philosophy were all ordered to present ourselves at the Ludovica Military Academy for a medical examination. After the physical, we were grouped according to the subject we studied. Once they had sorted us, they informed us when and where we should report the following day. They instructed us to bring our kit box (a large wooden container that held all of one's personal belongings) with us to Budapest Nyugati Pályaudvar (Western Railroad Station) and to be prepared to be away for the entire summer.

As I left the Academy behind, a new era began for me. To paraphrase Somerset Maugham: "The bottom had fallen out of his world." But for now I still had Éva to think about and my family to console me. They bid me Godspeed and organized a farewell party.

For the last time before many of us were to part, we gathered at the Gunda Farm. The original members of our group were there plus the newcomers, the Szinyei sisters and István Kormos. All of the Viczián cousins showed up. The focus of the party was on Dezső Kemény, Jajó Faludy, and me, the three who in a few hours would say goodbye to Nyires and to all of our friends there. The thought that a sizable part of our gang would stay behind and that they would still be able to enjoy the summer while we were digging trench lines for the Army was hard to bear. And then there was the nagging uncertainty about whether we would be able to continue our studies at the university when we returned.

After the party broke up, Laci Rados, Balázs Kenderesy, and I escorted Éva and Sisi to Anti's grange. Laci and Balázs ran ahead with Sisi, while Éva and I followed them from a distance. It was a bright full moon, unlike the moon I had experienced the first time I walked Éva home. On that particular night, weeks earlier, I had not even been sure if I would be able to find my way home, as there was no moon or stars and people were strictly adhering to the blackout regulations. It was pitch dark, not a village or a solitary house could be seen. Never before in my life had I experienced such complete darkness. I had walked in the ruts left behind by the wheels of carts. The only thing that led me home that night was my instinct. After about a forty-five-minute walk I finally recognized the road that led to the Rados vineyard and gave out a tremendous sigh of relief when I reached my family's gate.

By contrast, on this evening there was a bright full moon. It must have had its effect on all of us. As we reached the Arcfalvi vineyard, a beautiful estate in the neighborhood of the Gunda Farm, I tried to kiss Éva, but she nimbly kept me at a distance. She didn't say a word; she just sped up her pace so that we would catch up with Sisi and the two other boys.

I sank into utter despair.

When I reached home, the moon was at the full, throwing a milky blue mist over the rows of Jericho cascading down from above the stairs of Uncle Rory's apartment and over the courtyard, while casting black shadows as in the song, "Moonlight and Shadows." Éva had turned me down, and I was devastated. I even contemplated suicide. I must have drunk too much.

On the following day, Dezső, Jajó, and I headed into the city. While we were on the train leaving Vicziántelep, we hung out on the brakeman's platform and sang "Moonlight and Shadows" at the top of our lungs. We were headed to Ferdinand Bridge, where a one-hundred wagon cattle train was waiting for us. There must have been more than two thousand college students there. I was miserable.

While I was away at the camp, Éva wrote me three nice letters. She began her first letter, "My Dear Ex-Groom!" She gave an account of the flirtations that continued, and she wrote with much humor. By the end of the summer, Anti had been called up for service. Consequently the Szinyei girls returned to their flat in Buda. So, by the time I returned to Veresegyház, Éva was not even there anymore. My feverish infatuation cooled and when I met Éva again in the fall, it was not the same. In the fifties, Éva married her childhood sweetheart, István Szapáry. Later, they lived in Vienna, where she was adored by many and held in great esteem by Viennese society. Éva died in 1988.

20

Hitler Occupies Hungary—Manhunt

On March 12, 1944, I received a postcard from Genovéva, a.k.a. Móki. It said, "Dear Károly, I look forward to seeing you on Friday, March 24, at five in the afternoon for tea. RSVP. P.S. Please bring along a few records to dance to." On the day that Móki sent this card neither she nor anybody else had the slightest foreboding of what lay ahead for us and how soon it would come. Móki's party was preempted by the drama that took place on March 19. It was to change the history of Hungary forever.

On the evening of March 18, as people were leaving the opera house, a fine mist hung over the city. The sky was heavily clouded, the blackout amplifying the darkness. The government of Prime Minister Kállay had an unwritten agreement with the Allies. They wouldn't bomb Hungary and in exchange Hungary wouldn't fire at Allied aircraft flying through Hungary's airspace. Nevertheless, a blackout was enforced. The people exiting the opera house had a strange, inexplicable suffocating feeling. Budapest was deadly silent. There was no traffic. An eerie stillness reigned in an otherwise lively city, giving the impression of a ghost town. People sensed that something was out of kilter.

The next day, March 19, at five in the morning, our telephone rang. My father's cousin Béla Hilberth was calling. He told my father that the Germans were in the process of occupying Hungary and he warned my father to be extra careful.

With the German occupation, our whole life changed. Gyuri Sághy bicycled around the city and told us that German officers had taken over the Hotel Astoria and were already having their breakfast there. The Gestapo had settled into the Hotel Majestic on

Swabianberg. Prime Minister Kállay had sought asylum in the Turkish Embassy. Gyula Náray, president of the Hungarian Broadcasting Corporation, like many others, had gone underground. The Nazi machinery had begun to arrest the people on its blacklists.

I was still studying for my exams, cramming for them with my friend Tomi Róna. A few days after the nineteenth, I visited Tomi in Hűvösvölgy (Cool Valley), on the outskirts of Buda, to bid him farewell. The university was closing and Tomi had received a summons to join a labor battalion. He was a convert to Catholicism, but that didn't matter; he was still registered as Jewish. In class, we had nicknamed him Tom-Bom. At the end of my visit, Tomi put on a record as a farewell song. It was "The Tarantulla," with "The Champagne Cocktail," played by the British band Ambrose, on the flip side. We wished each other good luck. Fortunately, he survived the war.

The German occupation of Hungary invalidated the agreement with the Allies about aerial bombardment, and on April 2 the bombing of Budapest began. The sky was now pregnant with the deep throb of airplanes. The whole country was a target; and carpet bombing was the rule of the day. As a result, the radio airwaves filled with warnings, repeatedly interrupting programming with the German code words "Crocodil Gross!" or "Achtung, Achtung, Lichtspiele!" The main targets were oil refineries on Csepel Island, bridges on the Danube, train stations, and factories engaged in military production.

People tried to leave the city at least for the night. The streetcars, the trolleys, and the railroad cars were packed with people who dragged themselves to and fro between lodging and workplace. The searchlights crisscrossed their rays above the city and a sinister murmuring could be heard. The night became the scene of macabre fireworks. During the day, we would watch fighter planes duel in loops and turns in the blue sky, leaving behind trails of white condensation. Veresegyház, some distance away from the city and with no military targets, was spared. If a bomb had dropped, it would have been a leftover one, jettisoned on a return trip.

In the early days of May, when we were already out at the vineyard, my father took in a man I had never seen before. When I asked, my father said that the man had been bombed out of his apartment. He lived in the apiary. The bees were long gone, but there was a little room in the building that in the old days had been used to store honey, sugar, and other supplies and now lay empty. This was the room he moved into. I only saw him a couple of times, when he went to the well for water or to the outhouse. It must have been tough for him in that small room without any comforts or cooking facilities. In retrospect, he must have been Jew in hiding. In those days and under those circumstances, it didn't occur to me to question why a person would move into an apiary devoid of light and comfort. By the time I returned from Transylvania at the end of the summer, the man was no longer there. With my father's help, he may have found a better arrangement, especially since, with fall upon us, the unheated structure would have quickly become unlivable

With the German occupation, the persecution of the Jewish population began. One day, I went to the Láng family's store to pick out a few records. The main entrance of the store was closed and the corrugated iron shutters were pulled down over it. I went into the courtyard and knocked on the rear entrance. The owners knew me and they let me into the darkened store, a place barren of customers. They told me that if I wished I could sit in a booth and try out or listen to records to my heart's content. The family,

The apiary at Veresegyház

meanwhile, huddled in the inner part of the store in semidarkness, seemingly greatly absorbed in a debate or discussion. I felt rather embarrassed, selected a few records, and left. A few days later, when I returned to buy a few more records, the entire shop was locked up, including the rear entrance. I was dumbfounded and saddened but not altogether surprised; we knew the Nazis were taking Jews to labor camps, though the full horror of it would remain unknown to us for some time.

As March turned to April, with every passing day, the screw was tightened one turn at a time on the Jewish residents. Their lives became strictly regulated. They were the last Jews in German-occupied Europe to be obliged to sew the yellow Star of David onto their clothing. Their interactions with non-Jews were restricted to a minimum, if allowed at all. They could venture out of their homes only between prescribed hours.

In normal times, spring was when residents moved, if they so desired. Burly helpers packed belongings onto horse-drawn coaches. In April 1944, an enormous caricature of moving took place. Jewish residents had to leave apartment houses in which the tenantry was overwhelmingly non-Jewish. Those evicted residents then moved into apartment houses in which the body of tenants was mostly Jewish, and from these, non-Jews had to leave. Jewish apartment houses were marked with the yellow star.

The streets teemed with people pulling handcarts, and here and there a horse-drawn dray piled high with clothes, furniture, and household items. These hand-towed contraptions crisscrossed the capital as one group moved from here to there and another from there to here. The balmy air, the change to the spring season, the blue sky contrasted with the somber mood of these unfortunate people seeking shelter in this wretched new environment, this man-made tornado. After the Jewish houses were established a walled ghetto was erected.

A close family friend, Artúr Elek, who had converted to Catholicism, refused to wear the yellow Star of David. He rented a room from a niece who was not Jewish, and was therefore left undisturbed in her flat, and confined himself inside instead. Under the cover of darkness, Artúr would occasionally still dare to slip over to see my father. On the second of April he handed over his will to my father. On the seventh he sent a letter to my mother:

"I am savoring spring from my window. Now that I am leading the life of a recluse the garden has grown in importance. I see the fresh greenery, the most beautiful green that only spring can produce. The irises are already in bloom; they grow more with each passing day. On the right side of my window the bent chestnut tree puts forth its buds. And what an orchestra of birds! In the early hours, the blackbirds, with their magical throats, begin to sing, and they do not stop until dusk.

Life is beautiful, regardless of one's destiny. Now that I have re-read your letters, I have re-lived your experiences: the pleasures of meadows and villages alike. I am glad that you are well, and I hope that you will stay well forever, never falling into despair or brooding.

I cannot say much about myself. My life is one of great monotony. The main trouble is that I cannot work. It would be a salvation to work in the yard, or do something that requires skill. To do mental work, concentration is needed, and that is not to be found. Resoluteness, preparedness for all sorts of bad luck, or even for the worst, is in vain. If only a week would pass without harassment. If only more rules and regulations would not follow day after day! The ultimate fate pending before us—the doom being dealt out in small doses—cripples one's nerves. Given this scenario, the hours I spend in the air raid shelter during the bombardment are relaxing compared to what goes on otherwise. Down there I am not aware of my nerves, as I am upstairs in the midst of the spring sunshine and the warbling of birds. In the shelter we are at the mercy of blind destiny, which can hit or miss its target. It does not differentiate according to race. Should it hit its target, it kills instantly, rather than piecemeal. Oh, I wish I were not alive! I have had more than my share of life. For that matter, it stretched out longer than either of my parents. I have long had no claim against life, nor any specific desire for it.

Now I have let my pen go again, although I know that it is a sin to depress those whom we like, in setting a weight on their hearts with the fore-knowledge of helplessness. It shows ingratitude to answer your nice letter with such sorrow. I will stop complaining. I will take your advice: to be wise, a big word; to have the upper hand; and above all, to strive to be strong and determined. I do hope that I will have the strength to confront what is yet to come.

My warmest regards,

Artúr"

Artúr Elek was a writer and the art critic for the literary journal *Nyugat* (*The West*). One of his early works was *Álarcosmenet* (*Procession of the Masquerade*), published in 1913. He had given a signed copy of it to my father. Uncle Artúr had an encyclopedic knowledge of art. He had visited artistic, historic and archaeological sights all over Europe, but especially in Italy. He spoke fluent Italian and when I was studying Italian in high school, he had helped me with my homework a few times. His face radiated intelligence and understanding. The white beard enveloping his chin created an impression of a wise man, a persona in one of his favorite art pieces. One of his legs was shorter than the other and even though the heel on one of his shoes was thicker than the other, he still had a limp when he walked.

One evening after we received his letter, my parents, Aunt Blanka, and I went to visit Uncle Artúr on Mátrai Street, only a short distance from our house on Logodi Street. He had a simple small room. Since he didn't have enough chairs, we were ushered over to sit on the edge of his bed. Above his bed hung a landscape painting by Tivadar Csontváry Kosztka, a contemporary. My parents, familiar with Artur's code of ethics, which prohibited him from accepting any paintings from a living painter (as a critic he deemed it a conflict of interest), asked him how it was that this painting was hanging over his bed. He responded that since he was not going to write art criticism anymore, conflict of interest had become a moot question. We left in the somber gloom of that spring night, a foreboding that this might have been the last time we would see Uncle Artúr gripping at our hearts.

A week after our visit, Uncle Artúr received a note from the Jewish Council requesting his presence on the following day on the island of Csepel on the Danube. This was a place where Jewish journalists and writers were interned, and where Allied bombing was heaviest at the time. Uncle Artúr never showed up. His body was found slumped before his desk, a small revolver at his side. We imagined him sarcastically smiling over from the other side, or down from above, as if to say to his pursuers, "You couldn't get me, I tricked you."

Albert Gyergyai was another close Jewish friend of my father's. He lived on the same street as us, a short distance from our house. He was a well-known translator of French to Hungarian. His translations included the works of Jean Giraudoux, Duhamel, Gide, and many others. He translated the entire work of Marcel Proust's *Remembrance of Things Past*, for which the president of the French Republic honored him with the Légion d'honneur. The house where Uncle Albert lived was marked with the Star of David, designating its tenants exclusively Jewish. My father would visit Uncle Albert and drop off food packages, but Uncle Albert was soon called up for labor battalion duty. I once biked to the address where the camp was located with a package of food, but when I reached the camp it was empty. Its occupants had been evacuated to an undisclosed location. Luckily, Uncle Albert survived and returned home after the war. My father later related how at their first reunion they had extricated gold Napoleons from the lining of Uncle Albert's overcoat, which had been stored in our closet.

After March 19, the Official Gazette published new regulations. Day after day, order followed order. Employees of corporations, businesses, and government offices had to present their birth certificates verifying their Aryan ancestry going back to their grandparents. A flood of correspondence ensued to obscure parishes, requesting baptismal documents. Those whose forebears were unquestionably Jewish were immediately discharged from employment. These regulations, of course, applied to the Radio Broadcasting Corporation as well. My father called in his sales force, which was made up entirely of Jewish employees—approximately two dozen people. He told them to keep working; as long as they were able to move around, he would keep them on the payroll.

In the ensuing weeks, Aunt Blanka sheltered three Jewish girlfriends, former classmates of hers, Juci, Panni, and Sári, in her small apartment on Böszörményi Avenue, #3B. At the time I was unaware of all of this. My parents likely felt it better not to let me in on these things, lest I blurt something out at the wrong time or place.

Since Aunt Blanka's flat was fairly small, Grandmother Róza, who had been living there, had to move out to Veresegyház. From there, she went to stay with her stepson, Antal Dabis, in Ács in Trans-danubia. Blanka's apartment consisted of a living room, a small win-dowless kitchen, a bedroom, and an adjoining bathroom. For safety's sake, the shades in the living room were drawn at all times to ward off prying eyes. Blanka had no problem coming and going. She was working as a technical draughtsman for the Danuvia Corporation on the outskirts of the city and got home only in the late evening. Weekends she spent at Veresegyház. It was rather crowded in her flat, but the apartment was on the sixth floor and secluded. The greatest danger was that the concierge or another tenant would get wind of the women hiding there and inform the authorities. During the air raids, Blanka's friends could never go down to the air raid shelter since that would have given away their presence. It was a hairy situ-ation, especially one particular day during the siege in January 1945, when the house received a direct hit and the stairwell and elevator shaft collapsed.

In May 1944, the deportation of Hungary's Jews to Auschwitz began. In rural environs, in the villages, there was no chance to hide. In the countryside Jews were mostly dispersed, with only about one family per village. From Veresegyház Árpád Házi, the veterinarian, was deported. From Őrszentmiklós the Spitzer family was deported. In small localities like these, it was next to impossible to hide and shelter Jews because everyone knew exactly who they were.

Mr. Spitzer had a general store—a grocery and hardware store in one. He was generous and extended credit benevolently to anyone who asked for it, but after a while things got out of hand. He decided to help his customers out of their debts in a way that would benefit him at the same time. He was about to build a house adjoined by an enlarged new general store, so he suggested to his debtors that they contribute manual labor in exchange for a reduction of their debts. He showed his debtors the layout and purchased bricks, raf-ters, roof tiles, windows, and doors. Then he assigned each person a task, according to their skill and the size of their debts. Some of his customers dug the foundation; others did masonry and carpentry. Soon the Szűcses, the Barsis, the Lehotzkys, and other families were busily involved in his home-building project. In the end there stood a spacious, stylish red-tiled new store, and his customers had been absolved of their debts.

Meanwhile, down in Veresegyház, the father of our friend Jajó Faludy, whose family was Jewish, tried to commit suicide. Luckily he was saved. This happened right before we students were called up to go to the Transylvania labor camp. Since Jajó was Jewish, he joined us surreptitiously, thereby avoiding having to join a Jewish Labor Battalion. In the ensuing weeks, his younger brother, who somehow finagled himself out of any labor camp, took over management of the household.

"The deportations in the countryside were accomplished by Adolf Eichmann and his henchmen with brutal efficiency and lightning speed. Over 450,000 Jews, 70 percent of the Jews of greater Hungary, were deported, were murdered or died under German occupation. Within the boundaries of lesser (pre-1938) Hungary, about half the Jews were annihilated. Some 144,000 survived in Budapest, including 50,000 racial Jews, and about 50,000 to 60,000 survived in the provinces."[1]

Istvan Deak explains these events in his book *Essays on Hitler's Europe*:

In March 19, 1944, the German army and SS marched into Hungary. There was no resistance, largely because Horthy had been summoned to Germany earlier and was held there on the night of the invasion. In any case, he and Kállay had previously decided not to resist in case of invasion, if only because Hungary still desperately needed German protection against the Red Army, which was then only a hundred miles away from the border. Kallay and Count Bethlen went into hiding; numerous other conservatives and liberals were arrested by the Gestapo. Under threat of complete takeover by the German Reich, Horthy then appointed an unconditionally pro-German cabinet that proceeded to remobilize the nation for war. With Adolf Eichmann's assistance the Hungarian authorities also began to roundup any Jews living in the countryside for immediate deportation to Auschwitz as the last installment of Hitler's "Final Solution."

In his memoirs Horthy claimed that he was powerless to stop these deportations. He also claimed to have known nothing of the real goal of the transfer of the Jews. He had,

---

1. Lucy S. Dawidowicz, *The War against the Jews, 1933–1945* (New York: Holt, Rinehart and Winston, 1975).

in fact, been informed several times of the true nature of the deportations but he was unable, Sakmyster writes, to imagine that, "with the war at such a critical stage, the Germans would simply kill these Jews rather than use them as workers." He chose to dismiss the reports as "the usual gossip of cowardly Jewish sensation-mongers," until June 1944, when his son passed on a firsthand account written by two prisoners who had managed to escape the systematic murder of Jews at Auschwitz.

Soon Horthy began to receive messages from Pius XII, King Gustav of Sweden, Franklin Roosevelt, and other world leaders urging him to act to protect the remaining Jews in Hungary. In July 1944, when it came time to deport the two hundred thousand Jews still living in Budapest, he took military measures to oppose Eichmann and the gendarmes, who he feared were also planning a coup d'etat against him. The smoothness and speed of the deportation of the Hungarian Jews from the countryside was unique in the history of the Holocaust; so was Horthy's decision to order armored units to prevent the deportation of the Budapest Jews. Ultimately, over 40 percent of the Hungarian Jews survived.[2]

---

2. Istvan Deak, *Essays on Hitler's Europe* (Lincoln: University of Nebraska Press, 2001), 156–57.

21

In Transylvania

But though lean Hunger and green Thirst
Like asp with adder fight,
We have little care of prison fare,
For what chills and kills outright
Is that every stone one lifts by day
Becomes one's heart by night.

—Oscar Wilde, *The Ballad of Reading Gaol*

In the early summer of 1944, my school peers and I went to the Ludovica Military Academy for physical examinations so that we could be enlisted in labor battalions. We were all assigned to go to Transylvania. I should have been grouped with my fellow law students, but I wormed my way into the architectural students group instead, where I had Jajó Faludy and Dezső Kemény as traveling companions. In my state of gloom, this was a stroke of luck, since it was far easier to face the unknown future with longtime friends, and they were both down-to-earth, pleasant fellows. Thus, we were sent off to Transylvania to build the so-called Árpád Line, a chain of fortresses in the Carpathian Mountains.

At Ferdinand Bridge, close to Budapest Nyugati Pályaudvar (Budapest West Railroad Station) we boarded a train of cattle cars. It consisted of one hundred wagons, into which smelly bales of mildewed straw had been thrown to serve as our sleeping accommodations. Each wagon was supposed to carry twenty-five boys. Dezső, Jajó, and I, guided by our instinct, lured a few sympathetic characters into our wagon. One of them was Endre Fehér. He was the foster son

205

of Professor Zunft, director of the Institute of Radiology in Budapest. After the siege of Budapest, Dr. Zunft took the institute's entire supply of radium and carried it with himself wherever he went in order to prevent its looting and scattering by the Russians. He, of course, was well aware of the consequences of his action, and died shortly thereafter, a martyr to science.

Jajó and Dezső were both Jewish. Other Jewish boys became our traveling companions as well. For all of them, it was far preferable to join the student labor battalion than a Jewish labor battalion.

While we were away in Transylvania, we made new friendships. I became pals with Gábor Ambrózy, who slept next to me on the straw at the start of our journey, and would continue to do so later in our little bungalow.

After we had situated ourselves in our wagon, we decided that we would disregard the instructions and wouldn't allow more than fifteen boys in, including ourselves. Meanwhile, Endre Fehér occupied the brakeman's cab on the train and insisted that he would ride there the whole time. We managed to convince him to rejoin us and gave him the nickname "Brakeman," which lasted until the first night, when he began wandering through the cattle car and caused one of the boys to yell out, "This guy keeps stepping on me with boots that weigh a ton!" From then on, we called Endre "Tonner." With seven boys on one side of the wagon, eight on the other, and the center of the wagon clear, we were able to preserve our splendid seclusion.

The sides of the wagons were marked with chalk designating which university department the travelers belonged to—Architecture, Engineering, Philosophy, or Law. The train of one hundred cars was long and moved forward sluggishly. This journey of ours stretched out longer than we had anticipated. Whenever a military train came by, our train would be derailed to let the former pass. The train would also come to a halt during air raids, when we would quickly leave the cars and scatter into the meadows. Allied airplanes had demolished the largest train stations along our route. Fortunately, when we were leaving the Budapest train terminal each of our wagons had received a dozen or so five-pound loaves of bread.

On our third morning, we stopped at a station near where Hungary meets Transylvania. On the track parallel to us stood another cattle train This train had exactly the same number of wagons as ours, but it faced in the opposite direction, toward the West, and was jam-packed. The wagons were dark, but we could make out the sweaty faces and bodies of some who thronged before small windows. Each wagon had a single window, whose dimension was approximately four feet by two feet, that directly faced our doors. These windows were criss-crossed with barbed wire. The wagons were locked up and the people inside were half-naked. They must have been either Russian prisoners of war or Jewish deportees. There were probably seven or eight thousand people on that train, three or four times more than we had on ours.

As soon as our train came to a halt, all of us, in unison—as if by unspoken agreement—began to throw our five-pound loaves of bread over to the other train. Although the windows were criss-crossed with barbed wire, the openings were sizable enough for our loaves of bread to sail through.

A German guard was pacing beside the wagons. Once he had passed a wagon, the boys in that wagon would spring into action. When we anticipated his reversing course, we would all immediately freeze. It was then the other boys' turn to throw while the guard's back was to them. I don't remember how long this whole maneuver went on, but after twenty minutes or so we must have run out of bread, so we began to throw over packs of cigarettes. We had no opportunity to communicate with the other train; thus our identity was as much of a mystery to them as theirs was to us.

Around the time that we made the switch to cigarettes, our commandant, a sadistic young lieutenant, a shavetail and a moron, noticed what we were doing. He gave instructions to our military escort to lock our doors and pull down the crossbars as punishment. Now we traveled like the prisoners we had just seen. The air became stifling, so we lay down and placed our faces against the cracks in the floor to feel a little breeze. One day passed before the sliding doors were opened again.

We were now in Transylvania. We sat in the open door, dangling our feet out and enjoying the evening breeze and changing scenery. Before long, the towering mountains of Transylvania and the Carpathian mountain chain came into view. They were simultaneously magnificent and intimidating.

After a weeklong journey, our train came to a halt at the Maroshéviz train station. It was a beautiful, bright morning. A gentle breeze shifted the dark green shrubbery, and some birds broke the serenity with loud chirping. We climbed down from the cattle cars with our kit boxes and suitcases in hand, and boarded a small choo-choo train. This mountain climber took us up to the village of Székpatak. The locality behind the name was more invented than real, since there was no infrastructure to the place; nonetheless, this became our postal address.

Our new commandant, a first lieutenant in the reserves and a high school teacher in civilian life, was there waiting for us. Along with him were cooks, military escort personnel, and about one hundred law school students from the University of Kolozsvár (Cluj). These were our forerunners, our trailblazers. The commandant addressed our group, briefing us on our daily chores. He pointed out that although our food was tasty and plentiful, it would be a wise idea if we each gave up eight pengő out of our daily wages to be used to improve our diet. Unanimously we gave him our consent, only to learn after a few days that the food was indeed tasty and plentiful. We also learned that the relinquished eight pengő had simply gone into the commandant's pocket.

When we arrived, the camp was situated on top of the mountain where the trenches were to be dug between newly built concrete bunkers. The kitchen, on the other hand, was down in the valley by a brook. Thus, the students would come down into the valley every morning for breakfast and then climb back up the mountain to get to work. In the late afternoon they would descend again into the valley for the evening meal, and then climb back up the mountain to the camp again for the night. Eventually, the military realized the absurdity of this layout. Thus, one of the first things we had to do when we showed up was to move the camp down into the valley next to the kitchen facilities.

Our dwelling spaces were called Finnish wood huts. They had a circular foundation and were somewhat similar to an Indian teepee, only made out of wooden planks. The fifteen of us boys who had traveled to the camp in the same wagon stuck together and had just enough living space in one hut.

We carried the planks down from the top of the mountain on our backs. Due to my bicycle racing, my legs were muscular, but those muscle groups were different than the ones I needed to climb the mountain. In a short while, I suffered mercilessly excruciating muscle pain. Whenever I could, I sat down to take a respite, but then my pals would pass me by and there would be no one left to put the plank back on my back.

By the end of the day, a good night's sleep was guaranteed. We took pride in knowing that we had re-erected the buildings in the valley on the same day that we had dismantled them. When night fell, we positioned ourselves in these huts with our heads against the walls and our feet pointing toward the center of the cabin. Like slices of cake, we lay side by side. At the center of the hut was a round platform on which we placed our boots.

On the first day we received our work clothes, foot cloths, and boots. We were also handed our tools—pickaxes, shovels, and kerosene lamps. Later, to supplement our meager lighting, we fabricated floating wicks, which we placed on top of bookshelves improvised out of wooden storage boxes.

Before we picked our places in the hut, we unanimously elected Jajó Faludy as our cottage commandant. He thereby got the spot to the immediate left of the hut's entrance. Next to him came Dezső Kemény, then Tonner, followed by a boy we nicknamed "Bricklayer." I don't remember his actual name, but I still remember his girlfriend's name: Henrietta Mészáros (Henrietta Butcher); such a combination of first and last names one cannot soon forget. Next to him was Blazsek, the son of the owner of a cutlery shop in a posh inner city district in Budapest. I chose a place next to Gabi Ambrózy. Gabi—in his plus fours, or knickerbockers, with a pipe filled with scented Club tobacco hanging out of the corner of his mouth—looked like F. Scott Fitzgerald or one of the personalities described by Evelyn Waugh in *Brideshead Revisited*. I received the nickname "Cacao" since, according to my pals, I reminded them of a well-known advertisement in which a small boy in the buff is drinking chocolate milk out of an enormous jug as the overflow drips down onto his naked belly. Another of our companions was called "Little Csáth." His last name had been changed to Csáth from Csauscher. Next to him came Józsi Drechsler, whose hobby was running.

Besides a few students of philosophy, almost all of the boys were students at József Nádor Technical University. As for me, only Dezső and Jajó knew that I was not an architectural student. One other boy, Józsi Szende, a member of the national hockey team, had been known to me previously, but he lodged in a different hut.

Our supervisors, who were regular soldiers, were with us from the break of day until sundown, when they went back to the main fort. Ranks represented among them were corporal, sergeant, buck sergeant, and sub-lieutenant. One of our buck sergeants was a sadistic monster. Later, we learned that after we had left, when the Russians took the fortified lines—not by direct confrontation but rather by detour, brazenly marching up from behind on the highway—this buck sergeant threw a hand grenade at them. Through sheer clumsiness, the grenade hit a tree, bounced back, exploded, and tore him to pieces.

As far as nourishment was concerned, our first breakfast, consumed sitting cross-legged Indian-style on the ground, consisted of a mess tin of bean soup, bread, black coffee, and Hitler's bacon. The latter substance fully deserved the derisive cognomen we gave it. It had the consistency of cheese and was a cherry-red preserve—a concoction of tomato paste, red and blue plums, and who knows what else. It came in neatly sealed wooden boxes that, once emptied, we would utilize for a number of purposes. We soon learned that our bread and coffee were laced with bromide. This was a standard practice in the army, now extended to our student labor battalion; the goal was to suppress our desire for the opposite sex (basically, making us impotent). After breakfast we scrubbed our mess tins with sand and rinsed them off in the brook.

Sunday was a free day, our respite from work. Those who wished to attend religious services at the camp could do so. Most of us would write letters, play bridge, or go into the town of Maroshéviz. There, we discovered a pastry shop and a bookstore. We splurged and bought a multitude of anthologies—poetry and translations of Villon, Rimbaud, Verlaine, and Valéry. Sometime later, my mother mailed me a volume of Mihály Babits, one of the most outstanding Hungarian poets. I obligingly lent it to one of our corporals, who was especially interested in one of the poems, "Before Easter," a pacifist's cry against war. The poem had been written during the First World War and Babits had been indicted because of it, but the charges were dropped. Our corporal gave himself away when he quizzed me about this particular poem. It put me at ease to know that he and I were on the same political wavelength.

While I collected all the mail that was sent to me, my father collected all the mail that I sent him and my mother. Szabi Viczián wrote to me from Taktaharkány, where he was working as an intern for a land steward at a large estate. Gyuri Sághy wrote lively letters about the BMW motorcycle factory in Székesfehérvár, where he was working as a technical draftsman. Judit Rados also wrote to me, as well as to Dezső. At this point, Dezső was still at the front of the pack vying for Judit's favor. Móki sent long, gossipy epistles with fictitious, but easily recognizable, names. My father suspected that the letters to me were a ruse—that they were intended for Dezső, since she was well aware that Dezső and I were swapping her correspondence. Aunt Blanka also wrote, recounting the activities of our family—occasionally in a satirical vein. My father and my mother, both born writers, wrote colorful and engaging letters sprinkled with humor. The odd postcard or letter would also come through from Uncle Rory, Grandmother Róza, or my office at the consortium.

I received three letters from Éva. The contents of her letters contradicted the fearful impression that my parents had formed of her. My family thought that she might be a flapper, a wicked demimonde, or a gold digger. Her first letter began, "Dear (Ex-) Groom," and then went on about the local gossip, and tried to give me solace for being separated from our little gang. She knew from my parents how eagerly I read all the letters coming from home. Minci Alemann wrote one letter. It sounded rather cool and a bit bitter, which was understandable, given the way I had treated her.

These letters were our lifelines from the civilized world, much as they were for those caught on the front lines.

Our work in Transylvania was backbreaking. We weren't used to manual labor, and handling the pickax and shovel caused us hardship. The muscles that we had developed biking, swimming, or playing tennis were of no use to us in mountain climbing and construction work.

Our supervising soldiers marked the outlines for the trenches (as it turned out, out of either stupidity or sabotage, we started off digging in the wrong direction). One boy would loosen the soil with a pickaxe, while another would shovel away the dirt, throwing it over the side and creating a mound in front of the trenches. We took turns with these jobs. In the beginning, I couldn't decide which was worse—pickaxing or shoveling; as it turned out, both were equally excruciating. Breaking up the rocky clay with the pickaxe was drudgery, and so at first shoveling seemed to be the easier activity. As the trenches became deeper and deeper and the mounds taller and taller, however, one had to throw the clay soil that much higher every time. Of course, nobody wanted to do the harder task. Those who had started with pickaxing insisted on staying with it, since the deeper we went, the more malleable the earth became; those shoveling, on the other hand, found their task increasingly difficult.

If we hit a rock deep in the trench it would have to be blasted. The soldiers would place dynamite sticks called *paxit* under the rock and connect them to detonating equipment. We would retreat to a safe distance and lie down on the ground. As the explosion took place, pieces of stone and earth would erupt, occasionally even showering down upon us. At times like these, lying on the ground meant a few minutes of good respite.

Soon, our hands and feet had blisters on them. The heavy sapper boots chafed our feet. The soldiers advised us to urinate on our wounds. At night, we put our foot cloths on top of our boots to dry. The smell emanating from them would have made a lions den seem like a perfumery by comparison.

We washed ourselves in the brook that was a few steps from our little shantytown, and dug a latrine just as we had learned to do on our Boy Scout camping trips.

It was in Transylvania that I discovered my obdurate nature and what a shrewd, cunning, sly character I was. I began to refuse to follow orders that were not to my liking, such as shaving. Seeing my defiance, my companions became irritated and conspired against me with the secretariat of the camp. They made certain that I would be assigned as duty officer or orderly of the day. As duty officer, I would have had to face our commander during the evening and morning drill, requiring me to be clean-shaven. So every time that they tried to charge me with these duties, I would secretly bribe someone with a pack of cigarettes to take my place.

Figuring that this was the perfect place to grow a beard, I had given up shaving, but eventually an order was issued making daily shaving mandatory. When the supervising soldiers made sarcastic remarks about my fine crop of a beard, I would recite the army service regulations to them. According to one section, special branches of the services—the air force, the river force, etc.—were exceptions to the daily shaving requirement. Those forces were allowed to wear beards as long as the beards didn't hide one's badge of rank. We were obviously a special branch of the services, I explained, tongue-in-cheek, and I was certainly not covering up my rank with my beard. Thus, I successfully saved my beard until I returned home.

Step by step, we were broken into the wretched work. We got sunburned, then tanned; our bruises healed, our muscles grew stronger. Packages and mail arrived from the outside world and our lives gradually improved. It was a gathering of boys with intelligence and excellent senses of humor. Of course we were all homesick, and we could hardly wait to pull up our stakes and rush back to our homes. Our desires, our longings, were attested to in our correspondence; nevertheless, the tranquil beauty of the landscape stayed with us as an everlasting memory. In retrospect, it turned out to be an interesting and memorable summer, and was more like being in a large Boy Scout camp than a military establishment. Some of the boys daydreamed about a great reunion at the campsite, when we would bring our families here and reminisce. But this was not to be, especially since the Allies would return Transylvania to Romania after the war.

Over the course of these days, I kept improving my performance as a trickster or prankster. My adventures resembled those of *Tyl Uilenspiegel in Köln*. One day a slender wooden box arrived for one of the boys. Inside was a pair of *beigli* (a type of long strudel), one filled with poppy seeds and the other with ground walnuts. Unfortunately, by the time they reached us these pastries were covered in a thick dark green mildew. The owner of the package dejectedly proceeded toward the brook to throw them away. I followed him out of the camp and asked him to give the moldy pastries to me instead, because I needed the box. When he obliged, I ran back to camp for my shoe brush. Returning to the brook, I took out the pastries and gave them a thorough brushing. Bit by bit the green-colored mildew turrets disappeared and the *beiglis'* beautiful, shiny egg yolk–varnished brown coats reemerged. When the former owner saw that I had conjured up the original beauties, his mindset changed. First he demanded that I return the strudels to him. When that didn't work, he switched tactics and cajoled me until I returned half of each strudel to him.

My next caper involved the distribution of kerosene for the lanterns. Upon our arrival in the camp, each hut sent one boy to the storage building to receive a kerosene ration. I suggested that all fifteen of us show up from our hut and line up behind the supply depot. The first of us stepped up to the quartermaster sergeant and handed him our hut's kerosene lamp, which he filled up. Behind the depot, the lamp's contents were poured into an empty can. Then another one of us jumped into line with the newly emptied lamp. We managed to present the same kerosene lamp fifteen times to the quartermaster sergeant. Consequently, we were able to read at night by the splendor of the light of many small homemade kerosene wicks.

Slowly, our work conditions improved. We finished digging the trenches, and lined them with planks and boards to keep their earthen walls from crumbling in. There were no electrically driven tools then, so everything had to be cut with handsaws and hatchets. We felled huge pine trees and made pillars, sidewalls, and flooring out of them. Then we nailed it all together.

Early each morning we hastened to cut down our quota of pine trees. Then, with any time left over, we would go into the forest and pick wild strawberries. During these illicit breaks, we would drop our clothes and sunbathe, tanning ourselves. Consequently, we noticed that we were not all exactly alike; it seems that Dezső and Jajó were not the only Jewish students who had joined our group, a far safer solution than a Jewish labor camp. Around noon, we returned to the felled pine trees to drag them down to the trench lines and saw them into pieces. I finagled the position of counterweight, sitting on one end of the tree to facilitate less strenuous sawing. It was an exhilarating sight to see how those tall trees came down. The only thing we didn't do was shout "Timber!"

One of our supervisors, a sergeant who was a tailor in civilian life, played the guitar and sang popular American tunes in English. Among our favorites were "Some of These Days," "If You Knew Suzie," "Out of Nowhere," "Sweet Sue," "After You've Gone," and "Moonlight and Shadows." Each day after work, we would go down to the brook and sit around and sing these wonderfully enchanting melodies.

There were no newspapers in the camp, nor were there any radios. All of our news arrived through the mail. We were clueless about the great success of the Allied invasion in June. We didn't hear until much later of the botched attempt on Hitler's life in July. Our isolation continued into the fall, and in fact most of the time we were in Transylvania.

We had only been at the camp for a couple of weeks when Dezső Kemény, our friend from Nyíres, received a telegram. The commandant of the camp informed Dezső that his mother had died and gave him a leave of absence to attend the funeral. A few of us escorted Dezső to the Maroshéviz train station. Dezső was benumbed and in a somber mood, especially since there had been nothing wrong with his mother when he had left. So, with a heavy heart, he set out for Budapest. Once there, he rushed to his family's apartment on Bors Street, rang the bell, and with a lump in his throat, waited for someone to answer. Lo and behold, when the door opened his mother stood before him. They looked at each other dumbstruck. Finally, Dezső blurted out, "But Mom—you're alive?"

"Why on earth wouldn't I be?" she replied, perplexed.

A few days after Dezső's arrival, my father was talking with Mrs. Böttkös, our superintendent's wife, who lamented the fact that poor Dezső *Kémery* wouldn't be able to attend his mother's funeral, because the telegram had arrived too late at the labor camp in Transylvania. A lightbulb went off in my father's head: Dezső *Kemény* had reaped the benefits of this confusion over names.

Dezső had not been in a hurry to return to our camp. After all, the arrangements for a burial, are time consuming, and all the more difficult when it is one's mother who is the deceased! Having ensured that his mother was safe and sound, Dezső took the train out to Őrszentmiklós. There, he called upon the various summer residences, including my parents' at Veresegyház. He gave an account of life at the camp, which my father listened to keenly. He assured my father that our camp was secure and that we would all return soon. According to my father, Dezső saw everything through rose-colored glasses. After Dezsős's return, one day in late July, as we were walking up to the trench line we met a group of soldiers searching for partisans. Their bayonets were fixed. They checked out various little thatched huts, called *esztenas*, which could have served as hiding places. We boys also went out reconnoitering but with a different purpose—to find an *esztena* from whom to buy some goat cheese.

As the days passed, we began to have some misgivings about our return home. Our supervising soldiers began to tease us that soon we would be issued firearms and find ourselves in the very trenches we had just built. This was a scary prospect. We tried to reassure ourselves that the school year would begin soon and in a few weeks we would be holding in our hands books, rather than shovels or firearms. However, soon after we had been teased in this fashion by our supervisors, military trucks arrived bearing crates of well-greased infantry rifles, Mannlicher and Mauser types. We had to unload the crates and carry them into the storage depot.

The next morning, the rifles were distributed. This was a bad omen. It looked as if we really were going to be kept there to man the lines. I went to see Miklós Pálos, the secretary of the camp (we had nicknamed him "Seltzer Head"; his hair looked like soda water squirted out of a bottle—not unlike the hairdo of Professor Einstein).

I asked him how many students were in the camp. Then I went to see the quartermaster sergeant. I asked him how many rifles had been delivered. "Why do you want to know? It's none of your business," he barked at me. I replied, "The secretariat of the camp wants to be informed." That did the trick. Once I had learned the numbers, even with my limited mathematical ability, I could see that there was one more person in the camp than there were rifles. So, on the day that we were to receive the rifles I made sure to be the last person in line. One by one, every boy, the cooks, the secretary, and all the others who belonged to the camp, picked up their firearms. When it came to me, the quartermaster looked at me dumbfounded. "What do you want?" he again barked at me. "A rifle," I answered proudly. "We are out of them but I will try and get one for you." "Don't bother," I said, and tried to disappear as fast as I could, hoping he would never find me. From then on, while my comrades had to carry their rifles daily up into the mountain, I could stroll along leisurely—to their endless aggravation.

The arrival of these rifles spoiled our beautiful summer afternoons. The attempt was to transform us into grim warriors. Lucky for us, ammunition was not sent along with the firearms.

The supervising soldiers were not housed with us boys. They stayed in nearby barracks, only to reappear in our camp every morning. They were a mixed bag. Most of them were decent folks, but there were a few mean-spirited, Nazi sadists among them. They tried to torment us, while we tried to repay the favor by playing tricks on them. Gradually, our technique became more refined, and we managed to exert ourselves less and less.

One early morning, a messenger came to us with the news that the fortified line had lost a handful of horses and ordered that some of us boys should find them and bring them back. This was a splendid opportunity to skip a working day. Thus, we set out—among us Gabi Ambrózy, who still looked like F. Scott Fitzgerald, and Tonner, who on the other hand looked like Wallace Beery and had been so eager to join in this pursuit that he hadn't even taken the time to get dressed. He came along in his pajamas. We proceeded in the direction that we thought the horses might have gone.

Around noon, we came upon a group of soldiers, and had a nice chat with them. Shortly thereafter, still without the horses, we ran into another patrol that was far from friendly and, with fixed bayonets, escorted us to the headquarters of the fortifications, which were in the main barracks. There we sat until our identities were cleared over the telephone. We must have been highly suspicious-looking—with no military escort or guns, and I with my beard, Tonner in his pink pajamas, and others in their various quirky apparel. No wonder they thought we might be roaming partisans. Needless to say, we returned to the camp without any horses.

On another morning, Gabi Ambrózy and I were sent to the fortress to draw our bread rations. We carried a heavy blanket with us. This we were going to utilize as a stretcher, placing the bread inside it, folding its ends, and carrying the load back, one end on each of our shoulders. As soon as the cooks began to throw the four-pounder loaves into the open blanket, however, we realized how unprepared we were strength-wise for the task. Gabi and I looked at each other and broke out into uproarious laughter. The more we laughed, the more annoyed the cooks became and the more bread they threw into the blanket. Once this bread throwing had ceased, Gabi and I grabbed opposite ends of the blanket until we had it in the shape of a taco. We then dragged this pyramid of bread over the ground. The cooks back at our camp, seeing us arrive with our enormous pile of loaves, were stupefied.

Some of our supervisors were reenlisted noncommissioned officers. Since they weren't graduates of a military academy, they would not be able to advance past the rank of lieutenant. Nevertheless they enjoyed the military life, free of everyday worries, strutting around in a uniform, which gave them an added advantage in impressing and winning the heart of some lonely schoolmistress.

One of our sergeants had the reputation of being an outright sadist. Whenever he discovered the slightest irregularity, be it a dirty mess tin or garbage lying outside a hut, he would awaken the entire camp and have everyone line up with their weapons and supplies for a heavy march. Then he would have the whole contingent climb up the mountain to the trenches and back down again.

One day, we learned that he had been assigned duty officer. We knew then to expect a night inspection, since that was when most of this sergeant's inspections took place. That night, when we went to sleep, we were quite restless.

Sure enough, at midnight our young sergeant lifted the canvas at the entrance to the hut and woke up our hut commander Jajó. Jajó jumped to attention and made his report. "Wake that man up," ordered the sarge, pointing toward Blazsek, "and lift the plank up from under him." By that point we were all wide awake, but we pretended that we were sleeping. In the meantime our blood froze. It was a custom in our hut that empty cans, old papers, empty tubes of toothpaste, and all sorts of other garbage was disposed of under the triangular plank beneath Blazsek. It was eerie, as if the sergeant had an uncanny intuition as to which of the plank beds covered up our misdeeds.

As Blazsek was awoken, the rest of us still didn't dare open our eyes, but we couldn't help but hear the sergeant's explosion of words. "What the hell is this?! Is this a leper colony?!" Jajó stiffly saluted and replied, "Sergeant, Sir! I report that all of this happened without my knowledge or my consent!" The sergeant cracked up, laughing so hard that his tears were flowing. "Listen, that's all we need—that all this has taken place with your knowledge or consent. Now make this mess disappear right away!" With that he turned around and left. Jajó's presence of mind thus saved us that time from a miserable excursion into the night. From then on, "It happened without my knowledge and permission" became an everyday saying for us and Jajó's rating soared to an A-plus among his fellow tenants.

Some days later, all of us were marched up to the fortified line to observe a military exercise. Of course, we were happy to escape another day of digging and dragging. We sat down on the grass, on a fresh balmy morning, and enjoyed the production as if we were sitting in a box at the opera.

Captain Darvas, the commander of the fortified line, put in an appearance as well. He had allegedly participated in the Spanish Civil War, on Franco's side. He was tall and elegant, and had an impressive personality. I remember I took special note of his boots. While members of the Arrow Cross mostly wore the so-called *pac*, laced-top boots, or bilgeri, he wore fashionable boots with buckles on their upper edges. Captain Darvas was accompanied by two women in dressing gowns. They were beauties of the lower class. Apparently, one of them was the captain's girlfriend, with whom he cohabited in the fort.

Two sergeants came forward to explain the purpose of the exercise. We were facing three small concrete pillboxes lined up in a row. These pillboxes were relatively small, about the size of a garage. They could very well have been called bunkers. The middle one was supposedly in the hands of the Russians. Soldiers in the two side ones were to retake the center one. The attacks began, from right and left. The soldiers leaned a ladder onto the side of the middle building. One of them directed a flamethrower into a window. A second soldier aimed at another window with a smoke flare, while a third one opened up the rear door of the bunker and dropped a hand grenade inside. It took the soldiers less than half an hour to retake the concrete pillbox.

I was stunned. I imagined being a soldier, any soldier, there in that cramped bunker, on the receiving end of the dropped hand grenades and the scorching heat of the flamethrower. If there had been soldiers inside those bunkers, death would have been certain. They wouldn't have had a chance to defend themselves. Moreover, there was every reason for the Russians to attack our fortifications exactly the way Captain Darvas had just demonstrated. That no one else saw this as an obvious lesson was beyond me. After all, the Germans had taken the large Belgian fortresses simply by dropping parachutists on their roofs. And those fortresses were not like our measly contraptions. But then, the Russians hadn't the slightest intention of attacking the fortified lines head on. A few weeks later, they marched leisurely up the highway smack into the rear, exposed side of the defensive line.

A few days after this military exercise, those of us born in 1922–23 were called up by the army. Students in their junior year, born in 1924–25 like Dezső Kemény and me, were not yet affected. The majority of the boys in the camp had to take their leave, return to Budapest, and join the army. Those of us left behind were downcast. Our numbers had dwindled and we sorely missed our good friends.

Of course, none of us knew which of the two groups had fared better. Was it our group that had to stay on, unable to see our families, or was it the ones who were able to visit their families, but then had to join the army? After all, no one wanted to join the army, but no one wanted to get stuck in Transylvania either.

In honor of those who were to depart, Captain Darvas temporarily suspended the blackout and gigantic bonfires were lit. The cooks prepared sumptuous breaded veal chops and trucks arrived from town with cases of beer. A great festivity took place. The camp, which was normally enveloped in the deep blackness of night, was flooded with the light from the burning piles of wood.

Shortly thereafter, we became aware of the buzzing of an airplane. It was not particularly unusual, since every night a so-called Tito-bus flew over our heads, but that plane came at almost the same time each night—and this was not that time. By the characteristic drone of it, this was a Russian plane likely delivering ammunition and supplies to partisans (many of whom were Yugoslavs operating behind Axis lines). In the soldiers' view, Captain Darvas had suspended the blackout not just for our celebration but also to see what action the airplane would take as it flew overhead. He probably wanted to find out whether a drop would be attempted, as this could have given away their methods. The airplane seemed to be confused by the unusual brightness, circling overhead repeatedly. Perhaps it was waiting for some confirmation from the partisans on the ground that they should drop their packages there. It is also conceivable that the location of our camp didn't jibe with the flyer's routine. In the end, the plane flew away without dropping any supplies.

With the departure of our upper classmates, our morale sagged considerably as well. Within a few days, our workload dwindled. It seemed that time stood still at the camp.

One day, a young man arrived at the camp. Our camp secretary, Miklós Pálos, told a few boys that an evening meeting was planned where the visitor would talk about the political situation. He was said to have come from Brazil, and would talk about the free Western world. No one objected to his presentation. Perhaps it was a "secret mission."

Another afternoon, a few of us boys went out to gather some hay with the soldiers. While the soldiers piled hay on the drays, we lay down in the grass and took pleasure in the mountainous scenery of Transylvania. On those August days, almost every afternoon there was a little sprinkling of rain, but it never lasted longer than ten or fifteen minutes. The landscape, the invigorating air, the serenity were all ideal contributors to a venturesome vacation.

Every now and then I decided to skip work. On one of those days, Dezső had called in sick and gotten permission to convalesce in our little cottage. I had earmarked the day for reading and quiet conversation with my friend, and after the other boys had left, I took up my station in a corner. To play it safe, I positioned myself behind a pile of suitcases and kit boxes. I wrapped my body from the waist down in a blanket and prepared to pull it over my head should I need to quickly hide. These precautions paid off when one of the staff sergeants came in and sat down to chat with Dezső. I barely had a chance to cover myself and create a pose with the help of my arms to look like another suitcase.

After the sergeant had been there for a while talking with Dezső, I began to wonder whether he suspected that there was a person hiding beneath the blanket and if he were purposely staying such a long time so that I would be forced to suffer with my arms at the same level as my head for a half hour or more. Perhaps it tickled his sense of humor, or maybe he was just talking to Dezső to chase his boredom away. When he finally left, my arms were completely numb. Had I been discovered, it would have been a scandal.

We boys were in splendid seclusion. Thus, the events of August 23, and the way the front dissolved into chaos, caught us by surprise. On that day the Romanian government changed sides, signing an armistice with the Allies and rejoining the war, this time against Germany. All this happened with lightning speed, entrapping the Germans in Romania. Those who could extricate themselves left in headlong flight.

In the days that followed, the remnants of the German forces appeared on the highway on the opposite side of the brook from us. It created a colorful picture. This was not an orderly withdrawal, but a full-blown flight turning into a stampede. Trucks were jam-packed with soldiers; the exodus went on for hours on end. Long pine trees had been attached to the rear ends of the trucks to increase their carrying capacity; soldiers lined up on top of them, hanging onto one another's shoulders to keep their balance. As the pine trees were dragged along they stirred up an enormous cloud of dust behind them. This sight left us flabbergasted and anxious about what would become of us in the near future. A couple of days later, the Hungarian troops also retreated. Horse-drawn drays were filled with the wounded.

The tension in our camp grew by the hour. One more day had passed when trucks stopped opposite our camp. They carried Hungarian law students fleeing from the Borszék, Tölgyes, and Ojtoz passes. The boys told us that here and there they had already run into Russian soldiers. At first they had not been hostile, but soon they began to fire on them, and the boys decided to escape. Another truck pulled up, and more boys shouted at us: "What are you waiting for?! The Russians could be here any minute!"

By the time dusk fell, I had made up my mind to strike out. Come hell or high water, I would get myself home. That evening Miklós Pálos, our secretary, informed us that a telegram had come ordering the whole camp to march over to Borszék—where the

Russians already were. This directive only strengthened my resolve further.

I went to see the camp commandant, disclosed that I in fact belonged to the faculty of law, not of architecture or philosophy, and requested a military pass. As he drafted my discharge papers other boys arrived with the same intention. Soon, a small group of students had formed that would depart together.

In his last letter to me, my father had sent some good advice. In a disguised manner he more or less let me decide what to do. His advice was to follow my instinct. His letter, especially the last lines, brought a lump to my throat. He had written, "When you come home, it will be swell to be together and we will never part again."

Just before taking leave of the camp I executed my last prank, placing my repulsively stinky footcloths in a wooden box originally intended to contain fruit preserves and mailing the box to my family's address in Veresegyház. I insured it for three hundred pengős, a sizable amount of money. I figured that the package would get lost in the chaos of war and I could then make some easy dough. But one can never predict what will happen, even in the most harrowing situations. To my utter astonishment, the box arrived at Veresegyház long before I did. My mother, upon opening it, almost passed out from the stench and was puzzled. Not until later did she learn that the intent was not that the package should have arrived, but rather that it should never have arrived. In the sixth year of the Second World War, neither bombardment nor fleeing armies could keep the Hungarian postal service from executing its duty—especially when a package was insured.

22

Homeward Bound

Under the cover of darkness, I said goodbye to my companions in our little bungalow. Then, I and Tonner joined the small group of other boys who were ready to depart, and all of us boarded the mountain train. Tonner was busy with the brakes; he released them while the rest of us gave the carriages a push. We jumped on and the little train began to roll toward Maroshéviz. At the station we learned that there was one more civilian train leaving for Budapest. An hour passed, and a string of carriages arrived from our camp carrying the rest of the boys. Apparently, once the news of our small group's departure had spread, the rest of the boys had hurriedly followed.

As we stood by the station waiting, the eerie buzz of airplanes above us disturbed the silence of the night. When the aircraft were above the station they dove. We all ran right and left. Some of the boys crowded under the wagons of a sidetracked train. Others jumped through windows into the station building. One of the boys, wearing red-striped pajamas, landed in a barrel of rainwater being collected at one corner of the building. It was a moonlit night. The murmuring Rata fighter planes strafed the wagons and buildings; then they left.

Shortly thereafter, we heard the shrill whistle of our eagerly anticipated train. It was packed with people beyond belief. It was out of the question that we would be able to squeeze ourselves into one of the coaches, to say nothing of our kit boxes and suitcases. I told a pal that our only recourse was to climb on top of one of the carriages. The inspiration for this solution came to me from a Jack London story. My friend, whose nickname happened to be Jack, climbed a ladder on the side of a railway carriage and I handed him our luggage to place on the roof of the train. Then I followed him up. Looking around we saw that other boys had done the same. Within a minute, all of the carriage roofs were occupied.

As we traveled, red sparks from the locomotive's burning coal occasionally lit up the surrounding landscape. The train meandered through the mountains and we became conscious of a light mist of drizzling rain, covering our faces and our bodies. Jack and I fastened ourselves with our belts to the carriage's ventilation pipes. Thus, we managed to stay on top of the now-slippery surface. The wide top of the Pullman carriage gave us ample space for our belongings and we had plenty of room to ourselves. We imagined that we were riding on the back of a benevolent elephant. The monotonous rattling of the train soon had us fast asleep.

We woke up to the rising sun. We pushed our suitcases together to serve as a table for breakfast. We laid out bacon, bread, green peppers, a salt shaker, and a canteen of brandy. As the scenery spread before our eyes we felt as if we were in an observatory car. The fresh air invigorated us and gave us a good appetite.

In 1941, when northern Transylvania was reunited with Hungary (reversing the loss of territory that had occurred as part of the Treaty of Trianon following the First World War), the railroad lines between the two territories had to be reconnected and a tunnel carved through the mountains. The two localities at each end were then connected—Szeretfalva at the northern entrance and Déda at the southern one. We reached the tunnel on the second day of our journey. As we neared it, we lay down flat and covered our upper bodies with blankets. Once in the tunnel, we could feel wet steam from the locomotive's funnel licking our arms. There we lay, flat on our stomachs and sides for seventeen minutes, until we suddenly became aware of fresh air and the sun shining in our faces again. From here on out, the mountains were behind us and we began to travel among flat parcels of farmland.

Before the town of Dés one of our companions eight or ten cars ahead of us stood up suddenly. We looked on in disbelief as he was lifted up in the air by a low hanging wire and thrown down to the ground. Luckily he fell to the side of the railroad tracks into a cornfield. Somebody pulled the emergency brake and the train came to a screeching halt. We could see the boy lying unconscious. A wide cut was visible across his chest, through which seeped dark-colored red blood. A German military doctor on the train hastily bandaged the boy and we waited until an ambulance arrived to take him to the hospital in Dés.

As we continued our journey and reached the vicinity of the Tisza River, the number of passengers dwindled. At a certain point, there were plenty of seats inside the cars, and the railroad personnel decided it was time for us to come down from our scenic perch. Although we would have preferred to keep traveling on the rooftop, they insisted that we come down, so we did. We had traveled a little while longer, when an air raid siren sounded. The train came to a halt, and we dispersed into a meadow. Then, after about fifteen minutes, we returned to the train. A few hours later we arrived at Budapest Nyugati Pályaudvar (Budapest West Station) in the early morning hours.

At the train station, I boarded a bus. I headed to the rear, and as the bus wended its way through the city I stood, holding a ceiling strap and swinging to and fro. Next to me stood a very pretty young woman. She wore a cherry-red summer dress that revealed an exquisite figure. Her white sandals had a unique look, with soles made of rope. She stood close to me and I couldn't take my eyes off her. In my mind her beauty conjured up a beautiful apricot. As we rode on, an air raid siren began to howl. Hurriedly everyone exited the bus and ran into the nearest air raid shelter. The young lady was behind me.

In my short-sleeved military shirt, ski boots, my father's First World War riding britches, and my perky dark beard, I must have given a martial impression.

In the shelter, the commandant of the house asked me to take over as its temporary air-raid warden. Soon the all-clear sounded, and I had missed an opportunity to strike up a conversation with the pretty, young woman. This brought to mind another possibly missed opportunity from a few years earlier. At that time too I had been riding on a streetcar, on its perron, when a working-class beauty pressed herself quite close to me while the rest of the platform was unoccupied. Hesitancy kept me back.

After the air raid had ended, I hurried home to Logodi Street. My father was aghast at my appearance and urged me to shave off my dignified beard before I went to Veresegyház, so that I wouldn't scare my mother. The next day, with a more respectable appearance I took the train to Veresegyház. My entrance into the house generated an outburst of joy. My mother, Aunt Blanka, Aunt Ancsurka and Uncle János, Ilonka our cook, and Grandmother Eveline all overwhelmed me with an outpouring of hugs and kisses.

23

Autumn in the Vineyard

I spent the first two evenings back at home at the Gunda farm with the usual gang. The third evening was on my mother's name day, the day of Saint Rosa De Lima, and my family entertained all of Nyires. We young adults spent the fourth afternoon at Móki's, the fifth at the Rados house, and the sixth there as well. On Saturday, a party was planned at the Alemanns. In the midst of these parties, on one of the days I ran into the city to meet up with Gyuri Sághy. My head was spinning with all of these activities and seeing Nyires again. When we left Transylvania, the wise Miklós Pálos forewarned us that after the euphoria of arrival a letdown would inevitably follow.

We had a number of other lively gatherings, at various other houses. Our last convivial evening took place at the Viczián grange. Our frolicking was most memorable, with tables groaning under the weight of various delicacies and with the relentless flowing of wine, followed by repeated rounds of Uncle Tóni's zesty espressos. In the course of the evening, István Kormos challenged my father to a drinking duel. The end result was a draw; notwithstanding my father's best efforts, István stayed sober. During the course of the evening János Brencsán played the piano while all the guests, including mothers and grandmothers, whirled wildly round and round on the parquet. This last merriment was a "danse macabre" on the edge of a volcano. When we departed, we skirted around the Vicziáns' huge white sheepdogs. The moon lit up the road guiding us on our walk down the hill to the valley. It had been an evening of amusements in an enchanted house.

A few more beautiful days followed. The government of Prime Minister Géza Lakatos was a great improvement over the Quisling

Sztójay. Machinations were underway, however. In June, gendarmerie units under the direction of interior minister László Baky began to surreptitiously infiltrate the capital in preparation for a putsch. In early July Horthy caught wind of the plot. On July 7, a phantom Hungarian army division (the Germans were unaware of its existence) commanded by General Ferenc Koszorus entered the capital. By July 9 they had ousted the gendarmerie. The gendarmerie units were ordered out of Budapest just in time to stop them from executing a final roundup of the Jewish population of Budapest and from ousting the governor from the Royal Palace. The regent's son Miklós Horthy Jr. and the governor's entourage weighed the question of when to present the request for armistice that they had readied over the previous year—about all of which Hitler was well informed.

The war rolled on inexorably. American bombers filled the sky, their contrails stretching behind them, bound for targets in Ploesti or other locations. A gigantic tank battle—one of the Second World War's largest—took place in Debrecen. In October, the Russians crossed the Tisza River to the west of Debrecen.

As long as we could, we tried to maintain the semblance of ordinary life. We kept biking in the countryside and taking dips in the lake. Then the harvesting of the grapes began. In the evenings we listened to our records, and Aurél Dessewffy played "In the Mood" on the Viczián's piano over and over again. I went to visit János Brencsán at his family's villa in his subterranean room, where we played Artie Shaw's "Begin the Beguine" and "Pastel Blue."

The fall weather was gorgeous. It was still balmy and I was sad to leave Veresegyház and go back to work at the Hangya Consortium. The apartment of Uncle Béla Hilbert, my father's cousin, had been destroyed by aerial bombing. Thus, he moved in with us, taking over my father's study. As the chief executive officer of Hangya, he was driven to the office by chauffeur in a red Studebaker. Now I got to ride along with him, emerging with some pride from the CEO's car.

On the weekends, we went out to the vineyard and helped with the harvesting. But the crop that year was meager, as two hailstorms over the course of the summer had decimated the vintage. In my mother's opinion this also was Hitler's fault. Slowly we approached October 15.

24

October 15, 1944—
The Arrow Cross Grabs Power

Winters during the war years were extremely harsh. At the outset of the war Hungary lost approximately one hundred thousand men by the Don River in Russia. But that was only the beginning. Food and manufactured goods were shipped to Germany, leaving the country's population deprived. Schools were closed for a lack of heating fuel (it was called a coal break). Copper sulfate and raffia, necessities for a vineyard, were nowhere to be had. There was no glue to patch up flat bicycle tires either. Menyus Hajós invented an adhesive to patch the tires by soaking the rubber sole of his old sneaker in gasoline until it became a gooey spreadable fluid. Clothing and footwear were rationed. Gyuri Sághy went to see General Alajos Béldi, the head of the Levente Organization (a paramilitary youth entity for boys in the villages and students in senior high schools in the cities), to ask for a coupon for a pair of boots for a boy who belonged to our Levente group and had shown up barefoot for military training. On top of wartime hardships, Mother Nature knew no mercy. In parts of the country, flooding destroyed sizeable communities.

My father was not called up to serve in the military, because of his age but also because he had already served during the First World War. Thus, he remained the spiritual guide for the family, while my mother was the doer and mover in the vineyard. We were, nonetheless, wary of the intensifying war.

On October 15, we woke up to a warm and sunny morning in Veresegyház. My parents and I were out at the vineyard. Harvesting was winding down. We packed like maniacs. We dug holes and hid as much as we could in them.

At nine that morning, after a short firefight, Miklós Horthy Jr., Regent Horthy's son, was kidnapped by the Gestapo in Pest. He had reportedly been lured to Pest, and was wounded in the process of being kidnapped. The incident was reported to Governor Horthy during a Crown Council meeting in the Royal Castle at eleven. Shortly thereafter, Governor Horthy entered the studio of the Hungarian Broadcasting Corporation on Sándor Street, read a peace proclamation, and asked the Allies for an armistice. The announcement was made into a wax recording. He left the studio, and his proclamation was broadcast at around one in the afternoon.

Perhaps an hour later, the radio began to broadcast military marches. The sound of this martial music filled us with apprehension, especially since the proclamation by the regent was not repeated.

During the course of the afternoon, Gyuri Sághy bicycled out of the frenzied city. He had earlier cycled around the Royal Castle and witnessed some of the military action. Gyuri described members of Otto Skorzeny's German SS storm troopers sitting on the sidewalks on Lovas Avenue and on Atilla Street in their camouflage field suits with panzerfausts and machine gun bandoliers hung around their necks, waiting for the order to attack the Royal Castle. Tanks were lined up on Lovas Avenue. There was a short exchange of gunfire between the SS and the palace guards, which ended in a ceasefire and the occupation of the Castle by Skorzeny's troops. The guards hadn't wanted to give up their defense of the Castle, but the regent personally walked down to those in the first firing position and ordered them to stop fighting.

At the same time, the German SS took over the Radio studio on Sándor Street. There was only a solitary policeman there, who used his revolver to try and hold the Germans back from entering the building. When his ammunition ran out, he escaped through a rear entrance. The Germans turned the studio over to the Arrow Cross.

The Hungarian Army had for all practical purposes betrayed the regent. The leader of the fascist Arrow Cross, Ferenc Szálasi, who had the support of the Germans, came into power. He wanted to keep up constitutional formalities, so he asked for an audience with Horthy. By then, Horthy was under arrest and in no position to refuse to see this man he loathed. At their meeting he did not offer a handshake and did not engage in discussion; he listened passively to Szálasi. As Szálasi was about to take his leave, Horthy had but one admonition: "*Szálasi, vigyázzon a Zsidókra!*" ("Szálasi, you must protect the Jews!"). (This episode was relayed to me after the war by my mother's cousin Dr. János Lauringer, who heard it from his friend Elek Versegi Nagy, former ambassador to the Vatican.)

Another good friend of mine, Pali Groschmied, a blood relative of the famous Hungarian author Imre Madách, explained to me how the Arrow Cross had manipulated the putsch to install Szálasi. He told me this in 1947, while we were burning brandy at the Őrszentmiklós distillery. Pali had been chief constable in the small town of Rétság. He was good friends with Gyula Ambrózy, the head of Governor Horthy's cabinet bureau office. Ambrózy had been with the governor when the SS occupied the Royal Castle and arrested the governor. Ambrózy's office was in the entrance hall outside the governor's living quarters. Customarily he kept one blank sheet of paper with only the governor's signature on it at the bottom of his desk drawer in case of any unforeseen eventualities— and when an issue was not of such importance that Horthy should have to be inconvenienced for his signature. Ambrózy watched as a member of the Arrow Cross went through his desk and pulled this piece of paper out of the drawer. The Arrow Cross simply typed the text of Horthy's resignation and transfer of power to Szálasi above Horthy's signature. Thus, it looked as if the change in government had been a constitutional one. The Arrow Cross knew that Horthy would never abdicate his position and authorize a change in leadership of his own volition—especially not to Szálasi, whom he despised.

Thus, 1944 became another tragic year in the history of Hungary. The fifteenth of October sealed Hungary's destiny and closed an era that had begun when Horthy came to power in 1919. Horthy and his family were deported to Austria.

A social class ceased to exist. Its traditions, its wealth, and with these, its complexity, its virtues, and its sins, disappeared. The upper class and their way of life perished. This was a *Gone with the Wind* experience for all of us. What followed 1944 was an entirely different era. Separating the new era from the time that came before it was the period between March 19 and October 15. While the Red Sea was the savior of the Israelites in ancient times, in modern times the sea of the Red Army, as we soon found out, did not save us. Rather it engulfed us.

After the fifteenth of October, as the weather changed, so too did the political atmosphere. The sky turned overcast, the horizon was dark and gloomy, and it began to rain. One morning, I was riding the streetcar. As we reached Döbrentei Square my eyes caught sight of the marble statue of Gyula Gömbös. Normally gleaming white in color, the statue had been coated in thick black tar. Gömbös, the prime minister of Hungary from 1932 until his death in 1936, had been a demagogue whose concealed goal had been to propagate Nazism with himself as the leader. He had made every effort to build a Nazi party by appealing to the masses, and had tried to poison public opinion from day one of his ministry. His efforts resulted in new ties between Germany and Hungary and ultimately the coming together of the Rome-Berlin Axis in 1936. His illness and death in 1936 prevented him from seeing any further results.

Seeing Gömbös's statue disgraced filled me with secret glee. He should never have been honored by having a statue raised for him. But my delight was short-lived, since the next day there was scaffolding around the statue and workmen were diligently cleaning it.

That same day, at eight in the evening, a tremendous explosion shook our neighborhood. The next morning, as my streetcar passed through Döbrentei Square I was pleasantly surprised. Gömbös's statue had disappeared. In its place was a vacant space. The people in overalls who had been cleaning the statue with such élan the day before had been drilling holes into the statue while they cleaned it. They filled the holes with sticks of dynamite.

Today, at the spot where the statue once stood there is a plaque on a pedestal with an inscription reminding the public that this is where the statue of Gyula Gömbös, the former prime minister of Hungary, once stood and was blown up on October 6, 1944, by the Resistance. Some people have pointed out the irony of Gömbös's name being thus preserved for posterity.

One sunny afternoon, I was headed home on the streetcar when, as we passed Antal Szebenyi Square, members of the military police boarded the streetcar. These units carried as identification quarter-moon metal shields with the words "Military Police" on them hanging from small metal chains in front of their chests. They were looking for deserters. Since my identification papers from the Hangya Consortium were of questionable value, and strictly speaking I should have been in military service, I speedily retreated to the rear of the streetcar and managed to step down before it took off.

Not only was I vulnerable to being discovered on the streets, but one day the danger skirted me at the office. In the morning, an announcement was circulated requesting all male employees to report to the meeting room at eleven. In the front of the room standing on a dais was a uniformed Arrow Cross man with the usual armband. As soon as the meeting room had filled up, the storm trooper began his sales pitch, asking for volunteers to enlist in the Hungarian SS divisions. While the Archer was speaking I surreptitiously gravitated toward the rear door and scurried back to my office. My colleagues were amused.

As the front neared the capital, my family decided that it would be safer to move from Veresegyház back to Logodi Street for the duration of any siege that might occur. We carried some food with us into the city while we left valuables of all shapes and forms behind. There was antique furniture, oil portraits of ancestors, household items, carpets, Altwien silver, and Meissen porcelain that we did not take with us. Barrels of wine stayed in the cellar; lard was buried in the ground in firkins; potatoes, vegetables, and bottles of brandy and champagne were hidden in the cellar. As we departed Veresegyház for Logodi Street, we naively thought that our belongings would remain safe at the vineyard.

Soon, everyone at Nyires and Vicziántelep was hiding, digging, and walling up portions of their wine cellars. My father decided that before our final departure we should also wall up a section of our wine cellar and place our valuables, first and foremost wine, in that secluded area. Had the Russians had easy access into the capital this plan might have worked. But since the Germans put up a stubborn resistance, the Russian forces got bogged down on the Pest side of the city and had plenty of time to discover our clever hiding spots.

It was the first week of November already when we frantically completed our preparations to leave the vineyard. Father hired Mr. Cinkota, Grandmother Eveline's loyal helper, to build a wall splitting the wine cellar into two. We filled our biggest barrels with wine and rolled them into the hidden vault. We also placed some of the tools and supplies that we would need to restart the following year, such as copper sulfate, fertilizers, a small wine press, rubber hoses, and the wine pump into the secret enclave. When the "Great Wall" was finally completed it was November 4, my name day. The wall was built quicker than we anticipated, because our whole family, including Aunt Blanka, as well as Gyuri Sághy, assisted Cinkota in the project.

Then, as an afterthought, my father sent me over to the Viczian's upper grange with a wheelbarrow full of valuables. Since Aunt Bözsi was also building a wall in her wine cellar my father thought it might be wise to send her a small portion of our valuables, and thereby hedge the chances of losing everything. We were convinced that if anybody could succeed in saving anything it would be Aunt Bözsi, who was staying behind in the countryside and was always more enterprising and resourceful than the rest of us.

In the midst of our hustling and bustling, building and hiding, on November 4, a Saturday, Margaret Bridge in Budapest blew up in a series of explosions. It happened on an early afternoon when the bridge was crowded with commuters on streetcars, buses, and pedestrians. Aunt Ancsurka, the wife of my father's good friend Uncle János Benel, was riding in one of the streetcars. After the first explosion, she got out of the streetcar, but she ran headlong into a second explosion, in which both of her legs were wounded. She fell into the

Anna (Ancsurka) Benel, nee Anna Bánás

Danube. Since she was a good swimmer, she succeeded in reaching the shore. She was taken to Cave Hospital beneath Buda Castle. Unfortunately gangrene set in and her legs had to be amputated. She died the next day from an infection. All of this sad news awaited us a few days after its occurrence upon our arrival at Logodi Street.

Meanwhile, my mother was busy gathering, harvesting, and packing. One day, a good friend of Aunt Hansi and Uncle Rory, Ágota Kállay, stopped by the vineyard to see my parents. She and my mother walked through the upper tract of the house, where Aunt Hansi and Uncle Rory lived. Ágota surveyed the scene, took one look at the family portraits on the wall, and said to my mother, "All of these paintings will be stolen." Her statement was the manifestation of one thousand years of wisdom condensed in her Kállay blood. My mother thereupon took the portraits of Moritz O'Donnell and Prince Cantacuzene and his wife, off the wall. She removed the portraits from their stretchers and rolled them up tightly, making sure that the painted side faced outward in order to better preserve the painting. Thus the paintings were taken to Logodi Street.

My father looked for someone to move into our house so that the building wouldn't look forlorn or deserted. He was desperate. He cajoled, he begged, he tried to persuade peasants who had served our family for decades, but to no avail. Understandably nobody was willing to leave their households, their animals, just to be the guardian of our manor house. Under no circumstances would people part with their families and leave their farms unattended.

At last, in an act of desperation, he sent a message to Illés Hamar, a homeless vagrant in Erdőváros. This was the same man who had stoically watched one Easter Sunday as my dog Mackó delivered a ham to his shanty. Hamar had nothing to lose. Thus, he was happy to oblige my father. He and his two daughters moved into our vacant coachman's flat. The situation reminded me of Robert Louis Stevenson's *Treasure Island*, when the squire hires Long John Silver as a cook, who becomes confidante to the naive protagonist. Only a brigand like Hamar was willing to move into our estate.

The first snow flurries arrived. The crows were cawing loud and bitter. The sky was dark and foreboding. We shivered in the November wind as the weathervanes creaked on the chimney tops. One could dimly hear the faraway sound of artillery fire.

After we had locked everything up, Hamar came into my father's room and was given the keys to the house. We grabbed our suitcases and demijohns, and left for the train station. At the vintner's empty cottage, situated at the entrance to the courtyard, we turned back and took one last look at the manor house, not knowing when we would see it again. Hamar stood in the courtyard, his eyes following us as we departed.

We left the vineyard with sunken hearts, but it was high time for us to return to the city. Gunfire sounded ominously closer and closer. It reminded my mother of a story that Juliska Kvassay had related about the booming cannonade that could be heard through the open door of the church in Vácbottyán in 1848 while her parents were getting married. Then, the gunfire had been the sound of General Ernő Kis's troops fighting the Austrians at the battle of Vác during the Hungarian Revolution. In this case, our Hungarian troops and the Germans were fighting the Russians. By the first week in December the Russians had taken Vác.

I was torn about leaving Veresegyház, but I was looking forward to the comfort of our apartment on Logodi Street. It was always cozy, warm, and bright. Uncle Béla, my father's cousin, had gone to Transdanubia in western Hungary, but had left his beautiful Orion radio behind with us. This gave my father the greatest delight, since he could now listen to BBC broadcasts and keep up with events of the war. I, on the other hand, got my greatest pleasure from using its electric turntable. The quality of its electro-dynamic sound was far better than that of my hand-cranked Radiola portable phonograph. My joy was short-lived, however; the turntable soon stopped, when the electricity went out.

∽

After Gyuri Saghy helped us build the great wall in the vineyard, he bade us farewell and cycled back to his family's home on Vadorzó Street in Hűvösvölgy. He planned to take off on a unique bicycle trip. He intended to go as far south as he could and to connect with the Anglo-American forces. It was a risky undertaking. Only someone like Gyuri could have entertained such an adventure. I was not surprised, and to be sure, staying in Budapest carried its own risks.

On October 20 orders had been issued calling up those from eighteen to twenty years of age to join either the army or a labor battalion. We students at colleges and universities had enrolled for the fall semester, but since the schools had closed again student status could no longer be used as an excuse. Thus, Gyuri's scheme wasn't as mad as it seemed. Gyuri expropriated Mussolini's slogan *"vivere pericolosamente"* ("to live dangerously"). He was its embodiment.

I went to Vadorzó Street to bid Gyuri bon voyage. He handed me his favorite records for safekeeping. His first stop was to be the summer home by Lake Balaton of the Igaly family. János Igaly was a classmate of ours. The next time I saw Gyuri was in the spring of 1945.

Szabi Viczián had also enrolled in college and was in limbo just like Gyuri and me. Not knowing what might happen to him during the course of the siege, Szabi handed me his will, bequeathing his rifle and bicycle to me in the event that he did not survive. He also brought over to our apartment on Logodi Street a half-dozen bottles of wine, which we hid in the bottoms of our large plant boxes. He entrusted us with his wine, but his trust turned out to have been misplaced.

On December 3, the so-called Kiska-Kisegítő Karhatalmi Alakulat (Auxiliary Police Detachment) was established. It was intended to resemble the Volksturm in Germany. But in reality, the disguised aim was to surreptitiously give cover to absentees and prevent these young Hungarians from being seized and used as cannon fodder by the Reich.

One of these Kiska detachments was formed on Bástya Street with its headquarters at Péter Pázmány University. Since its members included my classmates and relatives of the Viczián cousins, I joined them. From then on, every morning, instead of going to work I showed up at the detachment's headquarters at the university. We were a motley group of about seventy-five boys. Some were still in high school. We conducted infantry drills in the courtyard to make our outfit look more legitimate, though one of our leaders wore a black derby hat. As the group grew, its leaders decided that it was time to look for military barracks where the young men could lodge, instead of having to go home every afternoon and present themselves the following morning.

At that point, I decided that even if I was courting danger I would rather sleep in my cozy bed on Logodi Street than in unheated barracks that were not much safer and where the provision of one's next meal was uncertain. As it turned out, the team wasn't able to stay in barracks for long, because the military authorities soon began to ask unpleasant questions about the outfit's legitimacy.

One morning, Tóni Viczián Jr. got word that a military train was at Budapest Nyugati Pályaudvar (Budapest West Railroad Station) loaded with firearms and canned food. Tóni and the two other leaders of the Kiska outfit, Pál Tomcsányi and Kristóf Kállay, conjured up a truck and filled it with as much loot as possible, returning several times. To be more exact, as Krisztián Ungváry writes in his book *Budapest Ostroma*, "Tóni Viczián, Aurél Dessewffy, János Brencsán, János Széchy expropriated five wagons containing: ten thousand items of clothing, twenty thousand hand grenades, three ak-ak guns, two thousand crates of ammunition, five thousand boots, and canned food."

The success of this raid made it possible for the battalion to move into a building whose basement had been designated as a hiding place for Jewish refugees by the Swiss Embassy. This small palace was in one of Pest's narrow streets at 17 Sándor Wekerle Street (Sas Street today). It was located in a crowded, elegant part of the inner city. Thus, the members of this Kiska outfit became the defenders of the Jews. But the deserters also had to defend themselves. On the thirtieth of November, the army posted another order on billboards throughout the city instructing all undergraduates not yet in uniform to present themselves at the army's Selective Service Centers. Tóni's battalion had false papers, and they were armed to the teeth.

The boys, numbering around one hundred, found lodging on the top floor of the building, in the library. They removed the books and slept on the empty shelves as if they were berths in a sleeping car. From then on, any attempt by the Arrow Cross to enter the building was denied. Once, when an army captain demanded to be let in, the sentry in the entrance hall sounded an alarm. Within seconds a large heavily armed group showed up. The captain, confronted by this formidable force, thought it best to make himself scarce. Thus, the group was able to provide safety for the Jews, and to stay put, until the Russians arrived.

By the time the Russians took Pest, only one toilet in the whole house was functioning. It happened to be on the top floor of the building. Since there was no running water, anyone who wanted to use the toilet was required to bring a pail of water to flush. To make sure that everybody abided by the rule, a guard stood outside the toilet at all times.

On the last day of the siege, it was Andor Beőthy's turn to be sentry. He stood by the toilet, minus his helmet, with a bandage on his forehead covering his oozing boils. Gradually, the bandage became soaked with blood. Nevertheless, he stood there unperturbed, with hand grenades in his belt and a machine gun hanging on his shoulder. In the background one could see the burning Royal Castle, the searchlights as they swept ceaselessly back and forth trying to ferret out the enemy, and the planes circling as they tried to evade the light beams and red tracer bullets.

On the ground floor, a group of young men stood transfixed at this hellish sight, which surpassed even the imaginative paintings of Vazul Verescsagin, the famous Russian painter before the First World War. One of the men, Antal Czettler, pointed up at Andor and cried out, "Look up there! There is the last of the Hungarian shithouse guards!"

Another Kiska unit was made up of former classmates of mine and Boy Scout companions from the Balassa troops. It ended up being thrown into the front line at Vecsés. Soon, they were retreating. Finally they arrived at Krisztina District and stationed themselves in the basement of the August Konditorei. This once most-elegant pastry shop was now crowded with the horses of the Wehrmacht. They stood there gloomily chewing the wood and neighing sadly, surrounded by glitzy pink marble tables and gilded gold mirrors. In the back of the shop, narrow steps led down to a first-aid shelter, dirty with soot and blood. There, Jumbó Csongrády and Böbe Binder, who were medical students, administered first aid to the wounded and operated by the dynamo-powered light of a stationary bicycle. When I asked what they had done on the front lines, Jumbó proudly declared, "It was we who surrendered Vecsés!"

25

Reminiscences

A s an only child, I was always on the lookout for playmates. Over the course of time, I befriended kids from across the social strata, including the working class. One of my friends was Laci Gangler, whose father was a waiter. Another was Sanyi Hajek, whose father worked in the Viczián brick factory. Through these friendships, a window opened up for me into the lives of families of much less means than mine. My parents may well have intentionally steered me toward these types of friendships.

I clung to my mother more than a child in a large family might. My mother was sensitive to my needs and able to communicate with me at my level. Sometimes we would sit down to play cards. I would wear a cowboy hat with my Smith and Wesson revolver hoisted on my belt, and she would be transformed into a cowgirl. We had drinking glasses on the table. They were only filled with water, yet they helped create the atmosphere of a Western saloon.

As a child, I was frequently bored, especially at formal dinners when I had to be on my best behavior, such as when we were invited over by Aunt Hansi and Uncle Rory. One summer afternoon, after I had suffered through one of these elegantly boring dinners I ventured into the garden and aimlessly loafed around. My mother soon joined me and we sat down in the park on a green and white garden bench. My mother conjured up Karl May's novel *Winnetou,* written in German. It was a book from my cousin Henry's library. We tried to understand the story, but after a while we reverted to small talk and had the best laughs over silly little sayings.

At this point, my parents were still very young, very much in love, and frequently flirtatious. For me this was embarrassing. I viewed my parents in an idolized, platonic dimension. Several decades after my parents had passed away, I still felt some embarrassment when I inadvertently came upon a letter my mother wrote to my father. In it, she laughingly recalled how my father's fountain pen would always end up falling out of his shirt pocket during their encounters. Even in later years, they behaved as a romantic couple. Yet it still took me a little time to grasp the reason for my father's request after the war that I not come out from the city on the midnight train without advance warning.

My other main companion in early childhood was Grandmother Eveline. With her, I would have simple conversations; perhaps she herself was a simple soul. When I was at Grandmother's house, people would stop by to buy wine. I would follow her down to the cellar and observe her handling the transactions. Afterward, we would share some small talk about the customers. At the end of one of these chats, we came to the conclusion that it was interesting that while we had all of this wine at our disposal neither of us had a desire to drink it.

Every year, one day after St. Stephen's Day, my playmates left Nyíres. During these rainy and cloudy days—September in the rain—the vineyard became a truly boring place for me. We had no electricity yet, and I often ran out of reading material. Excursions to the outhouse were a nuisance. Drops of rain dripped down from the leaves of the trees and the landscape became so gloomy and somber that even the most cheerful person could not have helped but feel downcast. Returning to the city was redemption. There, the kitchen maids sang while attending to their chores. On the street, cars honked, streetcars tinkled. Reaching home, the phone rang and the illumination of electric lamps dissolved my dampness and gloom. But coming into the city also meant the end of summer vacation and the beginning of another school year.

Trudging back from school on a warm and sunny afternoon, to my pleasure, I might find my mother at home. She might be by her drawing table coloring stacks of copper lithographs. Or she might be sitting in her favorite armchair reading her favorite daily *Az Est* (*The Evening*). Once I snuck up behind her and tried to read over her shoulder. She told me that reading over someone's shoulder is impolite. All in all, my early years went by with an ever-present loneliness and solitude.

When I was about fourteen years old, my mother took me to spend a Sunday afternoon with Erzsébet Hacsó, a friend of hers and

Aunt Blanka's. Erzsébet had a small secondhand bookstore some-where on the outskirts of the city. It boggles the mind how she could have made a living out of this tiny enterprise. After spending the afternoon at Erzsébet's, I borrowed a couple of Zane Grey and James Oliver Curwood novels. This was my first exposure to Zane Grey, and I was somewhat disappointed. I had been anticipating more action, like that of the Max Brand novels that my father forbade me to read in my salad years. Only later would I discover Zane Grey novels' special charm and flavor.

But the main attraction of a Sunday excursion with Erzsébet was going to the movies. One of the films we saw was a good slapstick comedy, a German film starring Willy Fritsch and Lillian Harvey called "Hét Pofon" ("Seven Slaps"). It was based on a story by the Hungarian writer Károly Aszlányi. As we were leaving the movies a newspaper boy in the street shouted, "They've killed Stalin!" (this was around 1935). Of course, this was a ruse, only to get people to take the flyer, which had an advertisement on one side. Passersby eagerly grabbed it. In those days, every day around noon, as the last papers rolled off the presses, the newsboys would gather in the editorial room for a conference to decide what slogan would be the best one to shout.

My parents were colorful personalities and had excellent senses of humor. Through the years this served my family well. During even the most trying times, my mother would find something to laugh so hard about that her tears would flow. My father was the poker-faced comic who would relate an outrageously humorous anecdote and then await the applause. My parents enjoyed all kinds of humor—word plays, slapstick, verbal puns, and comic situations. My father would say that humor was a part of his life to such an extent that he could not imagine an afterworld without it. He said that if Heaven doesn't have humor but Hell does, he would choose Hell as his residence. Although I felt that this statement went a bit too far, he had made his point.

Once, I made up a small poem during dinner. It went like this:

I sit before a bowl of beans. (*Bableves mellett ülök.*)
The innkeeper is a good man. (*Jó ember a kocsmáros.*)
He gave me this. (*Ő adta ezt.*)
And though it lacks veal, (*S noha nincsen benne csülök,*)
I eat it with zeal. (*Én megeszem örömest.*)

To which my father immediately tacked on:

Since it still holds appeal. (*Mert én mindent megbecsülök.*)

My father's mind worked as fast as lightning. His view of jokes was that the best ones are those that occur naturally in conversation. Once, when we were at the Kenderesy family's house for dinner, Iduska Viczián suddenly cried out, "*Hol van a villám?! Hol van a villám?!*" ("Where is my fork?! Where is my fork?!") *Villám* is a homonym, however, which means both fork and lightning, so her words could also be interpreted as, "Where is the lightning?! Where is the lightning?!" Thereupon my father promptly replied, "But Iduska, it hasn't even thundered yet." Of course, this violated a law of physics, but it made people crack up nevertheless.

Once, a friend of mine was given a bicycle made by a mechanic named Velvárt. To this my father remarked, "But surely it was '*Hév-vel várt*'"—meaning "longed for intensely." When I was playing one of my Borge Fries jazz piano records, he said, "Oh, I didn't know that Dörge Frigyes played jazz piano so well." The Dörge to whom he was referring was the director of the Hungarian state lottery.

The humor of others was also appreciated. After the war, when the train was not running yet all the way to Veresegyház, we commuted from the city to Szent Jakab. From there we would walk to Veresegyház, but on the way we would stop off at the local apothecary. There we would change out of our city clothes, and leave our clothing, shoes, money, and watches behind, because we never knew when we might face marauding Russians at our vineyard. The pharmacist and his wife, Mr. and Mrs. Ernő Csomay, were very kind, and we soon became good friends with them.

On one occasion, before we set out on our journey from Budapest, my mother asked Aunt Iza Rados what Mrs. Csomay's first name was. "Oh, that's easy. It's Kamilla," fibbed Aunt Iza. With that we took off. Midway, we stopped once more at the pharmacy and had a nice chat with Uncle Ernő. After we had changed clothing and as we were about to take our leave, my mother said, "Dear Ernő, please convey my greetings to Kamilla." Uncle Ernő turned around and shouted, "Jolanda, Jolanda, come on down. The Farkases are here." In an instant my mother realized she had been duped and felt a wave of embarrassment wash over her. But once we had left the pharmacy she laughed at her own gullibility and how she had fallen into Aunt Iza's skillfully prepared trap. (Kamilla is not just a female name in Hungarian, but also means chamomile, and chamomile tea was the equivalent in those days of chicken soup, a remedy for any ailment.)

After the war, during the era of my father's long journeys, partially on foot, commuting to and from the city, my mother and I used to eagerly await his arrival. On one occasion, my mother decided to spruce herself up for my father. She drew water, placing a large metal vat on the edge of the well. Normally this vat was used for preserving; jars filled with compotes or jams were placed inside it in boiling water. As my mother was filling the container, it tilted and fell off the edge of the well. One of its metal corners landed on my mother's foot. Blood, bruises, and an unsightly bandage were the result. She couldn't even wear a shoe.

Minutes later, her next mishap was a fall; this gave her a black eye. She was beginning to resemble a champion boxer after a fight. As if all of this wasn't enough, when she went to wash her hair, it stuck together in an indivisible mess. She didn't have any shampoo, and her fine silken blond hair had a tendency to get knotty. Looking in the mirror at her crazed hair, she said laughing "This is how a loving wife ends up when she tries to pretty herself for her husband."

Even in the most somber and worst of times one can find humor. Winston Churchill, in his multivolume history of the Second World War, describes one such episode. Once, after the all-clear siren sounded, he went out into the city to survey the damage of the air raid. The façade of one apartment building had fallen down, leaving the inside of the house visible from the street. It was like a dollhouse. High up on the edge of a crumbled wall stood a man laughing hysterically. Churchill and his assistants surmised that the man who stood there looking into the abyss had gone mad. But they soon found out that this was not the case. The man had been sitting on the toilet when the bombs began to fall. At the precise moment when he pulled the chain to the water tank to flush the toilet, the wall in front of him fell down.

My parents had a good ear for humor in everyday life. This held true during the siege in the air raid shelter. While eating soup one afternoon, my father asked what had happened to the croutons (in the size and shape of dice). My mother replied, "The die has been cast." Another time Aunt Hansi went outside to scrub the chamber pot clean in a bomb crater in the center of the street. Coming back, she tripped on the stairs, and broke the pot. My mother comfortingly said, "Well, at least it was clean when it broke." One other morning at the height of the siege, Aunt Hansi put on a pair of brand new snowshoes that for years she had been saving "for better days." My father couldn't help but remark, "The better days must have arrived."

My father had perfect pitch. He could hear and see the humor in every event. He observed the different tenants of the air raid shelter, and enjoyed the absurdity and spiritual panorama that resulted from the random social mix of the people enclosed together. It was this humor that enabled us to get through the various adversities of the siege.

In the fall of 1944, a weekly satirical magazine was published entitled *Pesti Pósta* (*Pest Post*). Its publisher was Stephen Pesthy, a dentist. The magazine survived for nine issues, from August 20 until November 10, which was remarkable considering its tone. With biting sarcasm it highlighted the utter stupidity of the Arrow Cross Party, which did not realize right away that the magazine's jokes were frequently at its expense. On the front page of the September 1 issue was a drawing of Ferenc Szálasi, the self-proclaimed leader of the Arrow Cross Party, with his upper body facing the reader and his hips and legs walking in the opposite direction. The caption read, "Szálasi's coming as if he's already going." Of course, this was not what happened, and the jubilation of *Pesti Pósta* was unfortunately premature. Mocking the Arrow Cross' persecution of the Jews, a line at the bottom of the same page read, "Just try to place a Jewish advertisement here."

In those days, Szálasi's position was precarious. Horthy was still in power, and Szálasi was hated by the Horthy establishment and despised even by some segments of the right wing. Szálasi was in the protective custody of the Germans, who treated him as a standby for use in case of an orchestrated takeover of the government. Even the Germans considered him a last resort, since they too knew that he was some kind of a nutcase.

Another issue of *Pesti Pósta* included two drawings side by side. On the left was the face of the French premier Clemenceau, who went by the nickname "the Tiger." He was considered an archenemy of the Hungarians for presiding over the 1919 Treaty of Trianon that dispossessed Hungary of two-thirds of her prewar territory. The caption beneath his picture read "Tiger 1919." The picture on the right depicted a German Tiger tank. The caption read "Tiger 1944."

In the next issue, a drawing appeared with a map of Hungary resembling an apple tree, with the rivers of the Danube and the Tisza serving as branches of the tree. At the point where Budapest would have been, an apple hung from a branch. At the base of the tree were two farmers pulling back and forth on a whipsaw and a passerby. "Tell me brothers," the onlooker says, "Does it make sense to chop down the whole tree just for that one apple?" The defense of the capital would indeed result in the entire country's destruction.

After the fifteenth of October a new government was formed, comprising members of the Arrow Cross and other radical right-wing supporters of the Germans. At the new government's first meeting, the ministers were photographed by the press. The photo revealed a dreadful group of morons. It might as well have been taken straight out of a gangster movie or a police lineup. When the next issue of *Pesti Pósta* appeared, its headline read, "Sometimes even a photographer is a caricaturist." This caption's allusion also apparently surpassed the mental capacity of the Arrow Cross.

The last issue of *Pesti Pósta* came out while the battle between the Russians and Germans raged between the Tisza and Duna Rivers. Now that most of the Hungarian plain had been overtaken by the Russians, it was only a matter of time before the capital would be encircled. The front page of the last issue of the journal depicted a motorcycle with a sidecar attached. A passenger seated inside it is shouting, "Watch out, Malvin! Sharp curve ahead!" And so it was.

This became an idiomatic expression, a part of the country's daily lingo. Even for the Arrow Cross regime this was too much. It finally woke up and ordered the paper's closure. After the war, *Pesti Pósta* reappeared under a new name, *Szabad Száj* (*Free Voice*). It was just as short-lived as its predecessor, only this time it was the Communist regime that banned it.

26

The Siege of Budapest
and the End of Nazism

My father began his diary on Christmas Eve, 1944. He knew that if the Germans intended to defend the city the siege would take weeks, and it would make sense to jot down daily events. But he didn't anticipate such a lengthy struggle, ending only on February 12, 1945, when the Swastikas and Arrow Crosses were replaced with the red star. He continued writing his diary during the Russian occupation, making his last regular entry on Christmas Day, 1945.

Our home was still cozy and warm, and we still had electricity. We had a decent meal, finished off with an espresso coffee, the aroma of which lured Aunt Hansi to our dining room within minutes. This was our last such gathering in the apartment house on Logodi Street.

On December 24, 1944, Budapest Radio stopped broadcasting. The city's military commandant called the studio and was outraged. "The situation is not at all so bad that you people would need to stop broadcasting." By that afternoon a group of Russian tanks were already at St. John's Hospital and Pasarét (Pasha's Meadow).

My father got a ride home from the studio before the curfew began. By Zerge Stairs, a shell hit the wall above his head. He fell and lost his silver cigarette case. He was covered with white dust when he entered the apartment.

Ilonka, our cook, was still with us. She prepared a fine evening meal just like in the old days. Grandmother Eveline stayed overnight. Blanka went home after dinner. Almost everything was still normal; the blackout was enforced, but inside, bright light made everything cheerful. My father tried to get the BBC on Uncle Bela's large Orion Radio. On the radio we heard, "The Russians took Vác." This meant

249

they had very likely taken Veresegyház too, and that people there would now at last be able to breathe easier. This, at least, is what my father thought.

I don't remember giving or receiving Christmas presents. My father always bought books for everyone. My mother was so modest, I'm sure she didn't desire to receive anything. As far as my mother's gift giving went, I was an exception. My mother had been working on a triptych during the previous winter but had been too busy to finish it. The center piece depicted Saint Columba, our famous ancestor, sitting in a church in a white monk's robe, a blue sash around his waist, a halo above his head, and a dove resting on the halo. Before him on a stand is a Bible, and a pen is in his hand. The side panels showed scenes from his life; their corners were decorated with flying angels.

For me, this was a complete surprise. When I turned the altarpiece over, I saw an inscription: "To Károly Farkas, painted by his mother Rosa Dabis and completed by his aunt, Blanka Dabis, for Christmas 1944." According to my mother, at my baptism I had been wrapped in the altar cloth of St. Columba. Uncle Rory, who was my godfather, loaned the sacred relic with some slight trepidation for the solemn occasion.

St. Columba altarpiece triptych

This was the last Christmas on Logodi Street. What followed were the pale, ghostly visitations of a sunken, vanished world. But for now a long siege was still before us, and everybody tried to hunker down in a place they deemed most conducive to surviving the storm.

For me, a young man of nineteen, the siege was a great adventure. Fear of the Arrow Cross could not diminish my exhilaration at being a witness to historic events. It wasn't as if the aerial bombardment wasn't scary, but I enjoyed the siege as a social event and a piece of military history. I could imagine that I was a reporter in disguise for a world-famous paper. And because I was constantly with my family—my father, my mother, Aunt Blanka, and our cook, Ilonka—unlike routine daily life prior to the siege, it meant an ever-present social hour. In addition, I felt empowered and useful, since without me not one nail would have been hammered into place when things fell into disrepair. And if a task was beyond my personal ability, I could mobilize our neighbors and my newfound friends the Béres siblings—first and foremost Béla, nicknamed Buci; then Mátyás, the deserter (Matyi for short) ; Vili, the fussy and pompous one; and Ottó, whom I knew from college and who had introduced me to the whole clan.

Ottó and I bonded over a joint escape from House No. 8, where the Béreses were residing. I happened to be visiting them when the Arrow Cross raided, looking for deserters. Someone must have informed them that the shelter's inhabitants included a group of young men. Luckily, the shelter had two entrances, so when the Archers came in at one end we were able to slip out the other. Thus, Ottó, Matyi, Ferenc the watchmaker's apprentice, Buci, and I escaped and hid in the empty Beres house, which was about six or seven houses away from No. 8. We only returned when we were sure the coast was clear. We had much to fear, since according to the placards posted on billboards all over the city, every young man should have been either in the army or in a labor battalion.

It was inconsequential what time I got up each morning. I didn't have to attend classes, nor did I have to go to an office. It was like an extended vacation. I could sleep as long as I could stand being without tea. I could go to bed whenever, however late I felt like it. I had plenty of time to read. Down in the cellar, it was warm and relatively cozy, aside from the days when we were desperately trying to get rid of the smoke from incendiary bombs or fumes that occasionally seeped in from the street. Every now and again I went out foraging, roaming around, with the Béres boys. Automobile tires and tools began to pile up in the ground floor apartment. I rescued a 350cc Puch motorcycle by dragging it out of a barricade with the help of the Béres boys.

In retrospect, I daresay that the siege was the best time of my life and also the worst time of my life. When I tell my friends this, they either want to beat me up or call me crazy. Yet for me, the siege was the greatest event in which I was a spectator, participant, and beneficiary. Of course, it helped that at the time I was only nineteen years old and largely free of any real responsibilities.

For a while after the siege ended my father didn't dare to venture out onto the street, but there wasn't much cause to do so anyway. The bridges had been blown up and people who did go outside were kidnapped off the streets by the Russians. Some women took the risk of going to the bakery for bread or to fetch some water.

In March, we moved back upstairs into our apartment, which was in shambles. It had been greatly damaged, but we had one room that was relatively unharmed and that we could heat. There, during his self-imposed exile, my father began to write the first few chapters of a novel about the siege. Later, after he returned to the Radio, he continued writing, but only sporadically, until his forced retirement in 1947. By devoting most of his ensuing free time at Veresegyház to the novel he was able to finish it the following year.

But at Christmas 1944, the events of the siege still lay ahead of us. Soon incoming artillery fire and the constant activity of airplanes would chase us down into the basement. I managed to break my nose while we moved odds and ends into the shelter. I had been carrying a large pot of boiling water when I lost my footing on the stairs. It didn't help that from our door you had to take a spiral staircase to get to the floor below. This staircase was about the same size as the one in Donegal Castle in Ireland or in the Cathedral of Esztergom in Hungary. Feeling myself start to slip, I thrust the pot forward to avoid scalding myself, and ended up hitting my nose into the wall. Breaking my nose marked the beginning of the siege of Budapest, and as it turned out would mark the end of it as well.

After the war, in 1945, my father sent me to do an interview. He was working at the belles-lettres department and wanted to write a eulogy in memoriam to his good friend, Artur Elek, who committed suicide in April 1944. Since my father needed more information about the circumstances of Uncle Artur's death, I was to find out more details, such as the make of the revolver that he used.

I went to his former apartment on Mátrai Street where a young lady, a relative of Uncle Artur's, was lodging. She invited me into the dining room. There, seated at the table, I began to ask questions and take notes. In the midst of my interview, darkness fell. A storm broke out. The wind swept through the dilapidated apartment with such force that the door behind me was pulled off its hinges and fell on my head, knocking my nose against the table. Thus was my poor nose broken for the second time, but broken nose notwithstanding, I spent another half-hour there to finish the interview.

At the onset of the siege for a time my father and I defied danger and stayed in our fourth-floor apartment, even though the rest of the family had already moved down to the shelter in the basement. My father's philosophy was that he would rather face the greater dangers and not be inconvenienced by small nuisances than live in relative safety but be exposed to a multitude of small aggravations. Thus, for a few more days, we held out in our windy tower room, until the morning when an artillery shot knocked us out of our beds. Aunt Hansi, whose bedroom was directly beneath ours, met the same fate. The hit bored an enormous hole in the wall of the house. Thereafter, we hastily joined the others in the cellar. But before long, my father's concern for comfort won out again over safety, and he was bivouacking in luxury on the superintendent's couch on the ground floor. He spent his nights there. Only the most vehement artillery fire and aerial bombing would force him below ground. In the cellar, a cot was fabricated for him on top of piles of coal and firewood.

I was the only young man in the house. Whenever an emergency arose, such as when the air pressure from a bomb blast ripped out the blackout curtains, I would be summoned to make the repairs. When the chimney was blocked, again it was me to whom everyone looked for help. But since this task surpassed my abilities, I turned to the Béres boys for help. Their father was a well-known stove maker, so I figured they would surely know what to do.

Jumbó Csongrády's auxiliary outfit was called into action when an artillery shell hit a crowd of people standing in line for water at a school in the Krisztina District. After the explosion there were about fifty dead and wounded. At the First Aid shelter there were no gloves, surgical hats, pain killers, or dressing material. Jumbó proudly showed me how a stationary bicycle served as a source of light for the operating table. While someone pedaled away, a dynamo bicycle lamp generated electricity, and a mirror projected the light. It is very likely that they got the idea for this improvisation from the movie *Young Tom Edison*, where Mickey Rooney, as Edison, collected kerosene lamps from throughout his parents' house and put a mirror behind them to reflect the light onto the table where his mother was being operated on.

Each day was somewhat different. One day, Mrs. Szedlacsek, one of the new tenants in our building, who had occupied the Töröks' apartment (when the Baron and his wife left the city), remarked, "We have had a noisy day, haven't we?" About fifty bombs had fallen in our neighborhood that day from the morning until four in the afternoon. One had landed in Aunt Hansi's bed. Uncle Rory kept nagging my father to move the bomb out of his wife's bed, and my father, having no better idea of how to take care of this, informed me that it was my job to get rid of the bomb. I vehemently protested the idea of carrying this unexploded behemoth down the stairs on my shoulder, but my father was adamant. When I pointed out that it might explode on my shoulder, he calmly responded, "Don't worry. By then you will feel absolutely nothing." With that, the argument was closed and I carried this one-hundred pound pig-like monster down to the street, where Buci and Ottó lifted it off my shoulder and placed it on the ground. The three of us gave it a push and sent it rolling down onto the neighboring tennis court. While all this was taking place, my father strolled behind us watching the action and smoking his cigarette with philosophical aplomb.

One of our unexpected daily nuisances reminded me of Rudolf Erich Raspe's *The Adventures of Baron Munchausen*. In one part of the novel, as a stagecoach arrives the coachman attempts to sound his trumpet, but, due to the cruel cold, the sound freezes. Thereupon the coachman brings the horn into the inn and places it next to the fireplace. Once the trumpet warms up, it sounds off merrily by itself. I had a somewhat similar experience when Jumbó Csongrády visited my family and he, my father, and I went up from the air raid shelter into my family's apartment for a chat. I was yearning to hear and to play for Jumbó my latest acquisition, a record of Gershwin's, "The Man I Love." I dragged the phonograph out from beneath the couch. There in the windowless room, in the middle of January, I put the record on the turntable, but no sound came out of my good old Radiola phonograph. I took the head of the record player off, warmed it in the palm of my hand, and, lo and behold, when I put it back in its place music poured out. We sat around listening to the music and chatting, well nigh oblivious to the bitter cold.

Our life in the air raid shelter, which was definitely not meant for the purpose that the name implied, but rather for the storage of coal and firewood, linked us up with new acquaintances. The social atmosphere lent itself to the establishment of a warm friendship between my family and Péter Váczy, a university professor who had ended up in our shelter by default. He taught history at Péter Pázmány University. As it happened, he had been the guest of two of our neighbors in the building, the Torday Molnár siblings, for Christmas dinner. That afternoon the Russians unexpectedly charged into Buda with a few tanks, reaching as far as St. John's Hospital. The streetcars had stopped running, so after dinner the professor set out on foot for his home in Pasarét (Pasha's Meadow). On his way, he found himself in the middle of the firing line. German troops had gathered helter-skelter to try to push the Russians back. At that point, Dr. Váczy turned back and returned to the Torday Molnár's, where he stayed as a temporary houseguest until February 14, when the siege ended.

Péter Váczy made our life in the cellar more colorful and entertaining. When the siege was over, he presented me with a small German children's picture book about cars, called *Das Autobuch*. He had dedicated it to me: "To Károly the Lionhearted. With love during the eight weeks of the siege. 1945, February 12, Péter Váczy"

While foraging with the Béres boys I collected booty in a spiritual sense, as well as a material one. In the latter half of January, we met a gentleman who lived in the same house in which Uncle Albert Gyergyai had previously lived. Not knowing his real name, we referred to him more formally by his profession, "Mr. Teacher." He was a stocky young fellow and wore a blue steel helmet and an armband with a red cross on it. His building was at the opposite end of Zerge Stairs. For a time, the bodies of two Hungarian infantrymen lay before the building's entrance on the sidewalk. The professor collected their identification papers, made a wooden cross, and fastened the names of the fallen men onto the cross. The earth was frozen, it was excruciatingly cold, and digging a grave had to be postponed.

Much earlier, the Béres boys and I had dug a grave for two young girls, about seventeen and eighteen years old, who had been killed by an artillery shell while queuing for water. One of them had been decapitated. After hearing about the tragedy, we brought the bodies up from Krisztina District to Logodi Street on a stretcher. There, we proceeded to dig a grave in the garden. The ground was as hard as rock, and we sweated in spite of the cold. The girls lay inside the house in the company of their sobbing, heartbroken mother. In an adjoining room, a carpenter built two coffins out of dresser drawers.

One day, I struck up a conversation with the math teacher who lived on the other side of the Zerge Stairs, whom we referred to as Mr. Teacher. I mentioned that my family's cellar was running out of candles. On an impulse, he suggested that the two of us search for kerosene near the Déli Pályaudvar (Southern Railway Station), roughly a thirty-minute walk in normal times. Before we set out on our foraging expedition, the teacher's pretty wife knelt down on a hassock and said a short prayer for our safety and success.

We headed off in the direction of Márvány Street (Marble Street). At its entrance, in front of Erzsébet Szilágyi Girls' High School, was a sizable group of Hungarian soldiers. Behind them a bunch of white parachutes lay in a pile, making my mouth water. So far, we only had red parachutes in our possession. White ones would be suitable for shirts. I made a feeble attempt to purloin one of the parachutes, but unfortunately these soldiers seemed to have been positioned there specifically to guard the parachutes, so it didn't work.

On Márvány Street, we peered into a courtyard and saw a long line of gasoline cans. I picked up an empty one and began adding to it any gasoline that I could find sloshing around in the bottoms of the other ones. By the time we had decanted the remainders, we had a Jerry can full of gasoline. Just as we had finished draining the last can, a German guard approached from the outside. With a simple, "Danke schön," he took the can of gasoline out of my hands and left. I could have exploded, but instead I grabbed a couple of empty cans and Mr. Teacher and I took off with them. We reached the bridge on Márvány Street and trudged along on the side of an embankment. A Hungarian infantryman passed us by, running down the center of the road. He was fully armed; he carried a machine gun and had handgrenades strapped to his belt. He was running as if he were under fire or partaking in a military drill, falling flat on his stomach every forty or fifty steps. The two of us looked after him perplexed.

When we reached Pálya Street (Railroad Street), we descended down the embankment. On the railroad tracks stood a tanker car full of kerosene. We went into the office depot looking for someone to whom to show our allocation paper, signed by Mr. Vaszkó, the air raid warden for our block. Nobody was there, though, besides a Russian POW who was busily sweeping the corridor. We went back to the tank wagon and turned on the faucet. Kerosene spilled forth in a wide stream. By the time our containers were full we were standing in a pool of it.

As we were heading home, a staccato burst of machine-gun bullets chased our heels. We climbed over ruins and tried to take cover under hanging balconies, collapsed balustrades, leaning walls, and hastily erected barricades. This eventually successful expedition made it possible for us to have some light in the dark evenings and for my father to continue writing his diary. My mother sent three bottles of kerosene over to Mr. Vaszkó. I was livid at her practicing charity at my expense. Earlier, when Mr. Vaszkó had asked for a volunteer to fetch kerosene, an air force officer who bivouacked in his cellar grumbled, "There's no amount of gold that would make me go out into that hell."

Most of the time I went on my excursions with the Béres boys, and we all agreed to share our booty. Our plundering was directed at the German and Hungarian armed forces. When all four Béres boys, Buci, Matyi, Vili, and Ottó, came, they were entitled to four parts while I took one-fifth of the finds. We collected with an eye to the future. The Béres boys looked for truck parts, so that they could replace their truck that had been destroyed by a bomb in the courtyard. I, collected truck and automobile tires and inner tubes. The 350cc Puch motorcycle landed in Mrs. Böttkös's kitchen. Later, I was able to sell it to Mr. Vass and Mr. Halász, who had served as my bicycle mechanics. They also bought my tires and inner tubes.

At the end of January, we went foraging on Lovas Avenue (Horseman Avenue), which was behind the Béres family's one-story house. It was a bit scary, because a group of Archers trudged right by us, headed in the direction of the Royal Castle. On Lovas Avenue, we discovered a beautiful automobile tire. We could only see a small section of it, since most of it was pinned under a collapsed wall. The Béres boys conjured up a few crowbars and we got to work. With superhuman effort and determination, we dragged away the crumbled stone wall and freed the tire. Then to our despair, we saw that the section that had lain beneath the rubble had been shot to pieces. On the other side of the street, a German guard, observing our deflation, could hardly hide his mirth.

On Logodi Street, between Mikó Street and the Zerge Stairs we found a decrepit bus. We skinned the seats and took out a few glass windowpanes. (Later, it turned out that the seats were not made of real leather and the glass panes were useless as civilian windows.) The bus could have exploded at any minute because it was jam packed with hand grenades in wooden boxes. Thus, we risked our lives for useless objects.

German cavalry units had lodged their horses in shops, including the August Konditorei. These unhappy creatures, now abandoned by their owners, were to us an emergency food supply. There was no fodder for them, and so they perished either from starvation or from incoming artillery shells. Each time one of the horses expired the news spread like wildfire, and people would scurry over from all directions with butcher knives and washbasins. Then the carving would commence in earnest. I extricated a bottle labeled with the red letter "E" for *eper* (strawberry) from under the hooves of the horses standing in the store window. Later, I presented the find to my mother. It was a condensed fruit syrup meant for making ice cream. After the siege, my mother went to a hospital and gave it to a nurse to share among the children.

The next major feat took place when we noticed a fire in the Putsay's bakery behind our house. The distraction of the fire gave us an opportunity to drag a few sacks of flour out from beneath the flaming and collapsing roof of the workshop. Some of us pulled away sacks; others helped with pickaxes to extinguish the fire while Mr. Béres and my father tried to divert the attention of the Germans. We hauled these sacks to our house's light shaft, where Gyuszi the paramedic lifted them up and placed them in our washhouse. From there, we carried all but one of them over to the Béres's shelter. After the siege we realized that our sack was the one sack that contained not flour for baking but rather the swept-up residue from the bakery floor. It looked like the real thing, and my mother was able to exchange two pounds of it at a bakery for one pound of bread. She went to a different bakery every time just in case her "dirty deed" should be discovered, which of course meant that she had to go farther and farther away every time. But at least we were able to have a few decent loaves of bread when it was hard to come by even one.

Next, Ilonka, our cook, and I ventured out to an empty lot where soldiers' uniforms were scattered about helter-skelter. We collected a load of them and planned to use them to make clothes after the siege. We were unaware that they were infested with lice. Thus began the war on lice. Soon they would be all around the cellar, and since soap and water were scarce, it took a good while to get rid of them.

Mr. Holéczy had a drug store on Atilla Street that had collapsed. I collected a number of items like toothpaste and soap from what remained of the store and carried them home in a blanket. My father took an inventory and priced the items, with the intention of reimbursing the owner after the war.

The eighth of January was Judit Rados' seventeenth birthday. I decided to go visit her and wish her a happy birthday. Aside from the interlude during the early summer of 1944 when I was infatuated with Éva Szinyei Merse, I steadily harbored strong feelings toward Judit. Thus, on the morning of the Epiphany, a rare event occurred: I shaved. I got ready while murmuring pious psalms. I put on a clean shirt and lowered a small gift into my pocket. My family members watched me suspiciously and when they learned of my intention to leave—on a long, dangerous trip, almost to the other end of the city—they pounced on me in an effort to persuade me not to do so. I had made up my mind, however, that I was going to visit Judit, and there was no turning back.

The journey turned out to be a veritable joyride, as I bicycled my way through the labyrinth of the city. Even before I had mounted my prancing little charger, I felt rejuvenated and exalted to be able to get away from the previous days' tension, pressure, and work, and to escape from the dark pit of the cellar. My muscles began to work; my lungs filled with air. High above, the sky was dove-gray, snow enveloped the landscape, and my escort was the fanfare of Russian rockets. These trumpets of triumph blew a chord in quintet, celebrating the holiday, and the modern salute of the Russians added relish to my joy. It was beautiful and uplifting to be free again.

Within minutes, I had left behind the familiar cobblestones of the Krisztina District, skirting the corpses of horses, overturned automobiles, bombshell craters, stiffly dreaming soldiers lying at the base of a crumbling wall, and dead civilians. Soon I was on the Elizabeth

Bridge. I felt as though the bridge's tall, slender arms were waving to me, and then embracing me high above the Danube. I rode with the wind behind me. Rákóczy Street, St. Rókus Hospital, and Baross Place rose into view as if in a fairy tale where a sunken city emerges out of the depths of the sea before one's eyes. The city of my ancestors, with its bleeding stones, stones resonating with a metallic ring, saluted me—their prodigal son.

On the righthand side of the street by the rubber factory, German and Russian tanks were firing at each other. I turned into a side street to avoid the square. From there, I paused briefly to watch the hullabaloo. I reached Aréna Avenue; Stefánia and Hermina Avenues were now only a stone's throw away. The area had received an intensive thrashing. The houses were in ruins, yet the din of battle went on. At times, steel and stones showered the streets like an April storm. At the corner of Gizella and Thököly Avenues stood Judit's house; behind it ran the Circuit Railroad, the line of defense for the German and Hungarian forces.

I looked for the familiar doorway, but couldn't find it. I circled around the building; there had to be an opening somewhere. Sure enough, my hawk eyes discovered a side entrance. I entered the courtyard, left my bicycle there, and went to the basement door. I knocked.

My unexpected visit made for much amazement and surprise. These first reactions were followed by an outburst of joy. As for Judit, it was a pity she couldn't have seen herself. She stood in a polka-dot apron, a kerchief over her head, holding a large, steaming pot in her hands. Her eyes, blue like forget-me-nots at dawn when the bell first tolls, enlarged and darkened. The pot of soup began to tremble in her hands. She quickly put it down on a white chest. At last, a smile dimpled at the corners of her mouth as she accepted my greetings with grace.

Her brother Laci was not his usual suntanned gladiator self, slashing about, but a pale motionless invalid with a high fever. Seeing him refuse chicken soup, I realized that he must be very sick. The meeting was short, like the sudden flash of a falling star on an August skyline. Judit looked at me. I searched my pockets, lifted out a brown sandalwood bracelet, and presented it to her. Her little red, heart-shaped mouth opened, "Oh, Oh." She smiled and blushed. She put it on and rattled the tiny bracelet.

Her mother, grandmother, and grandfather all began to speak at once. They talked of their misfortunes: the collapsing wall and the crushed windows. They pointed out the dangling iron traverses. They showed me the spot where Judit's aunt had stepped out of her room; a minute later, the whole room had sunk like a crazy elevator from the fourth floor to the ground level. They showed me where a shell had broken through the wall, just above their shelter. They were thankful that their pots and plates had been spared. As they spoke, a shooting contest was taking place. It resulted in the acquisition of two new gaps in the rear of the house.

Time—which Coleridge had once compared to two beautiful children, a boy and a girl racing each other (the girl was ahead and looking back; the poor boy, blind, set his feet at a given pace and never knew whether he was winning or losing)—was sometimes superfluous. I felt like I had just arrived only to already have to return home. Judit escorted me out. She went up the stairs, as if in a Debussy opera, stepping from step to step, somewhat stiffly. In the courtyard, with a graceful motion of her hand she pointed out the ugly scrapes on the walls of the house. She stopped in front of the side entrance door.

She begged me not to come again while the siege was on, but this I wouldn't promise. She left her hand in mine for perhaps a fraction of a second longer than necessary. I reached for my bike; she smiled like one who weeps. She looked like she was on the verge of speaking, but then the thought seemed to have slipped her mind. I told her not to worry. In the end, she never said a thing. She lifted up her small, dainty hand close to her face. She gave a farewell greeting at half-mast. It was accompanied by a calm murmur of waves in the shadows of her sea-blue eyes.

"See you soon. Take care . . ." she said faintly. Her words still resounded in my soul as I opened the wrought iron crossed-bar door of our old house at the foot of Castle Hill. My family had anxiously awaited my return.

This account of my journey freely quotes from my father's description of it in his novel *The Siege and the Besieged*. He described this jaunt in a more charming manner than I ever could have.

January went by in constant turmoil. My whole family, with the exception of my father, was under the impression that the siege would never end. It had become the steady state of affairs, and we wondered how much longer we would live this subterranean life before dying from hunger or bombing. By the time February came around, our depression had hit a low point.

As January departed, with every passing day the noose around the German forces got tighter. By now it had become impossible to resupply the German troops with air drops, since even their last "airfield," Vérmező (Blood Meadow), was under fire. Air-dropped parachutes swung in the night sky, while searchlights' crisscrossing rays tried to catch the plane. Then the packages would land in places that were already in Russian hands.

One evening we ventured out to see the spectacular fireworks, the red tracer bullets, and the landing of a container in a bomb crater next to Zerge Stairs. A German soldier ran down to the pit and had just begun to open the metal drum when an officer appeared at the edge of the crater with an escort and hollered down at the squatting soldier. The soldier ran up as fast as his feet would carry him and stood at attention. Tension was in the air. My impression was that our presence, the Béres boys and I, saved the life of this trooper. He could have easily been executed for attempting to plunder the unit's supplies. Some of these containers were filled with ammunition, others with food. In the last few days, many of the ammunition packages were left untouched; the defenders were no longer interested in anything they could not eat.

In our neighborhood there were a number of young men who were either deserters or shirkers, meaning they never showed up for service at all. Matyi Béres and his friend Nándi were among the former, while Ottó and I were two of the latter. The last warning placard on the street demanded that men between the ages of eighteen and forty-eight report for enlistment (fortunately, my father turned forty-nine on January 8, 1945). According to the billboards, deserters would be impaled on the spot. At this time, Buda was infected with despicable rabble like Pater Kun, who wore the cassock of a Catholic priest and an Arrow Cross armband. He led the Archers in hunting down fugitives and Jews in hiding. His henchmen were constantly on the lookout for absentees. I voiced my anxiety to my father about being caught and impaled. My best excuse, the fact that I was an employee of the Hangya Consortium, was rather flimsy. "Just stay put," said my father. "Don't go anywhere." "That's easy to say," I said, "but if the Archers catch me they'll kill me on the spot." "We'll figure out something then," said my father phlegmatically.

Toward the end of the siege, to mislead the Arrow Cross and Germans from a distance, I took to wearing a self-styled military uniform, a one-man military outfit. This consisted of a steel helmet, my father's First World War field-gray britches, my Boy Scout wind-breaker, and a belt whose buckle was engraved with the words *Gott mit Uns* (God be with Us). The difference between my buckle and the one worn by the Wehrmacht was the imperial crown on mine and the Swastika on theirs. On my feet, I had ski socks and ski boots. In my camouflage attire I became a sort of Walter Mitty (a fictional character with a vivid fantasy life in a James Thurber short story).

A couple of days after my first visit to Judit, I decided to pay her a second one. By then, I was biking practically across the center of the battle, and I was even more scared to be on the road than I had been the first time. Until January 11, the front line had matched up with the Hungarian Circular Thruway. In its close vicinity, the multistory apartment house of the Gunda-Zahár family still stood, but by now an entire corner of the building was missing. Amid all the rubble, finding the air raid shelter became difficult.

Once again, Judit's family was overjoyed to see me, but they begged me not to repeat the journey again. Laci, Judit's brother, still lay there feverish, battling pneumonia. As I took my leave, Judit escorted me to the top of the stairway. Just as I got to the street, a German Tiger Tank took a right-hand turn five steps from me and flattened a telephone booth into a pancake.

Until January 17, the Chain Bridge and the Elizabeth Bridge still stood, although they were heavily mined. These two remaining bridges served the German and Hungarian forces, allowing them to retreat to Buda in a panic-like headlong flight. On the night of the seventeenth, the flight across the bridges was an apocalyptic sight. The next morning, the bridges were detonated.

On my way home, I biked over to 12 Wekerle Sándor Street where the Kiska auxiliary outfit resided in the protected Swiss embassy building. I was let in by Szabi Viczián. Just as I arrived, the distribution of lunch began. In the courtyard, a long line of Jewish refugees, many of them fugitives from labor battalions, stood before a huge cauldron. They waited their turn for a mess tin of soup.

I had a scheme in mind that I proposed to Szabi. "Why don't you guys come over to Buda as a patrol," I said, "arrest me, and bring me back here." Szabi replied, with his imperturbable calm, "Look, you're already here. Why don't you just stay? Why should we take the risk of bumping into a group of Archers? To venture all the way out to Logodi Street could be the kiss of death for us." In my mind I had to admit that Szabi was right, yet I couldn't persuade myself to stay. I knew that on Logodi Street the tenants of our house were mostly old and helpless, and if I failed to return I would cause my parents agony, leaving them to speculate that I had fallen or had been captured by the Arrow Cross. Thus, with a heavy heart I said farewell to my good friends and went ahead on the last leg of my journey.

Before the German attempt in February to break out of the Russian encirclement, my main source of information was an SS sergeant named Graetz. He was a typically arrogant, indoctrinated Nazi. When I asked him what would happen if the German relief force didn't arrive, he replied, *"Das gibts nicht"* ("That will never happen").

On the night of the breakout, many Hungarian members of the SS whose families were ethnically German tried to obtain civilian clothes and desert the German forces. Thus, behind our house uniforms piled up in the big bomb crater. Many suspicious characters prowled the streets during those last few nights. My father ruefully discovered that several items were missing from his desk. These cat burglars were well aware that during the night apartment dwellers would be in the cellar so they had free rein to rummage through the empty rooms. Our house was easily accessible to them too, since the piled-up rubbish behind it yielded a direct path to the Torday Molnár's apartment. Next to it was the stairwell that led up to our apartment. We tried to create a barricade.

On the evening of the eleventh of February, the German attempt to break out began. At this point, the Hungarian and German troops were crowded into a small area consisting of the Tunnel, the Citadel, the Royal Castle, and parts of Krisztina District. The troops gathered for one final onslaught. Artillery fire originating from the Castle began in the early part of the evening; the last ammunition was being expended. A long line of German soldiers exited from the Castle through the Tunnel marching down Logodi Street toward Széll Kálmán Plaza. Soldiers carried *Panzerfausts* (bazookas), machine guns, and stretchers bearing their wounded comrades. Some of the soldiers were young boys, perhaps no older than fifteen or sixteen. Many of those walking by did so only with the assistance of others.

As the Germans passed, I stood at the entrance of our house, wearing my usual camouflage outfit designed to confuse the military police, the Archers, and similar hoodlums. But now I had to face the Germans. A lieutenant leading troops stopped and asked me, *"Von wo bist du?"* ("Where are you from?") Luckily, I had the presence of mind to blurt out, *"Von diesem Haus"* ("From this house"). It was a very tense moment. The German officer wouldn't have hesitated to execute a deserter. I presume my Hungarian accent came in handy. Right after this, I speedily went over to the Béres boys' house, seeking safety in numbers.

In the cacophony of the firefights, the burning buildings, the rattling of tanks, the purring of car motors, Ottó and I went over to the air raid shelter at 8 Attila Street. There, two solitary soldiers from a German SS cavalry outfit sat by the light of a single candle. They begged Ottó for civilian clothes so that they could escape to their village. They were Hungarians of Swabian origin, whose families lived in Swabian villages on the outskirts of Buda. Ottó told them the best he could do was to put civilian clothing on a truck that was parked in front of the Zerge Stairs. The mood in the cellar with the two Swabians was like being in a condemned cell. Although Ottó put the clothes on the truck, the two soldiers never dared to venture out onto the street to retrieve them.

I heard that on the following morning a Russian officer entered the courtyard of 8 Attila Street and spotted the two German soldiers. They told him that they were Hungarians. The officer asked, "Then what about your German uniforms?" On hearing their answer, he pulled out his gun and executed them on the spot.

The breakout was like a storm above our heads. Ottó took possession of a beautiful Mercedes with the help of his collection of ignition keys. He wanted to move it to safety, so he parked it on the corner of Attila and Roham Streets. But shortly thereafter, a tank came around the corner from the direction of Krisztina Square and crushed the car, breaking Ottó's heart. A crowd in the street quickly dispersed and some people began shouting, "The Russians are here." But the tanks lighting up Roham Street with their headlights were still German.

Mátyi Béres found a truck on Attila Street, put it in reverse, and backed it up the Zerge Stairs until he reached Logodi Street. There, he left the truck, as its proud new owner. In the morning, the Russians happily took possession of the truck, and Matyi didn't dare poke his nose near his find again.

The night of the breakout was like a grand finale in an opera house. People came and went, converging and marching in the midst of infernal noise. The sky was lit up by burning houses and by the headlights of cars and tanks, while searchlights crisscrossed the sky. The noise was the chaos of this last big effort and we knew it was all coming to an end. For me, this was the most fascinating night of my life.

On the twelfth of February, at around ten in the morning, the first Russian appeared. I was still wearing my semi-military outfit. On my finger I had an aluminum ring, in the center of which was inlaid an Iron Cross, a German military emblem. These rings had been given out during the First World War to those who had been willing to part with their gold wedding bands for the war effort. One of the Russians I encountered in the entrance hall of our house pointed at the ring and yelled that I was an SS. I had a hard time convincing him otherwise. Thereafter, I promptly removed the ring from my finger, hastily shaved off my beard, and shed my quasi-military garb.

From 9 Logodi Street came forth the Hungarian artillery unit that had been residing there. They lined up, and under light escort marched away in the direction of the tunnel. Only a few Russian soldiers guarded this sizable group; had some wanted to, they could have escaped.

The streets thronged with Russian soldiers, quite a few of whom were women. The whole scene, with the soldiers' diverse uniforms, faces, and races, gave the impression of a gigantic Persian marketplace, minus the market. Some of the soldiers used swords as walking sticks; others studied street maps like tourists. The residents of Krisztina District rubbed their eyes as they watched these descendants of Genghis Khan. Seeing them up close, we began to wonder how it was possible that they could have destroyed the most disciplined and formidable army in the world.

I heard about a scene that had taken place in Prague. One morning, the residents were greeted with a surprising sight in the main square. They looked out their windows to see a row of horse-drawn drays. On the carriages, female soldiers could be seen breastfeeding, and changing and dressing babies. There in the early morning was something resembling a maternity ward on wheels. The babies, which had been born during the long war, were apparently being transported from battlefield to battlefield.

Olasz Allée (Italian Allée) was covered with dead Germans. They had marched there without any armaments, hands raised, intending to surrender, but had been machine-gunned down. At the mouth of Ördögárok (Devil's Canal), the Germans emerged one by one, hoping to escape through this treacherous route, but as they climbed out of the canal they met the same fate as those marching on Olasz Allée. Despite the knowledge of their doom, they kept piling out, because there was no way to turn back. Each one was pushed forcefully ahead through the canal by the pressure of the marchers behind him. They were greeted by enfilade. Thus, this process went on until the last of the marchers "died with his boots on." Of course, at the tail end of the line a few soldiers stayed hidden in the canal, but in the end they too were rounded up. According to the statistics in a book by historian Péter Gosztonyi, only 785 Germans made it to the German lines.

There was house-to-house fighting on Széll Kálmán Square. Houses were burned down; their windowless hulks stared blindly at the square.

One morning, our cook, Ilonka, quite possibly saved my life. A soldier in Russian uniform came into our cellar. As it turned out, he was a Romanian. He shepherded me into the washhouse. Then he pulled out a grenade and told Ilonka—who was from Transylvania and fortunately spoke Romanian—that if I didn't promptly give him a wristwatch he would throw the grenade into the washhouse. Ilonka was able to explain to him that all of our wristwatches had already been taken by his comrades. This soldier may have been bluffing, but one can never be sure. So once again we were able to save our skins, and also the wristwatches that my mother had hidden inside balls of yarn in her sewing box, which she kept with her in our dreary dungeon.

In Mr. Török's second-story apartment the Russians found the baron's uniforms, medallions, and swords. This caused tremendous excitement. It gave the Russians the perfect excuse to continue their plundering, as it proved their point that the populace was either fascist, *Germansky*, or bourgeois. In their view, ownership of even a water closet qualified a person to be labeled as a bourgeois-capitalist. Whenever the marauding soldiers came upon a photograph of someone in uniform or a print depicting some historic personality, they vented their ire on the whole family.

It became my father's daily pastime to sit on a stool in the attic before a small hole in the half-moon tin window and watch the pillaging of the Russians in the house across the street. While I hammered away on the rafters and slipped tiles into the roof's latticework, he would entertain me with his comments on the progress of the looting: "Now they are scrutinizing the women's panties. They put their hands into the panties and turn them toward the sun to make sure that the buttocks are not worn out."

Downstairs, my mother could hardly shoo the loitering Russians away. They kept coming to look at my cherished Puch motorcycle, like bees buzzing around a jar of honey. But this motorcycle had no batteries and its tires were blown out. Thankfully, they finally left it alone. These soldiers were mesmerized by any mechanical gadgets. Some of them had never ridden a regular bicycle before and would continuously fall off as they tried to master riding on one. Others rummaged through the many decrepit automobiles.

One scavenger pulled my father's precious Waterman fountain pen out of his breast pocket, but my father, with a marvelous presence of mind, made a swap with him, giving him Aunt Blanka's old, useless Montblanc fountain pen in exchange.

One morning, two soldiers were walking on Logodi Street, seemingly in a heated debate. My father followed them at a distance, out of sheer curiosity. The soldiers were pushing and shoving each other, and somehow a large pack of cigarettes fell out of one of their pockets. On that day my father was the happiest man in all of Buda. He was constantly short of cigarettes, so this was a Godsend, one that he shared with Aunt Blanka. After this pack was gone, he sliced up some of my grandfather's old cigars and manufactured his own cigarettes.

Simultaneous with the robberies, the chase for women began. The nights were soon filled with shouts of "*patrul, patrul*" to get the attention of the Russian Military Police, but often to no avail. Later, other noises were employed, such as ringing cowbells or hitting pots and pans, but also usually to no effect. Occasionally a patrol arrived, but after chasing away the soldiers they would finish the job themselves.

At this time I was unaware of the fact that women were being raped. Soon, however, it happened in our shelter, an episode after which the younger women in our cellar were dispersed to safer shelters. The men of the house built a brick barricade to block the main entrance.

My father, with his bushy eyebrows, long black beard, and an angry face, must have approximated in his looks a Russian orthodox priest—a so-called "Popa"—which at times may have worked in his favor. On the night that the rape took place in our cellar, my father did his utmost to protect his women. He covered up the three of them, buried my mother under him, shoved Blanka behind him, and put his feet on Ilonka, who was lying on the ground. She was whimpering and begging my father not to let her be dragged away. My father explained to the leader of the incoming gang that any woman dragged away would only be taken over his dead body. It was a risky stance, since Bishop Apor at Győr had tried to do the same with a group of young girls who were hidden in his palace. He, however, was shot on the spot.

The Russians finally turned their attention to Mrs. Szedlacsek. Since Mr. Szedlacsek didn't dare stand up to the Russians it was his wife who ended up being gang-raped.

Violating a woman in our society was an unforgivable crime, the shame of which was shared by the family of the victim. There is a large oil painting by Mihály Munkácsy titled *Dobozi Mihály megöli hitvesét* (Mihály Dobozi kills his wife). The scene depicts a man fleeing from the Turks, with his sword raised to kill his wife. He does this to prevent her from being violated.

We inhabitants of the house were repulsed by Szedlacsek's cowardice. I believe that my father thought that if one didn't try to save their spouse, their own life would not be worth living. After this incident, we kept a distance between ourselves and Mr. Szedlacsek. Soon thereafter, he and his wife moved out of the house, and we heard that Mrs. Szedlacsek began to experience morning sickness.

Pali Viczián on Lónyay Street built a wall in the cellar out of firewood and hid a young relative named Judit Bolgár, who was seventeen at the time, behind it. The girl was safe from Russian brutalities, but she had to stay for quite a while behind that barricade—like a prisoner. Uncle Pali, like a prison guard, would empty a pail every day and hand food across an opening in the wall that would promptly be closed after each exchange.

Aunt Iza Rados went to the headquarters of the Russian general staff during the siege to protest. They politely heard her out, but that was it. Afterward, Aunt Iza told us how intrigued she had been by a large city map hanging on the wall of the headquarters. Little flags demarcated the firing lines; the positions of the German and Russian forces were mapped out street by street.

A good friend of mine, Márta Visky, was seventeen years old at the end of the siege when she was crossing the Danube from Buda to Pest. She ran into a group of loitering Russian soldiers who grabbed her and raped her on the spot. Bystanders hiding nearby counted about eighty Russian soldiers. Márta had to be rushed from the scene to a hospital, bleeding heavily. Her life hung by a thread for three months.

People soon came to the conclusion that artillery fire and aerial bombardment were more bearable than this violence against women. Then, at least a person's dignity was not involved. Jews who had returned from camps and captivity didn't fare any better. In their everyday conversations, the Russians frequently made derogatory remarks about Jews. Even people who were adamantly anti-Nazi and the most eager to greet the incoming Red soldiers, like Pál Pátzay, the famous sculptor, or Péter Váczy, having witnessed their sheer brutality remarked, "This was not how we envisioned things for ourselves."

In the following weeks the Russians began to round up civilians, snatching them off the streets of Pest and later from Buda as well. One of those caught this way was Tamás Csink. When the Russians scrutinized his papers, they saw the appellation "Dr." before his name, deduced that he must be a medical doctor, and ordered him to line up with other captured doctors. To no avail, he tried to explain that he was not a medical doctor but an economist with a Ph.D. The Russians would not listen. He was now forced to participate in medical operations, flanked by real surgeons. In 1948, when he returned from Russian captivity, his brother Loránt Csink, who happened to be the chief medical doctor at Miskolc Hospital, pleaded with him to enroll in medical school. But Tomi's reply was, "Having done hundreds of complicated operations, I can't imagine sitting on a bench studying the basics of medicine."

During these turbulent days, the Russians kidnapped a real doctor wearing a Red Cross armband as he was on his way to see a patient. He was told that he was needed for "*malinki robot*," just one little job—to drive hundreds of cattle down to the Black Sea. There weren't enough cowboys, so the doctor was forced to join in; a few soldiers went along as guards. So there he went, shepherding the herd to the sea. Once the herd had reached its destination, he was told that he was free to go home, so he made the same trip back on foot all over again, all the way to Budapest.

Gödöllő, to the north of Budapest, became a collection point for those kidnapped off the streets. There, the long cattle trains were packed with civilians that had been rounded up, including women. They were all sent to Russian camps. To venture out onto the street alone at night was a very dangerous undertaking. Stripping civilians of their clothes during the night—a new level of robbery due to the extreme shortage of clothing after the war—became the order of the day. There was always at least one group of hooligans on the lookout for any solitary person. They would grab anyone found on the street alone and rob them of their clothing. However, this activity was not the exclusive sport of the Russians; Hungarian hoodlums turned out to be good students. A contemporary joke told of an incident in which a poor resident is running toward a police officer in his underwear and shouting, "Officer! Officer! The Belgians took the clothes off my back!" "The Belgians? The Belgians?" asks the officer doubtfully. "Are you sure they weren't Russians?" "You said it. You said it—not I," responded the frazzled victim.

On the eighteenth of February, a Sunday afternoon, Gyuri Sághy came to visit. He looked like a dapper English gentleman, with a silk tie and well-creased pants. It made for a stunning contrast as he trudged across the remains of the battlefield, scattered with fallen German soldiers. We listened to his stories with bated breath, and dubbed him the Hungarian Rhett Butler.

Due to the constant fear of being picked up off of the street, my parents and I tried to stay in the house and not venture out unless we were going for water or to the bakery. In the midst of our involuntary incarceration, our fountainhead of stories was Gyuri, who moved around fearlessly. He had already visited Éva Szinyei Merse, who had become a housekeeper and cook for the British Military Mission, which at that time was located in the Italian Embassy. Gyuri had checked in on my father's office at the radio studio on Sándor Street and found it intact, miraculously having escaped the damage of the siege. But he also had a sad story to tell us about our friend Jumbó Csongrády's family. A few days before the siege ended, Mrs. Csongrády was looking out the window when a stray bullet hit her, killing her instantly. At the very same moment, Mária, Jumbó's sister, was out in the building's courtyard feeding their little puppy when a bullet penetrated her heart. A few days later, Jumbó came by, and we expressed our sorrow and condolences.

The constant fear of the Russians forced my mother to seek temporary refugee at the Kollár's. Since Pali Kollár was a British subject, they lived in relatively safe circumstances. Their house, at the beginning of the occupation, was a good safe haven for some of their friends. They had a heated room and were not harassed by the Russians. My father visited the Kollár family with a pail in hand as if he were a laborer, although even that camouflage wasn't sure-fire protection against abduction. When the concierge saw him, he remarked that his brother-in-law had also carried a pail and spade with him when he ventured onto the street, and they hadn't seen him for several days.

By now, my father had long ago left behind the physique he had had while serving in the First World War. Throughout his married life he had led a sedentary lifestyle, sitting at his desk in the office or carrying home some of his work and then sitting again at his desk at home. The only exercise he did was when he went with my mother down to the lake at Veresegyház for a dip. When my father started to worry about putting on extra weight, someone suggested he start smoking. He followed this advice, but the end result was not the desired one. Not only did his weight not diminish, but also he became hooked on nicotine. Ironically, the only time he managed to lose weight was during the siege. He described this achievement as if he had gone down to the cellar like Falstaff and melted away like a snowman—despite the lack of sunlight.

In this seclusion, he planned the future. Mentally, he rebuilt the manor house, enlarged the vineyard, and imagined brighter vistas. Yet he had his qualms, knowing that the estate was too small to assure us the living standard that we had had. He realized that he would have to either go back to the radio studio or freelance to make ends meet.

Gradually, we were able to move from the cellar back upstairs. We made one room, my father's study, habitable. There, the windows were intact, and since there was no shortage of wood we crowded around the stove. Aunt Blanka went back to her apartment on Böszörményi Street. Ilonka, our cook, took off to find out the fate of her missing husband. She received word that he had fallen on the front lines in an engagement at Ócsa. The news nearly broke her heart. Grandmother Eveline found sleeping accommodations in the vacated apartment of the Töröks. My parents referred to these makeshift sleeping arrangements as "Nachtlager beim Granada" ("Night Camp at Granada"). I used to think of this as a reference to some well-known painting; later, I discovered that it was the title of a musical composition.

The countryside had its own share of vexation and looting by the Russians. At one of the peasant houses in Veresegyház, a Russian tried to open the door in the middle of the night. Since the door was bolted by an iron latch it wouldn't give. A farmer inside pulled aside the latch, which emitted a sound like someone readying a rifle. Hearing the noise, the Russian strafed the door with bullets from his machine gun. The peasant on the other side was hit by a fusillade of bullets and died (one machine gun contained seventy-two bullets).

The Russian authorities vehemently denied all charges against the soldiers of the Red Army. Béla Illés, a writer of Hungarian origin who served in Russian uniform, came the closest to admitting any wrongdoing in a visit to the radio studio after the war. He pointed a finger at the Hungarian vineyard owners. It was on their wine that the Russians got drunk and committed these horrible acts. In his view, the wine cellars should have been drained before the troops arrived. It took decades before these atrocities by the Russians came to light. One of the first mentions of it was by Aleksandr Solzhenitsyn, who acknowledged the raping and plundering committed by comrades in his book *Prussian Nights*.

When things quieted down and people began to move about, their main pastime was telling stories. Everyone had a special one, their unique adventure, and people would narrate for hours. After a while, I grew tired of hearing these dramatized events.

Judit's family had their own share of stories. Aunt Iza kept lamenting about the three generations' worth of dowry that she had cherished but that was all gone now, plundered by the Russians. All the china, silverware, and linens that had been in safekeeping in their city apartment were gone. The Russians who robbed them would have enough dowry for a whole village somewhere on the Don.

When a bomb fell on the Rados's building during the siege, it hit the part where all of the pantry rooms (*spajz* in Hungarian vernacular) were, aligned one above the other from floor to floor. The only pantry that was not aligned with the rest was Aunt Iza's, which made it the only remaining food supply for the entire building of about sixteen apartments. From then on, it was Aunt Iza's "soup kitchen" that kept all the tenants alive during the siege. In fact, it wasn't really soup but rather the preserves from her "compote archives" that sustained them. The menus for the lucky residents varied from cherry and apricot compotes to dilled pickles, plum jam, apple and pear compote, and everything else that the family's Nyires orchard had produced over the prior decades that had been able to be canned. These became their lifesavers, along with beans, lentils, and split peas. In 1944, Hungary allegedly had had the largest bean crop of her entire history (well, if not the largest, a fairly sizeable one at any rate), which no doubt helped to save the population from starvation. Without those crops, starvation would have been epidemic. But as doctors say that they have yet to find a grateful patient, so it was with the bean farmers. The first graffiti that could be read on city walls after the siege jokingly read: "Death to the bean growers!" The populace had obviously had its fill of beans.

Gradually, normal life took hold—first in Pest, then in Buda. The great boulevard, the squares, still gave the impression of a picturesque, monumental Persian market, however, and it took a few more weeks before I ventured farther than the immediate neighborhood.

A couple of days after Gyuri's visit, Tóni Viczián Jr. and Szabi dropped in. It was a great surprise for us, since this meant that travel had been at least somewhat reestablished between Buda and Pest. We noticed that they both wore black neckties. After we embraced each other and Tóni and Szabi had greeted Aunt Hansi and Uncle Rory, my father and I took them upstairs into our apartment. There, they related us what had transpired since we had last met. They told us that their mother, Aunt Bözsi, died during the siege. When the Russians came to the upper grange, Aunt Bözsi tried to convince them that she was only a servant of the family. To her dismay, someone gave her away, and the soldiers harassed her and chased her out of the house. Then the building caught fire, and her beautifully renovated, restored residence burned to the ground. At this point, her secret enclave in the cellar was exposed. The Russians broke into it, drank the wine, and looted the other contents. While the Russians were drinking, another fire broke out that spread to the cellar. Next, the Russians excavated the caskets of wine that were buried in the vineyard. But even after her house and cellar had burned down Aunt Bözsi couldn't stay away. One evening, on her way to Veresegyház in a snowstorm, she was hit by a Russian truck. She died instantly, and was buried in the cemetery at Veresegyház.

Tóni and Szabi also told us that all of the boys who had been with them at the Swiss Embassy building were safe, with the exception of Lajos Kenderesy, who was in captivity. When the Russians lined up the group by the side of the Swiss Embassy building, Tóni sent Szabi up into the attic to hide and he, in turn, made himself look busy stacking up firearms on the sidewalk. The Russians led the group toward Gödöllő, but the enterprising Viczián cousins, Balázs

Kenderesy, János Brencsán, and Aurél Dessewffy, slipped away at St. Ilona's and returned to the city. Now they were camping out at the Kenderesy's apartment.

Their next account was about our manor house, which had also been ransacked. Illés Hamar, who had been left behind as our caretaker, was nowhere to be seen. The place was empty and desolate. Ágota Kállay's admonition came back to my mother. How right Ágota had been when she said, "My dear Boyka! All the paintings here will be stolen!"

On January 22, around eight in the evening, an enormous explosion took place at the corner of Margit Boulevard and Mechwart Square in Buda. It was in the vicinity of where the Germans had been storing ammunition. A corner house with an air raid shelter thought to be bomb-proof had collapsed. In there, underneath the rubble, the remains of about three hundred people languished for some time. When the excavators got to the body of a young girl, they found a note underneath her wristwatch that read, "at four in the afternoon I was still alive."

Marica, Toni Viczián's wife, and her parents were in a corner of the air raid shelter that miraculously held up. With some help from the outside they were able to extricate themselves unhurt. Toni and Szabi came for Marica and then returned to the safe haven of the Kenderesys at Bajza Street in Pest. The next move was for Szabi to cross over the Danube again so that he and I could help Marica's parents over.

At the time of their visit, Toni and Szabi already had impressive partisan papers with the red sickle and hammer and with a Russian text that might have given them some confidence as far as their safety was concerned. The bilingual identification cards were fine until you had to present them; at least they helped to maintain your mental equilibrium.

My parents and I decided that I should join Szabi and Tóni and go out to the vineyard, see if I could get some food from the mill, and assess firsthand the condition of our estate. But this plan got derailed for a while because of an unforeseen mishap. Before I was to take off for the trip, I went searching for usable rafters and tiles in the attic of 8 Logodi Street. On my way back to our building, I had to jump from the neighboring building's attic onto our terrace, which was one flight lower. I landed on my right foot and sprained my ankle. Consequently, I had to postpone my plan to walk to Veresegyház until it healed. This happened at a most critical time. It must have been a blessing in disguise, since the random arrests and kidnappings of civilians was then at its height. Had I been on the street in either Buda or Pest the chances were astronomically high that I would have become a captive myself and landed in the Soviet Union for at least a couple of years. An estimated four hundred thousand Hungarians were transported at this time to Russia, only half of whom returned. Some of them would only come back after Stalin died, some just before the Hungarian revolution of 1956. During my recovery, the worst part of the occupation was slowly passing by. I awaited the day when my ankle would be healed and Szabi would return for me so we could make the trip together.

By the time the calendar turned to March, we had run out of food, just like the majority of the city's population. Conversations were narrowing down to the subject of food, menus, and cooking. My father observed that this was a typical symptom of hunger, with which he was already familiar from the aftermath of the First World War. By now, more enterprising spirits—our cook Ilonka, my good friend Szabi—were already crossing the Danube and becoming the carriers of news—most of which was overwhelmingly depressing.

My mother lined up seven small boxes of powdered soup, the last of the remaining food supply for Grandmother Eveline, my parents, Ilonka, and myself. It became imperative for me to hit the road, ankle and Russians notwithstanding.

An enterprising soul in the Krisztina District set up a "food exchange." He made a chart listing each foodstuff with its equivalent value in relation to other food items. In theory, one could have taken to his location, for example, one pound of flour and received in exchange for it one-quarter pound of bacon, and so forth. His fee for a transaction was set at 10 percent. It served him well, but it was of no help to us since we had no food to spare, or to offer in exchange.

On the seventh of March, Szabi arrived. The plan was for the two of us, along with Marica's parents—Uncle Pista Kovács and his wife Mariska—to cross over to Pest. We were to pull a handcart loaded with the belongings of the Kovács parents as well as our own things. I put together a package with items like white pepper, matches, and some trinkets. I felt like a pilgrim on my way to barter with the natives. With a heavy heart I said goodbye. The whole undertaking was rather risky, and I wasn't sure when I would see my parents next.

The four of us, with our cart, successfully arrived on Bajza Street, where friends and relatives of the Kenderesys had huddled together in the storm. There, again we went over our plans and came to the conclusion that it would be a better idea, instead of going to Veresegyház, to go somewhere where we knew that we could get some food. We decided that Balázs Kenderesy and I would go to Püspökladány, a locality that was about two hundred kilometers from Pest. There, the Kenderesys had an acquaintance, a widow. Our reasoning was that because Püspökladány was somewhat farther from the capital, their food supply would not be so depleted. I liked the idea, and Balázs and I made a good team. He was a slim blond boy, with albino features and blue eyes, and was a couple of years younger than me. We used to bike together and enjoyed each other's company. I appreciated his impish sense of humor.

When we set out, despite the fact that it was March already, the weather was still wintery. To travel, we used our old routine—the rooftops of trains. The landscape was covered with snow and the trains were crowded with bundled up, shivering women. Men in those days still shunned the open air, anxious of being captured. We met a few Russians here and there. At one station, a soldier came to our wagon and did his best to persuade a young peasant woman to disembark and go with him on some unspecified excursion. The woman, who was hardly enticing, sitting in the center of a bunch of blankets and scarves, adamantly refused the soldier's siren songs. She knew that she was safe in the midst of the similarly bundled-up group of women. At last, the Russian waved his hand despairingly and contemptuously remarked, "Ach, papa gypsy, mama Jewish." With that he left.

Reaching Püspökladány, Balázs and I went to see our hostess, who showed us our sleeping accommodations. My roommate, I was informed, was a Russian officer. I was deep in sleep when he arrived late into the night and I woke up as he entered. I still remember how he held his boots in his hand as he came into the room, not wanting to wake me up with their noise. Out of politeness toward me, he made no move to switch on the light, but I flipped it on. At that point, he introduced himself, we shook hands, and as we did so, he blushed. It made me realize that one should not have preconceived notions, even of the Russians.

The next day, I went out with the widow to visit some peasant families. Balázs, meanwhile went to the marketplace to barter for food. He caught the eyes of the local police, however, with his blond hair and blue eyes, and the bearing of a young gentry boy that was quite out of place. It didn't help that his last name was Kenderesy, since it sounded like Kenderes, the principality of former Regent Horthy's estate. They put Balázs in jail and our hostess had to go to the slammer to extricate him.

In the meantime, I managed to conduct a few transactions. Business acumen was definitely not my forte. Equipped with an artistic temperament, I began with the wrong target in mind. When I stepped into the kitchen, the first important room in a farmer's home, my eyes caught sight of the pretty ceramic peasant plates hanging on the wall. Temporarily forgetting my original mission, I began to bargain for those plates. Luckily, after securing two or three of these old and beautiful plates, I succeeded in remembering my mission, returning to earth and obtaining for my starving family some flour, lard, and a small piece of ham. The ham was timely, since my return to Logodi Street ended up coinciding with Easter. My parents were delighted to see me and happy to be able to have a decent meal. My mother conjured up some cake and made some coffee. I regarded this as a pleasant interlude, since I knew that I would have to keep up with my peregrinations—to go back to Pest and out to the vineyard.

During my short stay, my father could hardly sleep. He became so excited hearing my travelogue that he skipped writing in his diary entirely, waiting for a quieter time—meaning, for my absence.

During this period, Grandmother Eveline and Ilonka, our cook, were still living with us, although Ilonka left frequently, to search for food and any news about her husband, who had allegedly fallen at Ócsa. Ilonka was from Transylvania; her last name was Bagoly (Owl). She had married her husband János during the war, but had remained with us for the duration of the siege and was like a member of the family. I always think of her with fondness; she was a tremendous help to my parents. She was petite, blond with blue eyes. Her voice was on the higher side and whenever she became agitated or angry, it would become shrill. After a dreadful interval, it turned out that Ilonka's husband was, after all, alive, while her colorful brother-in-law Nőci Kostin had either fallen during the breakout or had been captured. Either way, he was never heard from again.

Our whole building was in a rather shabby condition; most of the dividing walls had collapsed. The windows were broken and the wind kept howling through the rooms. Our only safe haven was the library, situated in a tower-like corner of the building. When we moved up to my father's library we placed a large wood-burning stove in it. This kept us warm to a certain extent, as long as we kept plying the stove with wood. Firewood was not a problem, since it was readily found scattered about on the streets and on rooftops. In addition, we had one winter's worth of wood and coal supplies untouched in the cellar; since we had been living underground all winter, we hadn't used the firewood and coal to heat the apartment. Unfortunately, though, the protruding square turret-like structure of this part of the apartment was more directly exposed to the elements, which made it harder to keep the library warm. There was no electricity or running water. While I was away, my mother had to fetch water from the Krisztina Mission House, approximately four city blocks away. We improvised lighting by floating wicks in kerosene. We regretted not having had the foresight to bring at least one of the kerosene lamps out from the vineyard into the city. Four decades later, when electricity was finally introduced in Veresegyház, my mother still kept kerosene lamps in her bedroom, ready for any unforeseen eventuality.

Aunt Blanka had moved back into her flat. Her Jewish girlfriends, all three of whom had survived the war, began to put their lives back together. Eventually, in 1956, after the Hungarian revolution, they would each seek refuge in the West. Blanka, meanwhile, was now trying to keep Uncle János Benel, my father's best friend, alive. For weeks he hovered between life and death.

The second time I ventured away, it was with Szabi who came and offered to go with me to Pest. From there, once again, my traveling partner was Balázs Kenderesy. On the return from our first trip he had been caught on the street by the Russians, but had managed to sneak away. Fairly soon, almost all of us had an escape story or two. An anthology could have been written of these adventures of captivity and escape.

The first rule of thumb, as soon as one had been captured, was to try to immediately escape. Trying this at the outset was best, since the captors usually weren't all that organized yet. There were no roll calls with names or numbers. At the Zahár apartment building on Thököly Avenue (where Aunt Iza and Judit lived), the main entrance door was left open during the night. When the Russians marched their captives by, there were always a couple of prisoners who noticed the open door and, utilizing the cover of darkness, jumped out of line and scurried through the open door into the courtyard. People escaped from all kinds of situations but the hardest was flight from a camp with electrified barbed wires, watchtowers, searchlights, dogs, and guards day and night. But, of course, even from such a place someone always got away. Two Hungarian soldiers in a Soviet prisoner of war camp offer one example. Their job every day was to load trucks with corpses, the victims of hunger, typhoid, and cholera. One day after filling up the trucks they climbed up into one of them and lay beneath the corpses. It was a risky undertaking, but it worked for them.

On another occasion, a German POW in a Russian camp scrutinized his legs and put his toes together in a "V" form, purposely making them uneven and putting them in awkward positions. All day long he stood there murmuring, "*Es stimmt nicht*" ("This isn't right"). After a while, the Russian guards came to the conclusion that the young man had gone insane. He was put on a train to be sent back to Germany along with other gravely ill prisoners. As the train left the station and there were no longer any guards around, he looked around and said with a satisfied smile, "*Es stimmt schon*" ("Now this is right.").

When Balázs Kenderesy was captured walking on the street, he and a group were herded into a basement. It looked like the intent was to deport them, since they were not lined up for any kind of immediate work. At the end of the corridor Balázs noticed a pale light and a window. He broke the window, climbed out, and found himself in a deserted side street.

All of the boys at 17 Wekerle Sándor Street who had guarded the Swiss building were lined up after the Russians took Pest. In January, they were marched under Russian guard down the Kerepesi Turnpike toward Gödöllő. By St. Ilona's, there was a lengthy slope where some of the boys slipped away. Balázs's brother Lajos, not being wise to the situation, ended up walking all the way to Gödöllő, where he was put inside a train filled with prisoners. Over the summer just before the train left Hungary he was discharged, as by then he was in a precarious physical state.

While the boys were marching toward Gödöllő, a man came by on the opposite side of the road carrying a wooden washtub on his head. One of the captives quickly glided out of the procession and joined the man as second-in-command under the washtub.

Another incident occurred when a middle-aged father (my future father-in-law, Dr. Ferenc Novák) and his eight-year-old son Péter were caught in a roundup on the street. Dr. Novák, realizing the soft spot that the Russians had for children, ordered his son to break into heart-rending crying, an order that Péter executed promptly and to perfection. Needless to say, it worked and the two were released.

A usual Russian ruse was to tell people that they must come to receive their identification papers. They were told that they would be free to go after a short spell of interrogation. Obviously, this wasn't what happened; instead, they found themselves in the Soviet Union.

Since my family agreed that I would go out to the vineyard, I had to cross the Danube once more to get to the Kenderesys' to team up with Balázs for the trip. On March 25, a Sunday, I left Logodi Street in the morning. My parents hoped fervently that I wouldn't be captured. I headed off in the direction of Ferenc József Bridge (by then the newly renamed Liberty Bridge). By a twist of fate, in front of the Gellért Hotel I literally ran into a so-called *kapdova*—meaning "custody" or "arrest." I was surrounded by a bunch of Russian soldiers and in a long line of captured men. While standing there waiting, I tried to take a quick "French leave," but an officer ran after me, grabbed me by the ear, and led me back to the group. From the hotel, the Russians marched us down to the Southern Railway Bridge. The German detonations of January 17 had sunk all of the bridges over the Danube that connected Buda with Pest. The Russians were hastily trying to rebuild as many of them as they could. A temporary pontoon bridge had been erected from Buda to Margaret Island, which sat in the middle of the Danube, and from there over to Pest. The Liberty Bridge had been patched up, since only its center part had been destroyed. As we arrived at the Southern Railway Bridge, it too seemed to be nearly restored. The Russians directed us to a huge pile of rocks and told us to carry them over to the base of the bridge. There were a few familiar faces in my group. None of them were female, since no women had been rounded up for this job; the rocks were inordinately heavy.

After a few turns, a Russian showed up, took my arm, and led me away. He took me to a floating pontoon, on the top of which, inside a gasoline drum, a bonfire was burning. Around the fire sat a half-dozen Russians. One of them put a tin can in my hand and explained my job to me. From time to time, I was to descend to the bottom of the floating barge and bail out any water that had seeped in. This was a "sinecure," a job invented almost for my leisure. I had only to take care of the water every hour, while the Russians played an accordion, sang, and smoked cigarettes. Day turned to night, but none of the Russians appeared to be sleepy. As I watched my compatriots, many of them elderly, embracing sizable rocks and trudging along before my eyes all night, a guilty feeling crept over me. After a while my chore became boring, so I decided to teach my captors a few Hungarian folk songs. I chose the old ones, the ones that can be played on the "Pentatonic" scale—the black keys of the piano. These were the ones that our predecessors had brought with them from the Asian steppes and thus were deemed by me to be the most appropriate. I selected *"Elmegyek, Elmegyek. Hosszu Utra Megyek"* ("I'm leaving, I'm leaving. I'm going on a long journey"), a song that was traditionally sung at graduations. Another song I taught them was *"Tizenhárom Fodor Van a Szoknyámon"* ("Thirteen Ruffles on my Skirt"), which is the lamentation of a young lassie about the frustrations of being unable to find a husband.

After a while, as day broke we became aware of an approaching train. It was moving very slowly, solemnly, over the newly completed bridge. Pandemonium broke out. The Russians threw their caps up in the air like cadets at a graduation. They let out a round of small arms fire and a few sorties from their machine guns as a salute. Red flags flapped in the air from the front of the locomotive, while gigantic billboards on its sides sang the praise and glory of socialism and the record speed with which the bridge had been rebuilt. The same billboards were also displayed on the caboose and on the bridgeheads. I bid an affectionate farewell to my captors and joined my fellow forced laborers in a line. We were led back to Liberty Bridge, which was a gesture on the part of our Russians to prevent us from being captured again by another of the *kapdova* outfits. From there I sped onward to Bajza Street and the Kenderesys' apartment, where I found a citadel of civilization, good friends and relatives huddled together in the storm.

The world into which I arrived was a surreal one. At the Kenderesys' one could clean up and even take a bath. This was in great contrast to the squalor of the two months during the siege. Back in my family's apartment, my father had been elated when he discovered a shirt in the hamper that he could exchange for the dust- and soot-covered one he was wearing. There, relativity was in action. The

Kenderesys' bathroom was in full working order; we had only to fetch some firewood. Marica, Balázs, and I promptly set out to collect some wood for evening baths. We went out into the residential section behind Bajza Street and climbed up to the top floor of an elegant villa whose roof structure was fairly dilapidated. We began to pull apart the loose beams. After a few swings to and fro several of the beams came loose at once and a sizable part of the roof crashed down onto the street below. As the beams fell down, they ripped asunder the telephone lines of the nearby Russian *kommandatura*. Within minutes, a Russian patrol arrived to repair the rupture. We tried to make ourselves scarce as fast as we could. On the street, we found a small carriage with its wheel chained and padlocked. With the help of our hatchet, we broke the chain and loaded our loot. On the way back, not far from the Kenderesys' building, the owner of the cart caught up with us and angrily repossessed his vehicle. The three of us dragged the collected beams home, where other members of the little colony set about sawing them up.

The next day, Balázs and I set out for the vineyard. The electric train was running from the city out to Gödöllő. We stayed on it until Szent Jakab, one stop before Gödöllő, from where we could reach Veresegyház on foot. Our first stop was the home of Miss Olga, who lived in a small house very close to the Viciántelep station. We hoped to be able to spend the night there.

A few years back, Miss Olga Erdélyi had bought a parcel of vineyard from Uncle Rory and settled down there in a small cottage. She was among the first owners of land that Uncle Rory parceled out. In the past, we would meet her as she was either coming from or going to her vineyard. She had a key to our gate and the right to pass through Uncle Rory's property. She wore her hair in a tower of buns, high above her head. Her other trademarks were her high-laced black boots, long narrow skirts, and stiff military gait, like that of a staff sergeant. She lived with her friend Margaret, who was very quiet, soft spoken, and ladylike. Miss Olga had a textile store in Budapest, but when the siege threatened the capital she and her friend decided to sit it out in Viciántelep and await the Russians' arrival there. As we soon learned, they had had harrowing, horrible adventures during the weeks of the siege.

The two ladies received us with open arms and provided us with a couch on which we slept side by side, head to toe. For dinner, we got *Zvekkerli*, noodles with cabbage well laced with lard. Since my stomach was no longer used to greasy food, I bore the consequences over the course of the night.

The next morning, Balázs and I set out to see first the Viczián estates and the various vineyards of the Viczián siblings. I postponed the visit to my family's home to the afternoon. At the Vicziáns', the upper grange was the picture of a sorrowful disaster. It was like a painting by Vazul Vereschagin, the Russian artist whose war pictures made him famous—especially the battle scenes of the Russo-Turkish war in 1877–78. A heap of reeking ruins faced us. The remains of the walls pointed toward the frigid blue sky like singed fingers. The once elegant and inviting country house was in shambles, burned to the ground. The colorful tile floor of the patio was a grotesque sight, exposed and surrounded by rubbish instead of walls and a roof. On the other side of the courtyard stood the only building still standing, the vintner's house. Walking around the ruins, my eyes caught sight of an object—a painting leaning against a pile of bricks. Its frame was missing and the painting itself was greatly damaged. Scrutinizing it more closely, I realized it was the portrait of the young Prince Charles de Ligne that I had carried up to Aunt Bözsi's for safekeeping. De Ligne's face was shattered; it was a customary practice of Russian soldiers to smash their jackboots through any painting or portrait they discovered. I picked up the trampled painting and took it back to our house.

When I arrived at our house, my first impression was that of a place where a giant vacuum cleaner had sucked up most everything except for the dirt. The walls were completely bare; not one painting, portrait, or etching remained. Ágota Kállay turned out to be an excellent oracle.

Every one of the tile stoves that served as our radiators in the winter was damaged. In each of the rooms, including those in Uncle Rory's wing, the upper half of every stove had been broken to pieces. Right before the siege, Emőri the architect had hid his gold Napoleon coins in his yellow tile fireplace. As soon as they were discovered by the Russians, for good measure all the tile stoves in the neighborhood were busted open as well. I found only a few large armchairs, canapés, in the house; even they had been denuded, the leather hides sliced off of the frames. The stable was empty. All of the light carriages, including the more elegant one in which Henry, my father's cousin, had been born, were missing. The dray wagons had been taken from the outside shed as well. Our large pantry was barren.

Only an empty wooden box for storing flour remained. Gone were the hamstrings with the silver O'Donnell coat of arms. A few of the heavy carved bookcases in our corner room escaped the looting, but damage they could not. The ones that had had glass doors now stood there deprived of their glass, staring blindly into space. The large dining room table, which ghosts had at one time skillfully levitated, had escaped the plundering; it had apparently proven too heavy for humans to lift. The pretty couch, newly reupholstered before the siege with a colorful flower motif, was also gone. The doors and windows were unharmed.

After I walked through our empty rooms, I went to see the main wing where Uncle Rory and Aunt Hansi had resided. The walls there were also barren. From the entry hall, the carved wooden furniture decorated with red tulips, the chest, the wall hanger, and the matching plates and jugs were all gone. Uncle Rory's tract had been converted into barracks. Every room was stuffed with cots and straw mattresses. The floors were scattered with empty cans of butter. There were five or six sleeping accommodations per room. Incredible amounts of trash lay all around. I was walking ankle high in a mixture of straw and paper. Uncle Rory had had a set of Russian classics in German translation by such authors as Tolstoy, Gogol, Dostoevsky, Goncharov, and Turgenev, printed on rice paper and bound in beautiful red and gold. As far as the usurpers of the place were concerned, they saw only one good use for these literary gems. The rice paper had likely proved to be excellent for rolling cigarettes, which they called *papirosi*. They filled the *papirosi* with cut tobacco they called *mahorka*.

Uncle Rory was a member of the Order of the Rosicrucians, a semi-secret society similar to the Masons that had originated in the Middle Ages. He regularly received the order's publications. These bright-green pamphlets were also scattered about.

During the German occupation, two old Jewish ladies, Ida and Márta Gyulai, had visited my father and given him for safekeeping their correspondence with Ernő Osvát. Osvát was the editor-in-chief of *Nyugat* (*The West*), a literary monthly featuring the works of preeminent Hungarian writers. The letters from Osvát had been written on miniature parchment-like paper in exquisitely miniscule handwriting. Due to the material of the paper and its small size, the Russians probably hadn't been able to use the letters for cigarettes or for kindling, so they littered the rooms with them instead. Painstakingly

I gathered them up. My father later met up with the two ladies—who had survived the Germans, the Archers, and the war—and returned the letters to them.

Next, I went up into the attic, where I hit upon a wooden box filled with embroidery and lace. The box was under a pile of tiles, the remains of an oven. My mind began to race through the various possibilities of what worthy objects like silverware or gold or anything else we might have salvaged in place of this useless old embroidery. There were also some old traveling trunks filled with several generations of accumulated bric-a-brac. But my toys—cars, soldiers, little trains, Meccano automobile assemblies—which had also been stored in a wooden box had disappeared. My father's various manuscripts—bound texts of an opera, typed-up stories, skits for radio presentations—were all scattered throughout the manor house.

As best as I could, I gathered up my father's papers, but a manuscript that my father had had only one copy of, *Testvérek* (*Brothers*), which had been left in the attic of the vintner's bungalow, was nowhere to be found. *Testvérek* was a historical novel set in the Middle Ages during the reign of the House of Árpád. It was about the three princes—Géza, László, and Lambert—and was a manuscript over which my father had labored for years. Despite my father's minuscule handwriting it had become a hefty tome, yet not a page of it could be found. My father was aghast when I told him. He said, "I will never have the strength to write it again so please make every effort to find it or parts of it."

Then I went to the press house, to do some reconnoitering. Of the four large wine presses, one was missing. All the presses had been manually operated, requiring a couple of men to crank them (electric power was still far off in the future for most Hungarian vineyards). Removing one of these presses must have taken the strength of half a dozen men. I learned later that a neighbor's dray had carried the press to Erdőváros (Forest City), to the Roheim Vineyard.

My next exploration took me down into the wine cellar, which had an all-around foul smell. The gigantic barrels were tilted on their stands (the gantry), and the small doors at the bottoms of the barrels were pushed in. The tartaric wine stone on the inside of the barrels had melted away due to the humidity of the cellar. Wine slurry sat at the bottom of the barrels like red mud. The soldiers had drunk to the last drop. As I scrutinized the barrels, tilting them on their transoms, the longitudinal beams carved from locust trees, I caught sight of a parchment lying in the dirt and tugged a few large pieces out from beneath the barrels. On closer inspection, I saw that these parchment pieces were fragments of a scroll of the O'Donnell family tree, with a dangling red wax seal that had been issued by the magistrate of Dublin. The sheets displayed the family's coats of arms in beautiful color, listing ancestors by name and year from generation to generation, from the year 500 up until the eighteenth century. Included were the coats of arms of those who had intermarried with the O'Donnells. I also found the sheepskin diploma from the city of Vienna that had been presented to Maximilian O'Donnell, adjutant to Emperor Franz Joseph. (Due to a spelling mistake O'Donnell was written with one "n." Out of reverence for the emperor, from that time forward the Austrian branch of the family used the new spelling, O'Donell.) In 1852, Maximilian had saved the life of His Majesty when a Hungarian named Libényi attempted to assassinate the emperor. Even though the parchment and the diploma had lost some of their original luster sitting in the mud under the barrels, they were still legible and their colors had only scarcely faded.

A gaping hole yawned in the wall to the secret room that we had built the previous November with Gyuri and Uncle Cinkota. The wall had been discovered on day one when the Russians arrived. We had stupidly made it quite easy for them to find our hidden treasure cave. They had only to knock on the wall, in which case a hollow sound would have given it away, or to stroll in the park alongside the house and count the cellar windows. Thus, they found their Eldorado. They drank the wine and feasted on the roasted potatoes, using our silverware, and for good measure they also consumed our champagne and brandy. Then, for entertainment, there were the two Hamar girls, professional prostitutes.

When we had hidden our treasures, we had counted on the Russians executing a fast rush to the capital, bypassing small villages like ours. But to be on the safe side, everyone frantically dug and hid what they could. It didn't cross our minds that the front would stagnate just outside the capital. As it turned out, the fighters settled in throughout the countryside for a long haul and had ample time to scrutinize and find most of the hidden valuables. These soldiers came from the east, heading across Bukovina, Moldavia, and Transylvania; by this point, their skills had been honed. For example, they would pour water on the ground. If it ran freely into the soil they began to dig. They also carried iron rods like walking sticks and took random earth samples. They would push a rod into the ground here and there. Where it gave way, they would start digging. A hollow-sounding knock on a wall would give away any secret enclave.

In 1919, during the first Bolshevik regime, Aunt Erzsi Kenderesy utilized her apiary. She hid cans of honey—some of which were filled with honey, others with jewelry and silverware—underneath the beehives. It turned out to be the perfect place to hide things, since no one wanted to irritate the bees. When it came time to hide valuables again, Aunt Erzsi laughingly told us that since she had been bragging about her old hiding place for years it had become completely useless.

The peasants—silent witnesses to the thousand-year-old Hungarian history—had the wisdom, the shrewdness, to trick the occupiers. András Lehotzky put his meat in a large pot, tied it to a rope, and lowered it into his well just above the level of the ice cold water. He also threw his tools into the well, knowing that as long as they were submerged they wouldn't rust. The peasants dug up the dirt in the stables and created hiding places under the hooves of the horses and cows. They also hid objects under hay stacks. Since animals couldn't be hidden, the Russians took them, but the peasants would run after them and swap a bottle of brandy for each livestock's return. Whenever a bunch of Russians started to dig and came dangerously close to a hiding place, the owner would transfer everything to a new location during the night. The farmers, having no other place to go, had remained there. This gave them the advantage of monitoring the moves of the Russians, enabling them to take the necessary preemptive steps. It was like a game of chess.

One of our neighbors had a unique idea for hiding his gold coins. He looked for a metal pipe and hammered it flat on one end, forming a wedge. He poured his coins into the pipe and hammered the whole pipe into the ground wedge-side first without disturbing the surrounding soil. As a result, it passed the water test and the pipe with the gold coins survived.

Since, unlike the farmers, we could not stay, we therefore did the next best thing and found someone to watch our house. When my father chose Illés Hamar to act as caretaker, it was an act of desperation—like hiring a yeggman, a safe cracker, to be bank president. However, it may have been a blessing in disguise. The Russians, having had such a good time with their pleasant bivouacking, may have been less inclined to burn the house to the ground. The neighbors later told us that when the Hamars left our house, Hamar loaded up our dray and made eleven trips with his loot.

After this "postmortem," Balázs and I set out to go back to the city. Darkness had already fallen. We were seized by hunger pains, so Balázs pulled out two slices of bacon and a piece of bread. He instructed me to chew the bacon very slowly and thoroughly, explaining that this was a Japanese method to alleviate the sense of starvation. We trudged up to Szada, and from there to the railroad station at Gödöllő. On the road to Gödöllő, while the full moon helped us to see our way, it also gave us away. We soon found ourselves face to face with a group of Russian soldiers working on a telephone line. They had great fun with us, amusing themselves at our expense. First they liberated me of the tools that I was carrying. I nearly froze when they pulled two bloody rabbits out of Balázs's knapsack. Balázs had received them as a gift from a local poacher. But never underestimate a Kenderesy. After the first few minutes of excited shouting over where the rabbits had come from, Balázs explained that we had gotten them from some Russian soldiers. "After all, who else could have a rifle nowadays?" asked Balázs of the soldiers. That saved our skins and got us the rabbits back. The Russians broke into laughter when I told them that Balázs was my "sistra;" they corrected me, he was my "brat."

In Gödöllő, we had to wait a long time for the train to arrive. Since Gödöllő was the large collection site where Russians replenished their supply of captives, we sat in the train station in silent terror. Late at night we finally arrived at the Kenderesy house, where the two bunnies were most welcome.

Over the following weeks, we continued to hear stories that increased the volume of the never-ending lore about the siege and its immediate aftermath. It was as if we were continuously listening to *Arabian Knights* or Bocciacco's *Decameron*. Everyone had a story. Edgar Nagy, for example, was walking from Kispest on the outskirts of the city to Eskü Square, quite a distance away, to visit some of his relatives. With no other foodstuffs on hand to share with them, he carried a large sack of red beets. As Edgar walked, the beets bounced against one another and against his back. After a while the beets were ready for revenge, and they let their juices out, coloring the back of his coat bright red. People on the street must have thought that he was shot and bleeding from his wound.

Another family acquaintance, Nándi Salzberger, sent his family out into the countryside just before the siege while he stayed in Pest. Even though he didn't cook and didn't have any household help, his agricultural expertise helped him to survive. When I visited him shortly after my peregrinations searching for food, he showed me his ingenious system. He led me into his bedroom, where I saw wires running along the walls like clothes line. At intervals there were strings attached, from which dangled smoked horse tongues. The strings were arranged systematically to make sure that each tongue had the proper amount of space. Whenever a crowd had congregated around a poor demised charger, he had run straight to its head and cut out the tongue. At home he devised his own rudimentary smoking apparatus where all these tongues were treated before he hung them on the strings. His apartment looked like a butcher shop. He told me that at one time he had no other food to eat than these tongues and a big jar of candied cherries.

Szabi Viczián had his own characteristic episode. One morning, while walking on Andrássy Avenue, a slow-moving Russian truck passed him. He noticed something fall out of the truck. It turned out to be a leather wallet. He picked it up and inside, to his amazement, was a stack of various paper currencies. There were dollars, pounds, and Swiss francs. It must have been a small fortune. The sight of so much money made him ponder what he should do with it, but before he could decide, the truck had already turned around and was slowly driving in his direction. He waited until the truck reached him. Then he politely handed the wallet over to the Russian driver.

27

Vanished by the Danube

During the months of severe fighting, our building on Logodi Street suffered greatly. That ultimately we survived and the building withstood the vicious bombing and artillery fire was a miracle, one that my father credited to his favorite saints: Saint Francis of Assisi, our ancestor Saint Columba O'Donnell, and Saint Rita, the patron saint of impossibilities. As the siege went on, my father would pray more often and more emphatically. For additional protection, he placed a black wooden baroque crucifix in a window facing in the direction of the fighting. This cross had participated in a number of previous Farkas family adventures. During the great flood of Pest in 1838, my great-grandfather Károly Farkas' house had collapsed; the only object he had been able to save and carry with him in the rescue boat was this cross.

Our building on Logodi Street had been in danger of a similar fate—albeit on account of different hazards, as it faced defenselessly the front lines on Naphegy and Gellérthegy. The cross, which suffered some splintering from bullets itself, by and large came through for us. The fact that the neighboring building, No. 8, was much taller than our building may have provided us with some extra cover, but that did not detract from the merits of our saints, who for two months worked overtime on our behalf.

One day in January 1945, Blanka and I ventured out in the middle of the raging siege. On Atilla Street, we glanced back toward our building. To our horror, we saw that the back wall lay completely exposed in the direction of the warring parties. Of course it had been this way the whole time, but seeing it now brought home the realization that nothing on the outside of that back wall protected us—no fence, no tree, no other building. It was only a thin brick wall that separated us from the outside inferno, from the firing. Thus we tried to sleep.

On one particular day, my father counted more than fifty bombs dropping around us. Most of them exploded only a few feet from our walls. Some of them were duds, which landed with a dull thud. Whenever a bomb did explode, it felt as if the whole house was being lifted up and dropped back down again. At times like these I placed myself under an iron crossbeam, Blanka's tears silently flowed down her face, the cooks covered their heads in blankets. Father smoked cigarettes, Uncle Rory his cigars. We were silent the whole time.

In March, we decided to move back into our apartment. We were happy to leave the underground life behind, but it wasn't so easy for the elderly. Oddly, by now they felt more at home in the warm nooks of the cellar and, with their built-in inertia, were reluctant to move out of these dreary dungeons. Uncle Rory ventured out and went to see Mr. Ősze, the roofer, who soon rebuilt the roof at an exorbitant price.

Still, there was no electricity, no running water, and the gutters were clogged. The bathroom door was blocked and disguised by placing a wardrobe in front of it. We used the bathroom to hide our valuables. All of the tenants except for my family moved out of the building. It was a miserable existence in that ruined house. One evening as my father and I sat down for our supper by candlelight and were cutting up some bacon, a mouse climbed up onto our table. He must have been even hungrier than we were to take such a dangerous risk.

Regretfully, we decided to bring this chapter to a close and quit our city dwelling. During my high school years the apartment on Logodi Street had been our cozy, warm, friendly, and cheerful haven. Now, sorrowfully, we took on the role of Scarlett O'Hara, escaping to our Tara, the vineyard at Veresegyház.

Ilonka said goodbye to us. She was still looking for her husband Jani's remains, unaware that he was in fact alive. My father kept busy working on his novel of the siege and keeping up his diary. In between writing, he read Robert Louis Stevenson's *Treasure Island* and *Kidnapped* and Gottfried Keller's *Green Henry*. Grandmother Eveline went back to Pest. During her absence her apartment had been expropriated, and she was left with only the small maid's room in which to lay down her head. Most of her possessions were also gone.

With my first excursion to the vineyard, it became obvious that it was time to permanently settle in the countryside and begin a new life. Nature wouldn't wait. The buds were opening; the vine stalks awaited their pruning. The kitchen garden was ready to receive seedlings and plants. The estate was still in its wintry dream, but the calendar was rushing toward spring. Our farmhands came into the city looking for us, and urged us to get out to the country and take care of the springtime work.

The local farmers were puzzled by our hesitancy about swinging full force into spring preparations; when nature calls, a farmer must obey. But they were also driven by their personal interest to get us out to the countryside. They wanted to rent parts of the estate, and they proposed becoming sharecroppers, whereby we would supply fertilizer and spraying materials and they would put in labor. They would keep half the crop; the other half would be ours.

When we finally made it out to Veresegyház to start over, the sight that greeted us was like a movie when the projector stops and everything stands still. The vine stalks, which by now should have been uncovered, lay still buried beneath their winter blanket of sand. It was time for us to get to work, to free the small buds, rescue them from suffocation, and enable them to bask in the warm rays of the sun. We needed to prune the vine stalks, and the orchard anxiously awaited our attention. The trees had to be pruned and sprayed. Adjoining the kitchen garden, the asparagus patch also needed care. Finally, we had a few acres of arable land on the other side of the Viczián hills, down by the road to Veresegyház and close to the Egervári watermill, that needed to be seeded. Thus, we stood there, like naked orphans in a thunderstorm.

On March 23, the day I returned to the city from my second trip with Balázs to Veresegyház, I gave a thorough briefing on the status of the vineyard to my father. On March 27, since our family was still short of food, I set out to Pest to sell my wristwatch on the black market. Approaching two Russian soldiers at the grand boulevard, with naiveté I showed them my Swiss Cortebert wristwatch. One of them took the watch from me, and they both hopped onto a truck; I hopped in alongside them. The truck took off, but made a stop at the corner of Dohány Street (Tobacco Street), where two women stood on the curb with bottles in their hands, motioning toward the truck. The driver pulled the truck to a halt and engaged in a negotiation with the women. This brought back memories of my teenage years, when on Easter Monday boys would go around visiting girls and sprinkle them with Eau de Cologne (a symbolic act meant to keep the young ladies blooming). The girls would then offer us sweets and lilac- and green-colored liquor seemingly similar to the contents of these bottles. One of the Russians told the women that he wanted to have a sip before he made a purchase. One of the woman handed a bottle over. The next minute the driver floored the gas pedal, leaving the two outraged and cursing women behind.

Bearing witness to this dastardly act, I realized the predicament I was in. My mind raced to devise a scheme whereby I could extricate myself along with my wristwatch. As human weakness would have it, the Russian had put my watch on his knee, so that he could happily look down and enjoy the sight of it while gulping down great swigs of the newly acquired suspicious-looking liquid. Seizing an opportune moment, with my left hand I grabbed the watch from his knee, with my right hand I opened the truck door, and I jumped out. Luckily, my landing didn't cause me any physical harm. The truck came to a screeching halt, but by the time they tried to catch up with me I was in the attic of a six-story walk-up apartment house. Since I knew by now that the attics of buildings were the least likely places that a Russian would venture to, I felt pretty safe. Nevertheless, I spent half an hour there in quiet meditation before emerging from my hideout.

Soon thereafter, I ventured over to Pest again to see Aunt Iza and Judit. It was a joyful reunion. I hadn't seen them since my second January visit during the siege, and I still very much had a crush on Judit. We decided that Aunt Iza and I should go out to Nyires together. We would set up a household in my family's home. My parents could not come out yet because my father, having lost half his weight during the siege, was too weak to walk and my mother didn't want to expose herself to the marauding Russians.

Once we were at Veresegyház, during the day Aunt Iza worked in her vineyard pruning stalks. In the evening she would come over to our house, prepare something to eat, and sleep over. She did not want to be alone in her house at night, which was probably wise because Aunt Iza was an attractive woman. Szabi Viczián came over from the Viczián grange and planted some pea seeds in our kitchen garden, with the agreement that we would split the crop. The Vicziáns' soil was clay (which is why a brick factory had been built there) and thus not suitable for vegetable gardening.

Aunt Iza's parents, Uncle Lajos and Grandmother Iza, stayed in the city, along with Judit and her brother Laci, who had since recovered from his near-fatal bout with pneumonia. Judit went back to high school as a senior, while Laci entered as a freshman. Their maid Aranka stayed with them. Aranka was a pretty, petite blond lassie whose last name was Major. Hearing people address her as "Miss Major," the Russians became reverential, believing that she was a major in the military.

Aunt Iza and I quickly set up house at Veresegyház. From the neighbors, we repossessed a *"Sparherd"*—a simple cooking stove or range. We looked for some food, and we collected essential tools for a rural life. Aunt Iza took over my parents' bedroom, while I fabricated a cot in the corner room, my usual abode. I also found a night table. In the garden, I found the doors to the house, which the Russians had thrown into the trenches they dug for their tanks, trucks, and field guns. I filled the trenches and leveled the field once more. Luckily, the doors had withstood the abuse and I was able to re-hinge them back into place. Aunt Iza and I decided that as soon as our Robinsoniad proved its mettle we would send messages to my mother and Aranka to follow us.

One evening, after finishing work in her vineyard, Aunt Iza came back to our manor house with a portion of cottage cheese and sour cream she had obtained in Vácbottyán, a village not far from the Rados orchard. Using about two pounds of flour, she prepared noodles for dinner. In those days we were so hungry that eating served not only as nourishment, but as a psychological necessity as well. The two of us couldn't stop eating. Even once we were satiated, we kept eating until the whole pot of noodles had been finished. The worst part was that while we were preparing the evening meal, I had knocked over a kerosene wick (a tall gadget, not very stable on its stand), pouring a sizable quantity of kerosene into the pot of noodles. A wicked spirit must have been directing my hand. The noodles tasted completely disgusting; even to this day, sixty years later, I can still remember the revolting taste of the kerosene.

One afternoon, a storm broke out. In the heavy downpour, I figured that Aunt Iza would be forced to stop working and would come down to our house from her vineyard. Recalling my father's scolding when Minci and Judit had left Veresegyház in a storm and I had neglected to escort them home, I began to worry about Aunt Iza. I scurried around until I found a weather-beaten umbrella and went out, hoping to meet her on her way.

In the meantime, Aunt Iza had reached the "small forest," an area of locust trees adjacent to our vineyard. The main road divided our vineyard from this small grove, which was on the Rados's property. In this wooded area, Aunt Iza unexpectedly came upon "the hatchet man" busily chopping down her acacia trees (he had earned the name "hatchet man" when I found him dismantling our pantry shelves with his hatchet the first time I visited the vineyard after the siege). Seeing the man trespassing and looting, Aunt Iza began to yell at him, delivering a verbal fuselage. The man raised his hatchet to attack her. I arrived precisely at that moment, whereupon "the hatchet man" lowered his hatchet and left. Aunt Iza was convinced that my arrival had saved her life.

On April 11, Aunt Iza went back into the city. She took with her a letter from me to my mother urging her to come out and join us. On April 23, I ran into Uncle Károly Brencsán and sent another message with him, again urging my mother to come out to Veresegyház. On April 27, my mother and Aranka finally decided to hit the road and join our company.

Two days later, on the morning of April 29, Aunt Iza and I had an unpleasant surprise. A dray wagon full of Russians showed up. Since the weather was overcast, Aunt Iza had decided not to go up to her house, but rather to stay with us. The Russians marched through the house as if we weren't even there. They grabbed my decent pair of shoes and a small carpet. Their eyes fell on the Omega wristwatch that lay on my night table. This had been a present from Aunt Blanka, my Dabis grandfather's watch. Naturally, the Russians pocketed that as well. One of the Russians, a small, blond, blue-eyed hoodlum of the type that harassed the women in our cellar at Buda noticed Aunt Iza and tried to grab her. Aunt Iza was slightly plump, but ran very nimbly around the dining room table. I ran out to the porch where I had previously hung an iron bar just for this kind of emergency. I picked up a large hammer and banged the iron rail, the sound of which carried quite a distance and would alert the neighbors. I was still in my pajamas, and as I kept on banging a soldier ran out, grabbed my hammer, and tried to hit my head with it. With his other hand he grabbed my pajamas, which were fortunately in such a worn-out state that the sleeve was left in his hand, while I got away. I ran toward the train station where Mrs. Cserepkai, a widow, lived in a small cottage with her two sons. They lived next door to Tivadar Bucs and his wife Eszter and their children. I gathered the Cserepkai boys and Uncle Bucs, and we returned to the house, armed with hatchets. When we arrived, Aunt Iza received us greatly agitated but unharmed. We had a short consultation and decided to go down to Vácbottyán and file a complaint with the staff officers. The idea originated with Aunt Iza, who had done the same when the Russians were harassing her family in Pest. I was skeptical.

We went down to Vácbottyán, where the Russians were thronging about like bees in a hive. There, I noticed Uncle Rory's water tank serving as a showering device. We looked for an interpreter and told him the reason for our visit. After a while, we were led into a room where three staff officers sat around a table. One of them was, again, the blond, blue-eyed shouting rascal type with which we were already familiar. The next one was a Mongolian-looking officer, while the third looked like a university professor from Germany. As a matter of fact, the latter spoke fluent German. Aunt Iza narrated the events of the morning, the Russian interpreter conveyed our story, and we were ushered out of the room. After a short wait, we were ushered back in. According to the interpreter, the officers wanted us to return the next day at noon. The garrison would be lined up then and we could pick out those who had robbed us in the morning, including the soldier who had grabbed my hammer and tried to hit me with it when I sounded the alarm.

Aunt Iza and I then walked home. I had mixed feelings, since I was convinced that our morning visitors would not be on display. They would be sent out to the forest to pick wild strawberries and we would stand there with egg on our faces, having only created more trouble for ourselves.

When we got back home, a new surprise was awaiting us. My mother and Aranka had arrived from Pest. Hearing the events of the day, they were aghast. Here we were sending out these messages urging them to come since it seemed safe enough and the work was too much for us. Now, because of our assurances and urging, here they were and yet suddenly the situation had drastically turned for the worse.

When we finally went to bed my mother, Aunt Iza, and Aranka lay down, all three of them on the large gothic bed, but they stayed dressed. In the middle of the night, I woke up to a Russian lighting up my face with his flashlight through the window. Like a madman, I jumped up and ran into the next room. Every window had iron bars on them, which in peacetime served us well by keeping burglars away, but now turned out to be deadly traps. I alerted the three women and called them over into the corner room where I slept. Its entrance door was a double door, but instead of glass it was made of solid oak. It opened onto the porch and was bolted in place by two large sliding iron bars, one at the top and one at the bottom. I squatted down and lined the women up behind me. I whispered to them that as soon as I pulled the latches out, they should make a mad dash in separate directions.

Those few seconds were nerve-wracking and hair-raising. I waited until the soldiers at the other end of the porch broke the glass door with their rifle butts and entered the house. A few seconds later, I could hear the jackbooted steps of the intruders. When I heard them reach my parents' bedroom, I pulled out the latches, opened the door and pushed the three women out on their way. At this point I could do no more. My immediate concern was to get to the Cserepkai's house as fast as I could to alert a group of men to help. I did so and gathered the rescue squad, made up of the Cserepkai boys and Uncle Bucs, all armed with hatchets. We speedily returned to the house, and walked around the building. There was no light coming from inside, and we didn't have any flashlights. After an extended period of time, Aunt Iza came forward. She had been reluctant to show herself until she was sure that the voices were ours. The Russians had been caught by surprise when they saw the shadows of so many people fleeing. They expected to find only one woman, Aunt Iza, there, not three, and they had not noticed that there was another entrance off of the courtyard. My mother had run to the railroad station and spent the night there at the watchman's cottage. Aranka ran in the opposite direction, to Mrs. Bredl's vineyard, where she found shelter with the family of Bóta, the vintner.

Early in the morning we gathered in our macabre mansion. We mulled over our predicament and concluded that we must return to the city, since we were now in a situation where we could be harassed on a daily basis. We gathered our belongings, packed everything into a wheelbarrow, knowing that the house could be fleeced again, and walked down to Veresegyház. The pharmacy was our regular stopover, a safe haven, whether we were coming or going. From there, we walked to Szent Jakab, where we caught an electric train into the city.

Sometime later, our peasants told us that the Russian commanders were outraged when we didn't show up the next day after they had lined up the entire garrison.

On April 30 my mother and I arrived back at Logodi Street. This ruined, shot-up building was our fortress where safety beckoned, where we were not in danger from nightly attacks. For a long time I slept restlessly, with nightmares every night. Over time, the nightmares faded, but not the memory of those events.

The next day was May 1, a dreary, joyless day. Residents were organized block by block and marched out to celebrate the greatest holiday of the proletariat. My parents and I were also expected to take part in the procession, which started in the morning. Our first stop was before the Gellért Hotel, where loudspeakers transmitted a speech by Marshal Voroshilov to the amassed multitude. Its opening line was: "*Tovarishi, Drazvushitye*" ("Greetings, Comrades"). Thus, we were greeted as comrades for the first time. After a long speech in Russian, we trudged on to City Park, where boring speeches followed one after the other. Late in the afternoon we were finally free to leave. Since we hadn't had anything to eat or drink all day long, we dragged ourselves home. We released a heavy sigh, but the dark cloud of uncertainty kept hovering over our heads.

In the spring of 1945, Uncle Rory became psychologically addicted to selling the family's treasures and relics. Due to his experience during the siege, he was afraid of dying of hunger. He fell victim to carpetbaggers who bought his house on Logodi Street for a pittance, a mere four hundred dollars. Then he sold his antique furniture, a portrait of Prince Charles de Ligne with a quill in his hand, and a beautiful triptych with all of the O'Donnell coats of arms depicted on its side wings.

In the midst of this frantic selling, Uncle Rory handed me the book *Goethe und Gräfin O'Donell* (*Goethe and Countess O'Donell*) and a painting by Johann Wolfgang von Goethe with the words "Teplitz 1811 Gothe" on the matting. He indicated that he wanted me to use the book as proof of the provenance of the painting, and to sell the landscape to a dealer in the inner city. As I got ready to leave, my father warned me not to sell the painting to the dealer under any circumstances. "Listen," he said, "Whatever the dealer offers, I'm willing to pay. Uncle Rory doesn't have to know about it. You just bring the painting right back to me."

My father's worry about this transaction ended up being unfounded. What the dealer told me was in essence that he wasn't even interested. "You see," he said, "I have not the slightest doubt that this landscape was painted by Goethe. It is very much in line with how he painted his landscapes, and the provenance of it coming from the O'Donell family only makes the case stronger. However, since the signature is not on the painting itself, but rather on the passé partout, to me as a dealer it has no commercial value." I was relieved, having accomplished the mission without forfeiting the painting.

Uncle Rory sold many beautiful pieces of furniture at this time, including Biedermeyer chairs, cabinets, a secretaire, an armoire, a chest, and a beautiful triangle-shaped china cabinet. All of his antiques changed hands for a meager amount of lard, flour, and bacon. He made the worst possible deals. In the end, the flour became infested with vermin, the lard and bacon went rancid.

Uncle Rory had a few gold coin relics of the old Monarchy and a few gold Napoleons. These he habitually kept in the pocket of his fur coat, but the pocket had holes and the coins kept falling out of it and into crevices in the apartment's parquet.

Ink landscape of Teplitz by Johann Wolfgang von Goethe

In the spring of 1945, Aunt Hansi and Uncle Rory moved out of Logodi Street. They found a villa on Lejtő Street in Hűvösvölgy, which they shared with Princess Clementine Metternich-Sándor. Shortly thereafter Uncle Rory's health deteriorated, and by the summer he had passed away. In late fall Aunt Hansi emigrated to her homeland, Austria, to live with her sister. We stayed on Logodi Street longer, but in November 1945 we moved out as well. At that point there still wasn't any electricity or running water. The bathroom was still out of order, the dividing walls collapsed, and the walls facing the street were pocked with sizeable holes. We couldn't use the fireplaces, the windows were missing; the wind whooshed across the forlorn and depressing apartment. My father and I were the last remaining tenants in the house.

28

Home Again in the
Old Manor House

In May, my mother and I finally set out again from Buda to Veres-egyház. On our way, we stopped at Aunt Iza's house in Pest. From there we took the electric train to Szent Jakab and trudged down to Veresegyház. In Veresegyház, we had a short respite, as usual at the Csomays' local pharmacy. We changed out of our city clothing into tattered country rags. This way, if we encountered any loitering Russians, we would blend in.

At the Csomay Pharmacy, we ran into Ernő Jr. He was a year or two younger than me and studying to become a pharmacist. As for now he was busy in earnest defusing mines, which were littered higgledy-piggledy in the nearby fields.

He led us into his bedroom and showed us a macabre sight. Neatly lined up underneath his bed were land mortars, bright lemon-colored beasts, each one roughly the size of a baseball bat. I counted thirty pieces or more. We were stunned.

Ernő told us how he decided to take this dangerous job upon himself. A couple of weeks ago, as he was walking in his family's vineyard, crossing a little grove, he caught sight of a yellow object on the ground. As he watched, a little bird settled on it. In the next instant the little creature was blown up, ripped to pieces. This horrendous sight inspired Ernő to search for a bomb disposal squad to learn how to defuse the mine—by screwing off the igniter key.

I immediately thought of a scene I had witnessed on a previous visit to Veresegyház. On that occasion, Laci Rados and I had set out to try to reclaim my family's stolen dray from Illés Hamar. As we ambled along in the morning sunlight among the hills and vines, the sound of an explosion hit our ears. Shortly thereafter we heard wild ululating. The best writer would not be able to do justice to this scene. Two little boys—they must have been five or six years old—had come across an abandoned hand grenade, which in the midst of their playing had blown up in their hands. The children, like two little worms, lay wriggling on the ground. The explosion had ripped open and torn apart their innards and in total agony they squealed and writhed on the sandy ground. Next to them were two peasant women, clearly the mothers, wailing and clenching their hands, stuck to the spot like magnets. The horror had paralyzed their capacity for action; they didn't say anything to us, nor did we to them. Laci and I saw that no kind of medical attention would be of help here. There was no surgeon in the world who would be able to patch up these torn-apart inner pieces, and by the time an ambulance were to arrive both of the boys would have bled to death. Not that calling an ambulance was an option—there wasn't a telephone nearby. We quickly departed. Afterward I wondered what we could have done differently and whether we could have done anything at all.

Leaving our city clothes and shoes behind at the Csomays', we set out again. We passed the cemetery and stopped at the Cinkota's house. Everywhere we went, we lent a sympathetic ear to various gruesome stories. This era had a long life in everyone's memories, at least until newer calamities washed away these reminiscences.

By the time we reached the railroad tracks close to our house, we were quite worn out. The railroad line passed by Erdőváros Station; its next stop was Vicziántelep. We crossed the rails and kept going toward our house on the path that led to our kitchen garden. Passing by the row of weeping willows, by the poplars, silver birches, and sumacs, we could see the yellow gables of our old manor house beckoning toward us.

On this day, as mother and I sluggishly walked home, we didn't run into anyone working the land. Many of the men were missing, and the women didn't dare to show up by themselves. The peasants wouldn't bring their horses out yet for fear of losing them to the plundering Russians. One exception was our neighbor Mr. Bucs.

On one fine day, Mr. Bucs discovered a horse, a dying nag, in his meadow. This poor horse was nothing but skin and bones. Mr. Bucs asked the Cserepkai boys to help him. They placed two long poles under the poor animal and succeeded in lifting him onto his legs. He was given water and some fodder. The faithful creature later paid back the loving care when he dragged Mr. Bucs's jalopies, and he played a vital role when we moved out from the city to Veresegyház. By then he had a partner, in the form of a mule. They formed an odd couple. Mr. Bucs gave them just enough food, keeping what they ate to a minimum to ensure that the Russians wouldn't be enticed to steal them away.

29

"In the Meantime,
Back at the Ranch . . ."
and Our Daily Russian "Visitors"

In old Western movies the audience would be transported back and forth to the ranch where a fight was on between the Indians and the pioneers or the farmers and the horse thieves. In the spring of 1945, peregrinations between the city and the vineyard defined a period where my mother and I repeatedly returned to the ranch. As we neared the manor house, an eerie silence would prevail. There were no dogs incessantly barking; the Russians had shot them dead. The cawing of crows was absent for the same reason. There was no sign of any life on the landscape. The clinking of the hoe, the rattling of the carriages, or the sound of a human voice; they were all gone. The only sound that greeted us was the song of the blue titmouse, with its attention-getting cry: *"Nyitni kék, nyitni kék."* To Hungarian ears it sounded roughly like, "Need to open, need to open," reminding farmers that it was time to uncover the vine stalks.

The house with its yellow walls, long honeysuckles hanging in cascades over the stairs, greeted us with utter quiet. The wind traveled across the rooms unhindered, but it was a godsend because it helped push out the stench left behind by the occupying army. When we finally reached our destination, we entered the same side wing of the building from which a few weeks ago the Russians had chased us out. Exhausted, we dropped the load of supplies we had carried out of the city in knapsacks to save us from starvation. As we went from the kitchen into the bedrooms, we made a dreadful discovery: in every room the floorboards were missing.

307

This was the beginning of a new adventure. Like the pioneers in Zane Grey's novels, we warmed bricks in the fireplace and, to fight the winter chill, put the hot bricks into our beds. At least we had bricks.

Soon, some of the neighbors showed up, courageous souls who had remained in Nyires during the siege. They tried to give us moral support while informing us of the latest rumors. Mrs. Cserepkai dropped in. She lived by the train station in a small house, a widow with two sons. Her news was that on the day that we arrived, three thousand Russians had simultaneously arrived at Vácbottyán. Our blood froze.

There were signs that something was amiss. Not only were the floor planks missing, but walking through the rooms I noticed that a few planks from the ceiling in the last room were also missing. They might have been taken by the old marauders, or perhaps it was a new act of piracy.

My mother and I again had to make a quick decision. We decided to stay no matter what. We could not keep on coming and going. If the others could stay here—Miss Olga, Mr. Bucs, the Cserepkais— somehow we should have the courage to do the same. We reasoned that the Russians wouldn't have the guts to kill us in cold blood. We decided to stay away from the main tract of the upper house; to stay there would have given away our relationship to the owners. We would have been automatically stigmatized as the bourgeois oppressive class enemy, exposing us to unnecessary harassment. Of course, even in our more humble environment we were vulnerable.

It was obvious that if we wanted to stay, I would have to construct a makeshift floor. I filled a vat with straw and clay, mixed it with water, and plastered the ground, thumping the mixture down with my hands. The three rooms opening railroad-style from the kitchen thus all got a clay adobe floor. The first room adjoining the kitchen was the dining room, the second was my parents' bedroom, and the third, in the corner, was my room with its separate opening onto the porch. These were the double doors that had served as an emergency exit on the night of the Russian "visit."

My mother behaved heroically. She agreed to stay, risking further encounters with Russian soldiers that could, of course, be particularly dangerous for women. The only precaution she took was to leave the house at sundown to stay with Miss Olga, whose little cottage was no longer harassed by the Russians. I kept my sleeping cot in the last room, in the usual spot in the corner.

I was convinced that we must not show fear or anxiety. We had to pretend that we were not the wicked bourgeois who owned the house. Those people had fled with the *Germanski* or *Nemeczki*. Nevertheless, I was completely scared. I was scared of the uncertainty, the possibility of a new onslaught of Russian hoodlums. I was quite aware of my vulnerability, but at the same time I also knew that if we wanted to work the land, to cultivate the kitchen garden, to plant and be able to enjoy the fruits of our work then I must stay. I was also serving as a deterrent to homesteading by strangers in the empty house. As the days went by, I kept hoping that Aunt Iza would show up again with Judit. My friend Szabi Viczián was staying nearby in the old Viczián grange, anxiously waiting for our pea crops to appear. I was in weary shape, a weakling, when I started to work the land. Every few minutes I had to take a break. I felt ashamed that I didn't have the strength for digging and pickaxing. The strength that I had gained during the summer of 1944 in Transylvania had long dissipated during the siege.

So I kept myself together, not unlike Scarlett O'Hara at Tara with her dramatic pledge never to starve again.

In May 1945, none of the gentleman farmers, aside from Szabi and myself, dared to venture out from the city. The Faith siblings had their vineyard on the same road as the Gunda-Rados family. There, only Uncle Jenő stayed in the house during the siege and the Russian occupation. Uncle Jenő was clubfooted and therefore not fit for the army. He ended up playing an important role in my life, launching me on my moonshining career. He was willing to lend me his special cauldron, an alcohol distillery container, which was a double boiler; the hot water boiled the fruit mash, preventing it from scorching. (Most Hungarian homemade brandy had a burnt taste unless the distillation was done slowly and carefully on a low flame.) But this secret activity began only later that summer with the ripening of apricots, blackberries, cherries, plums, and peaches.

∾

I was covered with mud up to my ears when through the window my eyes caught sight of a large Dodge truck in our courtyard. I was plastering and trampling down the clay, straw, and water mixture to create the improvised floor. My heart began to beat faster, my throat felt dry; a gripping fear came over me. This fear and agony remained with me all through the summer because from here on out, Russian soldiers visited daily.

No sooner had I caught sight of the truck than a Russian officer was already coming into the house. His jackboots didn't make the customary noise, since we no longer had any floorboards; therefore, he took me by surprise. Luckily, by that time I had a rudimentary command of the Russian language. He asked me who I was. I came up with a sob story. My family was murdered by the Germans, we were bombed out of our flat in the city during the siege, only my mother and I are still alive, and now that the former squire left with the Germansky we were homesteading in this place. The saga of our vicissitudes seemed to move the officer; he gave me a warm handshake and a package of cut tobacco. I had laid the foundation of our acquaintanceship while making the foundation for our rooms.

This first meeting with the Russian officer was pivotal to us being left in the house unmolested. From here on, I would see my Russian friends almost every day. They would drive into the court-yard with their huge Dodge trucks and go straight into the upper house, the tract where Uncle Rory had lived. They would come with crowbars and iron hatchets to loosen up the ceiling planks and the floorboards, which they loaded onto the truck. In Uncle Rory's apart-ment the attic floor was laid with two-inch-thick planks, on top of which a thick clay cover served as insulation. For the Russians to reach the planks they had to remove the clay (clay that came in handy for me while I was installing the floor of our rooms). I had to bear painful witness to these beautiful pinewood planks being stripped from their beams and hauled away. Once they had filled their truck, the soldiers pointed at the well for me to draw water. The weather was hot and they were sweating profusely. I felt somewhat akin to an Ali Baba who not only saw the forty thieves, but had to help them wash up. Most of the time they didn't carry any weapons, but on one occasion I saw a pistol poking out of a soldier's pocket while he busily splashed himself with water.

In our vineyard, the ground was made of sand. The sandy roads of our vineyard posed problems for the Russians. Their wheels would spin like they were on an icy road, or in the mud. Their trucks would get stuck in our vineyard, and then, to stop their wheels from spinning, the soldiers would pull up vine stalks and push them under the wheels. Each time a Russian truck got stuck it created an infernal noise until the truck finally reached more solid ground. This loud noise had an added grinding effect on our already frayed nerves. Our hearts would start beating faster and we would scurry about, looking even busier than usual.

During one of the Russians' unexpected visits, my mother was sitting on a small stool on the porch surrounded by pots and pans and baskets of fruit. As summer passed, the apricots, apples, and plums followed one another in ripening. Now my mother was in the process of making them into preserves. There she sat, looking haggard, while her heart throbbed wildly. She kept on peeling, chopping, and stirring the fruits on top of the stove, her hands shaking.

As the days went on, our desperation and bitterness grew. One afternoon, after the roaring of the truck's motor died away, I climbed up into the attic to survey the scene. A gigantic hatchet lay across the beams. An idea took hold of me, a revelation. If the Russians can steal our planks, why can't we do the same? The big hatchet lay there invitingly, left behind by a careless Russian. It proved to be the best tool for the project. Still, it was hard to rip up those two-inch-thick, twenty-foot-long planks. I had to make sure to stay on the beams, or face the possibility of falling through the gypsum ceiling into Uncle Rory's bedroom. Here and there, I could see holes in the stucco ceiling where the Russians had slipped. I had to work fast to utilize the remaining daylight, since I knew that the soldiers would be back the next day. I unfastened the planks above Uncle Rory's bedroom and study. I took the risk that the Russians would notice the gap, but I figured that they would suspect their own comrades before they suspected us. I was prepared to tell them about another group of Russians who also took a couple of truckloads of planks. It was critical for me to make them believe my story. If I could get away with that, I planned to continue stealing and hiding the boards.

As these beautiful, long planks gave way, they bade their farewell to the beams that had served as their cushions. After I finished prying them free, I had to drag them down and hide them. Since I couldn't do this chore alone, I needed my mother's help. Thus, the once elegant, pretty artist, the intelligent writer, who with the unexpected turn of events became a thin, almost emaciated woman in her worn-out skirt and torn blouse, climbed up into the attic to lend me a hand. She was utterly exhausted by the siege. Her nerves were on edge, and she had tried to spoil her looks even more to deter the Russians from any unwanted approach. She grabbed one end of a board and I the other; stepping from one beam to the next, we dragged the planks down.

As I looked around the house, I found just the right hiding place. Behind our house, in between the irrigation canal for the kitchen garden and an overgrown, bushy area, lay a little swamp surrounded by weeping willows, sumacs, and celtises. The water, which we normally used to irrigate our kitchen garden, was swelled up in the canal. I slid the boards into this improvised little pond. The depth of the water was just right to hide the planks. Anyhow, the Russians didn't walk around the back of the house to explore the park or the garden. When the Russians were coming daily for the planks, I presumed that they needed them to build barracks. To my great astonishment I later learned that they were selling the planks to farmers for brandy.

While the planks were quietly resting in the pond, my mind began to race, imagining what else we could possibly save from the marauding Russians. It occurred to me that the next items that would be taken away were the doors and windows. I visualized the trenches in the park, each of them lined with the heavy oak doors of Uncle Rory's residence. In desperation, I turned to András Lehotzky, Grandmother Eveline's faithful farmhand.

I went to look for András and found him at home. At my request, he harnessed his only horse to a carriage and drove down to our house to pick up the doors and windows and take them over to Grandmother Eveline's wine cellar. Her house had been plundered and her wine barrels were empty, but since her cellar was very deep it had proved to be too cumbersome to take the barrels. We slid the doors and windows down there as well.

Thus, Uncle Rory's tract was just about emptied. The wind had free access to the rooms. During days when I became too tired or the heat was too stifling, I would go up to Uncle Rory's rooms and sort through the mounds of scattered paper piles. Most of these papers ended up in our fireplace or stove as kindling.

The daily visits of the Russians took place during the daylight hours, except for one occasion. It was toward the end of the summer, when one night I awoke with a start. I heard the familiar droning of an army truck at our gate. Its headlights lit up Apple Allée, which led toward our house. I was frightened and confused. I picked up a heavy stable blanket and slipped out of the house. I hurried into a far corner of the vineyard, dug a hole for myself, and decided to spend the night. As I lay there in the sand, despair took over. My mind went through the what-ifs. What if they went into the house and found no one there? My mother never stayed for the night but now I was not there either. My whole carefully contrived sob story about homesteading might be blown. Yet I couldn't bring myself to return to the house, since the bars on the windows would prevent any escape, should things get ugly. Memories from a few weeks earlier, when the previous Russian garrison members had broken into our house and I was there with the three women, came rushing back. Now I had no choice but to stay where I was, even though I ran the risk that they would nab me as a hiding partisan. From my hiding place, I could see them go straight into the attic. The headlights of the truck illuminated the scene. I heard the heavy cog roof tiles landing on the ground and breaking into pieces. After a while the truck departed with its usual struggling sound on the sandy road.

After this episode, I feared that these nightly visits would become commonplace, so for several nights I slept in the vineyard under the starry moonlit night. I became quite comfortable with this new mode of slumber. The sand gave way to my body's contours and my sleep was sound until the early dawn. As daylight broke, the dew descended and birds began to sing, beckoning me from my slumber. Luckily, we didn't have any more "night visitors," so eventually I ventured back into my usual nook in the house.

Even though the nights were quiet again, during the day there was no shortage of visitors. Early one morning, a carriage pulled up before the porch with a half-dozen Russians. On our porch stood a Maria Theresa period piece, an escritoire. This piece of furniture had been in the family for generations. It had originally belonged to either Count Joseph O'Donnell, finance secretary to Emperor Francis I, or to Prince Charles Joseph De Ligne. Half of its drawers were missing, but its three large sections were still intact. The top section had a tabernacle-like center piece with four drawers to the right and four drawers to the left, plus one below the tabernacle itself. The middle section had a folding upright writing desk. The bottom section, similar to the top, had three drawers to the right and three to the left, while a recessed part in its middle was covered by a door. Both sides of the secretary had an iron rod that connected all of the drawers. These rods could be operated from inside the tabernacle, each locking six drawers simultaneously into a closed position. Then, by locking the tabernacle's door, the whole secretary could in essence be locked with one key. Originally, the secretary had had fifteen drawers. Looters had taken all but the frame and a few of the drawers. I had left the piece on the porch, waiting until I could get some help to move it elsewhere.

The newly arrived Russians went straight to the porch and began to pull out the secretary's few remaining drawers. They intended to use them in lieu of bags to collect apples from our orchard. My mother was inside the house, oblivious to the Russians and the commotion. As I ran into the house and began pulling out drawers right and left from the furniture inside, my mother was startled, but there was no time for explanation. I ran out with my replacement drawers and explained to the soldiers that these were better suited to their purpose than the others. They smilingly remarked that I am a *durak*, a crazy, but they gave me back the other drawers. Thus was I able to salvage the few remaining drawers. The carriage rolled out of the courtyard with its load of unripe little green apples. One could only imagine what those apples did to the Russians' stomachs. Or perhaps not, since they seemed to have iron stomachs. They were known for gulping down aftershave lotions for the alcohol content.

For the time being, for us, life was primitive. We couldn't make any repairs to the house, since that would blow our disguise. On the other hand, demolishing structures didn't risk our cover. I began to take apart a shed-like construction adjoining the rear of the coachman's apartment. I saved the roof tiles, with the thought that they could come in handy in the future. Similarly, I saved the lattices and the rafters. I demolished the adobe walls; the good clay improved our sandy paths outside. Next, I took down the apiary. I sold its bricks, likewise the tiles of its roof. These were large red tiles, different from the beige tiles on the house. I also sold its windows and doors. While the Red Army was utilizing our house as a checkbook, I also attacked our buildings with a vengeance. I razed the outside car shed; since all the drays and coaches were gone, it had no purpose anymore. I left the poultry farm fixtures and the pigsties in place, hoping that they might be useful in the future. I took apart the ice pit that had served Uncle Rory's household so well. The beautiful bricks lining it could be sold for good money, but its thatched roof was worthless. The greenhouse proved to be useless. It was made of concrete and its windows were broken. In the course of all of this work, I came upon four hundred ceramic pipes, which could be used for irrigation. I went to Mr. Kertész, the miller, and made a deal. He gave me a sack of flour in exchange for the pipes.

Our lifestyle was like that of the shipwrecked Robinson Crusoe. We made soap in a cauldron by boiling lye, ash, and animal fat. We also boiled water from Őrszentmiklós. A thermal well in the center of the village had water with a high salt content. We managed to condense a two-inch layer of salt in the pot.

We brought kitchen utensils out from the city, along with some washbasins, pots, and pans. We missed the running water that we had had in the city. Out in the countryside we had to use our draw well. In the kitchen stood a bench with a couple of pails of water on it. I bought a kerosene lamp, a luxurious round burner, and somehow got a hold of kerosene. But we didn't need to use the lamp much. The days were long and tiring and we didn't have any reading material anyway. By the time night fell, we were quite ready to go to sleep. Sleep was the narcotic that we looked forward to for escape. To wake up was a disillusion. Our days were burdened. Looking ahead we could see only problems and uncertainty.

One day, as the weekend approached and my father was expected from the city, my mother inquired in the neighborhood about where we could get some poultry. She came back with a rooster, and since the rooster was to serve as my father's arrival dinner we were faced with the task of killing the poor creature. My mother declined to participate. She had never killed an animal in her life and didn't intend to start now. She handed the task over to me, not that I had killed any animal up to that point either. I went behind the house into a secluded area shaded by trees and shrubbery that was used for storing firewood. I looked for the tree trunk that I used to chop firewood. I proceeded to lay the rooster on the trunk, but he must have sensed his doom and he refused to stay still. In my right hand I held my superb hatchet, courtesy of the Red Army, ready to strike the rooster's neck. In over-arming myself thus (the thought had apparently escaped me that a regular knife would have done the trick) I had made my task cumbersome. I then made it even more so because I didn't want to see the hatchet cut off the rooster's neck. So I did the deed somewhat as a blind man would, by averting my eyes. Somehow, I managed to complete the task. Luckily, never again was I faced with the same predicament, as Grandmother Eveline's old cook Rózsi joined us soon thereafter.

At the end of the summer, a small boy showed up at our door. He was around five or six years old. We tried to find out who he was, where he came from, and where he was headed, but he wouldn't speak. We were glad to have him with us; even his small hands could help around the farmyard. He spent a few days with us, and then one morning he disappeared. He never said goodbye, just took "a French leave"—as suddenly as he had appeared, he disappeared.

30

Exploring Our Newfound Domain

When I returned to our estate at Veresegyház in 1945 after the siege, I began to look at the property from a different perspective. I realized that from then on this was going to be our permanent home, providing us with perhaps our only livelihood. I walked around the land making mental notes about its possibilities. We had about four acres of arable land, separate from our main property situated about halfway between Veresegyház and Őrszentmiklós, opposite the Egervári water mill. To reach it, we passed by the Viczián estates and by the Brencsáns' orchard. The land was not very fertile, and since it was farther away from our premises our surveillance of it was limited; thus it was exposed to thievery. With that in mind, my mother decided to plant potatoes, corn, and rye on it, the usual staples.

Grandmother Eveline's vineyard and house was an independent, self-sustaining entity. It consisted of two acres of vineyard plus my mother's half-acre of vineyard and fruit trees. My grandmother also had fruit trees, but they were not systematically groomed. To get to my grandmother's house took about a half an hour on foot. Now that my grandmother had turned her little vineyard over to us, we had an added chore of going there with tools and baskets to harvest the fruit and carry it back. All the while, thieves had a free hand, knowing that nobody was guarding our house.

Our estate at Veresegyház had been a small earthly paradise. We cherished our remembrances: the landscape with its varied slopes and haystacks, the overpowering sense of spring, the wild orgy of grapes, lilacs, linden trees, and wild carnations.

We made every effort to regain our former standard of living, to create a new home imbued with ambiance. My mother loved the estate so much that she gave up her career as an artist and a journalist in order to devote her full energy and attention to the land. My father also loved the house and vineyard, though he had a different perspective. While my mother characterized our living quarters as "a small hidden wing of a large castle," my father felt enchanted by its surroundings. During our involuntary incarcerations immediately after the siege, he began to dream about the estate becoming more beautiful, larger, and more modern. He visualized a picturesque, impressive manor house in the center of a rejuvenated vineyard. The imaginary picture he drew of his longings stayed with us as "*Le Temps Retrouvé*" ("Time Regained"), a film on our minds' screen.

Fall came and the Russian garrison finally left Vácbottyán. We began to breathe easier, but for a while during the weekdays when my father was in the city, my mother still didn't dare sleep in the house. As evening fell, she would return to Miss Olga's cottage. By then, I didn't encounter any nightly visitors anymore, but I was overcome by loneliness. Although the trees and the plants were surrounding and protecting me, offering consolation in the windswept garden, I was alone and overwhelmed by the thousands of tasks and challenges.

The world began anew, slowly evolving out of the chaos, and although we couldn't yet see what shape it would take, we fervently hoped that it would not be drastically different from the old.

31

Working the Land

By the spring of 1945, I had fallen in love with the vineyard. I became just as infatuated with our land as Scarlett O'Hara had been with Tara. The full force of my imagination revolved around the modernization of the estate and the intensification of our farming. I dreamed about rebuilding the manor house and modernizing it with the installation of a bathroom, so that we wouldn't have to brave the elements each time Mother Nature called.

By this time the Russians had left Vácbottyán, it was time to bring back the doors and windows of the main house. András Lehotzky once again met me at my grandmother's house in Őrszentmiklós with his dray. We brought the doors and windows up from my grandmother's cellar and returned them to the manor house. The upper part of the house gave the impression of a moveable set in a theatre. The rooms were empty, and one could see the sky through the gaping holes in the stucco ceiling and the missing roof tiles. Behind the thick beds of clouds, the moon soared radiantly bright.

In the city, my father moved to a small rental room by Apponyi Square. The room had been the servant's quarters for a maid (an endangered species, which, by the end of the war had become extinct). The apartment owner was Dr. Endre Tüdös, chief medical officer of an orphanage, the Foundling Institute.

Once we had decided to move, it became imperative for my mother and I to create a warm and inviting new home at Veresegyház. All signs indicated that we shouldn't have to fear the Russians any longer. With the passing of time, a few of our old neighbors also returned to Nyires, among them the Gunda-Rados family.

I pulled the floor boards out of the shallow wetland behind our house, and Mr. Cinkota got busy laying a new floor for my parents' bedroom and my corner room. This flooring was less attractive than the previous jointed floor, but far better than tamped-down clay. In the third room, we removed the clay, and laid the floor with ceramic tiles. To the left of the entrance room was a storage room, a large, bright, enticing area that we transformed into an elegant dining room. Once we had finished with the floors, I asked Buci Béres, the oldest of the Béres boys, to come and build us large tile stoves to heat the rooms.

My mother and I planned to have a ceramic stove built in one corner of the library. The tiles were maroon colored. Buci Béres and his bride cut the wires that would hold the tiles together, and they mixed clay and water in a vat. In the meantime, my mother went up to Grandmother Eveline's house. A half-hour later, as we were drawing the outline of the stove on the floor with a piece of chalk, a little boy arrived carrying a note from my mother: "Put the stove in the center of the wall." Her intervention arrived just in the nick of time. It took about two days for my stove-setter friends to finish the two fireplaces. The tall one had a small nook in its center, where a teapot or a bowl of soup could be placed to keep it warm. These fireplaces were our most loyal friends during the frosty weather, when the winds were howling and the snow was falling.

Now that we had a roof over our heads, doors and windows with shutters, fixed floors, and working fireplaces, we could take our next step. By the end of the summer, it became apparent that Grandmother Eveline could no longer go on in Budapest crammed into a small servant's room, crowded in by furniture. Her apartment had been looted, she had no provisions, and her pension had been devalued by inflation. The only solution was for her to join us at Veresegyház.

With the help of András Lehotzky, the remnants of Grandmother Eveline's household were transported to the vineyard. She settled down in the little bungalow at the entrance of our courtyard, previously the vintner's house. The house had a room but no fireplace. The entrance hall had a cooking stove, and there was a pantry and a small covered patio.

Fall set in and distributed its cornucopia with a blessed hand. Fruits and vegetables ripened. Our meals became ample and more varied. Mr. Cinkota and his wife went to the market and sold vegetables from the garden and fruit from the orchard. It was time to harvest the grapes. It was the first year after the war, and since we had sharecroppers tilling the estate, only half of the crop belonged to us.

Laci Lehotzky, who was my age, became our foreman. Money still had no value, so we paid him in wheat and rye. With Laci's help, we began to organize the wine cellar. We scooped the gooey material out from the bottoms of the barrels. Then we hammered off the hoops holding the barrels together. After that, we brought up the staves (the wood pieces that comprise the barrel) and laid them out by the well. We scraped off every stave, cleaning them of the tartaric wine stone residue. Once that was done, we built a bonfire and scorched every stave individually. We singed the surface, to kill off any harmful bacteria, and then put the barrels back together again, hammering the hoops back on. We slid long slender reeds between the staves, to soak up the wine and prevent its escape. Once the reeds were in place, and to make sure the staves held fast, Laci walked around each barrel and hammered the hoops back into their original places. With some rope, we then moved the barrels back into the cellar. Placing each barrel onto its stand, we lowered a few burning sticks of sulfur on a wire into the barrels in order to fumigate them. Once the sticks had burned down, we pulled them out and the barrels' corks were put securely into place. Now the barrels were ready to receive the most.

That blessed autumn, the golden harvest slowly filled up the tubs and vats with mash. Everyone saved their unsold or faulty fruit. They ground them up and stored them in vessels. There were apricots, cherries, plums, and peaches galore, often mixed together. These were mysterious concoctions; their smell would carry over to neighboring vineyards. Due to the war, the revenue officers were not organized this year; this led to a number of moonshiners all over the countryside.

The doyen of the moonshiners was Uncle Jenő Faith. He had a special cauldron for steam distillation, a so-called double boiler, in the back of his courtyard. All the other types of distilling gadgetry that people used—spray cans, milk cans, jerry cans—lent a bitter, stinging, burnt taste to the brandy. I borrowed Uncle Jenő's miracle cauldron and set out on the risky, but glorious, road of moonshining. From then until 1947, my main source of income came from illegal booze. My high-quality fruit brandy was sought after by local innkeepers. Uncle Jenő was frequently visited by the roaming pirates of the Red Army, so he had a special buzzer alarm installed. It worked on a small battery. Its push button was on the veranda, but the buzzer sounded at the far end of the courtyard in a shed. Whenever a cart full of Russians arrived and the distillery was in process, Uncle Jenő pushed the button. At that, his helpers would hastily put out the cooking fire, drag the utensils into the vineyard, and cover up the cauldron. The only thing left was the overpowering smell wafting away from the shed. But Uncle Jenő always had presence of mind and a large bottle filled with brandy, ready to be offered to his uninvited guests.

32

Farewell to Logodi Street

In November 1945 we completed our departure from Logodi Street to Veresegyház as best we could under the turbulent circumstances. There were no moving companies, but even if there had been, they would have been beyond our financial means. As it was, four drays appeared in front of 6 Logodi Street. One of these was Mr. Bucs's, with his ill-matched animals (the mule and the horse). The other three belonged to farmers from the village of Veresegyház. This was not an organized move. Nothing was properly packed. There were no boxes. Books were not tied up with string. Everything was in a heap. The makeshift movers did their best, but the drays were all uncovered. While we were packing, it became dark and snow flurries began to fall. One of the peasant coachmen disappeared, went into an inn on Attila Street, and began to drink. He had a large flatbed dray. Since his horses were two strong young foals, we packed my father's library onto that vehicle. Just as we had finished loading the cart, its owner showed up. He mounted his coach and started to make a u-turn onto Logodi Street going north. Halfway through the turn, the carriage toppled over sideways and all the books landed on the muddy street. The owner extricated himself from his seat and tottered back to the inn to continue his drinking.

With the help of the three remaining coachmen, we turned the dray around, picked up the books, and loaded them back onto the cart, but now there was no one to take command of the cart's reins. My father sized up the situation and ordered me to drive the dray out to the vineyard. I protested, with a vehemence equal to that with which my father was ordering me to undertake the task. I argued that I had never in my life driven a coach with horses. But it was to no avail. Resignedly, I climbed up into the coachman's seat, determined to close ranks with the next to last vehicle in the convoy. Desperately, I worked to catch up with the others. Mr. Bucs was in the dray directly ahead of me.

On the edge of the curb by the Zerge Stairs sat a neat pile of unexploded mortar shells, hand grenades, and mines. When Mr. Bucs's jalopy arrived at that spot, the left wheels of his carriage raked over the ammunition pile. For a minute I visualized Mr. Bucs and myself watching the bleak autumn landscape from "above," but in the next instance another near-mishap caught my attention. On top of the piled-up objects in the wagon ahead of mine lay a large portrait of Charles O'Donnell, a general decorated with the order of Maria Theresa. A stool leg had punctured the painting, poking toward the sky like a submarine periscope emerging from the sea. Decades later, I realized that had the leg not punctured through the painting that night, we might have lost Charles O'Donnell to the high winds.

6 Logodi Street, 1945 (1)

We were rolling down Margaret Boulevard toward the temporary pontoon bridge that had been installed on the tip of Margaret Island in place of the blown-up Margaret Bridge. Dusk had fallen, but military trucks lit up the night. Small, stocky female Russian soldiers, so-called *Barisnya*, directed the traffic, waving little yellow and red flags. Immediately I was surrounded by the thronging mass of Russians and cut off from the three drays ahead of me. Tanks, trucks, and cars struggled to get across the bridge in the snowfall. There was some moonlight, which was the only light, due to the absence of streetlights, other than that of the military trucks. The pontoon bridge was flat, floating on the icy surface of the Danube. It was a lucky convenience, since I couldn't have gotten across the patched-up Liberty Bridge, which had a steep slope.

At this point, my biking experience came in handy, because I was familiar with the various routes out of the capital. Darkness notwithstanding, I was able to navigate. I chose the hard surface

6 Logodi Street, 1945 (2)

6 Logodi Street, 1945 (3)

road toward Vác and, surprisingly, caught up with my traveling companions. My relief was short-lived, however. By the time I reached Dunakeszi about an hour later, all three of the coaches had disappeared from view. I was the single soul on the road. The villages were dark, like ghost towns. From Dunakeszi, I took a sharp turn to the right. Now I was on the road to Fót. Somehow, I didn't have any problem with the horses. They knew their duty. I had only to keep the reins in my hands, sit tight, and hope for the best. The road through Fót was paved with clinkers, ceramic bricks. We rolled smoothly across the hard surface as we went through the center of the town and across the grounds of Count Károlyi Castle. On each side, the castle walls and buildings loomed. Just as I reached the edge of the complex, a large group of Russians jumped out from both sides. They sent one round of machine-gun volley after the other right in front of my horses. Scores of bullets whizzed above my head. For a second I had the feeling that I was in the midst of the siege all over again. I stood up and whipped the horses. It was needless. The two colts were so bewildered by the shooting that they broke into a stampede. They could not have gone any faster.

When we took a sharp right turn toward Csomád, the horses drove into a ditch. Here, I needed to lash them. Luckily, the horses were so incredibly strong that in spite of my father's enormous library load they were back on the road again.

As we neared Veresegyház, I began to wonder how I would return the horses and dray, since I didn't know where, or to whom, they belonged. We were rolling along Main Street in Veresegyház at a good clip, when suddenly the horses took a turn toward the right across a small bridge. For a second, the two left wheels hung in the air. Then the horses stopped and snorted. They were home. The wife and the mother of Gerhard, the farmer and owner of the horses, were still awake. I stepped down, told them what had happened, and they promised to drive the dray out to the vineyard the next morning. I slogged home on the sandy path, across the railroad line, between the poplars and weeping willows, straight to the kitchen garden and into the house, where my mother also was still awake, waiting for me.

33

Settling Down at the Old Homestead
and a New Year's Party

Our loyal old friend, 6 Logodi Street, which we had been forced to abandon, had protected our possessions during the ravage of the siege. Whether it was furniture or paintings, the items we were able to salvage gave us a chance to beautify our ultimate haven, our final destination. The coarse wooden plank floors at Veresegyház were now covered with carpets. We installed my father's bookshelves into the corner room, which instantly took on the ambiance of a small library. All of us were drawn to its charm. From then on that room became our drawing room as well as a library.

The room opening off to the left of the entrance hall was earmarked as our dining room. The large dining room table was moved there and a fireplace built of bricks was erected in one of its corners. The room opening off to the right of the entrance hall became a guest room. From here opened a room that became my parents' bedroom. Inside it we placed my parents' couches and a washstand with a large pink marble top. From that room one could access the corner room, which became my bedroom. The dilapidated furniture, the armchairs stripped of their leather upholstery were sent into exile in Uncle Rory's section of the manor house.

We began to hang our paintings. My mother's artistic skill, her excellent taste, now came into play. In the end, a couple of her own paintings, *Landscape of Balaton* and a large nude, were sent cruelly into exile in the attic.

My mother had a good eye for spatial positioning. I would hold a painting up to the wall and she would tell me where to put the nails. She had no use for rulers or measuring tapes; she disliked being bogged down by details or exactitude. Uncle Rory and Grandmother Eveline's O'Donnell portraits offered us a great variety of superb paintings. Two huge portraits of Henrik O'Donnell and Malvina Tarnóczy, my grandmother's parents, went into the dining room. Every once in a while during the picture-hanging process, my mother and I would go out into the courtyard and come back in again just to get a feel for the impression a visitor might get upon entering the house. These old family portraits were painted by artists who had worked in the Austro-Hungarian imperial castle for the royal family. When we had finished hanging the paintings on the walls, my mother turned to me and said, "You know, you must keep in mind that these paintings should be cleaned and re-varnished every one hundred years." This daunting task shocked me for a second, until I realized that I would just as well pass this instruction on to my descendants.

By the time my father arrived the following weekend for Christmas Eve and Christmas Day, he would be received in elegant surroundings. In 1945 my father had both days off from the Radio. He came out to Veresegyház in an elated spirit. Before dinner, while I was out in the courtyard, I heard Russian voices. I ran into Uncle Rory's kitchen, where everyone was, and alerted the household. The broiled chicken hastily returned to the oven just as three Russian soldiers entered. They were polite. We served them a good portion of a tasty soup and gave them a bundle of apples. They behaved decently, said thank you, and left. They were the last Russians to visit our manor house. After they left, we took the chicken out of the oven and happily sat down to our Christmas dinner.

Gyuri Sághy and Szabi Viczián decided to celebrate the end of the 1945 and the arrival of the next with us. Our weatherbeaten family ship crossed the line of the old era into the beginning of the new. In the early part of the evening we went to a small gathering at the home of the Arczfalvi sisters. Szabi and I were due to meet Gyuri later at Óbuda, on Lajos Street, where a celebration was in progress at a local high school gym. Szabi and I left the party at the Arczfalvis' reluctantly, since Judit Rados had just arrived. She was accompanied by István Kormos, who had recently returned from a displaced persons camp in Austria, where he had been working as an interpreter. He had immediately thrown all his energy into wooing Judit. My curiosity for the unknown and my close friendship with Gyuri and Szabi won me over. Thus we departed for the next party. Gyuri arrived at the school with a beautiful girl named Klári. There was no shortage of adventures whenever Gyuri appeared on the scene. This time, we faced a school that was already over-crowded; its doors were locked. A few Russian soldiers with fixed bayonets sauntered up and down in front of the building. Gyuri was determined to get all of us in, and he came up with a plan. The side of the building was scaffolded, awaiting reconstruction. He climbed the scaffold until he hit upon an open window. He picked a board up off the scaffolding and laid it from the scaffold over to the window. As he went about his business on top of the scaffold in his formal evening attire we watched him with bated breath. He put the plank in place, walked across it, and disappeared through the window. He had told us that once he was inside he would open the door and let us in. He warned us to be ready to slither in as fast as we could once he opened it. His act was befitting a Hollywood detective movie. We ran over to the main entrance, where Gyuri was already awaiting us.

With a grandiose gesture, Gyuri informed Szabi and me that he didn't have any proprietary rights to Klári and he would not be offended if either of us left in Klári's company. We danced a lot; swing had its sway over us. But as the evening wore on Klári couldn't help but remark that on her own she was not enough for three boys. The earlier generous offer of Gyuri's inspired Szabi to action, while I passed. Szabi tried to kiss Klári in the middle of a wide stairway. Choosing the stairway was a strange choice, considering that a flood of youngsters were continuously ascending and descending. Szabi's attempt was nimbly staved off by Klári, who said, "Not here, please." Szabi misinterpreted the statement, and sadly escorted Klári back to Gyuri. I made a feeble attempt to explain to Szabi that "not here" meant somewhere else, but it was too late. It became obvious that Gyuri would leave the ball with Klári. Regretfully, I never met this charming young lady again. She remained only a fleeting New Year's memory.

34

An Adventure in the Life of Szabolcs

In the fall of 1945, the schools opened again. Szabi enrolled at the Economic Studies Department, while I continued my studies at the law school. Luckily, in the spring of 1945 I had been able to take exams for the year, so I did not lose any time due to the siege. Since I now attended classes regularly, I needed to find a room to rent near the university. A friend of the Viczián family, Árpád László, whose nickname was Lacika, rented a room to Szabi and me in his apartment on the sixth floor of 36 Lónyay Street. Our room was partially built into the attic.

Szabi, like the other members of the Viczián clan, was constantly on the lookout for good business opportunities; but that is where the similarities stopped. While his clansmen had good business acumen, Szabi's transactions almost always ended in disaster.

One of his more notable transactions took place while he was Lacika's tenant on Lónyay Street. On an early winter evening, as Szabi was walking home, a man stepped out from the Meinl delicatessen store at Kálvin Square and called after Szabi. He told Szabi that he was the manager of the store and that auditors were coming the next day to take his inventory. It just so happened that he had in a nearby storage room a twenty-five liter surplus of Maria Theresa brandy. He was ready to sell it for a pittance since it would be taken from him anyhow. The list price of a good quality brandy at that time was around ninety forints per liter (on August 1, 1946, the Hungarian forint was trading at one dollar to ten forints). The manager told Szabi that he would sell the liquor to him dirt cheap, just thirty-five forints per liter.

For safety's sake, Szabi asked the man for some identification. He memorized the man's name and address. Then they walked across the street to a pub. There, in one corner of a storage room stood an enormous demijohn. The demijohn is included in the price, said the man affably. Szabi asked for a sample, which was poured into a shot glass. Upon tasting it, Szabi concluded that this was indeed an exquisitely fine cognac, and so he closed the deal (it remains a riddle how the man picked out Szabi, who just happened to have enough money on him). In the end, he paid 875 forints for the booze.

Szabi trudged home with his heavy find to 36 Lónyay Street. Luckily, it was only a short distance since the demijohn was heavy and he had to carry it on his shoulders. As Szabi entered the apartment, he cheerfully shouted to its inhabitants: "Ili, Lacika, Kálmán, let's celebrate!" Everybody stood around Szabi in curious anticipation. "Let's get some shot glasses!" he exclaimed. He proceeded to pour the brandy into each of the little glasses until he came to his, at which point the demijohn refused to yield any more of its precious contents. He put it down to better investigate. In the neck of the demijohn he felt a cork, which, with a sigh of relief, he removed. Then he proceeded to pour a shot for himself, but although the brandy in the other glasses had a nice caramel-like hue, his was clear. He lifted the glass up to smell the aroma. Unfortunately, this was a fluid that had no smell. It was tap water.

The following morning, Szabi, being a stubborn and methodical person with a good memory, went to the house on József Street where the seller lived. On a nameplate in its hallway, he found the name of the person he was looking for. Just then the actual person for whom he was looking tried to sneak by him out onto the street. Szabi grabbed the swindler, but unfortunately for Szabi the guy knew how to present a real sob story. He promised to give the money back, but of course he had already spent it. In the end, Szabi's heart overtook his business sense and he let the man go scot-free.

35

Moonshining in the Moonlight

Gradually, our little community at Nyires began to grow. Pali Illés-falvi, Miss Olga's nephew, settled in with his wife Manci and their two-year-old son Péter. They were avid readers like us, and we exchanged reading materials with them.

Ilonka Dukony helped my mother with some of our household chores. Her husband Boldizsár worked in Ujpest as a technician in a factory. He set up an incredible distillery apparatus for me out of a two hundred liter copper cauldron, which we had been using for washing clothes and cooking plum preserves. Boldizsár made a dome-like hood, which we fastened to the cauldron with screws. A copper tube spiraled through the top of the hood and entered a water tank, which cooled the alcohol evaporating in the spiral and lique-fied the vapors. I was now able to make homemade brandy without having to borrow Uncle Jenő's double boiler. To be on the safe side and avoid prying eyes, we distilled only during the night. Notwith-standing our extreme secretiveness, the smell of the mash wafted out, around, behind, and beyond. One couldn't help but notice the overpowering stench. Another giveaway was the sound of us draw-ing water from the well. We had a steady need for cold, fresh water, and our well had to be cranked by hand. People in the neighborhood must have raised their eyebrows: Why in the world did the Farkases need so much water in the middle of the night?

Because I was busy moonshining at night, I slept during the day. We encountered an unexpected glitch when, after a while, my grandmother began to wonder what was wrong with her grandson, since I was sleeping all day. Since she was rather a naive soul, we decided to keep her out of the know. We couldn't risk her giving the show away. So when my grandmother asked my father why I

335

was not up and about during the day, my father said to her, "He's a young man who frequently visits maidens in the evening. It's only normal." To which my grandmother replied, "I understand that, but if a young man disappears every night that is most definitely not normal."

One evening, Uncle Tóni Viczián dropped by to see us, more precisely to make me an enticing proposal. At Őrszentmiklós there was a bona fide distillery that was temporarily closed. He proposed that I take over its management.

The next day I set out to Szada to consult with Pali Groschmied, a friend who had worked for Baron József Vécsey's distillery after the war. I enlisted Pali as a silent partner in this enterprise. He and I turned out to be a good team. I learned a great deal from Pali, and he benefited financially from our partnership. In those days, distilling brandy was an excellent moneymaking venture.

In the distillery, we burned apricots, plums, peaches, blackberries, cherries, sour cherries, pears, and mixed fruit. We also distilled the marc, the burned-out husks of the pressed grapes, and the lees, the sediments from the bottoms of the barrels—well-nigh a cognac.

While we sat by the fire, Pali entertained me with many colorful stories. He was a blood relative of the great playwright Imre Madách, author of *The Tragedy of Man*. Since Madách had lived most of his life in the county of Nógrád, a statue had been erected in honor of him in Balassagyarmat, the county seat.

According to Pali, one night after the local tavern in Balassagyarmat had closed a group of rowdy college students proceeded to the main square. One of the boys climbed onto the pedestal of the Madách statue and cracked a bottle of champagne open on Madách's head.

Shortly thereafter, the local police showed up, arrested the disturbers of the peace, and put them in jail. At noon, they stood before a judge who read the charge: disturbing the peace, desecration of a statue in the main square. He asked them what they had to say in their defense. By that point, the boys had begun to sober up. One of them replied, "Your honor, we had the best of intentions. No harm was intended, nor was any disrespect. When the champagne bottle broke, we all shouted, 'You, too, should have a drink, Granddad.'"

As it turned out, all of the rascals present were the grandchildren of Imre Madách. The Groschmied, the Butler, and the Hanzély boys were all straight-line descendants. Thus, the judge dismissed the case. Stories like these made time pass more quickly as we sat before the blazing fire night after night.

At our last monthly revenue inspection, officer Béla Medgyes, captain of the revenue service with two gold stars on his collar, came to check our business procedures. He was an outright gentleman, quite unusual for his profession. He was certain not to last long in the job. He hinted that his successor Ferenc Kátó was a member of the Communist Party and that he didn't get along with him.

Pali and I made our usual preparations for the inspection. It was ironic how these inspections—for a distillery or for any other operation—seemed routine for any regime. Preparing for our visitor, I thought of the episode where my friend Gyuri encountered the German Wehrmacht officers on the barges on the Tisza River. Here, we did something similar. At the completion of the inspection, we invited the captain to join us for brunch. There, on a slanted table attached to the wall before the window in our little office, we piled up various delicacies: bacon, ham, sausage, liverwurst, rye loaves, and to wash it all down wine and brandy. In this cozy atmosphere, we handed over our tax receipts, which were in perfect order, and after the official functions we got down to satisfying our hunger. Among the displayed goodies was a piece of headcheese, the size and shape of half a grapefruit. We were standing around the little table having a convivial conversation, when the headcheese suddenly flipped over twice from the center of the table and fell to the floor. The three of us looked at each other and said in unison, "A ghost!" I followed up my exclamation with the question, "Captain, do you believe in ghosts?" "Not only do I," answered Captain Medgyes, "but I am a regular participant in séances at Vác." "How does someone in your profession venture into such unlikely territory?" I asked. "I'll tell you why," answered the captain.

He began his story going back to his adolescent years. He was born and raised in Transylvania. When, at the conclusion of the First World War, the Peace Treaty of Trianon gave Transylvania to Romania after detaching it from Hungary, he decided to leave his native land. He went to the railroad station. Since the train was still hours away he decided to take a nap at a small bridge, a trestle under the railroad tracks. While he was asleep, he dreamt that he was standing on the rear platform of the last car of the train in a strange uniform unknown to him at the time, dark green with gold epaulettes and gold stars on his collar. As time passed, he forgot all about this dream.

In August 1941, an arbitration occurred between Romania and Hungary. The Axis powers, Germany and Italy, redrew the Trianon borders and awarded northern Transylvania, where the majority of the population was overwhelmingly Hungarian, to Hungary. Following that decision, Hungarians began to take over the administration of northern Transylvania.

It just so happened that Béla Medgyes, who at that time was already a revenue officer, was assigned to travel to Transylvania to organize the newly established revenue service there. It was beautiful balmy weather that fall as he stood in his uniform on the rear platform of the last car of a passenger train. As the train rambled across a small bridge and slowed before a station, the dream that he had had twenty years earlier came back to him. "From then on," he finished his tale, "I knew that there are things that we are unaware of, and I became interested in the occult. I joined a spiritual group to learn more about life, death, and destiny."

Unfortunately, our careers as distillers terminated abruptly six months later when the state nationalized our little enterprise and showed us the door. The distillery was reorganized into a cooperative association without us, the capitalist usurpers.

Inflation was constant during and after the war, but hyperinflation[1] only began in earnest after the November 1945 elections, when a new coalition government came to power. People on fixed incomes or pensions suddenly had virtually no money at all. The population worked for an entire year with hardly any remuneration. Pensioners didn't claim their pensions, because the price of the bus ticket to go to the post office and collect it cost more than their monthly pension. Factories distributed cooking oil or other foodstuffs in lieu of wages.

---

1. The inflation in "neighboring" Hungary, the worst in recorded history and far exceeding that of 1923 Germany, peaked at five quintillion (five to the thirtieth power) paper pengős to the dollar—meaning that by the time the pengő was replaced by the forint in August 1946, the dollar value of all of the Hungarian banknotes in circulation was just one-thousandth of one cent. Tony Judt, *Postwar, A History of Europe since 1945*. (New York: Penguin, 2005), p. 87.

36

A Garden in the Rain

In 1946 and 1947, my mother hired five young workers, cousins of our foreman Laci Lehotzky, from spring until harvest. Their wages were paid in rye and wheat. My mother said enthusiastically, "I like them. They are so good-looking, young and cheerful."

By 1946, we had only one share tenant, the Cinkota family, renting out our kitchen garden. They worked the land with the agreement that half the income from the garden would be theirs.

Every evening, Cinkota arrived with his dray, and we packed his carriage with fruits and vegetables. His horses stayed in our stable. At the first blush of dawn, he and I hit the road and rolled toward the marketplace on the outskirts of the capital. Mrs. Cinkota would take the train from Veresegyház and arrive at the market at the same time we did. By daybreak, the open air market was filled with carts, wagons, and drays. We took beans, peas, asparagus, strawberries, green peppers, raspberries, cauliflower, and cabbages. It was a fascinating experience for me. While Mr. Cinkota and I displayed our wares, Mrs. Cinkota walked around the market, scouting out the prices of produce. We knew what the prices had been the previous day. If more produce was rolling in than the day before, we lowered our prices. When fewer farmers arrived, we raised them. The Cinkotas were shrewd, and we never had to return home with vegetables. This was important because standing out for longer than a day would cause the Juliet beans to become rusty, the asparagus tips to turn from white to green or crimson, and the tomatoes to spoil. Carrying back any load also made the horses do extra work.

We would divide our daily income shortly after noon, when the market women, the housewives, and the storekeepers left the market. I would take the train back while the Cinkotas rolled home together.

As time went by, my father realized that he would have to suspend his dream of a larger, more beautiful manor house (my mother had always deprecated my father's high-faluting plans, saying, "Why on earth would you want to create Kettleby's monastery garden out of a practical farmhouse?"). There was no more talk of a blue-and-white checkered ceramic floor or of columns at the entrance to, or around, the courtyard. My father was forced to place himself into a more practical frame of mind and to be satisfied with interior alterations. He mobilized Laci Lehotzky to put on his masonry and carpentry hats and to modify the flow of traffic inside our tract so that we could move from one end of the house to the other without being exposed to the elements.

In the north corner of the kitchen we opened up the trapdoor that descended into the vegetable cellar. We broke down the wall that separated the vegetable cellar from the wine cellar. This gave us a direct entrance into the wine cellar—at least the portion of it that had been walled up in November before the siege. We closed the hole in the false wall that Russian soldiers had made when searching for our hidden treasures. Now we again had a secret annex for some of our wine. The only modification we made was a small opening that we left in the corner of the wine cellar and hid behind a large barrel. This hole was utilized to run the rubber hoses of the wine pump from one section of the cellar into the other. We now had two different ways to reach the wine cellar. One was the original entrance from the side of the house, reachable from the main road. This entrance consisted of two winged doors, bolted with an iron bar and secured by a padlock. The second entrance was the new opening off of the vegetable cellar.

The secret enclosure in the wine cellar was a matter of survival and defiance against the regime. Hiding some of our wine made it possible to evade some taxes. The government, which by then was under the thumb of the Communist Party, was pressuring independent farmers, through a confiscatory tax policy, out of business and into the government-established farming cooperatives.

37

A Phony Peace (1946–1947)

During the carnival season of 1947, Gyuri Sághy enticed Szabi and me to attend the law students' ball. As a rule, Gyuri preferred to crash such parties. We tried to enter the Gellért Hotel, where the ball was being held, but the defenses against gate-crashers were too strong. We then walked over to the Park Club, an elegant entertainment center in City Park (in those days, there were no cars or cabbies, so we walked a great deal). There several parties were taking place, but the main attraction was the farewell to the 1947 ball season, a gala that also honored the commander of the Russian garrison in Budapest, General Zamercev, who was being transferred back to the Soviet Union.

Here the gates were also closed, but Gyuri walked around the building and discovered a scaffold on one of its sides. This gave him a chance to repeat his performance of New Year's Eve 1946. He climbed up on the scaffold to the third floor. He aimed for a narrow, well-lit window, jumped over onto a small terrace, and climbed through the window. We waited a few seconds and when he didn't return, Szabi and I followed his lead. Gyuri's arrival, it turned out, had caused some consternation since he happened to land in the womens' bathroom. Luckily, by the time we landed, the shrieking and screaming had abated and Gyuri had already organized the girls to be a part of our venture. Three girls came forward to take our overcoats to the cloakroom. We sauntered into the grand ballroom without creating any suspicion. Just as we did so, General Zamercev marched across the room, decorated with numerous medals, his wife by his side. He was roly-poly, and his wife was a pudgy little dame. As they passed, the young students, most of them tipsy, jubilantly shouted questionable epithets. Luckily, the general didn't understand

341

Hungarian, and seemed to interpret the commotion as a sign of his popularity, not unlike a wedding day somewhere in his homeland.

After this episode, I went exploring. By the bar I found Ági Ács, playing the piano and singing along. In another room, I hit upon a great swing orchestra. Repeatedly I requested from different musicians that they play "The Man I Love" by Gershwin.

While I enjoyed the pulsating rhythm of the orchestras, I looked at the beautiful girls, the newly budding generation of the postwar era. These girls, who had grown up during the siege and were dressed in their evening gowns, were enchanting. However, I was not particularly enamored with any of them, except for Vera Nagy. We danced a lively swing. She was definitely very pretty. Over the next few weeks, I helped Vera a few times with her Latin homework while she prepared for her high school graduation exams.

At different times and places, life was lively and uproarious. In 1946, while the British and American military delegations were still very much present in Hungary, they would crisscross the city in their Jeeps, oftentimes with pretty women at their side. The cinemas showed American movies. The Metropole coffee house on the grand boulevard was a preferred meeting place for the international clientele. One evening, when the majority of the guests were American, British, and Russian soldiers, a brawl broke out. On one side were the Russians, while on the other were the Americans and the British. It was a spectacular sight worthy of a Western movie. Lamps, armchairs, café chairs, and other movable objects went flying across the room and crashed to the floor. The noise of heavy marble tabletops crashing from the balcony onto the ground floor was earsplitting. It was like Dodge City in a Budapest coffeehouse. The row finally came to an end when British and American MPs and a Russian KGB unit showed up. Each side collected its constituents, forced them into cars, and drove them away.

Another amusing episode took place in the Castle District. Right after the siege, the diplomatic missions settled down in different parts of the city, preferably at posh locations. The British ambassador found a palace in the Castle District that had miraculously survived the ravages of the siege. It was owned by Baron Berg's family. The baron kept part of the house for his family, while renting the top floor to the ambassador.

One night, the two Berg brothers went to a movie. It was a swashbuckling Hollywood feature with romance and lots of fights.

After the movie, they went to a pub and did some heavy drinking. In the wee hours, they called it quits and went home. As soon as they stepped into their palace's entry hall, their eyes lit on the armor decorating the stairway walls. Each grabbing a sword, they began to fence on the stairs, charging up and down. The great clanking and running about made an enormous ruckus. Suddenly the door on the third floor was flung open. Appearing on the balcony in his pajamas was the ambassador. He rested his arm on the balustrade and enjoyed a sight that up until then he might have only seen in the movies.

On January 1, 1947, my father received the news by telegram that his job at the Radio had been terminated. Until then, my father had rented a small bachelor flat at 1 Apponyi Square, but with his forced retirement he moved out to Veresegyház for good. Meanwhile, I had been sharing a room in Budapest with Szabi, but now I moved into the fourth floor room that my father vacated. In better times it had been a servant's quarters. It was just big enough to hold a bed and a clothes chest.

This house was referred to as *Királyi Bérház* (King's Rental House). It was owned by the Hapsburg family, but not for long, because it was soon nationalized. The maid's room that my father had occupied and I now lived in was part of an apartment rented by a well-known pediatrician, Dr. Endre Tüdős (Uncle Bandi to me). He was the director of the municipal orphanage known as the Foundling Institute. The Tüdős household was eccentric and bohemian, with the exception of Uncle Bandi, who was a serious type. He was a short man with thick glasses, resembling a combination of Gandhi and Pope Pius XII.

One night during the interwar years, Uncle Bandi received a frantic call from Magyar Street, where a rather elegant and expensive licensed brothel called Maison Frieda operated. This was an institution of prestige in the trade, a house where gentlemen selected ladies from a photo album. There had been an accident at the brothel, and someone, either a customer or a female resident, had been hurt. The brothel called Uncle Bandi because he was the closest doctor to Magyar Street. After Uncle Bandi had provided emergency assistance, he took his leave, receiving profuse thanks for his services.

In the morning, getting ready to leave for work, Uncle Bandi realized that he had left his umbrella at the brothel. He finished his coffee and set out leisurely for Magyar Street. He recovered his umbrella, but just as he was stepping out of the red-light building he bumped into three of his colleagues from the Medical University. They greeted Uncle Bandi with simulated outrage: "Good heavens, Bandi! Aren't you ashamed of yourself?! What would Ildikó think! And at your age, who would think that you would go into such a disreputable establishment!" Uncle Bandi, of course, hastened to explain what had brought him there—the need to reclaim his umbrella—but it was of no use. "Fine," they said. "But how did the umbrella get there in the first place?"

∾

"But are not the places where you spend your turbulent years closest of all to your heart."

—Solzhenitsyn, *November 1916*

Now that my father was no longer working, he concentrated his energy and attention on our rural life with interest and great gusto. He and I turned out to be a good team, willing to try out all kinds of ventures in our small paradise and wine enterprise. On a bitter cold January night, we filled a large vat on our porch with wine. By the next morning, there were chunks of ice floating on top of our zesty zinfandel. We threw the ice out and had a stronger wine than we would have had otherwise.

Our next experiment fell into a legal grey area. Hungarian wine law was rigorous. For example, there was a severe fine for adding salt to wine as a flavor enhancer. A few drops of lavender oil could make a wine taste like a Muscat or Muscadet, but this was also forbidden, of course, along with enhancing the sweetness of wine with sugar (unless the alcohol content of the wine was also raised).

With an abundance of apples too inferior in quality to sell on the market, we made them into wine. We ground up the apples and pressed out their juice, to which we then added a good amount of sugar. After fermentation, this mixture produced a beautiful greenish-colored wine. We could have made it into a so-called Calvados, a fruity, dry brown brandy favored by the French, but since we wanted wine, not brandy, we blended it with our Zinfandel. The blend made for a gently sparkling wine with a greenish hue and a higher alcohol content.

In 1947, when my father was fired from the Radio, he was still relatively young—fifty-one years old. His personality, his world view, his optimism kept him young and invigorated, and he was a *Europäer*—a European in the best sense of the word, a grand seigneur. His experience, his vision, his widely liberal humanistic attitude marked him as a gentleman. He began his Ovidian exile on what had been Uncle Rory's terrace.

Behind him, the empty house was a theatrical stage. He took out his ubiquitous Waterman fountain pen (he would never think of buying a Parker or a Montblanc) and began to write again. The years while my father sat there on Uncle Rory's terrace, working on his novel *The Siege,* were full of crossed hills and rude awakenings, but how beautiful they seem in retrospect.

Around this time, the older generation tried to re-tie the threads of social life where they had left off. We youngsters followed in their footsteps. In the early days of the summer of 1947, János Brencsán emerged from the city with three pretty girls, Mokka Spolarich, Ildikó Spolarich, and Éva Gervay. By now the trains were running again, though not the electric ones since the wires and poles had not yet been replaced. János's father, Uncle Károly, had died soon after the siege, and his mother Aunt Ida now resided in the family's villa at Vicziántelep. János was a member of the Radical Party, which had two members in Parliament, and was building his career in the publishing field.

On one day, the sky cornflower blue, I went up to the Brencsán villa. Aunt Ida, János, and János's three female guests were sitting on the terrace. Others were present as well, partially the old gang, but also a few new faces—namely Marica, Tóni Viczián Jr.'s wife, and Marica and Tóni's daughter Csilla, who lived with Tóni in the remnants of the burned-down manor house. Aunt Ida regarded the youngsters with delight, but couldn't resist motioning to one of the girls to uncross her legs, because her crêpe de Chine skirt was emphasizing the contours of her body at strategic places in a way that was not ladylike. We were still living in another world, and the dissolution of traditions and customs was a prolonged process. Only as communism permeated our lives did we, in chameleon-like self-defense, attempt to become part of the proletariat.

János confidentially informed me that Ildikó was not seriously attached to anyone. He was courting Éva Gervay.

In March 1944, when the Germans occupied Hungary, Aunt Gugu, Éva Gervay's mother, sent Éva, a young lady at the time, to visit their local parish and try to obtain baptismal certificates. The parish priest left the room, excusing himself for a few minutes. On his desk were a pile of blank certificates. Éva picked up a bunch of them and left the parish. Later Aunt Gugu prepared the baptismal certificates for Jewish families and members of the Jewish labor battalion. They were all saved. Years after Aunt Gugu died, the father of one of the saved Jewish families came to Hungary from London and took Éva to Israel where her name had been listed at the Yad Vashem memorial. The Holocaust Museum in Washington also lists Éva Gervay's name—under her married name, Brencsan—on a plaque memorializing Hungarians who dared to risk their own lives to save others.

After the introductory get-together at the Brencsán villa, a few of us visited the Spolarich family at their residence at Rákóczy Square in Budapest. Their apartment was inside a high school, because the girls' father was its principal. Besides us youngsters from Vicziántelep, an American boy representing a Quaker relief agency also joined us. While only János spoke English, it didn't seem to bother the young man, who enjoyed our company nevertheless. Ildikó played the piano, singing aloud to "The Man I Love," in Hungarian with her beguiling alto voice. That was all I needed to hear to develop a crush on her.

On the weekends, the girls would come out to the country, which had a negative impact on my assiduity. One afternoon, I set out for the city with an enormous hamper of sour cherries. At the Vicziántelep railroad station I bumped into our merry group. Ildikó was among them and she persuaded me to stay a while. Although it didn't take much to convince me to postpone my trip, she then lured me up to the Brencsán villa. Consequently, I left the basket with the truck watchman for the night, which, of course, didn't help the state of the sour cherries. My delay in delivering the cherries to Aunt Ildikó Tüdős until the following day came at the expense of the fruit; it was over-ripe and partially smashed.

I had a crush on Ildikó, a pretty girl with blond hair and blue eyes and a muscular body that looked especially good in a swimsuit. She had just graduated from high school and in her spare time she sewed and explored fashion design. She made her own dresses—to enticing effect, I might add.

Events followed events. One evening, we held a party on the other side of our house on Uncle Rory's terrace, whose ceramic floor was ideal for dancing. We carried the phonograph to the terrace and were dancing to tunes of those good old 78s such as "Mexicali Rose" and "Moonlight Serenade." While we danced, we flirted. We nestled close to our partners and held them tight.

Of course, the merry crew needed to be fed as well as be given plenty of fluids to avoid parched throats. The wine kept flowing. It needed to be replenished, so I asked Ildikó to escort me down into the wine cellar. We drew the wine into a wooden pail that served as a communal drinking goblet, thereby allowing us to dispense with wine glasses. We made an art out of drinking from it. We placed the pail on the balustrade of the terrace. Whenever one of us wanted to drink from it, we would squat down in front of it and tilt the pail to the proper angle. Then we proceeded to slurp the wine. Our Ezerjó (one thousand times good) sold itself. It was sweet, and in that year it was dangerously strong.

In the midst of our merriment my father dropped in. The ubiquitous Kenderesy boys danced with great élan. István Kormos, who had just returned from American captivity, wove his threads around Judit. Almost all of my friends were college students and free for the summer.

This was my frame of mind when I received an invitation from Ildikó to visit her for a week at Aszófő, a village adjacent to Lake Balaton where her family had a bungalow. I was glad that she had asked and I hoped to continue where we had left off a few weeks earlier on a romantic, moonlit summer evening.

38

Blue Skies Smiling at Us

I took the train to Aszófő. Ildikó was waiting for me at the station in a red dress with white polka dots. During my stay she mostly wore white shorts with white blouses. With her blond hair and blue eyes she was definitely attractive, especially when she smiled.

Aszófő, where Ildikó's family vacationed, was a village and a summer resort. The cottage of the Spolariches was a half-hour walk from the village center and train station. I arrived with a small suitcase. I always traveled light, a practice that I had learned as a Boy Scout camping and boating on the Danube. Now, when I went to visit Ildikó, I traveled ultra light. My present to her was a pack of Chesterfield cigarettes, which were very fashionable at the time— much sought after in those days along with Old Gold, Philip Morris, and Lucky Strike. She was happy to receive the gift, since she was a smoker (in those days it was hip for a girl to smoke).

On our way to the bungalow, we came upon villas and cottages showing signs of plunder and pillage. Even the windows and doors had been stolen from some of them. My night lager had been prepared in one of these ransacked bungalows. Ildikó had constructed a couch for me out of pine branches covered with blankets. This little bungalow was very close to the family's villa, which stood just before a hill. The top of the hill was covered with rock formations. Early the next morning, I climbed up and perched on the rocks, waiting to see signs of life at the Spolarich villa. At other times, when my patience waiting for Ildikó to wake up ran out, I threw a few small pebbles through the window of her room, hoping to hit her stomach.

At the Spolarich house, I was introduced to Uncle László, Ildikó's father. His wife had stayed in the city, so to amuse himself he had invited a friend of his over for vacation, a priest who was a teacher at the high school where Uncle László was the principal. Thus Ildikó and I were under constant supervision. The only times we could exchange gentle signs of intimacy were when we went to the village to pick up some milk. Those were occasions when we managed to slip out of the two elderly gentlemen's range of vision. The night of my arrival, we went for a walk as a foursome. We walked along the shore of the Balaton in Indian file. That night there was a full moon. It could have been romantic, but we had no privacy.

Near the Spolarich villa was a mom and pop restaurant where we were able to eat heartily at a reasonable price. A few days later, the priest took his leave and Uncle László was left as our sole guardian. Then even he had to leave for a day to look after some business in the city. However, this ideal situation was promptly interrupted by a letter from my father, in which he instructed me to take a quick trip to Somogy to see if I could buy some grain for our laborers. This letter came at a most inopportune time, but I felt obliged to carry out my father's request. In the meantime, Ildikó took comfort in Claire Kenneth's soft porn novels, favorite books of young women at the time: *A Night in Cairo, May in Manhattan*, etc.

After a day's expedition looking for grain I returned to Aszófő emptyhanded. By now, my visit was drawing to a close. We went swimming in the lake, basked under the sun, and enjoyed the magnificent landscape. The sky was blue and the sun engulfed us with bright rays. Lake Balaton mirrored the blue and green colors of nature, while a balmy breeze made configurations and ripples in the playful waves. It was invigorating and I became intoxicated with Ildikó. On the last day of my stay, sitting on the shore, I asked Ildikó to be my wife. Her reaction was a succinct sentence. In her deep alto voice, she said pensively, "I wish I could transform myself into a mouse and hide in your pocket." I was amazed at how a woman could utter such an inanity in such a strategically significant situation.

Shortly thereafter, a sailboat cast anchor in the harbor. On it were Uncle Huba and Aunt Livia, and their son Ákos Előd, a former classmate of Menyus Hajós. Ákos was a tall, handsome man, studying to be an architect (after the Cold War had ended, he would design Statue Park in Budapest), and he became Ildikó's next target. He brought an enormous leather trunk off the boat, and it reminded me of an advertisement by the trunk maker Csángó, whose trunks were sought after during the Austro-Hungarian Monarchy. The advertisement depicts the character Berci Mokány (Bert Plucky) standing on top of a traveling trunk in the ocean puffing on his long-stemmed pipe with his faithful hunting dog at his feet. He exudes a superior confidence and equipoise, as if nothing could go wrong for someone riding on top of a Csángó suitcase. This was the luggage Ákos arrived with, and I could only guess at its innards. I promptly said farewell to Ildikó and her father. I felt somewhat like Napoleon might have felt on the Island of Elba when he had finished his first meal in exile (laced with arsenic).

A few weeks passed by, after which Ildikó was courted by Bandi Matolcsy, a colleague of mine from law school. At one point, Bandi forgot his favorite fountain pen at Ildikó's. Feeling somewhat at a loss without it, he asked his brother Gyuri to go and pick up the pen for him. Since Gyuri didn't know the Spolarich family, he reluctantly agreed. In the end, he not only accomplished the mission of bringing back his brother's fountain pen, but he also ended up marrying Ildikó. The moral of the story is that if you leave an object behind at the home of the girl you are wooing, don't send somebody else to reclaim it.

After she got married I ran into Ildikó only once, on the bus. By then she had become the proud new mother of baby Eszter. Later on, she worked for the Magvető Publishing Company. She had a sunny disposition and was extremely popular; her colleagues adored her. They were deeply shocked when cancer took her from them; she was only around forty years old.

39

The Fall of the House of Roediger

He lay as one who lies and dreams
In a pleasant meadow-land,
The watchers watched him as he slept,
And could not understand
How one could sleep so sweet a sleep
With a hangman close at hand.

—Oscar Wilde, *The Ballad of Reading Gaol*

The title of this chapter could also have been "The Last Leap Year." In 1948 this designation had a double meaning for us. It was a leap year in a celestial sense, but by putting the words "the last" in front of it, it acquired a political meaning. That is, this was the last year before the Iron Curtain descended, and so it was also the last year people were able to leap over the border to emigrate, the "Year of the Escape."

Already in that year escaping from Hungary had its dangers. It was by no means a walk in the park, but it was still doable. We would hear the most fantastic escape stories. Some people managed to cross the border by putting on a railroad uniform and pretending to be a stoker in a caboose. Others floated down the Danube breathing through a reed as they came close to the border. One man, dressed as a racing cyclist, mixed in with the peloton of the Budapest-Vienna road race just before the Austrian border and then sweated it out entering Austria with the other racers. Some created berths for themselves beneath railroad wagons or under the seat of a railroad car. Others stowed away on Danube steamers. One driver drove his car right through the border barrier.

Gyuri Sághy left that year at the end of the summer. Not only did he escape himself, but he guided a dozen Romanian escapees to safety as well. Before Gyuri left Hungary he told me that he had been confidentially informed by the Ministry of Construction that the political situation would not improve and that he would be better off if he left the country while he still had a chance. He would have liked it if I had gone with him, but he knew that leaving Nyires, the vineyard, as well as my parents, would break my heart. My amorous adventures, the other argument against leaving my homeland, he lightly dismissed.

As time went by, it became clear that the newly established Communist regime would eliminate the private farmers, their orchards and vineyards. We were still unwilling to face the signs. Even if we were on a slippery slope we fervently hoped against hope that we could cling to something and stay put.

Around that time, Berti Roediger, the son of Miklós Roediger and confirmation sponsoree of Uncle Rory, married Zsuzsa Somssich, the firstborn daughter of a distinguished historic family, whose land at Sárd had been confiscated after the war. The Roedigers lived near Városliget (City Park) in a fashionable villa, befitting Miklós Roediger's position as president of the Hungarian-Soviet Shipping Company. Berti succeeded in obtaining a superb apartment in a villa on a side street of Andrássy Avenue. His bachelor flat in his parents' home thus became vacant. Berti offered this room to me for free in order to avoid having strangers squat in it.

By the spring of 1949, I was close to getting my diploma. I had one unit to go, which entailed exams in four subjects. Once I passed these exams, I would receive a double diploma—one in law and one in political science. One afternoon during this period, when I was studying for my exams as a lodger in the Roediger's household, I was in the bathroom shaving when there was a knock on the door. A man poked in his nose and asked if it would be long before I finished. I told him I would be out shortly, annoyed by the intrusion. I thought that perhaps it was a plumber, there to make some repairs. As I stepped out, it became immediately clear that I had not been talking to a plumber. Aunt Mia, Miklós Roediger's wife, and the Roedigers' cook were in the study with two men and a woman, who asked me as a witness to attest to the fact that no money or valuables would be taken from the apartment. I realized that these were secret police who had come that afternoon to search the apartment. Outside, dusk was falling, rain was drizzling, and a car was parked before the villa. A mean-looking woman in a green loden coat, favored by female Communist Party members, sat in front of Uncle Miklós's desk. I was certain that she was in charge. My later conclusion was that the house search had been only a formality, not a means for collecting evidence—a formality toward the family and the public. They already had all the information they needed about Uncle Miklós; his fate was sealed before the search began. The secret police must have planned the action sometime earlier, but postponed it until the Smallholders Party had control of the government. It served the Communists well to delay his arrest also because in the meantime Uncle Miklós would get the shipping company up and running again. Moreover, keeping him under surveillance for a while longer allowed the authorities to track and arrest his contacts as well. Once the Communists had achieved their aim and the political winds blew in their favor, they struck.

As the search proceeded the carpets were rolled up to see if anything was hidden beneath them. Candlesticks were taken apart. Paintings and lithographs on the wall were lifted from their hooks to afford a glance at their backs. Sconces were dislodged. Then the police turned their attention to Uncle Miklos's desk. One drawer had bundles of forints in it, a sizable bunch. Judging by their color, they must have been of high denomination. These were handed over to Aunt Mia. The plainclothesmen borrowed my suitcase to carry away the papers in the desk. Thus, although my suitcase visited the ÁVH (secret police) headquarters, fortunately I did not. (A few days later, they returned the suitcase.)

After the three ÁVH agents had left, Aunt Mia, the cook, and I stood there paralyzed. Aunt Mia told me that they had taken Uncle Miklós away. As he put on his overcoat to leave the apartment, he called over to her, "Mia, *sei ruhig*" ("Mia, stay calm"). The whole time the ÁVH was present, she kept her composure. Aunt Mia, born as Baroness Schluga, was a tall and incredibly beautiful woman. Her husband Miklós, on the other hand, was very short. They were cousins.

The following afternoon, I opened the door of the Roediger apartment for Herbert Thierry and his wife, Countess Erzsébet Csáky. Uncle Harry had been a co-organizer with Uncle Miklós of the Jewish rescue missions on Danube steamships from Budapest to the Black Sea.

Uncle Miklós had been a naval officer during the First World War and subsequently was employed by the DDSG, or MFTRT (Hungarian River and Sea Shipping Company). In 1939, he utilized cruise ships to transport fleeing Jews down the Danube. It was a sensitive, covert operation that required someone with the right experience.

After the ÁVH took Uncle Miklós away, nobody—not even his immediate family—ever heard from him again. Allegedly he was executed. My father's cousin Imre Tarnóczy saw an official death certificate at the prison on Fő Street in Budapest several years later, but there was no information on the whereabouts of his body.

Uncle Miklós's arrest had dire consequences. His father gone, Berti realized that the family could ill afford to have two apartments and two households. He sold his parents' apartment and bought a smaller one on Hegyalja Road, where he, his wife, his mother Aunt Mia, and his son Niki moved. As a result, I lost my rent-free room at the Roedigers.

~

In September luck smiled on me. My studies at the university were coming to a close, and in July 1949 I was solemnly accepted as a *Doctor utrimque*, having earned a doctorate in law and political science. An announcement posted on the unemployment office bulletin board sought an individual with a legal background and expertise in alcohol distillation. I was convinced that my pals sitting there on the bench beside me week after week were playing a practical joke on me, so I didn't apply right away. Eventually, they convinced me to apply for this mysterious job, which it turned out was at the Gyümölcs Termelési Nemzeti Vállalat (National Fruit Production Company).

On Monday morning, I went to the company's main office, where a lengthy interview process ensued. I was quizzed by the so-called company triad: the secretary of the Communist Party Bandi Kocsis, previously a fruit seller from Szatmár; Comrade Nagy, the president of the company; and Comrade Meizel, the head of the union. The interview went on all morning long. When it was over, I was hired to direct alcohol production in the various company orchards.

By the next morning, I was at my work station being informed of my duties. A young man, a controller of the Trust, told me that over the course of the next few days we were going to visit a number of nationalized farms, primarily in the Tisza River region. I was somewhat taken aback by my prospective traveling companion. Up until this point in my life, I had been spared from having to associate with this type of socially inept, roughneck person (in short, a moron). The young man with whom I was to be paired up seemed to me as if he had just emerged from the gutter (my father's favorite term for characters like this was "sewer dude").

A short while later, Bandi Kocsis, the young party secretary, appeared. He must have sized up the situation and, consequently, promptly changed the plan. My traveling companions became Comrade Bukova and Comrade László (or Laci) Ausch. I learned that Comrade Bukova had been a member of the Communist Party in 1919. After the demise of the Kommune in Hungary, he had lived in the Soviet Union. At the end of the Second World War he was parachuted into northern Hungary. His assignment was to organize partisan activities. On our trip, he would be in charge of inspections. Laci Ausch would serve as our driver.

The following day, I went to Comrade Bukova's tiny house on Kerepesi Avenue where he lived with his wife. There we were picked up by Comrade Ausch, in a Warburg automobile. We headed toward northern Hungary, intending to stop for the night in Miskolc. From time to time, we stopped by the different nationalized orchards. At each orchard, my job was to find out whether there was a distillery, and if so, to prepare a makeshift inventory of supplies and installations.

I was on friendly footing with my colleagues at the company, and eventually sat in at the meetings of all the department heads.

I made other trips to various parts of the country. I assisted in the transfer of two tank wagons of apple wine to a state spirit facility, to be utilized in the production of Maria Theresa brandy. It was fascinating to see how the process of blending Calvados, the apple wine spirit, with a regular brandy could be accomplished without any trace of apple flavor. Apple wine is essentially flavorless, in contrast to apricot or plum, where the smell and taste, the bouquet of the plum or apricot, is drastic right up until the last stage of the deflagmator.

I worked in different wineries throughout the country, transferring wine from the company's estates to the state-owned bottling plants. The work taught me that tasting wine in cool wine cellars and then emerging into warm outside air could be trouble. The reverse, drinking wine in a warm room and heading outside into a wintry night, could have a rapid sobering effect. These were the conclusions I distilled from those events.

Occasionally, I traveled with Communist potentates. They all enjoyed these trips since they were catered to like princes at the various state farms. They also received an extra bonus in their paycheck for each day that they were away on a business trip. In January, Comrade Mérő, one of the department heads, and I visited an orchard in Mezőcsát, where we familiarized ourselves with the problems of apple growing. The executive of the company enjoyed Mezőcsát because the wife of the agricultural engineer was strikingly beautiful. We were their guests.

With the start of my new job, I rented a room in the inner city, at 5 Régipósta Street, from Felix (or Lexi) Hetés and his wife Ilonka. Lexi Hetés had lived in France for years but had repatriated. After the war, he became a member of the Social Democratic Party. He didn't have a job, which to me was odd, since being unemployed was dangerous; the Communist regime treated nonworkers with suspicion. He served as his building's house warden, but this wasn't a job and he didn't get a salary. His wife Ilonka was an administrator at the Fővárosi Tervező Intézet (FŐTI) (Metropolitan Planning Institute).

My room in the first-floor apartment overlooked a courtyard. Access to my room was through the only bathroom in the flat, which was a bit of an inconvenience, since if any of us happened to be using the bathroom people would have to wait to come in or to go out. To get to work from the apartment I took the speedy No. 2 electric train, the "Stuka," which ran along the shore of the Danube and stopped near the National Fruit Production Company.

40

Liquidation of the Kulaks

On a morning in early January 1950, a customer left my parents' house with a ten-liter demijohn of wine. He had hardly left before he returned escorted by two revenue officers, who began quizzing my father about the sale. My father realized immediately that he had a big problem, because he didn't have a permit to sell wine in quantities of less than twenty-five liters. He tried to explain to the officers that the buyer had in fact purchased a larger quantity of wine, but because he didn't have a larger container—and would not in any case have been able to carry a larger one even if he had—he had intended to come back for the rest. The officers were unconvinced, and they asked my father to take them down to the wine cellar. My father knew now that he was in great trouble. As it happened, the previous day's drawing of wine had necessitated the removal of the large barrel that customarily covered the small opening in the corner of the wall. The rubber hose sneaking through the wall would promptly betray the fact that he stored his wine in two separate cellars.

As the officers entered the cellar, their eyes grew wide. The wine pump stood before the wall, utensils lay helter-skelter in front of the wall's opening. Nothing remained to be explained. It was obvious that my father was hiding part of his wine to avoid taxation.

The revenue officers went about measuring the wine stock in a slow methodical manner. They sat down at our large kitchen table and took copious notes in a long drawn-out fashion. They even made an observation that made my father laugh with bitter black humor. They reported, "Given the physique of the owner, the opening in the wall was not suitable for regular access to the other parts of the cellar."

From then on, revenue officers showed up every few days to reinspect the wine cellar. Such large-scale tax evasion was unusual, and here it was coupled with the misdemeanor of selling wine at retail without a permit. These bureaucrats could now justify their employment. The wonderful large wall, the product of Cinkota and Gyuri Sághy's, on which all our hopes had been pinned and which began its solemn debut on November 4, 1944, let us down for a second time. Only now the consequences were far more dire. The secret of the wall had held out for nearly four years, from 1946 until January 1950. The revenue officers assumed that wine had been hidden in the partitioned-off section of the cellar since the war, and accordingly calculated our tax evasion for each of these years, plus a penalty. It was an astronomical figure. Interestingly, revenue officers never came to check on a farmer without first receiving or obtaining denunciation.

These events ground on my mother's nerves. Years later she told me that every morning when the train came in from Vác and whistled before Vicziántelep, she went to the large cupboard, took out a flask of brandy, and poured herself a shot. It was the only way she could withstand those daily visits.

My father secured a lawyer, Dr. Lajos Kéri, an attorney from Budapest who also had an office in Vác. He would later become president emeritus of the Hungarian Jewish Community, and be awarded a medal of honor by Pope John Paul II when he visited Budapest in 1991.

Dr. Kéri had excellent connections and was widely respected. He was not an inexpensive solution by any means, but that was the least of our worries at the time. He and my father went to the revenue office in Vác and sat there from early morning until late into the afternoon. If it hadn't been for Dr. Kéri's tenacity, my father would have given up. But Dr. Kéri held the front like Kemal Pasha against the Greek Army, and with his legal skill and stubbornness haggled the original 36,000-forint fine down to approximately 10,000 forints. For us, this was still an astronomical sum, and didn't include the retainer we owed Dr. Kéri. My father had the shock of his lifetime. This was not only a financial disaster, but a psychological one as well. He felt his naked vulnerability, and his habitual optimism was badly shaken. He also had to witness the impact on my mother, notwithstanding her effort to present a strong front. She was an artist, not accustomed to such confrontation. During the siege, she had withstood the vicissitudes, but that was a hardship that visited everyone indiscriminately. In this case, we were singled out.

Then another problem crashed down upon us. The National Fruit Production Company was forced to declare bankruptcy and forfeit its orchards and farms to the Ministry of Agriculture. This didn't come as a big surprise. Its management had racked up a multimillion-dollar forint deficit. The original owners had not been allowed to keep their land and invest their own money in it, they had not been mindful of what they spent, and the administrative overhead had been overwhelming. As a result, in March I became unemployed.

At some point, I went to see Uncle József Emőri, who was vice president of the Országos Lakásépítő Nemzeti Vállalat (Countywide Apartment Building Company). The best he could offer me was a manual job. Luckily, the construction site was close to my flat, at Molotov Square (previously Vigadó Square), which allowed me to go home for lunch and walk to work. The site was a demolished bombed-out hotel. My job was to clean the bricks, chiseling and scraping off a heavy coat of Portland Cement. The bricks then had to be bathed in water. The handling of the bricks, the scraping and bathing, resulted in big bloody blisters on my hands. I was soon issued rubber gloves, but these just made things worse. My hands sweated inside the gloves and the blisters burst open. Soon, I couldn't even touch a brick. The sight of one, alone, made me sick. In addition, I was a slow unskilled worker. This was reflected in my paycheck but also put me in real danger. The supervisor put my name on a blackboard, labeling me a lousy worker, and therefore an enemy sympathizer. Young women at the worksite helped me fulfill my daily quota by stealing bricks for me. This job didn't last very long, but long enough to get on my family's nerves.

Meanwhile, Uncle Józsi asked his friend, the architect László Szpierer, to help me. Szpierer's business, like Emőri's, had been nationalized. I went to the offices of the Épület Bontó Nemzeti Vállalat (National Building Demolition Company) at 26 Szent István Boulevard. There, László Szpierer greeted me warmly and took me in to see the president, who was a frightening-looking low-level worker cadre type with squinty eyes. Szpierer told him that the company needed an industrial statistician and that I was available. I quickly told them that I had taken a course in statistics at the university and that my last job was as a planner at the National Fruit Production Company. The president thought for a moment and said that there was no difference between counting apples or bricks. I couldn't agree more. I got the job, and with it began an era of my life that was turbulent and traumatic, but as far as my subsistence was concerned, relatively placid. I didn't earn much, but I augmented my income with the sale of some family valuables.

László Szpierer skillfully talked the president into bringing Ágoston Lengyel, the previous head of the planning department for the Gyárkémény és Gőzkazán Építő Nemzeti Vállalat (National Smokestack and Steam Boiler Building Company) into the office. Comrade Lengyel was working at the time as an unskilled laborer on the demolition of a military hospital. He was one of the white-collar communists who were assigned manual labor as part of their ideological reeducation process, an alternative to being purged. Comrade Lengyel knew statistics, planning, and payroll procedures inside and out. For him it was a salvation to be able to put down his pickaxe and return to the office. For me his coaching was an absolute necessity.

The pressure being applied by the Communist Party began to have its effect. All around us, circumstances deteriorated. Jobs, wealth, positions, pensions were melting away like snowmen in March. As stability disappeared from my parents' lives, I tried to spend as many weekends in the vineyard as possible. It felt like that was the only place where I could have a reprieve. I was like someone clinging tenaciously to a rope, so as not to drown. I also knew that my parents needed my presence as much as I needed theirs.

My father had finally completed his novel The Siege. But as the new year progressed, his legal problems and my unemployment increasingly deprived him of the enthusiasm and passion needed to sit down and keep writing. On one visit to my parents, to my great surprise I found my father in the stable grinding up corn for the animals. The work made him gasp for air, yet he still couldn't resist lighting up a cigarette. From time to time, he sat down to gather his strength. Then he went to the draw well, turned the wheel to fill the pail, and carried the water inside. I was shocked. Up until then I had never seen him do any physical labor. He'd never harvested the grapes or pressed them. He had lived the life of a benevolent autocrat, where nothing happened without his consent and everything revolved around him. He demanded good service, criticizing the cook when the spaghetti was not sliced thinly enough. But now, he stepped down from his Olympian heights to help my mother. His struggle with the corn grinder was a premonitory sign, a portent of a coming tragedy, and the closing of an era.

On many weekends during the early summer, after his retirement in 1947, through 1950, my father and I sat on Uncle Rory's terrace and chatted. This was my father's favorite place to be when he wanted privacy to write or to think. There he would sit with his blue beret on his head, his faithful Waterman fountain pen at his side along with his Gamma lighter (an imitation Dunhill) and silver cigarette case. Nature was waking from its long slumber and the slowly burgeoning green leaves began benevolently covering the wounds of the war.

Now that my father was not going to the office any more, when he came into the city on occasion it would be to meet some of his friends, mostly colleagues from the Radio. They would gather around and listen to the broadcasts of the recently formed Radio Free Europe (RFE). My father's optimism was reinvigorated by the broadcasts; he insisted that they could generate unrest, and eventually, a revolution. He was convinced that the West could not desert Hungary—a country of historical culture and parliamentary tradition—leaving it to suffer under the Soviet sphere of influence. He said every piece of propaganda has a goal and a targeted timeframe for the culmination of its impact. While he frequently erred on timing, my father's predictions mostly hit the spot. Soon enough, however, listening to RFE was forbidden by the authorities.

My routine was to visit Veresegyház on the weekends, returning to Régipósta Street on Sunday evening. I didn't particularly like to commute, since most of the trains still consisted of cattle cars, but I did this for a year. On Sunday evening, April 23, 1951, after escorting me to the Veresegyház railroad station, my parents took a stroll and visited their neighbors, the Szendrőses, for a short while.

On Monday morning at work, I was told that I had a visitor. As I walked along the long interior balcony that ran the length of the side of the building, making my way to the entrance, I came face to face with my landlord, Lexi Hetés. Lexi, in his long leather overcoat, looking like a Russian security officer out of *Dr. Zhivago*, looked grim. He pulled a yellow telegram out of his pocket and handed it to me. It read: "Your father has died. Come home. Mother."

I was shocked at the news, uncomprehending. How was it possible that my father had died, when only hours ago he had seemed to be in good health and spirits? At fifty-five years of age, it was an untimely sudden death.

Thus, the "*Annus Miserabilis*" continued. I went to see Miklós Sugár, the head of the personnel department, to ask for leave, and rushed to the Nyugati Railway Station to catch the next train. I found Grandmother Eveline and my mother at the manor house. My father's death must have been at least as hard on them as on me, but they weren't the types to display emotion—unlike my father. He used to say that feelings only make sense if we exhibit them to those we love. Nobody could benefit from being loved if it was not demonstrated and if the recipient wasn't aware of it. Now the three of us were consumed by silent sadness.

My mother recounted that after I had left for the city, she and my father had gone over to the Szendrős', the next villa over beyond our gate. My father had sipped some wine sparingly, as was his style, while discussing George Marshall's book *The True Glory*. They had left Gizelle and Paul Szendrő's house in a cheerful mood.

Early the next morning, my mother woke up to the startling sight of my father sitting on the edge of the bed on the verge of vomiting. After a while, he lay back down, but my mother sensed that he was not well. As she later explained, when two people have been married for as long as they had been, this was intuitive. She was not inordinately worried, but she dressed hastily and left the house to find help. Just then, our neighbor Ilonka Dukony entered the courtyard, to deliver our fresh linen. "Ilonka," called out my mother. "It seems that my husband is ill. Please do me a favor, and call Dr. Lakner to come over." Dr. Lakner had a motorcycle so he could make house calls quickly, but by the time my mother returned to the bedroom, my father was already rattling. When the doctor arrived, it was too late. Dr. Lakner told my mother that my father must have had a blood clot blocking the artery to his brain or heart.

Fortunately, Ilonka was there to help my mother. She washed my father, notified the funeral home at Veresegyház, and sent me the telegram. My mother and Ilonka ordered death announcements to inform friends and relatives of the funeral date. By the time I got to the house, a cart was arriving with the coffin. It was a warm day in April when my father died, and his body had begun to decompose by the time we laid him in the coffin. Its lid was promptly closed for good. We turned all the mirrors in the house face down, an old custom allegedly to prevent the ghost of the deceased from seeing himself, and the house was transformed into a virtual flower garden. On this day, the twenty-seventh of April, spring also unfolded outside. As if to honor my father, nature dressed up the whole landscape. Incredible scents wafted about, inside and outside. It evoked a Japanese Haiku, (translated by Dezső Kosztolányi into Hungarian):

> When all the roads are bedecked with flowers
> and the cherry trees are white
> all the past comes back to mind.

The coffin was difficult to move. Father was tall, and, even in his worn-out state, he was heavy. Many people, especially those in Pest, missed the funeral, because the announcements didn't reach them on time and there were no telephones around for us to contact them. Those who received telegrams in time all came.

We walked down to the cemetery across the railroad tracks. The cemetery was at the end of the village toward our vineyard, closer to our house than the Veresegyház train station.

Among my mother's many theories was that funerals take on the ambiance, the character, of the person who is being buried. She supported her theory with an experience she had had during her father Antal Dabis's funeral. Grandfather Dabis was a so-called *homo ludens*, a playful man, a practical joker. It was a strange trait in fact for a judge who served as chief justice of the Supreme Court of Hungary. At his funeral, as the parson, who was Calvinist—and they are famous for their lengthy speeches—began his eulogy, a little frog began to croak. It seems that while one carriage carried the coffin, a separate one transported the wreaths and the flowers, and inside one of them nestled the little creature. To find the frog was next to impossible, and no one could stop it from giving out a shrill croak every time the pastor finished a sentence. By the end of it all, people just concluded that my grandfather had hired the frog to croak throughout the ceremony.

The peasants of Őrzsentmiklós and Veresegyház showed up in great numbers for my father's funeral, about fifty of them. Uncle Rory, Grandfather Miklós, and my father were all well known and much liked in the two villages.

The funeral was choreographed by nature. Spring was unfolding in its full splendor. Bees buzzed by, chasing the fragrances of the various flowers. A gentle breeze blew, caressing the landscape. Everything resonated with bird songs and was bathed in bright sunshine. The weeping willows, the silver trunks of the birches, and the poplars were reaching toward the sky. The silvery oleasters were all alive. Even a haystack beckoned from the distance. Had the scenery been transposed into music, it would have made a great new Resphigi composition that could have been entitled "The Spring of Veresegyház."

On the surface, life at Veresegyház was undisturbed. The house, the vineyard, and the kitchen garden were still there. A barrel of Ezerjó was ready to be served to the guests at the burial feast.

As the funeral procession headed for the graveyard, the tiny voice of the bell began to toll, like at the end of Berlioz's *Symphonie Fantastique*. Standing by the graveside, Uncle Mihály Babinszky sang the old funeral song my father had offhandedly asked him a few years earlier to sing at his funeral. The coffin was being lowered into the grave, and as the ropes holding it were released, it let out a rattling noise. The gravediggers extended their shovels toward us, so we could throw clods of soil on top of the coffin. At this sight, Paul Szendrő began to sob.

My mother later surmised that these were tears of regret—that Szendrő had been the one to report my father's clandestine wine selling to the authorities. (We were stiff competitors of his in the wine-selling market and our wine was better than his.) Perhaps when he denounced my father he didn't realize the dreary consequences it would have for us. I covered my face with my gloved hand to catch the tears that began to flow. Father was fifty-five years old when he died, twenty-seven of those he had lived with my mother.

Once the burial service had concluded, we set out for home. As we came out of the cemetery, we passed by the Cinkotas' house. We walked up the sandy road, crossed the railroad tracks, and walked through the "Revetek," or as the old maps called it, the "Kigyóstó Dűlő," or "Snake Pond Ridge." Then we turned onto the road, went by the kitchen garden, and into our courtyard. My mother and Blanka set the table in the kitchen. We took the last ham in the pantry off its hook. Uncle Jenő Schármár opened a can of sardines.

The funeral party is the greatest invention of mankind. It bridges the abyss left behind by the departed, especially when death comes abruptly and at a relatively early age. While we gathered around eating and drinking, we reminisced fondly about my father. For the time being, it made it easier for us to bear our loss, and to get accustomed to the fact that he was no longer with us. As we sat around the large kitchen table and sipped the Ezerjó wine, our company became livelier, but outside it was quiet. On this day, no workmen toiled in the vineyard. They came to pay their last respects to the head of our family. The dogs refrained from barking at the moon, the frogs didn't croak, no whistle of the train could be heard. While we were reminiscing inside, a great, solemn, soulful stillness reigned outside. Perhaps we even lowered our voices. It was as if nature created a cathedral-like ambiance to honor my father. As the sun set, the mourners who came by train began to say farewell.

The day after the funeral, my mother's friend, Erzsébet Sárkány's sister Lilla came out to Nyires. Erzsébet told us later that when Lilla turned the corner at the crossroad, on her way to the Szendrős' house, my father came toward her with a small plate in his hand. Greeting Lilla, he explained that my mother had sent him over with a piece of meat for Gizi Szendrő. When they reached the Szendrős' gate, Lilla rang the bell and Gizi appeared. Lilla turned around, looked at Gizi puzzled, and asked, "Where is Jenő?" Gizi was stupefied, but answered quietly, "We buried him yesterday."

Now it was Lilla's turn to be flabbergasted. She said incredulously, "Don't say such nonsense. I spoke to him only a minute ago. He was on his way over here with a small piece of meat sent by Boy (my mother's nickname was Boy). I was certain that he had followed me right up to your gate."

Trying to make sense of this, we surmised that since my father had died so abruptly, his reappearance was intended to put us at ease. He had artfully selected someone from our immediate circle who would have no way of knowing that he had died, so he would not startle her. (My theory about the plate in his hand is that it served as a device so that he could avoid physical contact, such as a handshake, with Lilla.)

At a later time, when my mother and I were sitting in the library and talking about my father, she remarked that her life with my father had not been easy. He had such a powerful personality that it cast a shadow over her. She felt like a small flower unable to fully blossom under a tall oak tree. She said, "I feel as if a great pressure has been lifted off my shoulders. Yet, if I had to live my life all over again, I couldn't imagine living it with anyone else but him. I remember times when I was cleaning and he would come into the room and start telling me something, and the dust cloth would stand up in mid-air."

My father was a benevolent autocrat, perhaps another *Leopard* (from Giuseppe di Lampedusa's classic novel about an old Italian nobleman increasingly out of touch with modern republican times). His personality was enthralling and he had real presence. He was a grand seigneur, warm, intelligent, with an excellent sense of humor. A period of trials and tribulations followed. The *Annus Miserabilis*, which had begun with the revenue inspectors' discovery of the false wall in our cellar, didn't end with my father's death. A few weeks after my father's funeral, on May 21, 1951, enforced evacuations—otherwise called deportations—began. Targets were the middle and upper-middle classes, former officeholders in the government, officers of the inter-war army, aristocrats, and intelligencia—bourgeois members of society and their entire families.

These inhumane directives served two purposes for the new regime: (1) to get rid of "socially undesirable elements," i.e., those deemed unfriendly to communism; (2) to seize apartments and other living quarters for favored members of the government—Communist Party members, police officers, and members of the dreaded ÁVH, the secret police—and their families.

My future wife Edith's family received a deportation summons around six in the morning on June 19, 1951. The apartment doorbell rang and Edith's father found a policeman at the door presenting him with the family's deportation summons. They had not quite twenty-four hours to pack and be ready for an official pickup at the next dawn, around four in the morning. They were to take only what they could carry, be it furniture, bedding, clothing, or kitchen utensils. The head of the household was allowed to take 1,000 pounds and every additional member of the family was allowed to take up to 500 pounds (minutes from May 5, 1951, about deportations in the city of Budapest.) Everything else was to be left behind, forfeited to the authorities along with the apartment, unless they could find some neighbors who would safe keep a few of their most prized possessions.

At the next daybreak, they were taken by the ÁVH officers to an outlying railroad station, where they were herded into railway cars and escorted under guard to their assigned enforced destination. This would be a village east of Budapest, toward the Russian border. Rumor had it that the final destination would be in the Soviet Union.

Edith's family was told that their interim destination was the village of Egyek. All seven family members (my wife's parents and their five children) were bivouacked in an assigned "room," and given an outdoor kitchen on a porch in the home of a kulak, a farmer with a relatively sizable landholding, approximately twenty acres or more. Luckily, before winter arrived, they were reassigned to another dwelling where they had an indoor kitchen and one room for the family. Both of these rooms had dirt floors. Their kulak host lived in the house's remaining rooms. These living arrangements were calculated to punish the kulaks as well, by forcing them to co-habit with the deported families.

The deported families lost not only almost all of their valuables, but were also deprived of their livelihoods. The families were forbidden from leaving the vicinity of the assigned village, and local police knocked on their doors at all hours of the night to check that everyone was there. The deportees were forbidden to do any kind of work other than manual labor at various farmer collectives. It was backbreaking work and they worked for a pittance, and even those wages were sometimes stolen from them.

My wife was thirteen years old and still of mandatory school age (up to fourteen years), but that June, once school was out, she was forced to join the labor force with her father and two older brothers. The family was desperate for the wages. They needed all the earnings they could get to support her younger sister, toddler brother, and her mother, who was pregnant and unable to do manual work. Edith was assigned a job behind a threshing machine, gathering chaff with a pitchfork. By the end of the first week, her hands were blistered all over, but between her brothers and herself, they saved enough flour to provide the family with bread for the winter.

The following year, she was fourteen years old, and joined the work force full time. Getting up every day at four in the morning, she would walk to the station to catch the 6 a.m. train to Hortobágyi Halastó, a lakefront where she had a job as an aide to a mason. She would mix the mortar and carry it in a wooden box with leather handles. Lacking the strength to carry the box by its handles alone, she attached a strap to them and slung the strap over her shoulders. She was additionally tasked with throwing bricks up to the masons as they stood on their platform, building the walls ever higher. As the bricks left her hands, they scraped the skin on her palms mercilessly. Two years, from 1951 until 1953, passed in this fashion.

In 1953, Edith was fifteen when Stalin died and the deportations ended. The family was free to move, but to return to Budapest was forbidden. No matter how many times Edith's father petitioned the authorities to allow them to return home, the reply was always no.

Eventually, they were able to find an empty barn on the outskirts of Budapest. Her father and brothers transformed it into two rooms, one a kitchen. It was similar to the one at Egyek: a dirt floor, one bedroom, a kitchen, and an outhouse (no running water or bath). Water had to be fetched in pails from a well a couple of blocks away.

At sixteen, Edith began to work as an aide to an electrician. She carried hundred-pound sacks of cement on her shoulders up several flights of stairs and carved channels in concrete ceilings for electrical wires. She did this with a chisel and a hammer, but no protective gear for her eyes while she hammered against the force of gravity. It was done with brute force; no machinery of any kind was available. Then, in the evening, she attended high school classes. This is the situation she was in just before the 1956 revolution broke out.

The deportations occurred not only in the capital, but in other cities, towns, and villages as well. Among these other locations, Veresegyház was also included. From these locations the deportees were the millers, pub owners, innkeepers, shop owners, and village intellectuals.

The month of May had passed quietly in the vineyard. One afternoon in June, upon finishing our errands in the city, my mother and I took the train back to the vineyard. As the train came to a halt at Vicziántelep and we stepped down from it, Mrs. Cserepkai ran toward us as if she had been expecting us. She had an uncanny way of knowing when we would arrive, and she always greeted us with the latest news. As soon as we were within earshot, she blurted out, "My lady, you will be pleased to know you are being deported." Using the word *pleased* was a polite form of expression and not meant in a literal sense. We thought to ourselves, "Pleased?! Like hell!"

We later learned that the Veresegyház town clerk had departed with the same train on which we had arrived—just missing us—without having handed over a summons to my mother, according to which my mother was to present herself at a certain time and place in Veresegyház together with other deportees. They were all to be transported to the easternmost part of Hungary, where they would be forced to reside and their movement restricted to one village.

No deportees were ever taken to Transdanubia. All of the deportation end points were close to Záhony, a station on the Hungarian-Soviet border.

When we reached the house we sat down in the library in a dense gloom. My mother had run out of money and cigarettes, so she asked me to fill a pipe for her. We sat down in armchairs opposite each other and puffed our pipes, emitting billows of smoke up toward the thick rafters of the ceiling. My mother asked, "Now what? What should I do?" "Nothing," I said. My panicky mood in 1944 came to mind. Back then I had wanted to join the army or a labor battalion (terrified that my evasion of military service would be discovered), and my father had counseled, "Wait until they come for you." As we sat there puffing on our pipes, I gave the same advice to my mother. Eventually we agreed that this would be the best course to follow, especially considering the plight of Grandmother Eveline, who had already been displaced twice—first, within her own apartment in Budapest when she was banished to the maid's room, and then from there to Veresegyház. One day passed after another, but nobody came looking for my mother. Following my father's advice seemed to be working, though we didn't know for how long it would.

In fact, she never was deported. Decades later, we figured out why things had unfolded as they did. Around 1954, my mother was working in the city, living in a small room in her sister Margaret's apartment. This was temporary lodging, and she was obliged to request a provisional residency permit every year. Since this was inconvenient, she decided to apply for permanent residency status. In order to do so, she had to go to the village office at Veresegyház to obtain a certificate of her current permanent residency. When she asked for it, the clerk informed her that she was not in the village register. "What do you mean I am not in the village register?! I've lived here for the past twenty years!" she blurted out, outraged.

Then it dawned on her that her registration card must have been pulled and destroyed. It must have happened during the deportations. She had disappeared from the register as if she had never existed, and therefore no one ever came looking for her. My mother never found out whom she had to thank for this.

∿

A few months before my father died, he had met a new settler to our neighborhood, Lajos, or Lali, László. Lali was introduced to my father by Erzsébet Sárkány, who knew him from the interwar years. Lali had just been released from an internment camp and had been assigned a residence with his mother Teréz and his wife Gréti in Őrszentmiklós, close to my grandmother's former vineyard. My father visited them and was shocked to see their primitive circumstances. Lali had a menial job with the railroad company pulling weeds out from between the ties on the railroad embankment, and earned a pittance for it. The Lászlós were on the verge of a starvation diet. After his visit, my father told me to put a dresser and some household items on a wheelbarrow and take them up to the Lászlós'. This was characteristic of my father; when he saw a need, he tried to help.

Lali was a colorful individual. He had been born out of wedlock. My mother's theory about illegitimate children was that they have the strongest characters, since everyone is their enemy, everyone wants to destroy them, but still they arrive on this earth in spite of it all. Her theory befitted Lali, in any case, who was an incredible driving force and a veritable storehouse of ambition. He was a champion gymnast in high school.

Lali had ambitions. He had been bitten by the political bug and had joined the Smallholders Party. However, his political activity had a short life. The authorities cracked down on the party, and Lali landed in prison on trumped-up charges. He was assigned to the Kistarcsa Internment Camp.

After Lali was discharged from the internment camp and relocated to Őrszentmiklós, he became a daily visitor to our home. As long as my father was alive, Lali would frequently stop by our house on his way home after his grueling workday on the railroad. We would anxiously await his arrival, because he would transmit the most recent political news from the West he had heard on Radio Free Europe. We didn't dare listen to that station, since it was strictly forbidden and we feared being arrested for doing so. In any event, the government's twenty-four hour jamming made it difficult to receive.

Lali would blow in like a whirlwind, calling out exuberantly "Boyka, Jenő, Károly, it is terrific, it is stupendous what's going on." Then we would listen in rapt attention.

At other times, short of political news, he would start his never-ending stories, eloquently embellished, and we would be swept off our feet. He couldn't get enough of hearing his own voice. After he would leave, we would look at each other and ask, "What did he say?" None of us could recall.

We were still utterly elated.

Shortly after my father's death, and in the interval of my mother's suspense over whether she would be deported or not, my mother and I came to the conclusion that it would be a good idea to offer lodging to the László family. They would have decent living quarters and their presence would strengthen our very tenuous situation. Otherwise, with my mother the lone dweller, after my father's death, the village authorities would assign lodgers to the house. Consequently, I offered a section of our house to Lali's family. They would get the kitchen, the pantry, and the large dining room. All those rooms were furnished, equipped with beds, and, with family portraits hanging on the walls, they were pleasing to the eye. We proposed transforming our entry hall into a kitchen for ourselves. We weren't asking for rent; the thought never occurred to us.

The following Sunday, Lali, his mother Aunt Teréz, and his wife Gréti strolled down to visit us. They looked at the place and made their decision on the spot. Lali's recent past, spent in prisons and internment camps as a politically stigmatized individual, was of no concern to us. Having been classified as kulaks, we wouldn't be any worse off for having an ex-political convict move into our home. Thus, it was a win-win for both our families, and by then Lali's life had begun to take a turn for the better. He left his backbreaking weed-plucking job at the railroad for a managerial position at a car service station. A few months later, he obtained a position in Vác as a manager of a hardware store.

By June, deportations from the city had become an everyday occurrence. I only had the opportunity to visit the Roedigers twice at Hegyalja Road, because they also received the so-called pink slip. It came at six in the morning informing them that within twenty-four hours they would be picked up with their belongings—whatever they could carry—and taken to Hunya. Hunya was a small village, close to the town of Gyoma, near the Romanian border. Thus, Zsuzskó, Aunt Mia, Berti, and little Niki were again uprooted. The Roedigers wrote, informing us that visitors were most welcome, especially if they were able to bring food, coffee, or rum, not necessarily in that order.

The general situation was grim. Police went around daily delivering deportation summonses. Lexi and Ilonka Hetés, my landlords at 5 Régipósta Street, kept a large trunk in the entry hall at the ready in case they were also deported.

I went to see my second cousin Imre Tarnóczy and his family in Lágymányos District in Buda. They were in the middle of breakfast: ham, pork scraps, head cheese, sausage, smoked bacon, green peppers stuffed with pickled cabbage, and, of course, coffee. I met Imre's younger brother Rudi Tarnóczy who had just been released from prison. He was assigned to work at the Beloiannisz Factory, which manufactured radios, telephones, and telegraph machines. Before the war, it had been owned by an American firm called Standard, but like other private enterprises, it had been nationalized. Rudi worked there as a Bakelite pressman, pouring Bakelite powder into various forms to create the plastic communication units.

Soon after my visit, I received a call from Imre informing me that Aladár Tarnóczy, Imre's uncle and my father's cousin, wanted to see me. Uncle Aladár lived in a spacious apartment on Endre Bajcsy Zsilinszky Boulevard near the Nyugati Railway Station,. In the interwar years he had been employed as a legal council in a ministry. At that time he still owned the 120-room Tarnóczy Castle and surrounding estate in Laszkár, Czechoslovakia until the end of the war (afterward the estate was nationalized). Before the war, the Tarnóczys had been regular visitors to Grandmother Eveline's and they knew my parents, but I only began to get to know them now.

I had, however, heard many stories about them over the years. One of these concerned Uncle Aladár and a widow, Mrs. József Kunz. It was an open secret that they lived together. Their relationship had a sort of romantic tinge. Nowadays no one bats an eye at unmarried people living together in a communal household, but before the war such relations were stigmatized. It just so happened that Uncle Aladár and the widow Kunz had adjacent apartments. On one end of the corridor, the name plate on the door read Dr. Aladár Tarnóczy, Ministerial Councilor. On the other end the nameplate read Mrs. József Kunz. Those of us in the know knew that only one door needed to be opened on the inside between the two apartments and they would turn into one. They would have much preferred to get married, had it not been for Mr. Kunz's will, which stipulated that all the income from his houses would go to his widow but only as long as she didn't remarry. Aunt Klodine (Kuki) was thus condemned to eternal widowhood unless she was willing to forfeit a sizable income.

When I went to visit Uncle Aladár in his spacious apartment, I found Imre's wife Ila, Imre, and Aunt Klodine busily packing up the contents of the two apartments. Soon, I found out why they wanted to talk to me. Uncle Aladár asked whether he could move his belongings out to Veresegyház. After I gave my consent, the wheels began to turn. In a short while, six trucks pulled into our courtyard.

One of these towed a trailer that carried Uncle Aladár's firewood. Uncle Aladár had some gigantic carved baroque furniture. Among their belongings, hanging on a wooden contraption, was Aunt Kuki's bridal dress (the one she wore when pledging eternal faithfulness to Mr. Kunz). Another wooden crate held Uncle Aladár's Hussar uniform hung—just in case he would need to wear it again. The last time he had worn it was in 1914. Chandeliers had been hung up in a lattice framework, and infinite care had been taken with packing up all other objects as well. Their move out to the countryside with so many trucks and antiques couldn't have gone unnoticed, which put us in danger. Even the blind could see that this caravan was the result of a desperate flight to avoid deportation. The line of trucks was followed by a policeman on a bicycle coming from the Veresegyház police station to our house. He was curious about the large caravan headed to the manor house. Luckily, his scouting didn't generate any followup by the authorities, which surely would have made our lives more miserable.

Once the contents of the trucks had been unloaded into Uncle Rory's apartment, Uncle Aladár and Aunt Kuki began to bring their suitcases into the library and place their food stocks into the pantry. At this point, I felt that charity had reached its limits, and politely but in no uncertain terms told them that the library was regularly used by us and that sharing the pantry might create some confusion. Fortunately, my angelic grandmother offered to share the pantry in her little cottage. She sacrificed her kitchen and entry hall as well. Uncle Aladár promptly sat down on the porch and began to type a letter on his Hermes portable typewriter (presumably to his nephew Ádám Tarnóczy in New York asking for charity packages). Sitting on the porch typing away, he again raised suspicions in the neighborhood, as only subversives used typewriters. Sure enough, another policeman bicycled in to see what we were up to. This managed to keep all of us in a nervous state of mind.

After the dust had settled, Aunt Kuki set up her weaving loom and began to make beautiful shawls of vivid colors, which she sold for one hundred forints apiece. The first customers, of course, were family members. Thus, the Tarnóczys spent the summer in Grandmother Eveline's tiny bungalow until the fall, when Uncle Aladár discovered that the spacious house of a former miller by the Egervári mill had been vacated and could be rented. Uncle Aladár sold his gigantic, carved baroque furniture, lessening the load for transfer. As a farewell gift, he gave me two antlers. From then on, the antlers hung on the pillars of the porch, greeting visitors entering the courtyard. My mother and I breathed a sigh of relief upon their departure.

The miller's house that Uncle Aladár rented was close to the main road in Veresegyház, about a mile from us and on the other side of the hill from Vicziántelep. It was situated in the middle of a scenic landscape, and upon seeing it my mother became nostalgic, because her grandmother had grown up in a mill. But this mill hadn't been in use for quite some time.

As Uncle Aladár bid farewell to Grandmother Eveline, he asked whether she would like his two-pronged wooden ladder. My grandmother didn't need the ladder, but she must have figured that it might come in handy in the future. She promptly paid the 180 forints that Uncle Aladár requested. Then she picked up the ladder to bring it into the stable, so that it would not "inadvertently" be taken away with Uncle Aladár's belongings. On her way into the stable, she lost her balance on the uneven brick-paved entrance. She fell down and the heavy ladder landed on top of her. My mother and I ran over and discovered that she couldn't stand up. Someone called for an ambulance, which took her to the hospital of the Sisters of Mercy in Buda. The nuns, who had been the primary caretakers, had already been expelled. The medical director, Oszkár Wagner, was a former schoolmate of my father. Through that connection we managed to get Grandmother Eveline admitted. The diagnosis soon followed—a fractured femur. Her hip was placed in a plaster cast. When I visited her, I was told that she needed to be taken home. I was aghast. She had lost some weight and the plaster dressing had begun to rub her hip, creating an open cut. I tried to get some advice, some information from Dr. Wagner. I asked, "What comes next? What should we do?" He reacted strangely. He didn't prescribe any medication and he didn't tell me what he already knew—that this fracture would never heal (It would be decades before doctors would be able to surgically repair a broken hip.). He kept emphasizing that we needed to take Grandmother Eveline home, which we did, but he said no more. The hospital had strong Catholic traditions and therefore the discussion of my grandmother's demise could have been anathema to the doctor. Moreover, the hospital was now under communist management and any digression from the rules, or a shadow of medical malpractice, could mean years of imprisonment.

An ambulance brought Grandmother Eveline home, and we faced one problem after another in caring for her. The first challenge was to keep her clean. In those days, there were no such things as diapers for the elderly, and we didn't even have a bedpan in the house. Her wounds began to fester. About two days later, we found that the cast had become wholly useless. Another ambulance was called to take her back to the hospital to remove the plaster dressing. When she returned home, she required around-the-clock care. My mother, Aunt Teréz, Gréti, and Aunt Jenke Brédl alternated. I came out from Budapest after the end of each workday.

Grandmother Eveline was reluctant to eat, afraid of the consequences. The only thing she allowed herself was a little tea. And the only way she could take a few sips was to have the spout of the small teapot at her lips. She must have suffered immensely—partly from the smell of her foul sores, but more so from the physical agony she had to endure. She had always been finicky about smells. Now she endured tremendous pain, the stench of her own flesh, and hunger, all with the stoicism of a saint. Dr. Wagner never prescribed pain medication or any sedatives for her, even after her second visit to the hospital. I was deeply offended at the way he cared for my grandmother, especially since he had been friends with my father. I didn't understand the political pressures he was probably under. I felt helpless. One evening I sat by my grandmother's side and broke down in tears.

She, on the other hand, kept her cheerful disposition throughout. One afternoon, when Aunt Teréz was taking her turn sitting at my grandmother's bedside, prattling away, after a considerable period Grandmother Eveline said, "It is amazing, Teréz, how much you can cluck-cluck today." On another occasion, Aunt Jenke silently stepped into the room, carefully nearing the bed, where Grandmother Eveline lay with her eyes closed. My grandmother must have had an inkling of Aunt Jenke's frame of mind, for she suddenly thrust out her two emaciated arms and exclaimed, "Hah!"

Every day felt like a week until we were finally able to find a nun who was willing to come and stay with us. We gave her the tiled floor room next to my mother's, where my grandmother now lay. By this point, everybody was exhausted, and it was clear that Grandmother Eveline was not going to recover. Since she was not eating, she would die.

Sure enough, then came the night when the little nun ushered my mother and me into the room where Grandmother Eveline lay in bed with her eyes closed. There was no one else there other than the three of us. It was already late into the night. We sat down by grandmother's bedside, a candle in the room lighting up her face. Grandmother Eveline seemed to be asleep. Suddenly she emitted a deep sigh, and with that she returned to her maker. The experienced nun must have known how closely death was approaching. Once the last breath had left Grandmother Eveline's body, the little nun tied up her jaw and shut her eyes.

The next day, I went into the office while my mother ordered a coffin and made funeral arrangements. Our nun took her leave. It was a dreary, drizzling afternoon when a coach with the coffin arrived from the Veresegyház funeral home.

In about five minutes, half a dozen people had entered our courtyard. One of them was the mayor of the village, another the secretary of the local Communist Party, then a clerk, and lastly two policemen. When my mother saw the gathering, she quickly passed her handbag to Aunt Jenke, who hid it behind a dishpan. The mayor demanded that my mother hand over her cash and jewelry. My mother had the sales slip from the funeral home in her apron pocket. Holding it out, she said, "Perhaps on your way in, you folks saw the coach with the coffin on the road. That is for my mother-in-law, who just died. This is the receipt for the payment to the funeral home and the cemetery." This was my mother's proof that she no longer had any money. Hearing this explanation, the little group (who had already walked the entire house) became a tad subdued and left.

On the next day, November 19, the annual festival in commemoration of St. Elizabeth, my mother and I escorted Grandmother Eveline on her last journey, to the cemetery. She was buried in the same grave where her son had been laid to rest six months earlier.

The cemetery was forlorn. Besides the two of us, the only one present was the gravedigger. The sky was crying with us. Grey clouds veiled the cemetery; a fine mist, a drizzle, fell. There was no priest, no flowers, no eulogy, and no music. No bells tolled, either. The simple coffin sank into the sands of Veresegyház next to my father. This is how Countess Eveline O'Donnell, the last of the Hungarian O'Donnells, died and was buried in the Year of our Lord 1951.

We walked home in silence.

At that Christmas in 1951, neither my father nor Grandmother Eveline was with us. This is the last Christmas I can recall before the

Hungarian revolution in 1956. My mother wanted to carry on with the traditions, and she even got a Christmas tree, but not from our property. We had seventeen pine trees in the garden. For seventeen years, Aunt Hansi and Uncle Rory had bought living pines for the holidays, and after Christmas was over they had planted them out in the garden, their son's favorite place to play. By 1951, the tops of the seventeen pine trees had all been cut down, stolen.

My mother and Blanka decorated the tree and invited over our closest neighbors. We had no money for presents. We put candles on the tree, some sparklers, and our usual Christmas ornaments. As we lit the tree, I could barely fight back my tears. Sensing the pity of those around me, I found it even harder to choke back my emotions. I felt the discomfort of others and I was embarrassed. I missed my father terribly, along with his annual recollection of how he had traveled hundreds of miles during the First World War back home from the front to celebrate Christmas with his family. Even during the war, he had never missed a Christmas at home, but now, for the first time, he did just that.

41

Searches at the Ranch and
Another Dreadful Year

Now that my father had passed away, my mother was targeted by the authorities. We tried desperately to refuse to inherit the estate in order to escape *kulak* status, but the state targeted us regardless. Not only did we have to buy a hog to forfeit to the Village of Veresegyház along with wine and eggs (the latter of which we had to buy in the market!), but we were also obliged to volunteer a large sum of money as a "peace loan" to the government. We were down to a half-barrel of wine. My salary was barely enough for me, and certainly not enough for both of us. My mother was well aware that she had to find a job, or we would have to offer our property to the state and become paupers.

For the time being, my mother still had to care for the vineyard, the orchard, the kitchen garden, and the livestock. On one of these dreary wintery nights, another group of people came for a house search. This visit appeared to be of a more serious nature than the one upon Grandmother Eveline's death. My mother happened to look through the glass front door, when she saw a group of official-looking men, some policemen and village officials, approaching the courtyard. On a sudden impulse, she grabbed the nearest painting off the wall—a portrait of my great-grandfather Henrik as a young boy, with a drum and a sword—went into the library room, opened the door to the outside, and threw the portrait out into the snow. There was no time for any paintings to be unhooked from the library's walls. In the evening, Gizi Szendrő came over and took the painting of Henrik away with her for safekeeping.

The officials searched the house and sealed the door to the library. A strip of paper ran across the door with an official stamp; we were forbidden to enter. They didn't search the rooms occupied by the Lászlós, since the Lászlós were tenants and not related to us. The men went outside and around the corner to the other side of the house to the entrance of the wine cellar. They taped over the keyhole with a paper strip affixed with the village stamp. Then they taped a long strip of paper across the door that led to the cellar from the inside of the house, thereby barring us from entering the wine cellar and rescuing our last remaining wine. I still had a bottle of peach brandy in my father's desk, but since the desk was in the library, the brandy was tantalizingly close, yet unreachable. It was the last bottle from a sensational peach crop in 1946. That year we had distilled two truckloads of peaches from my grandmother's and my mother's orchards. Since the peaches had not been enticing enough to sell in the market, I decided to make brandy from the whole crop. When the cork was pulled out of one of those bottles, the whole room filled with the brandy's fine bouquet.

With this latest visit came fear of what would come next. When would we be evacuated from our house? So far, we'd been lucky. One night, my mother had an unusual—one might say, "occult"—experience. She asserted that it was more than a dream. While she was asleep, she dreamt that she was awake. She felt like she was being gradually, slowly, sucked through the wall. She explained, "Then I was standing in the center of the library. I was actually there physically, not as a ghost but with my body intact. I smelled the stale, dusty and somewhat mildewed air since the room had not been aired for weeks. Then I sucked myself through the wall again and woke up."

On another evening, my mother and I went out into the garden to hide my cousin Henry O'Donnell's headstone. Inscribed on the headstone were the words "Count Henry O'Donnell" and the years of Henry's birth and death. Given the circumstances, we felt that the tombstone, with its reference to an aristocratic background, needlessly complicated our already precarious position as landowners. I dug a sizable hole behind the tombstone and we pushed the headstone face down into it. We pulled the sandy soil back over the headstone and flattened out the earth.

The following night, we went out into the garden again. This time Lali László joined us. We counted out twenty-seven steps from the middle of the two guestroom windows. There, we dug a sizable hole, about two feet square, straight down. Then we dug a narrow channel off to the side of this original hole. Into this hiding place I placed a dozen wine bottles, head down, and a jar filled with jewelry. Then I placed a pot on the bottom of the large main hole and filled it with broken glass and shards. I figured that, should someone poke an iron rod into the ground or pour water on it, he would find a pit full of broken glass and shards. A couple of nights later, worried that this underground pocket still wasn't safe enough, I excavated our jewelry, but left the bottles of wine there.

Since we desperately wanted to get to the wine in the cellar, one night we went outside and scrutinized the outside of the cellar door. It was a double door, fixed in place with a padlock reinforced by a cross-bar. On the day of the house search, the padlock had hung disengaged and the crossbar had been pulled to one side of the door. Luckily, the officials had put the seal over the keyhole vertically instead of horizon-tally (which would have made it impossible to separate the two doors without breaking the seal). Now, Lali and I just shook the panels of the door until the inside latch on the top fell down. Then, by pulling on the doors from both sides, we created an opening for our entry. We rushed back into the house to grab wicker baskets and empty bottles, in order to steal our own wine. After the bottles were full and we were coming back up the stairs, the bottles began to tinkle like chimes. We were horrified that the noise might give us away. For our next trip, we deemed it better to carry down demijohns to avoid the tinkling.

The house search was followed by a summons. Since my mother had failed to comply with the law and had missed her compulsory deliveries of victuals, criminal proceedings were filed against her by the state. Between 1948 and 1953, some 400,000 Hungarian peasants were arrested for failing to deliver their production quotas and an extraordinary 850,000 were fined.[1] I immediately thought of Dr. Lajos Kéri, the lawyer who had helped my father the year before in the great wall affair. He was very expensive, but he had a good reputation for standing up to the authorities on behalf of his clients. Dr. Kéri agreed to represent us and advised us to deliver whatever we still "owed" the state in the form of livestock and wine, so that we would only be charged with tardiness rather than willful criminal negligence. He also began a disinheritance process, so that we would no longer be classified as kulaks.

---

1. Applebaum, Anne. *Iron Curtain*. (New York: Doubleday, 2012), p. 276.

I became not only a client but also a friend. Dr. Kéri was doing his best to help my mother, who was already under indictment. The date of her trial had been set and was just days away. Time was pressing and summer had arrived. Every Saturday I took the train out to Veresegyház to see my mother, Lali, and my other friends at Nyíres. On one particular weekend, I experienced a virtual Jungian synchronicity. Instead of following my normal routine, I decided to go to the Gellért Hotel for a swim on Sunday. I can't explain why an urge came over me to go swimming rather than heading home as usual, much less why I decided to go to the Gellért, since up until then I had only frequented the Rudas pool, mainly for its steambaths.

Walking around the edge of the Gellért's swimming pool, I bumped into none other than Dr. Kéri. He was holding his five-year-old son Lacika's hand. We greeted each other warmly, and he told me that we needed to meet urgently. He needed my signature because Monday morning he had to submit some papers to the court. That settled, we each had our swim, after which I went to see him in his office on Nyári Pál Street. Once we had concluded our business, I asked him how often he went to the Gellért. "Never," he said. "I don't like it. The only reason I went there today was because Lacika was nagging me to take him."

The next weekend, when I went to Veresegyház, my mother suggested that we go to the lake for a dip. It was early in the morning when we got to the lake, and it was deserted. The air was cool, so we decided to just sit in the sand and enjoy the sun. At first we thought we were the only people there, until we noticed a man some distance from us. He was about fifty-five or sixty years old with a bulging waistline and receding hairline. He wore glasses and had a rather unpleasant-looking face. My mother whispered to me, "He is the prosecutor representing the state against me." We didn't pay any attention to him. He was also reluctant to trudge into the water and just strolled at the edge of the lake. My mother was greatly amused. She remarked, "On a cool summer morning the stern representative of the law takes a dip in the same lake as the accused and hardened criminal against whom he has brought charges." At this point, she had already been sentenced to eight months in prison.

Dr. Kéri kept urging us to deliver whatever we could. Only then could he argue that our sole shortcoming was tardiness. We still had to produce a cow, which was a very costly undertaking, but with that the chapter of the compulsory deliveries would be nearly closed. At the same time, Dr. Kéri informed us that the sequestration of certain parts of our house had been cancelled. A new edict had been published in the Official Gazette: the properties of kulaks were not to be nationalized. The reasoning behind it was that spring had just begun and the state required the kulaks' participation in the new farming year.

I speedily removed all of the seals from the wine cellar doors, and we didn't have to steal our own wine back any longer. I also took the last bottle of peach brandy out of my father's desk drawer. As we removed its cork, the library filled with its heavenly scent.

After the harvest, the persecution of the kulaks began anew. There were compulsory deliveries to the village office, set unrealistically high, that gradually impoverished the previously well-to-do farmers. In our desperate attempts to avoid being designated kulaks, we employed various schemes.

My mother remained heiress to the estate and all its associated burdens. Unable to turn in the goods demanded, we then offered our property to the state. But before they would accept it, we had to sell some of our belongings so that we could clear up the remaining debt. First, we had to turn in a three-hundred-pound hog. We only had one hog (which we had planned to consume ourselves) and, complicating matters, the hog met its demise before we had a chance to turn it in. We begged the veterinarian to give us a permit for an emergency slaughter, so that at the least we could have it for our own household, but Daróczy, the despicable cowardly veterinarian at Veresegyház, trembled with fear and refused to help us. We felt he could have helped us without incurring any risk, and concluded that he was craven. There was nothing else for us to do but to bury this beautifully fattened-up animal in the garden. Now, not only did we not have the hog for ourselves, but we also needed to buy another one to hand over.

Only much later did my mother and I learn that it was strictly forbidden for kulaks to slaughter a hog. (We didn't read the papers, and neither did we read the Official Gazette.) Had Dr. Daróczy issued a permit to us for "emergency slaughter," he could have been immediately denounced for authorizing an illegal "black slaughter." Not only he but my mother and I too would have been imprisoned or sent to an internment camp. On the other hand, Laci Rados, Judit's brother, fattened up two donkeys, which the statutes overlooked, and slaughtered them, thereby supplying his family with lard, ham,

My mother and I at the lake at Veresegyház, 1940

sausage, and all. But he didn't belong to the kulak category, and I wasn't as enterprising or sly as he was.

Our hens fell ill with a plague, yet we still had to deliver a few hundred eggs. And as wine producers, we were, of course, expected to turn in several barrels of wine. Fortunately, we had had a good crop of apples. Out of those, we made eight hectoliters of apple wine that we blended into our regular wine. The apple wine enhanced the color of our final product, giving it a beautiful greenish hue. In January, with the roads covered in snow, we rented sleds to deliver thirty-six hectoliters of wine to the village. A stern-looking proletarian woman measured the maligan grade of our wine for its alcohol content. She declared that the Rizling Szilváni was worthy of an upgrade in quality. Rather than receiving one forint per liter, we therefore received one forint and forty-five fillérs per liter (thanks to the good apple wine). Of course, the price set by the state was still well below the fair market price, which was around ten forints. I was at the tender mercy of this woman and expected anything but this. My expectation was that I, as a kulak, would be fleeced by any and all means. Not to mention the fact that we didn't have Riesling or Szilváni. Only sixty-five years later did I realize that her decision to give me a better price was an act of benevolence taken at her own peril; if discovered, she risked going to prison or at least losing her job.

42

The Red Army Wants Me

In the middle of the nonstop blows that life presented, in the early spring of 1952 I got called in by the army for a physical. A few days later, I was drafted. The authorities' sudden interest in my person was because I was born in 1925, part of an age group that had never received any military training. During the war years, we had fallen by the wayside. Now we were called up for reservist army training. We had to report to the Ludovica Military Academy, where we received wooden infantry kit boxes to carry our personal effects, and then we had to walk to the Nyugati Railroad Station. As I bid farewell to my circle of friends, Tibor Bródy mentioned that Miklós Lehotzky, a friend of his, had also been inducted. Lehotzky had been a member of the Kiska outfit that had defended the Swiss Embassy building during the siege. In April, my unit was assigned to a training ground near Mór, west of the Danube in western Transdanubia. Our mailing address was a village called Pusztavám, but our camp was deep in the forest. When my mother heard that I would most likely be assigned to the signal troops, she waved her hand—knowing how much I loved to talk—and joked, "I should have known."

As a rule, those who were called up for service had to sacrifice one year of their lives. We "elderly" twenty-six and twenty-seven-year-old conscripts hoped to get away with less. The night before joining the colors (mainly red), I decided to make the most of the evening, especially since I had not been informed how long the training would last. At that time, Budapest was packed with entertainment places. Most of them even had dance floors. Musicians—one better than the next—played at the night clubs. I strolled over to Lajos Kossuth Street, and in a narrow side street behind it stepped into the

389

night club Jerevan, where Józsi Szabó played the piano. There, my escapade began, even though I hadn't intended to seek adventure.

~

Thursday evenings were reserved for my family. On those nights, Aunt Blanka had an open house for our closest relatives. My mother and I would meet at Aunt Blanka's flat, have some tea, and then go out to a pub for drinks. By now, my mother was employed, and had a small room in the city at her sister Aunt Margaret's. My mother had firm views regarding the restaurant and pub industry. One of her guidelines for figuring out how expensive the place she had entered was whether or not it had preheated plates. If it did, this would be a sign for her to beat a hasty retreat. Places like that would charge about three times as much as an ordinary establishment. Another of her tactics for eating out was to ask the waiter what the special of the day was. If she liked what she heard, she would order it, to speed up the service. By the time she had finished her meal, others would still be munching on hors d'oeuvres, with bulging, starving eyes.

On our way home from Blanka's on Thursday evenings, we would stop by the corner of Széna Square (Hay Square) at the Zöld Hordó (Green Barrel) on Csalogány Street. The place was crowded. People thronged before the bar; streetcar conductors, truck drivers, and other toilers elbowed in front of one another. On the opposite side of the bar were neatly arranged tables with white tablecloths. Waiters stood waiting for guests, but not a single soul was around. I suggested to my mother that we leave the bar section and take a seat on the other side. "You know what," said my wise mother. "I would rather have my drink here at the price charged here while looking at the sight over there, than sit over there and pay the price charged there while looking at the sight over here."

As André Malraux once noted, "Life cannot be lived without narcotics." In the 1950s our narcotics were these evening excursions. After our disgusting, hostility-filled days, we let ourselves be immersed at night in music such as Cole Porter's "Night and Day" or George Gershwin's "The Man I Love," certain that a country where such music was composed and played must be a marvelously different world.

While we felt deprived living in Hungary, by transporting the music of America into our world, these bars compensated in part for what we were enduring. When I was hard at work during the day, I kept humming along to the tunes from the night before. I began my day with this entertainment and sometimes kept on singing the same tune over and over, hits from the thirties like "Thanks for Everything" or "This Is the Beginning of the End."

Each love affair of mine, each flirtation, each fling or infatuation, was tied to a particular song. These songs stayed with me even after the romances had cooled off. Just one part of a song could awaken long-forgotten memories; a face, a body of a girl or a woman, a scene, would appear on the screen of my mind.

"Blue Skies" would conjure up Judit Rados; we had danced to that tune on her mother's terrace on a number of occasions. "Amapola" would bring forth Minci Alemann. "Is It True What They Say about Dixie?" and "The Naughty Lady of Shady Lane" would bring Eszter Hajós to mind. "Shall We Dance?" would remind me of Éva Szinyei Merse. "Ich Küsse Ihre Hand, Madame" was Móki Marosszéki's song. "The Man I Love" was Ildikó Spolarich's favorite. "Night and Day" was my favorite with Judit Hajós. When I first began to collect records, I played several of them one wintry afternoon on Logodi Street for Veronika Gábori, a petite dark-haired daughter of family friends, whom I never saw again: "Cinderella Sweetheart," "Faithful Forever," and "My Lady."

~

On this evening, my second-to-last before I was to enter the army, I went into a bar. In hindsight, I would have been better off staying home and getting a good night's sleep, so that getting up bright and early two days later wouldn't have been so painful, but at twenty-seven I wasn't yet old enough or wise enough for that.

As I looked around the bar, a small group of people caught my eye. Sitting at a nearby table was a middle-aged couple and a young woman. The woman was very attractive; she had an elegant bearing and an engaging appearance. After observing me sitting alone for a short while, they invited me to join them. I did so, and soon we were engaged in animated conversation. During the course of the evening, I mentioned to my new acquaintances that I would be joining the army the next day. I only learned the first name of the attractive young lady, Ilonka, and didn't know if she was single or married.

When the time came to close down the joint, it was already early morning and the sun was beginning to rise. The middle-aged couple bade farewell to Ilonka and me, and I offered to take Ilonka home in a cab. This turned out to be quite an excursion. We left downtown and soon we were on the outskirts of the city. Fortunately, I had enough money for the fare. After quite some time, we came to a railroad crossing, where to my dismay I saw the sign "Rákosrendező." We were now in the vicinity of Rákospalota, which meant that even Veresegyház was not too far away. Shortly after going over the railroad crossing, we turned onto a long, straight street, where Ilonka stopped the cab and we got out. The street was lined with small cottages, huddled side by side, in close proximity, on tiny lots.

Ilonka suggested that I wait outside for a few minutes. "My father-in-law will leave for work momentarily," she said. "Then I will let you in." Now it became apparent that if there was a father-in-law, there must be a husband as well. Shortly thereafter, a middle-aged man emerged from the house rolling out a weatherbeaten bicycle with a small lunch box fastened onto the luggage carrier. He cycled away and I was let inside. Of the surroundings, I can only remember the upright piano.

Ilonka told me that she had a number of errands to run in the city, and that if I wished I could accompany her. We decided that once she had finished her chores, we would part ways, go home for naps, and then meet again and spend the night, my last night, together.

Ilonka was about the same height as me. She exuded a simple, unaffected warm charm that I recognized right at the outset. I judged Ilonka's intelligence to be high above average. She listened to my conversation, my babbling, with an understanding and benevolent smile. All throughout the evening, I had felt that I was in top form; uninhibited, witty, cheerful, and sparkling. I took her quietness not as an indicator of a shortage of subjects that interested her, but rather as the result of an introverted nature. When I met her, her ladylike manner was enough for me to form a favorable opinion. Despite her sordid suburban environment, she had class.

As we trudged through the city's downtown, I learned that Ilonka had a husband who was in jail. Some of her errands were related to her husband's circumstances. Whenever she went into an office, I would wait for her outside, and as soon as she emerged we would continue our peregrinations. Despite our lack of sleep, we spent a splendid morning together. When we parted ways in the afternoon, we agreed on a place to meet in the evening.

I woke up from my nap rested; I showered, shaved, and dressed for the occasion, and set out to meet Ilonka at the Egyetem (University) Espresso. I spent an inordinately long time waiting to be sure that I hadn't missed her, but she didn't show up. I hoped that perhaps she was only delayed, and even as time went by I still didn't want to face the fact that she had stood me up. In my judgment, it was not in her character. But since she didn't have my phone number and I didn't have hers—assuming she even had one—things were all that much more complicated. Yet I wanted to find out what had kept her away.

I only had one way to find out, and that was to locate her house again. This, of course, meant a one-day delay in reporting to the military academy. I completely disregarded the consequences. They might declare me a class enemy and send me to work in a labor force as punishment, but right now that was not my primary concern. I discarded my anxieties, feeling a bit like Cary Grant must have felt in the three-hanky movie *An Affair to Remember*, when he waited in vain for Deborah Kerr to show up at the top of the Empire State Building.

I was determined to find the adored dame at any cost. This, however, was a challenge that required help and money. I couldn't ask Gyuri Sághy to help because he was already in France, so I set out to see Szabi Viczián, the only person I knew who would willingly undertake such an utterly mad adventure with me.

Luckily, he was home. I sketched out the whole situation, giving him the only points of reference—the name of the railroad station where we had crossed the tracks, the direction we had come from, and how soon we had arrived at Ilonka's house. It was all very much like a Jules Verne novel. We set out to investigate. We had one advantage: Szabi's father Uncle Tóni had a law office in Rákospalota. This meant that Szabi was somewhat familiar with the area.

Now Szabi and I took a bus headed toward Rákospalota on the outskirts of the city. At about noon, just as I was nearing the point of giving up, the bus turned into a long, straight street that I recognized as Ilonka's. We quickly got off the bus at the next station. I started searching for the right house, but it was difficult, since all of the houses looked alike. At last, I found it. I rang the bell, but no one answered. I jotted down the address, and with some satisfaction we returned to the city. After this, there was nothing else to be done but to write a letter to the object of my obsession.

Then I had to present myself the next morning with my green military kit box at the Ludovica Military Academy—just as I had done in 1944, eight years earlier. At the Academy, I was truly dressed down. "Tell us," the staff sergeant asked: "What would happen if those yelping dogs of Tito were to attack the country and everybody came in a day late?" I, of course, had my own ideas as to what would happen, but I was careful not to disclose my thoughts to an experienced clairvoyant staff sergeant. I said that I had been dead drunk and slept through the day. This, of course, was not far from the truth. Drunkenness was a regrettable but understandable bad habit, a common one. Starting with shop workers and leading all the way up to the first secretary of the Communist Party, everybody was drunk some of the time. It was a shortcoming not typical of, or unique to, a class enemy. I tried desperately to avoid giving the impression that there was any political motivation behind my tardiness and rule-breaking.

There was not much else to say. Soon, a huge contingent was formed. Among them I discovered Miklós Lehotzky, the person Tibor Bródy had suggested I seek out. Miklós observed me with some curiosity and anxiety. He later admitted that he felt some trepidation, thinking to himself, "Who is this strange bird that Tibor wanted me to link up with?" He was fearful of having to babysit me, but his misgivings quickly dissipated. As we started to trudge on foot to the Nyugati Railroad Station with our heavy wooden kits on our shoulders, I trotted along, cheerfully humming a tune, while quite a few of the others could hardly keep up the pace. From here on, our friendship was sealed. We were sorted into the same outfit and assigned to the same tent.

We got off the train at Mór, and from there went on to our camp near Pusztavám. The camp was located in a breathtakingly beautiful, mysterious locality. It was in the Bakony Forest. One hundred years earlier, the forest, like Robin Hood's Sherwood Forest, had been infamous for outlaws hiding there. My unit was assigned to an artillery battalion as telephone operators. Our lodging was a pit dug into the earth; our beds were straw mattresses on top of planks supported by wooden pillars. Three steps led into these trenches, and each trench held ten conscripts. A tent was placed above each trench as a roof, and draining ditches were dug around its canvas. By the time we got to our tents, our cots were ready for us. We changed into uniform and everyone was issued a Tommy gun.

We enjoyed the awakening spring in the wilderness and went about whistling our favorite tunes. We sat like children on benches that were dug into the ground and listened to different lectures. We might as well have been in a Boy Scout camp. We learned how to dismantle and reassemble our guns and how to clean them. We wore the red epaulettes of artillerymen, since our unit belonged to their battalion. Rolls of wires were attached to our waists, which we would unravel and connect to the artillery. We established our post at a farm nearby, promptly ordering scrambled eggs with bacon and green peppers from the farmer while we increased our technical readiness. From time to time, we marched out to do some manual work, felling trees and building barracks, reminding me of my time on the front in Transylvania in 1944. Our whole crew had an excellent sense of humor.

While I was in Pusztavám, the inheritance proceedings were taking place. Dr. Kéri represented my mother and myself and rescinded our inheritance. Thus, we were no longer the owners of the estate at Veresegyház. The house and the land became the property of the municipality, but my mother was still living in part of the house. The criminal charges against her for not turning in the required exorbitant amounts of produce and livestock still hung over her head.

April passed, and still I had experienced no repercussions for being late to the induction center. On the other hand, I did receive a nice letter from Ilonka. From her letter I learned that when we had parted, she had gone to bed dead tired and forgot to set her alarm clock. By the time she woke up, she realized that it was too late and there was no chance that I would still be waiting for her. Since she had no address or phone number, she could do nothing. She was glad that I had written, and her answer went further than sheer politeness. Looking back, I wonder why I didn't look her up after I was discharged, but at that time quite a lot was happening.

May arrived, and with it an official communication from the military court. I was ordered to appear for a hearing. I had to take a large brown envelope with me from the camp. It was somewhat reassuring to me that two other young men were sent with me. They had also been late presenting themselves. One of them had had to sell his horses before he could come.

When we arrived at the military court on Fő Street, it made me wince. In the corridors, soldiers were lined up facing the wall without belts or shoestrings, waiting their turns. I was directed to the office of a captain who presided over my hearing while his secretary took down minutes. I said the right things. I told the interrogating officer that I had never been a soldier before (that, of course, is why I had been drafted). I knew nothing about soldierly discipline (which was why I was in front of him), but in the interim in the training camp I had learned to take the military seriously (we hoped so). I told him that I was terribly sorry that I had joined my unit a day late and that it would never happen again (just what I needed—a repeat performance).

The captain was a shrewd fox. He tried to prove that I was late because I had hoped that I would be a supernumerary and therefore be sent home. I had my answer for that hypothesis as well. I described meeting an enchanting young lady and consuming alcohol excessively (a regrettable but understandable social shortcoming). Thus, I managed to skirt yet another trap the captain had laid for me. I was sent out of the room, given a new big brown envelope, and sent back to the camp. I traveled back in good cheer and turned in the envelope. The secretary, of course, tried to scare me. He said that the incident would cost me another year in the army.

Shortly after I returned from the military court, I went to the commandant's office to ask for personal leave. Upon hearing my request, the duty officer exploded. "Unheard of! You just came back, and now you want another leave?" "That's true," I responded. "I have been away, but I wouldn't call it leave when one has to report to the military court." "Get lost, you rascal," said the lieutenant, while filling out my paper and handing me the free railroad ticket.

Once I arrived in the city, I stopped by the Kárpátia Restaurant. This was a restaurant where everyone knew everyone. If a new person did show up, someone would inevitably know him or her and introduce him to the rest of us. Thus, there was a constant addition of people to my portrait gallery. I made acquaintances with a number of illustrious people of varied backgrounds. Some of them were aristocrats or landowners, notorious or otherwise well-known personalities of yore.

Now, as I settled down in the restaurant once more, in the course of the afternoon I was introduced to Judit Hajós, a relative of the Hajós family from Szada. Judit, whom almost everyone called Ditta, came into the restaurant with a stack of psychology textbooks under her arm. At first glance, she seemed somewhat nondescript. Pale-skinned, without any cosmetics, and simply dressed, she gave me the impression of a sleepy cat, rather than a woman of temperament. My mood may have had something to do with it as well, but she didn't seem attractive or exciting. Shortly thereafter, I took my leave.

When I rejoined my company, I consoled myself with the thought that it would soon be time for discharge. When the day finally arrived, the "Order of the Day" was read. First, the commanding officer read the names of those who had received reprimands. I heard my name called out, with the explanation that I had been a day late in joining the outfit. Then, to my utter surprise, I heard my name once again, but this time among a group of names of those who deserved honorary mentions. The commanding officer went on to state that I had received the citation for my exemplary discipline and diligence during my training period. This was the discharging ceremony.

After I had served my full term in the army, I returned home as a civilian and reported to work at the Demolition Trust. I was in my second year at the company when rumor had it that Szikla Kápolna (Cavern Chapel) would be demolished. The chapel was carved into the side of the Gellért Mountain, and a tall cross stood at the top of it. The cross was an eyesore to the communist authorities. Moreover, it was in close proximity to the "Szabadság Szobor" (Freedom Statue), which had been erected in 1947 to commemorate the so-called liberation of Hungary by the Red Army. The authorities' main intent was to make the chapel nonfunctional, in the same way that they closed the monastery of the Pálos Friars on the other side of Gellért Mountain. Since Cavern Chapel stood close to a busy thoroughfare, overlooking Szabadság (Liberty) Bridge and next to the Gellért Hotel the demolition work would take place at night to avoid calling any unnecessary attention to it. It was a politically sensitive task, and so it would be done by management. The crew consisted of the president of the company; Géza Takács, the assistant manager; Géza Biró, the party secretary; Miklós Sugár, head of the personnel department; and László Szpirer, a technical executive. The benches, the carved sculptures, the candleholders, the altar, the paintings, all were taken to the company's storage depot. The demolition of the large cross created a problem not only physical but psychological as well, until Géza Biró, the party secretary, climbed up on top of the cross and wrapped a rope around it. Then the entire group pulled on the rope until the marble sculpture came crashing down. Afterward, the entrance to the chapel was walled up. This was a hush-hush job. Like the monastery's removal it did not have any public reverberations, in part because people had grown fearful of speaking up and in part because the Communist regime was still not so sure-footed that it would undertake such an activity in the open.

Shortly after the demolition of the Cavern Chapel, an attendance sheet was circulated asking for volunteers. This day started out as a gorgeous summer day, but with the news that all office workers should "volunteer" to demolish the church of Regnum Marianum, I began to cringe. All office employees were to meet next Saturday at the end of Gorkij Allée (formerly Queen Vilma Allée) to demolish the church and make room for a statue of Stalin. In front of the statue, a rostrum would be built where members of the Politburo would greet marching toilers on May 1. This shocking weekend work was designed intentionally to break the backbone of the white collar work force, to force office employees into a demeaning, antireligious act. The object was not productivity, since people from the office were poor substitutes for regular laborers. This also served as a sort of unofficial poll to see how employees would react. I faced a major dilemma. I knew that if I didn't participate, I would expose myself and risk my job, especially if all the other employees were there. Nevertheless, I decided not to participate in the demolition of a church. I felt emboldened when I thought of László Kalmár, the famous movie director. Kalmár had been asked by the national film studio's management to direct a movie version of Kálmán Mikszáth's novel *Strange Marriage*. In the novel the protagonist is a village priest. The studio's management wanted the priest to be portrayed in a negative light, which would comply with the party's campaign against the Catholic Church. Kalmár accepted the job on one condition. In addition to the first priest, he wanted to add a second one who would be portrayed in a favorable light. Immediately the studio's management dropped him as a prospective director and gave the job to Márton Keleti, a Communist Party hack, instead. On the day the story broke, the studio's entire workforce went over to Kalmár and without saying a word they shook his hand. I had been impressed by his stance.

As soon as word got out that I hadn't signed up, the upheaval began. First, I was summoned for a hearing, where I had to face the so-called company triumvirate: the manager of the company, the secretary of the Communist Party, and the head of the personnel department. They asked me whether I was religious. I told them that strictly speaking I was not, since I didn't practice my religion. They demanded the reason for my refusal to participate in this volunteer job. I told them that if this building had been a synagogue or a mosque my conscience wouldn't have let me do it either. These places of worship are sacred regardless of denomination, and I didn't want to have any part in the desecration of their walls. At this, one of the members of the "triad" remarked, "We have our means to deal with people like you." I replied that I would not be the least surprised by any retribution. I knew that I was skirting danger with my refusal, but I counted on the management's desire to avoid having to resort to extreme measures. They definitely were not interested in creating martyrs.

In the ensuing week, I was put under psychological pressure. A few of my colleagues tried to persuade me to change my mind. Mrs. Katona, who had been persecuted in 1944, said she was surprised because she didn't know that I had such strong religious feelings. She was a gentle, good woman. I told her that I was not very religious, but I was unwilling to destroy houses of worship.

Mrs. Márta Radványi also approached me on the subject. She was a nice, roly poly woman of sunny disposition. Her father, Comrade Fisher, had been the model for the famous 1919 placard drawn by Mihály Biró of a naked man raising a hammer, with the caption "1919 May 1" on it. Márta had been deported in 1944 to the Ravensbruck concentration camp. She told me that her extra thick support brassiere was one of the things that helped saved her life in that camp by keeping her from freezing. We were good friends, and she tried to convince me that I was committing a great blunder. She was also a party member, so coming from her it sounded like a warning. Uncle Laci Frisch was another colleague who tried to talk me out of my decision. "Why make a hero out of yourself," he said. At last, even Uncle Laci Szpirer, who had hired me, tried to convince me to sign up for the job. He told me that he had visited a parish priest in Zugló who told him that no one doing this work under duress could be censured or blamed for it. Uncle Laci also pointed out that even fellow workers like Jánosdeák, the head of the accounting department, who was an old man, and Klara Apátfalvi, the plump accountant, would also be going, even though they couldn't be counted on to do any useful manual labor.

After listening to all these people trying to convince me of my pointless mulishness, I concluded that if I were to give in now it would be self-defeating stupidity. At this point, I had already ruined my reputation with the management. Besides, if I were to turn up at the building site I would lose the sympathy of those who were secretly pleased that there was at least one person who dared to rebel. On Saturday morning a crew set out with pickaxes and crowbars for Regnum Marianum. I, on the other hand, scared but relieved, strolled to the Nyugati Railroad Station to take the train to Veresegyház.

At home, I gave my mother an account of all that had gone on the previous week at the office. I told her that another obligatory volunteer communal work project was scheduled for next Saturday at the Regnum Marianum—a sort of makeup assignment for those who had missed the action the first time around. "I'm sure the pressure to participate will be even greater. What should I do?" I asked my mother. "You shouldn't go then either," she said. "Then I'm sure that I'll be fired," I said. "It doesn't matter," said my mother. "You just come back home and we'll manage somehow."

Considering that my mother didn't have a job yet, it was surprising to hear her support my seemingly irresponsible choice. But it was exactly what I wanted to hear. It gave me the strength to face the forthcoming week with all its consequences. I had another hearing with the company triumvirate, my colleagues tried to explain that playing the hero made no sense, especially when everyone else was going with the flow. But by this time I was far more adamant than on the first occasion. When the volunteer sheet was circulated at the beginning of the week, I signed it. I did it partly to avoid the constant nagging, partly to spare me and my fellow workers superfluous discussions. Then, on Saturday at noon, the workday concluded. Aware that quite a few people were watching my steps, I left my office, went into the entrance hall, signed out for the day, and left to take a train home. As soon as the company had reached the obligatory time for keeping me on the payroll, they fired me.

Now, instead of placing another phone call, I presented my complaint in person to the commandant of the First Army Corps. I was given a hearing by a young captain, who listened to me and then called up my former employer. Throughout the phone conversation, he kept looking at me and smiling in an amused manner. When he put down the receiver, he turned to me and, still smiling, said, "Comrade Farkas, my advice to you is to forget about a white-collar job for a while. Rather, try and find some manual labor." Thus, my career at the Demolition Trust came to an end. Now not only was my mother unemployed, but I was too.

43

My Move to Buda

D r. Kéri had successfully concluded the inheritance proceedings, by which we declined to inherit Veresegyház. Thus, my mother and I slipped out from being stigmatized as kulaks, and the court case against my mother was dropped. Shortly thereafter, my mother was hired by the Budapest Grafikai Alkotó Közösség (Budapest Graphic Artists Creative Cooperative). She remained employed there until her retirement. The atmosphere was convivial, and she earned a decent living.

At Veresegyház, safety lay in numbers. The Lászlós dwelled in one section of our old house and we put István Kállay up in a room adjacent to my mother's. The-more-the-merrier principle prevailed.

István, whom we called Ipi—or Ipike—felt threatened by deportation, and sought us out for safe harbor. His apartment was not the problem but rather his last name, which betrayed that he belonged to one of Hungary's historic families. He had been moving about, ducking the authorities, until he landed with us. When he put on a suit, he looked the part of a dapper gentleman, but most of the year he looked like an unemployed pirate. When the sugar beet harvest arrived in the fall, Ipi would quit his regular job and work at a weighing station where farmers sold their beet crop to a sugar factory. After the harvest, he would return to his old job at the Veresegyház railroad as a leveler or staff holder.

The railroad workers would go home on the weekends. During the week they stayed at a worker's hostel. Ipi came up with the bright idea of transforming the upper tract of the house, Uncle Rory's apartment, into a lodge for the railroad workers. As a result, the sandy rooms where the planks had been torn up got a cement floor, a huge cauldron was installed in the entrance hall, and a dozen cots were set up. It reminded me of 1945 when the Russians occupied the same quarters in a similar fashion. But the new lodgers were not troublemakers. They were diligent; they worked hard during the day, did their household chores, and went to bed. When the weekend arrived, they all went home. Converting the upper portion of the house also served as an insurance policy against any homeless person or family planting themselves in our courtyard.

∿

I was still living on Régipósta Street, but the monthly rent of 250 forints was too much for an unemployed class enemy. I was job hunting but getting nowhere. As the days passed, I grew increasingly concerned. Then a message came from my cousin Rudolf, or Rudi, Tarnóczy, who wanted to see me (up until that point I had never met him, although I knew his brother Imre). The following morning, I set out to meet him on Fehérvári Road, where Rudi was temporarily dwelling with Imre.

Rudi was three years older than me. He had heard that I was unemployed, and suggested that I join him at the Beloiannisz Factory (previously owned by the American company Standard, and expropriated by the Communist regime) as a Bakelite pressman. A pressman could make seven or eight hundred forints a month to start, and perhaps more later. His other suggestion was for us to rent an apartment together.

A young couple, the Gogoláks, had been issued an apartment on Szabolcska Mihály Street, near Zsigmond Móricz Circle. The Gogoláks didn't have any furniture and told Rudi that if he could get them some, they would be willing to sublet their maid's room to him for free. Rudi asked me if I could conjure up a few usable pieces of furniture from Veresegyház; if so, we could live in the maid's room together rent-free. Rudi's proposal was not incredibly enticing, but it was a workable solution to my employment and lodging needs. When I complained to my friend Pali Szabó about the paltry salary, he remarked that this would be seven or eight hundred forints more than what I was making now. That did it. I decided to plunge into an entirely different way of life.

With the help of my friends Julia Nádasdy and István Lukács, I moved my belongings on a handcart to the Gogoláks' "mansion."

Besides the two Gogoláks, Rudi, I, and a streetcar conductor and his wife resided in the same apartment. Thus, the apartment had nearly a Soviet-type arrangement, the difference being that walls separated us instead of blankets hanging from the ceiling. Rudi and I shared the maid's room. I had the better sleeping accommodations on a small couch at the end of the little room. Rudi had a mattress on the floor. When Ipi Kállay came into the city, he would occupy the rest of the floor without a mattress. We also had a dresser that the two of us shared. In order to reduce crowding in the little room, we tried to rotate our shifts so that while one of us was working, the other would be off. The entrance to our room was off of the kitchen, and from there some warmth also intruded, especially when one of the tenants cooked. The two of us only used the kitchen to toast some bread and boil water for tea. On occasion, we went so far as to make soft- or hard-boiled eggs. Our staple diet was bread spread with lard and sprinkled with paprika. Every day at work we received a bowl of chicken soup and a bag of salty biscuits. In exchange for our accommodations, I loaned two armchairs and a dresser to the Gogoláks, plus a few other items inherited from Grandmother Eveline.

Rudi had been incarcerated for nearly two years. He and his cousin Miklós Gosztonyi had been coming back on the train to the city from Erk, where the Gosztonyi family still had a house. As usual, they were pretty drunk and singing an old soldiers' song "*Horthy Miklós Katonája Vagyok*" ("I Am a Soldier in Miklós Horthy's Army"). Someone denounced them and they were arrested at the Nyugati Railroad Station as they got off the train. They were tried and sentenced, though there was an irony in the verdict. While Miklós Gosztonyi received three years, Rudi, whose family had owned about four thousand acres before the war, broke down into tears and sobbed to the judge that he was a "poor refugee" from northern Hungary. Hearing his plight, the judge gave him a more lenient sentence—two years. Although the Gosztonyis had owned some land, they had never had nearly as much as the family of the "poor refugee" from northern Hungary.

When Rudi was released, he was assigned to the Beloiannisz Factory. Sending freed prisoners there was a routine arrangement. I applied for Workshop No. 3, the Bakelite pressing workroom. The doctor who performed my physical was reluctant to give me a clean bill of health. He said that my heartbeat showed some irregularities; nonetheless, in the end I was able to cajole him into letting me pass.

It is conceivable that as a former bicycle racer I had an enlarged heart, which in those days was not considered normal, or that the doctor was trying to steer me away from work that he knew was excruciating and took a heavy toll on one's constitution.

The Bakelite powder permeated our clothes, our hair, and skin with an abominable odor akin to a cloaca. We also had a natural stench. Our hygiene was rather perfunctory. If we wanted to take a bath, we would have had to light a fire to warm water, but we didn't have any firewood. Our only recourse was to go to one of Budapest's many public baths. We frequented the Rudas Bath, where the hot and dry steambaths were conducive to expelling alcohol fumes from one's constitution, as well as the smell of Bakelite. These mineral baths had been left behind as a rare good deed of the Turks during their 150-year occupation of Hungary.

The bathing facilities in the factory were abysmal. At the end of our work shift, we would head to the shower. Just as we began to soap ourselves, the hot water would stop running. In unison we would clang on the pipes, shouting, "Water! Water!" but it was no use. The factory economized; they were stingy and they withheld hot water from the slaves.

With the passage of time, I became well acquainted with the whole "merry crew." I asked a young worker next to me where he had been before this. His answer almost blew me away. "I was a horn player in the ÁVH's (Secret Police's) orchestra." he replied.

I was unable to find out why an ÁVH trumpeter had been fired.

One evening, an elderly man with a somewhat more orderly appearance than the average laborer was working next to me. He caught my attention when he quietly began whistling the Jerome Kern song "Smoke Gets in Your Eyes." I promptly asked him, "Tell me, mate, where did you learn that tune?" "Oh," he said, "in the bar of the "Kékes Hotel." This had been an elegant place during peacetime, up in the Mátra Mountains in northern Hungary. "And what did you do there?" I asked. "I was the headwaiter," he replied.

After a while, I became more relaxed with my work comrades. Knowing their background helped, although that was not foolproof assurance either, since the ÁVH had embedded informants at every strata of society.

The scene in Workshop No. 3 was like a barge with chained-down slaves sitting side by side. If someone had glanced into the work-shop, he would have seen a dozen galley slaves or a virtual chain gang; half-naked people clinging onto machinery. We had to shed our clothes because of the heat generated by the Bakelite presses as well as by our own physical effort.

Supervisors walked between the machines and workbenches, changing the casts and checking our work. In the morning, they dropped a bag of salted crackers on our benches, and at noon a gigantic cauldron of salty chicken soup was wheeled in. Everything had to be salty, since we were sweating so much. Occasionally— more so during the evening shifts—we sang. Our favorite song was "Holdvilágos Èjszakán" ("On a Moonlit Night"). When we got to the last part of the song, "Hope will last forever—only the hope, only the hope," the whole workshop blasted out the refrain in full force. At the end of the song, Lajos Farkas, our evening supervisor who was a more understanding sort, walked along the workbenches and quietly warned us, "Keep quiet, men. Pipe down."

This repetitive piecemeal form of labor, at one time called the Bedeaux system, had already been forbidden for several decades in Western Europe and the United States. By the time I joined the factory, the quotas had been recalculated upward a number of times. I was never able to surpass 60 or 70 percent of the quota, and so my name was on steady display on the blackboard, or the so-called "pillory post."

Because I was constantly assigned different types of work, with varied baking times and finishing processes, I could never develop a steady rhythm. At a certain point I asked Comrade Burger, the workshop head, to give me a steady task. Luckily, he agreed with my reasoning and put me to work solely on connector plugs. Unfortunately, after a few months we stopped manufacturing plugs. My Stakhanovite career ended, and I asked for a position that would pay me by the hour, rather than by the piece. I received starvation wages and my efforts diminished as well, commensurate with the pay. My job was to transfer the finished pieces from the workshop to the storage room, which I did in my own leisurely way.

One day in the month of December, as I made my usual rounds collecting the previous night's production to bring to the storage room, I noticed a group of supervisors congregating around a large electric press and working together in a conspiratorial atmosphere. In response to my questions, I was told that Marshal Stalin was going to receive a white telephone on his birthday, December 21 (according to my mother, Stalin wasn't actually born on that day, but chose it because it is known as "the birth of light"). The supervisors pressed out at least ten phones, until they agreed that they had finally produced a faultless pristine white phone.

There was an interesting tidbit, a rumor that a Mozart composition recorded by the Moscow Radio Symphony Orchestra was playing on his phonograph at the time of his death. This musical piece may well have been recording made in deadly fear. No one knew for sure how much "the great teacher/master linguist/military genius" knew about music, since he seemed to know about everything. One evening as he was listening to the radio, a Mozart piece came on the air. He called the radio station and asked whether it was a live performance or a record. The hapless apparatchik who picked up the phone answered that it was a record, when in fact it wasn't. Stalin then requested a copy of the record. The pandemonium that followed surpassed any imagination. Cabs were speedily dispatched to the musicians' homes to bring together the orchestra. The orchestra played, the piece was recorded, and by early morning the record was delivered to the Kremlin. There was some speculation that Stalin knew that it was a live concert but got sadistic pleasure out of visualizing the excitement that occasioned his request. Allegedly this record was on his turntable the night he died.

I was working the morning shift when the "big event," with an impact on tens of millions of lives, occurred: Stalin died. He died on the evening of March 5, 1953, at 9:50 p.m. in his dacha in Kuntsevo. According to the official announcement, he died in his apartment in the Kremlin. I was at my work station when Kossuth Radio Budapest announced Stalin's death. Our party secretary was standing on top of a ladder adjusting a wall clock. When he heard the announcement, he jumped down off the ladder, ran to me, and shook my hand. I had not the slightest notion why he did that. After all, I was not a relative of the great leader. I was a class enemy of the regime. Perhaps he thought, not entirely illogically, that communism would now collapse and he might need my sheltering arms in the future. One will never know.

As it happened, the death of Stalin led to a political landslide. It took decades before the whole edifice of the "Evil Empire" collapsed, but from then on the political atmosphere changed. The prisons began to be emptied, political prisoners were freed. The Auschwitz-like camp system at Recsk, a labor camp in northern Hungary, was dismantled. It was a horrible installation, notorious for inhumane torture and treatment sufficient to cause all those who had been held there to leave Hungary the first chance they had. One of its former inmates, Count József Somssich, later remarked, "It was a holiday on the days when the guards didn't kick the tin mess out of our hands." The prisoners were regularly made to stand and be counted, no matter the weather. This took a long time because the guards' knowledge of numbers was so weak. Those who disobeyed any of the rules could be put in a punishment barrack and deprived of food or could be sent to spend the night lying on a plank in a "wet" cell, where water seeped in from the sides, sometimes kneedeep.[1]

Imre Nagy's government ushered in a more liberal atmosphere. There was a letup in the terror. One of the major changes was the elimination of the forced residency in the boondocks, to which many families had been deported from Budapest in 1951. The deportees were not entitled to repossess their former homes, however. They were not even allowed to live in the capital again. With this edict, many of the families that had been evicted returned from the eastern part of the country and settled in the outskirts of Budapest. Included in this group was the Roediger family, which came back from Hunya. My mother and I offered them safe haven in our home at Veresegyház.

---

1. Ibid., p. 281.

44

Haven for the Shipwrecked
at the Old Manor House

After my father's death and the voluntary relinquishment of our property to the state, my mother was no longer harassed. She had a prestigious past, not only as an artist but also as a journalist, and she had never been shy about expressing her political views. After the war, Aunt Blanka was called before the so-called Political Screening Committee, a kind of de-Nazification process, to be interviewed and quizzed about her past. The first question the head of the committee asked was, "Are you related to Róza Dabis?" "I'm her sister," answered Blanka. At that, the head of the committee turned to the other members and said, "This colleague is cleared. No further questioning is required." My mother had always been open in her disdain for the Nazis and their Hungarian counterparts.

My mother changed jobs and became a member of the Budapest Creative Co-operative of Graphic Artists. From then on, her life started to stabilize. She was not given creative work, design, or planning, so she was still working on the periphery of her first love, art. Once, she told me, "I adore the colors and love to paint. I even like the smell of it." Her colleagues were graphic artists, painters, exterior designers, and window dressers. They were aware of her past achievements as an artist.

My mother's closest friend, Erzsébet Sárkány, lived on Lövölde Square (Rifle-Range Square) near the artists' cooperative. As a result, my mother frequently went to visit her, especially when my mother's work extended into the wee hours of the morning. The two of them had much in common. Erzsike and her husband Oszkár were both so-called left-wing intellectuals. They were writers, and Oszkár was

409

a French language teacher. Oszkár had been called up for service during the Second World War and had disappeared in the great catastrophe of the Battle of Voronyesh.

Blanka could never understand my mother's love affair with the land. Yet the explanation was quite simple. My mother constantly sought beauty, and the landscape of Veresegyház fulfilled that need. Even when she was still working as an artist and a writer, she clung to the landscape—to the land of Veresegyház and to the countryside at Őrszentmiklós. She lived her life as if she were inside a gigantic picture frame, where some otherworldly Monet inspired the scenery and the lighting. She looked at every nook and cranny with the eye of an artist. In the mornings, she would throw open the shutters and step out into the fresh air. The shrubbery, the trees and bushes covered with icicles gleaming in the sunlight, scenery like Sisley's, the flowering apple trees of Pisarro, all were there to greet her. Then her eyes would fall upon the haystacks in the meadow, and in her heart she knew that she could never part with this beauty. She would sigh and say, "How beautiful."

Every segment of the day, every part of the year, provided her with material. In her imagination, she was constantly painting. When we were returning from a neighborly visit and the moon appeared in a mysterious light, she would sigh, "Even if I could paint something like this, no one would believe it was real." On another occasion, seeing the moon in a syrupy trite orange color, she said, "Anyone who would dare to paint this should be dragged over hot coals." Even though she didn't have the opportunity to paint the landscape, she could hold onto an image in her mind's eye. At least she knew what and how she would have painted. Toward the end of her life, knowing my interest in the occult, she asked me whether I thought she would have a chance to paint in the afterlife. Albeit my information about the other world was quite rudimentary and unsubstantiated, I assured her that once she was there she could paint to her heart's desire.

While our standard of living in the country kept deteriorating, our enchantment with the landscape never ceased. The vine stalks had been cut away, and hooligans had felled the fruit trees for firewood, but we still had a little refuge behind the house. There in the meadow we would stretch our blankets out on the ground and bask in the sun, enjoying the scenery. Where once we had our kitchen garden, there was now a meadow. It had not been possible to maintain the garden, and had we tried, the fruits and vegetables would have been stolen anyhow. In addition, the land was no longer ours to cultivate, because it now belonged to the state. I was extremely careful not to pick a single fruit from any of our former trees for fear of being denounced as a thief.

Lying in the meadow, we could look toward Szent Jakab and the mountains of Mogyoród, where the kings of the house of Árpád once fought their battles. Closer at hand were the weeping willows, the olive trees, the silver-trunked poplars, and the "Trembling" and "Lombardy" poplars. These had all been left alone, because they were unsuitable for firewood.

The flora and fauna were distinct. The breeze caressed the sandy slopes. You could bite the air, listen to the shrill chirping of crickets. The little wild white and pink cloves, or gilly flowers, held fast.

With Imre Nagy's ascension to power, people began to refer to his regime in Hungarian as "The New Deal-i" (which meant "The New Silliness," in a benevolent sense). Deportees were now free to move around. We extended an invitation to the Roedigers to move into our house, which they accepted. On an early summer morning, Zsuzskó, Berti, Niki, and Aunt Mia, Berti's mother, stepped off the train at Vicziántelep Station. They arrived in Nyires ready to make a new home for themselves.

The old circle of friends was reestablished. With Niki to look after, Zsuzskó stayed home. Berti joined the crew of Uncle Kovács's Railroad Repair Brigade, where Ipi Kállay, István Lukács, and even

Gräfin Zsuzskó Degenfeld-Schonburg nee Somssich von Saárd (formerly married to Albert (Berti) Roediger)

Uncle Kovács's daughter Marica were employed. Berti didn't make much money, but his family was relatively secure. Ipi was still living in the refectory-like room off of the kitchen, with its red and blue slate floor.

Our weekends became more animated, with lively social gatherings. A group of young friends and relatives of ours and the Roedigers' would spend Saturday evenings and Sundays in our old manor house reminiscing, joking, and drinking. If anyone wanted to spend the night, we were prepared to give them lodging. Whenever a big party took place, five-year-old Niki would be taken to a neighbor's house and the Roedigers' floor would serve as a temporary hostel.

Among the first guests that visited us after the Roedigers moved in were Baroness Mária Butler and her husband Tibor Bródy, Count Ottó Dégenfeld, Countess Aliz Esterházy, Melinda Huszár, Countess Margit Majláth, and Countesses Julia and Katalin (or Kata) Nádasdy, along with Kata's husband Pali Szabó. Other guests were my cousin Rudi Tarnóczy, a distant relative of ours Miklós Gosztonyi, János Thierry and his sister Polidur, László Máriássy, and István Lukács.

At the time, my mother was fifty-three years old, still very young in body and spirit. She had a wonderful sense of humor, a sunny disposition, and enjoyed having young people around.

Coffee on the Lászlós' porch in 1953: My mother, Lali László, myself, Erzsébet Sárkány, and Gréti László

It was amazing how good-naturedly my mother tolerated the immense mess, the cigarette smoke, the burned-out rugs, the dirty tablecloths, and the used bedspreads that followed our wild weekends.

During the week, I lived in the city, in the suffocating little maid's room that I shared with Rudi Tarnóczy. I looked forward to the weekends—to get fresh air and to be with our little coterie. In my mind Veresegyház was our fortress. Our hidden shelter was now filled with members of a forgotten world, flowers of the now-downtrodden class.

For the Roedigers, living in Vicziántelep, after their deportation to Hunya, represented a quantum jump in location and surroundings. Aunt Mia rented a room a few minutes' walk from us in the little cottage of Jenke Bredl. The corner room that used to be our library and had a separate exit became Berti's family's room. The Lászlós lived in what was Uncle Rory's former kitchen and our former dining room. For most of the year István Kállay stayed in the room adjacent to our former entry hall and current kitchen. This arrangement offered a safe harbor for all of us.

45

Workers Unite!

One day in Budapest, as I was heading toward the Kárpátia Restaurant, I bumped into Andor Beőthy. Although up until this
point I had never spoken to him, his was a familiar face, since I had
seen him at the Swiss Embassy building during the siege. He was a
member of the Kiska outfit led by my friends Tóni Viczián Jr. and
Pali Tomcsányi. He was a unique character, tall, with pitch black hair
and a handlebar mustache in the style of a Hungarian shepherd. He
was wearing a long leather overcoat that had seen better days.

Andor struck up a conversation, and I was taken aback by the
peculiar intonation of his speech. He spoke in a terse manner and
finished his sentences on a high octave. Andor suggested that I come
work for him as a bicycle-rickshaw transporter—a kind of rickshaw
coolie. His bicycle-rickshaw was a large contraption with a three foot
by six foot platform, balloon tires, and a three-foot-long aluminum
handlebar. He had two bicycle-rickshaws and offered one to me to
use. He would round up business for me, and every Friday I would
pay him 20 percent of my weekly income. His offer caught me off
guard. My gut reaction was that it was total lunacy and to be immediately refused. I wanted to stay in my stinky familiar corner of the
Beloiannisz Factory, which at least was warm, rather than venturing
out into the big, hostile world, where the air was fresh but cold and
I would be exposed to all kinds of peril. Since I hesitated, Andor
asked me how much I earned. When I told him that it was around
seven or eight hundred forints per month and a warm bowl of soup
at noon, he said that that would be how much I would make with
him in a week. I mulled over his proposal. In the end, I reasoned
that I would not be risking much by going to work for him, and if

it worked out, I would earn much more. Moreover, the job might offer some downtime, which was also appealing.

Before I could leave the Beloiannisz Factory, though, I needed to get my workbook stamped. This created a dilemma for me since I wasn't sure what the stamp would read, "Left with permission" or "Left without permission." If the latter were stamped in my workbook, every prospective employer would be obliged to send me back to the workplace I had left. Consequently I would never be able to get another job. On top of it, if I ended up jobless, I risked being sent to a concentration camp as a shirker.

When I requested a discharge from my department head, he denied it. So I went to see the factory doctor. I remembered how he had hesitated in approving my employment when I first came in, pointing out that I had an arrhythmia, and I was hoping that I could use his findings as a rationale for discharge. This ruse didn't work, however. This time he told me that my heart was as strong as a bull's. My next trip took me to the union secretary (not a union in the Western democratic sense that would negotiate wages, for example, but, rather, a rubber stamp for management). He sent me to the department CEO, who to my greatest surprise offered me the position in the stockroom held by my immediate boss, Imre Takács. I indignantly refused this offer and promptly informed Imre to watch his back, since his position appeared to be up for grabs. "What did you say?" he asked with an ashen face.

As a next and final step, I went back to the union secretary, who was a young and decent fellow. He warned me that the consequence of my departure would be the "Left without permission" stamp. My eyes were tearing, but I wouldn't budge. I turned in my work clothes and tools, and went to say goodbye to those for whom I had developed great affection. Among them was citizen Esztojka, the ex-headwaiter of the Kékes Hotel bar. I went to pick up my workbook. With trembling hands, I opened it. To my great relief, it read, "Left with permission." With that, my life as a member of the toiling classes came to an end.

As I took up my new calling, I established a daily routine. The key to success in my enterprise was Valika, Andor's girlfriend. Valika was an executive at the National Synthetic Materials Distribution Company, where she was in charge of issuing ration coupons for industrial materials like Polystirol, Monsanto, or Bakelite to various cooperatives and small independent manufacturers. Whenever she handed out these highly demanded allocation coupons, she would tell the customers that she knew a skillful young man who would gladly transport the material for them on his bicycle-rickshaw. Then she would add that, if it made it easier, she could give the delivery permit directly to this young man. If the customer agreed, I would go to the Kossuth storage depot with the coupons and either expedite the material to the given workshop or take the goods to the train station. As a rule, Valika's customers were more than happy to accept her offer. It worked out well for them, and it certainly worked out well for me.

My cycling soon became a lucrative business. Andor's prophecy was literally right on the money. I rushed through the streets of Budapest from dawn to dusk on my "Silver Arrow," which was fabricated out of the remnants of a shot-down German Messerschmitt fighter plane, and therefore larger than the average bicycle-rickshaw. It was built of aluminum, which made it lighter. It would gleam in the sunshine. I parked the bicycle-rickshaw in a courtyard on Reáltanoda Street, and early each morning I journeyed by streetcar to retrieve it. I dressed in quilted jackets and pants, and carried a canvas cover for the merchandise, as well as a bicycle pump. I would hop on my bicycle-rickshaw and off I would go to see Valika for my daily log.

With my new job, my living standard rose considerably. When working at Beloiannisz, my main course of the day had consisted of a slice of bread spread with lard and sprinkled with salt and paprika. Now I was able to eat lunch in buffets and dinner in restaurants. For the physical work that I was doing, I needed nutritious meals. My favorite pub was Bajtárs (Comrade) Restaurant, where the cooking was great and the meals relatively inexpensive. It was also where the shipwrecked people congregated in the evening. The hat rack was packed with Tyrolean hats, embellished with green and red bands, the unspoken sign that the owners belonged to the persecuted class.

At the restaurant, the head waiter, Uncle Gyula, knew each one of us, and we formed a "mutual admiration society." Once, when I ordered my favorite dish, Brassói Aprópecsenye (Veal Cutlet Brassó-Style), I noticed that a young lady at a neighboring table had ordered the same dish, but that her portion was only half the size of mine. Curious, I whispered to Uncle Gyula, "Why is her serving half the size of mine?" With a conspiratorial smile on his face, he whispered back, "I stole half of her portion for you. She doesn't need it anyway."

On one of these evenings, as we sat around waiting for our dinner, the ÁVH raided the restaurant. Luckily, Uncle Gyula had the presence of mind to quickly steer our friendly circle out of the restaurant's rear exit to the street.

As a rule, once I had finished my daily work I changed into clothes that transformed me into a dapper gentleman. I put on my favorite light gray trousers that I wore to death. Then I put on my tailor-made shirt, my custom-made jacket, my orange-red scarf that was the handiwork of Aunt Kuki, and my brown Swedish shoes. Finally, I would don a unique, out-of-this-world fur coat made by the tailor Dubány. Its removable lining had been made from Uncle Rory's Nutria pelt fur coat. The outside of the coat was one of my father's old coats specifically tailored to my body. With these preparations, I made my appearance with flair. Before heading to the restaurant for dinner, I would make short social visits. Most of the time I would drop by the Szabós', who had just moved to Irányi Street.

On a wintry morning a few months earlier, Kata Nádasdy and Pali Szabó had gone before a civil court to get married. Of course, beforehand Pali went to see Kata's mother to ask for her daughter's hand (Kata's father had died on the front at the end of the Second World War). Her mother's answer was, "Pali, I must warn you: My daughter has a colorful but tiring personality." Pali took the warning in stride.

On another wintry afternoon, after work, I was strolling down Fő Street under the gunmetal-gray colored sky when—fate willed it so—I saw an old man struggling by the curb with a four-wheeled handcart filled with firewood. As I scrutinized him, I noticed a priestly collar poking out from under his overcoat. When I asked him where he had come from and where he was headed, he mumbled something about having come from the Castle District and being headed toward Margaret Bridge. It was a chilly afternoon and it had begun to drizzle. Seeing the old man's frail body and his handcart piled high, I doubted that he would reach Margaret Bridge any time soon. Coming from the Castle District would have been easier for him, since it was all downhill, but now, on the flat terrain, he needed more strength to pull. Making a split-second decision, since the bridge wasn't that far, I decided to be a good Samaritan. I began to pull the cart by hand while the old man pushed it. Even for me, the cart was hard to pull.

In a short while, we had left Margaret Bridge behind us and were rolling down the clinker-paved highway parallel to the electric train heading toward Szentendre (St. Andrew). For a while, no houses could be seen near or far. I kept on pulling the cart and becoming angrier and angrier. It seemed like we were headed nowhere. Whenever I tried to prod the old man to tell me how much farther we had to go, he just growled under his breath that we were almost there. At least I was not cold, since the effort warmed me up. A good hour may have passed by the time we reached the outskirts of Szentendre. By then I didn't even want to say anything to the old priest. The adventure evoked a story from *Arabian Knights* where a devilishly cunning old man sits on the shoulder of a young man and forces him to carry him. The young man cannot free himself since the old ogre keeps his legs around his neck, even while they are asleep. Finally, the young man ferments an alcoholic beverage and offers it to the old monster to drink, which causes him to fall asleep. The young man then crushes the head of his tormentor with a rock.

At long last we arrived in a village-like settlement, a rather shabby and ugly neighborhood. We took a turn and left the clinker-paved road behind for a dirt road, crossed a small canal, went through a side entrance, and pulled the cart up to a small cottage. It was more like an old hut, obviously the home of the old priest. He said not one word of thanks to me, nor did he shake my hand. He just disappeared into the cottage.

I headed back to the highway to find a station stop on the electric railroad line so that I could get back to my beloved city. Luckily, I had enough money on me for a fare, and after approximately thirty-five minutes of journeying, I was back at the Margaret Bridge. From there, I took a bus to Irányi Street, where I arrived muddy and worn out. I related my adventure to Kata and Pali. With a wink in his eyes, Pali said, "Károly, you are such a good man."

My little transportation enterprise was working out quite well. It brought me plenty of money. By now, with the help of Valika, I was working with a long list of small cooperatives. One was the Optician Cooperative, which had its office on Ferenc Boulevard in Pest. Its workshop, where lenses were ground and polished, was in Pasarét (Pasha's Meadow) in Buda. I would take grinding powder to their workshop and bring finished lenses back to their office. The first time I rolled down the hill from Pasarét with my heavy load—about five hundred pounds—my brake proved totally inadequate. As an emergency measure, I headed for the curb. At the expense of ruining my right wheel, I came to a standstill.

Another of my customers was the Public Catering Cooperative. They had a crew in Pasarét that consisted of István Marthélyi, a former officer of the army, and Pali Nádasdy, the father of Barbara Nádasdy (who later became a movie actress in Germany). Ipi Kállay joined them at a later stage. They were nicknamed *mosómedvék* (literally "washing bears," or raccoons). They worked in the attic of a villa prewashing new tablecloths for restaurants. They rinsed the tablecloths in large vats, to get rid of the excess dye. Once they were dry, I shipped them to the central stockroom.

As my customer base grew, my bicycle-rickshaw business took off. One of the new additions was Miklós Hámori, a blind engineer. His office and workshop was in the center of Kálvária Square, situated on a little island, just big enough for a small building. Every Friday at noon, I showed up at Hámori's establishment and loaded my bicycle-rickshaw with his manufactured screwdrivers and electric irons. Then I rolled over to another workshop, where I left the screwdrivers and irons to be chrome plated. There, I would also pick up the previous week's load, which had already been plated, and take them back to Hámori.

Another source of my income was the Jewish religious community, to which Mr. Hámori referred me. An Orthodox temple managed a kosher butcher shop in Visegrádi Street, near the Nyugati Railway Station. Every Friday morning, I rolled over to Visegrádi Street and loaded my bicycle-rickshaw with kosher geese. I took them to the big marketplace on Váci Street, where the municipal health department placed its lilac stamp on each goose. Then I turned around and transported all the geese back to the butcher shop ready to be sold.

46

A Budding Romance

Through my bicycle-rickshaw job, I struck up a friendship with Antal Czettler (nicknamed Ciha), who was also a bicycle-rickshaw rider for Andor. As we became better friends, I learned that he was dating Judit Hajós. I used to bump into them here and there. I had met Judit about a year earlier at the Kárpátia when I was a conscript and just coming back from my military court proceedings. At the time, she seemed rather young, and gave me the impression of a sleepy cat. Now, when I saw her again, her presence touched a chord, but I didn't want to commit piracy in the waters of a friend. After some hesitation, one day I turned to Ciha and asked whether the two of them had a meaningful relationship, because if not, I would like to get to know Judit better. Perhaps I would invite her out for dinner. Ciha appreciated my openness and honesty and told me to wait for a short while until he gave me the green light. This was an interesting reply. I was somewhat puzzled, in a curious state of anticipation. After about two weeks, Ciha informed me that I could take the field. As far as he was concerned, Judit could do as she pleased, and he wished me good luck.

Now, when I met Judit Hajós for the second time, I felt that she had that missing ingredient I had been on the lookout for all along. She had a deep alto nasal voice, an elegant smooth neck stretching out of a turquoise cardigan, and a ready smile as she smoked long American cigarettes.

Judit, also known as Ditta, was a slender young lady with a nice figure. Her ash blond hair bordered on light brown. She was fair-skinned and had an oval face, symmetrically pretty with a slightly upturned nose. Her eyes were light gray, and she had graceful hands with long fingers. She was very attractive and comfortable in her skin.

In my mother's view, she personified the Marlene Dietrich song *"von Kopf bis Fuss auf die Liebe eingestellt,"* meaning, from head to toe for love attuned. She became "an object of my affection" for a long, long time.

Judit's father János belonged to the Calvinist branch of the Hajós family. The other Hajóses of Szada, whom I already knew, were Catholic. Ditta's family had an estate at Dömsöd and while they had lost their land, Uncle János's sister Aunt Julia still lived in the old *kuria*. Ditta's mother, Mária Biró, came from an extremely wealthy family. They had owned an apartment house at 5 Szép Street (Beautiful Street), but by the time Judit and I met it had been nationalized. Judit's mother was not only rich, but also beautiful. She had broken five engagements before marrying János Hajós. Uncle János was not particularly handsome, so it must have been his personality that won Ditta's mother over. Judit was unemployed.

People who had lived most of their life in the so-called *belváros* (inner city, or downtown)—a posh area—frequently drifted together like planets moved by some orbital regularity or celestial force. This

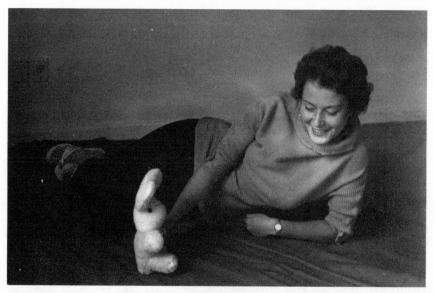

Judit Hajós

was especially true in the evening hours, and this is how I bumped into Ditta. Impromptu, I invited her out to dinner at the Százéves Étterem (One Hundred Year–Old Restaurant), which I hoped would be the perfect setting for our first evening together. The restaurant truly was over one hundred years old and still standing on the same street corner that it had for decades. Antlers decorated its walls, and a lady played romantic themes on a harp. The restaurant had the perfect ambiance, and proved to be ideal. Our conversation mainly revolved around Veresegyház, my father's writing, and the 1944 siege of Budapest. I learned a few things about Ditta's father and mother. Right from the beginning we were quite frank with one another, and talked openly about ourselves and our pasts. Ditta told me stories about the old manor house at Dömsöd during the Russian occupation, when she was not even in her teens. The conversation differed from ones I had had with previous acquaintances or with the "merry maidens" of Nyíres. I very soon realized the difference. Ditta and I shared a similar intelligence and humor, and our general curiosity about life was similar. It turned out that our musical taste was exactly the same. Ditta was absorbed and attentive when Guszti Ilosvay played the guitar and sang "I Thank You, Mr. Moon" and many other derivatives of the Big Band Era. We both adored "Night and Day" and all of Cole Porter's other creations. The star of my childhood had been Bing Crosby (by the time the Sinatra age arrived, the political earthquake in Hungary had pulled the rug out from under Frankie's feet; Sinatra was forbidden in Communist Hungary). During this era, some audacious medical students made recordings of big bands like those of Glenn Miller, Benny Goodman, Artie Shaw, and the Dorsey brothers on x-ray films; their voices and music would be carved over plastic pictures of lungs and kidneys.

By the end of the evening, all signs indicated that Ditta had enjoyed my company. From then on, we went out practically every night to a restaurant, a pub, or a musical entertainment locale. Most nights we would go out for dinner, then into an espresso to listen to live musicians such as Jenő Horváth, Ernő Vécsey, Gyuri Cziffra, Doris Vécsey, or Ági Ács singing and playing the piano. Our favorite night locales were the Jeep, the Pilvax, the Anna, the Old Firenze, and the Bristol. We greatly enjoyed each other's company, and swam in the nightlife of the city like two little fishes.

I was pleasantly surprised by how our friendship evolved. We understood each other completely; we never had any disagreements.

As I began to get to know her, I was exuberant, inpatient, and rushed headlong ahead. She already knew that I was head over heels in love with her.

I wanted my mother to meet Ditta, so one weekend I took Ditta to Veresegyház. From then on, Ditta frequently came out to Veresegyház, and her presence marked a distinctive era. She became well known in my circle of friends. For me, it was important to see how she interacted with the gang at Nyires. I wanted the object of my passion to be accepted by my friends.

The first time Ditta came to visit us, we were joined by my cousin Rudi. My mother was in an exhilarant mood, breaking the latest news to us: "Imagine! Uncle Aladár and Aunt Klodine finally tied the bonds of matrimony in the rural beauty of our village church." Imre Tarnóczy had served as a witness. The forbidding hand of the deceased József Kunz (her late husband) could no longer interfere with Aunt Kuki's plans, as there was no more income because all apartment buildings had been nationalized. Thus, there was nothing to hold the two back from marriage. My mother was amused by the event, since by now the newlyweds were quite advanced in age and had already spent several decades living together. My mother promptly proposed that we pay them a visit at the mill where they lived. "Let's go and steal a glance at the newlyweds billing and cooing at each other. Since the wedding took place a few days ago, the Tarnóczys must have just returned from their honeymoon," she said jokingly. Mother, Ditta, Rudi, and I trudged across the Vicziántelep hills. The landscape was snow-covered and crunched beneath our feet. Our mood was festive. Whenever my mother made this trip, the sight of the water mill on the way filled her with joy, reminding her of her grandmother, who grew up in a mill.

The Tarnóczys received us with open arms. Aladár was extra happy to meet Ditta, whose mother he had idolized a few decades earlier. Aladár, Rudi, and I mentally charted out our relation to each other. We were all descendants of Kázmér Tarnóczy, the immensely wealthy oligarch. Kázmér had owned about thirty thousand acres, most of them in the upper region of Hungary and in Slavonia, and had been a member of the Hungarian parliament. Uncle Aladár was his grandson, Rudi his great-grandson, and I his great-great-grandson (his daughter, Malvina, was Grandmother Eveline's mother).

Ditta and I were on the same wavelength, and we thoroughly complemented each other. Our relationship was harmonious but seemingly stagnating, until one day when she told me that she was willing to get married. I was elated, and since she was anxious to announce our planned marriage to her Aunt Julia, she left for Dömsöd. A few days later, I received a postcard from her stating that she could hardly wait to see me again. In retrospect, our whole marriage plan seemed to be devised by characters from *Alice in Wonderland*. We had no set date or location for when or where we would marry. We didn't think through how we would make a living. Although I was able to generate a steady income of 150 or 200 forints a day (which was more than most people earned), it was by way of a job that was far from secure, and Ditta was unemployed again.

Our betrothal was characterized by a total lack of preparation. My mother didn't make an appearance at Ditta's parents' house; they didn't honor our ancient domicile with a visit either. We didn't discuss where I would keep my wardrobe or where we were going to eat. Ditta knew that I frequented restaurants regularly, but to continue with that practice once we were married would be financial suicide. Ditta wanted me to move into her room with her, but her room adjoined her parents' bedroom. There were two ways to leave her room—both of which were far from ideal. She either had to go through her parents' room, or through a bathroom that was used by other tenants of the apartment. If the bathroom was occupied, she could only use the exit through her parents' bedroom. It inconvenienced and jeopardized her privacy. On the other side of the bathroom entry also lived another tenant, Mrs. Sáfrány (not her real name), with her son.

One bright warm sunny morning when Ditta's parents were out of town, I languished leisurely on Ditta's couch while she was reading. Our tranquil serenity began to get crushed by the sound of someone coming from the direction of the bathroom. Without bothering to knock, Mrs. Sáfrány entered Ditta's room. Ditta had the presence of mind to throw a blanket over me, and I tried to stay motionless.

Mrs. Sáfrány was a notorious gossip monger. Her pretense for coming into the room was to ask to borrow an egg or something. An amiable chat followed. I became aware that while my body was fully covered, my toes, clad in fancy red and blue-striped ankle socks, poked out from beneath the blanket. I could hardly contain my mirth and became quite anxious for the lady to leave.

Looking back on it, I can laugh at our lack of marriage preparation, but I certainly didn't at the time. Then, I just wanted to marry

Ditta and worry about the incidentals later. However, my joyous anticipation soon slammed to a halt.

Ditta returned from a two-week visit to Dömsöd and told me that she had changed her mind. She no longer wanted to get married. There were no explanations or conditions. She just told me, and there was nothing I could do to change her mind. I felt that despite what she said, she hadn't entirely given up on the idea, but, rather, wanted more time and definitely wanted our companionship to continue. She was happy in my company and if I neglected to call her, she quickly made her presence felt.

Ditta might have been thinking that if I truly loved her, I would be faithful forever, or at least for the long term. She was the type who wanted to have her cake and eat it too. I didn't have much choice. Either I roamed the nights of Budapest with her or we would break up. If I were to break up with her, although I might open the door for someone else to come in who would reciprocate my feelings, it might also open up the door for someone to come in and reciprocate her feelings.

She definitely had a hold on me. I couldn't visualize bumping into someone else with whom I could share my ideas and feelings as openly as with her. It became a strange relationship. Even though she said that she didn't want to get married, she didn't show the slightest intention of breaking up with me, and I didn't propose that either. As time went on, however, my anxieties increased. By becoming her friend on a long-term basis, I was in danger of losing my appeal as a suitor.

In the meantime, I left my small servant's room in Buda and moved to 2 Dimitrov Square in Pest. My new accommodation was close to the big municipal market in the heart of the city. It was also a small servant's room, one that Józsi Gosztonyi had just vacated, but it was still better than the little dungeon that I had left behind.

The owner of this third-floor apartment was Antal Szanyi, a retired attorney, who lived there with his wife Mariska and a few other tenants. My room had a window facing the inner courtyard. I had direct access from the apartment's entry hall to my room. It was furnished with a small iron stove, a desk, a hanging closet, and a radio. Berti Roediger gave me a queen-size bed frame without a mattress. My mother added a decorative touch. She passed on to me the portrait of Moritz O'Donell, Grandmother Eveline's grandfather. This oil painting had been rolled up for a decade, ever since my mother had stored it for safekeeping. This life-sized portrait greatly improved my living quarters.

The Szanyis were adorable people. Their landholdings had been confiscated in 1945, but as far as politics were concerned, Uncle Tóni's optimism exceeded that of even my late father's or Lali László's.

Uncle Tóni was a godsend for my small transportation company. He was home all day long close to the telephone, and he would take messages and organize my business schedule. He introduced me to another retired lawyer, who became my income tax advisor. A final bonus was that I was able to park my bicycle-rickshaw in the courtyard of the house for just a few forints that I gave to Misi, the super. That saved me time and hassle coming and going from work. I was paying rent, but Uncle Tóni wasn't charging me for his secretarial services. My night life entered a new phase. Living now in the center of the city, restaurants and night clubs were all within easy reach.

The second chapter of my friendship with Ditta began. It was longer than the first and lasted well nigh until the Hungarian Revolution of 1956, even a few days longer. It was a sequence of bohemian episodes. We appeared at various spots in the city—at bars, restaurants, and espressos—habitual customers enjoying the night life of Budapest.

My mother, however, was fed up with the fact that our friendship was not progressing. Disgusted at the stalemate, before we arrived for one of our weekend visits, she decided to avoid Ditta's company by visiting an elderly aunt of hers, Fanika Paller.

Thus, Ditta and I were left alone. Without my mother around, the old house felt forlorn. The Roedigers were away, and Ipike had by now left our safe haven, so his room was empty too. I was reading in the library, while Ditta was lying on the couch in the room that Ipi had previously occupied. We couldn't have been farther away from one another in that wing of the house if we had tried.

All of the books in our library enhanced the ambiance of the old curia. The house was infused with scents from the outside and the smell of the old on the inside. The aroma of the linden tree, lilac bushes, acacias, honeysuckle rose, and jasmine bushes intermingled with the smell of burnt firewood, cigar and cigarette smoke, and old leather. A concoction of these and other unidentifiable smells wafted around. A verse by the poet Mihály Babits to a certain extent reminds me of our house on that day:

Remete lakban óra nincsen.
Boldog a lak hol nincsen óra.
S nincs idegen kéz a kilincsen
S nincs idegen látogatója.

In the hermit's dwelling there is no clock.
Happy is the home where there is no clock.
No stranger's hand is on the doorknob
There are no strangers visiting.

It was also Babits who wrote, "Every portrait of an ancestor is a ghost on the wall." At Veresegyház, the walls of every room were covered with such ghosts. Nonetheless, surroundings of the house gradually began to show—to use Baudelaire's title—*les fleurs du mal* (the flowers of evil). The fruit trees were chopped down for firewood, and the same fate befell the vine stalks. The pine trees in the garden lost their crowns, to serve as Christmas trees in some filcher's home. It took a while before nature stepped in to replace the missing trees and bushes, haphazardly sprinkling the landscape with acacias and willow trees. The house became surrounded with wild greenery that cast a shadow over the windows, darkening the rooms. To someone who had seen the manor house when Aunt Hansi and Uncle Rory inhabited it, it would feel as if the whirlwind of war had blown away all orderliness and signs of cultivation.

Of course, my mother cherished the vision of those days, preserving it mentally. After running an errand in Erdőváros and walking home, my mother once said, "I can just picture Aunt Hansi sitting on the veranda in her wicker chair, laying out her cards and playing 'Patience,' while Uncle Rory reads *Pester Lloyd*. And then out comes Terka, dressed up, to serve them coffee and whipped cream."

Recapturing a picture of the past is well-nigh impossible. The memory and the reality are not quite the same. With time, some colors become sharper, the dimensions change, certain aspects come into focus, and some things, including the women, become more beautiful. Distance makes looking at things selectively, distinctively, feasible. We tend to highlight the interesting, the colorful, the gaudy, while forgetting the mundane everyday occurrences. Somerset Maugham once described this phenomenon when he compared life to an oriental carpet where the faded background is sprinkled with lively spots of happiness.

On this particular August afternoon when my mother felt the urge to visit Aunt Fanny, Ditta and I immersed ourselves in reading. Besides Ditta and me, only Gréti, Lali's wife, was at home in the other end of the house. Even though the weather was quite warm, the enormous width of the adobe walls kept our rooms cool. If a person wanted to slumber, he would reach for a blanket to cover up. Warm weather was never a problem for us. In the cold we would build a fire in the tile stove and crowd around it.

The stillness of the summer afternoon was broken by footsteps. It was Ditta's father Uncle Janos making a surprise appearance. He told Ditta that she had a possible job offer and should go for the interview as soon as she could. In the back of my mind I couldn't help but wonder if this was a ruse on Ditta's mother's part to send her husband on a scouting expedition. After all, neither of Ditta's parents had yet visited our home at Veresegyház, and they may have been curious.

Thus, our quiet, serene, afternoon came to a halt. Luckily, Gréti showed up just as Ditta's father was entering our courtyard. She assured Uncle János that we were being chaperoned despite my mother's absence (never mind that she was all the way at the other end of the house). Later on, when Ditta and I talked about this surprise visit, we chuckled at the thought that if it was an inspection we would have passed with flying colors. Before going back to the city, we went outside to show Uncle János the former garden and kitchen garden, to give him some idea of our past lifestyle. The three of us then started back to the city, but the urgency of the job offer faded. We headed to the Old Firenze café in the enchanting Castle district to spend together the little daytime that was left.

47

My Life as a Rickshaw Man

Gathering dark clouds threw a shadow over my one-man bicy-cle-rickshaw enterprise. As my business expanded, new regulations obliged me to pay taxes. I therefore needed a tax accountant. A friend of Uncle Tóni's, another retired attorney, agreed to keep my books and calculate my taxes, but Dr. Csernátonyi, unlike Uncle Tóni, didn't work for free. Now I was about to regret not having put any money aside for a rainy day.

One morning, as I was pedaling my bicycle-rickshaw over the Petőfi Bridge, a Wartburg automobile sideswiped me. My left wheel was destroyed, my bicycle-rickshaw was ruined. I stood beside it bewildered. The driver of the car was terrified and admitted that it was his mistake. He had looked down while changing gears instead of keeping his eyes on the road, but he begged me not to call the police. Since he was an officer during the war, he had spent some time as a POW and a political prisoner. He told me that if there was an official police report about this accident, he would surely lose his job and it could possibly cause him to serve another prison term. He assured me that he would go to my bicycle mechanic and pay for the repair. I didn't ask him for his name or address, and needless to say he never showed up. It cost me a small fortune to replace my wheel and tires.

Then the weather turned against me, bringing rain and snow, which made the bicycle-rickshaw business treacherous. Finally, the political climate changed again. Imre Nagy, the prime minister of reforms and new economic policy, was forced to step down. He was put under house arrest, and the revolting, disgusting gnome Rákosi regained his previous position. Rákosi proceeded to tighten the screws. The cooperatives, which had begun to boom, were targeted anew with a flood of regulations. During successive weeks, my clients wrung their hands. "Károly," they said "our funds for freelancers are depleted. Sorry, but we can't give you any work, maybe next week." In a fateful week, I lost seven coperatives. The old standbys remained: Mr. Hámori the engineer, with his electric irons and screw drivers, and the Jewish butcher shop on Visegrádi Street. But these last stalwarts kept me busy only on Fridays. Occasionally, I found some impromptu work, but the days when I would ask my friend Atilla Terstyánszky to help me out with his horse-drawn coach were gone. Even paying my rent was difficult.

I was at the lowest point in my existence in the middle of the winter when Imre Hunyor, another one of Uncle Tóni's tenants, knocked on my door to offer me a job. He proposed that I bring a load of socks from his weaving shop in Budaőrs into the city, and offered me twenty forints for the job, which was a pittance. I should have gotten at least one hundred forints, not to mention that it was snowing. He knew that I was broke, was behind on rent, and had lost most of my customers. I refused the job because I was insulted by his offer, and decided I would never work for him no matter what.

In those days there was scarcely anything that could cheer me up. Ditta was still unwilling to commit to me, and this didn't help. Nevertheless, we spent lots of time together. She came out to Veresegyház a few more times over the coming months. My circle of friends approved of and liked her, but I was urged by István Lukács to present an ultimatum, so that she would make up her mind. I knew that if I broke up with her we would be mutually deprived of each other's company and neither of us would be happier. Whenever I tried to loosen the thread that tied us together, she would quickly counter my scheme. At the end of the year, I decided that I would not go to her New Year's Eve party. It was a bitter decision, since all of my very good friends would be there. On the afternoon of December 31, however, Médi Gosztonyi dropped by my flat and delivered a note from Ditta. It was warm and heartfelt, and begged me to come to her party. My resolve evaporated, and I went.

Among the wintry days that followed, there is one that stands out as quite unforgettable. One night I had fallen into utter despair. I felt totally helpless and frustrated as I fell asleep. Negative thoughts raced through my mind. My rent was unpaid, I had no work lined up, my love for Ditta was unrequited, and so on and so forth. In total despondency, I sighed a short prayer, informing God that I was at the end of my rope. I simply could not stand it any longer. Then, mercifully, sleep robbed me of any further worries.

The next morning, when I woke, it was already daylight. In a half-awake state, a feeling of calm came over me. I felt that everything was going to be in perfect order, and an indescribable joy filled my whole being. This euphoric feeling was so powerful that I wanted to foster it, hold onto it. The impact of this esoteric event stayed with me for a while and only gradually faded as the day went on. I took this experience as the answer to my previous night's despondency. Perhaps this was what the occultists call "the cosmic consciousness."

This feeling was followed by some changes in my life that were for the better. Through divine guidance, I became the recipient of tools that enabled me to keep my head above water.

A few days later, Aunt Margaret sent a message informing me that a porter who had retired was selling his porter truck-rickshaw, an uncovered rolling cart. She asked me if I would be interested in buying it. I was surprised that my mother's sister would think that I aspired to expand on my transportation enterprise by becoming a rickshaw coolie. But, after mulling it over, I decided to look into it.

I ended up buying the cart. I rolled out this gigantic two-wheeler, ready to navigate uncharted waters among a group of porters who were smarter, seasoned old hands. I had to learn the secrets of the trade. I recalled Anti Zahár saying that once a society girl turns to prostitution it usually ends up in a debacle. Even a hooker has skills to learn, usually from her mother, and a well-brought up girl is a fiasco in such a situation.

I was hellbent on avoiding such a fate. I had to find customers. I found three greengrocers, for a start. Each of them was a strange character. My first recruit was Mr. Havasi, whose fruit and vegetable stand was on Dohány Street. He always wore a navy blue business suit but never a tie. Decades later, I found his name in the daily newspaper *Népszabadság*, where in an interview he recalled a time when he was in a sort of political exile, a former undersecretary of state who had fallen out of favor with the party. That explained his official demeanor, which was unlike a typical grocer's.

Usually, after dropping my load off at Mr. Havasi's stand, I would roll over to Mr. Katz's on Király Street. He was a professional fruit and vegetable vendor. He once sent me down to Csepel Island to bring back a load of apricots for two hundred forints. Oddly, the

the apricots were nowhere to be found. When I returned Mr. Katz wanted to pay me only thirty forints. Even though I protested that I had made the trip and that it was not my fault that the apricots were not there, Mr. Katz held his ground. He said that because I did not bring him any produce, the thirty forints should cover my trip.

My third shopkeeper was Mr. Halpern, in Gábor Bethlen Square. He was the last stop on my daily delivery route. From there, I rolled back to the Haller marketplace on Mester Street, where I parked my pushcart and stacked my crates to await the following day's produce.

The shopkeepers paid me by the crate or box. For one crate of produce I received two forints. It was a tough job. In order to earn one hundred forints I had to drag in fifty crates. Even if my strength would have allowed for more, the cart didn't have space for much more than fifty crates. But strength was an issue. Whenever the load surpassed my capacity, I would ask Béla, a streetcar driver, for help. Before Béla went to his regular job, trolley work, he would come out to the market early to make a few extra forints with me.

I was a rookie, and before I could become a full-fledged porter, I had to first learn how to load the cart. If I loaded the front of the cart down disproportionately, I would be unable to lift it. Or if I did the opposite and overloaded the rear of the platform, I would have a surprise awaiting me.

On my first morning, as I rolled along Mester Street and reached the corner of Grand Boulevard, the cart suddenly swung upward, throwing me into the air. There I was, dangling harnessed between the handles of the rickshaw, trying desperately to return to earth. Luckily, there was a traffic cop nearby who rescued me from my predicament. He held onto the rickshaw handles, pulled me down, and said with unconcealed mirth, "So, you think you're a pilot, eh?" "Well, my education didn't exactly prepare me for this job," I said. "I can see that much," said the policeman, grinning, as he waved me on.

I carried a variety of produce, depending on what was in season: green peppers, cauliflowers, cabbages, cucumbers, tomatoes, and other vegetables, though most of the time I transported fruit. I had to be extra careful not to drop the crates, because the cost of the damage would come out of my pocket.

I had to be at my post every morning by five. At five, Jenő the entrepreneur would show up. Strung around his neck was a tray carrying small shot glasses and a bottle of plum brandy. He would walk among the porters, offering each one of us a stirrup cup for credit, which he would collect on the Friday morning of our payday. This simple practice of capitalist enterprise kept our spirits up.

A few days after I made my first appearance at the marketplace, one of the porters offered me a deal. My pushcart had planks on each side as safety devices to keep the crates in place. He offered to remove all those heavy side planks if I was willing to part with them. I gladly gave my consent. He went to work hammering and pulling the boards off my cart, immediately rendering it at least one hundred pounds lighter than it had been before. My once immensely heavy porter's truck became far lighter and easier to pull.

As much as I disliked my employers, I was fond of my porter colleagues. They warned me from the start not to work in a wet shirt. They said that in the heat of the summer days I should get rid of my sweat by exposing my torso to the wind. I was not to wear a shirt at all. Otherwise, the sweaty shirt would keep my body wet and the wind blowing on it could eventually lead to rheumatism or arthritis.

Once I had finished my rickshaw business for the day and taken my carriage back to the marketplace, I hopped on a streetcar to get home. There, Uncle Tóni would be waiting for me, hopefully with some orders for my bicycle-rickshaw services. Whenever I came home and learned that there were more jobs to be done, my day felt complete.

48

Clouds on the Horizon

In the course of Hungarian history, a poet once wrote, "The earth shook, a star fell, the year of miracles commenced." The year 1956 became another year of miracles, and likewise began with an earthquake. The chandelier on the ceiling of my room swung wildly. Shortly thereafter, a comet passed close to earth. A bus crashed through the barrier on Margaret Bridge and fell into the Danube. Fortunately, unlike November 1944, no passengers were on board. For those of us who look for esoteric signs of mythical dimensions to draw their projections for the future, such calamities were warnings.

The political tremor that followed was gradual. The seething outrage of the masses forced the hated Rákosi out of power, but Imre Nagy was not rehabilitated. The old Rákosi coterie evicted Imre Nagy from the prime minister's seat and reversed some of the more liberal changes of the previous months. But the avalanche of events was unstoppable. Criticism of leading political potentates began to appear in newspapers.

Our household in Veresegyház was buffeted by the blowing winds as well. Around the end of the summer, as I was riding my bicycle-rickshaw, I got a message that Berti wanted to meet me at an inn in József District. We met on Rökk Szilárd Street, a few steps from the Győrffy bicycle shop. In the pub I met up with Berti and István Lukács. Berti informed me that he and Zsuzskó were going to divorce. He phrased it philosophically, describing life's roads and crossroads, meetings and farewells, and pointing out that now was the time for departure. I was stunned and saddened, albeit not entirely surprised. Berti wasn't exactly the husband type. Zsuzskó and their son Niki moved away from Veresegyház, and Berti looked for another place to live.

49

Revolutionaries Pull Down the Stalin Statue. Siege of the Studio.

"Rohanunk a Forradalomba" ("Rushing into Revolution")

—Ady Endre

Ady Endre, one of the most esteemed Hungarian poets, wrote a poem at the end of the First World War, *"Rohanunk a Forradalomba"* ("Rushing into Revolution"). Another poet, Gyula Juhász, took up the same theme in his poem entitled *"Magyar Nyár 1918"* ("Hungarian Summer 1918"). He faithfully described the mood in Hungary at the time. Every line of his poem is a sizzling picture of the slumbering passion, the anticipation of the forthcoming conflagration. In his verse he puts forward the question:

> *Mi lesz ha egyszer szikrát vet a szalma?*
> *És fellángol e táj, e néma, lomha?*

> What if the straw is ignited by the spark?
> And this mute and idle land bursts into flames?

The revolution that these two poets foretold, the Revolution of the Asters, erupted in October 1918. Its name derived from the revolutionary soldiers' custom of putting asters in their rifle barrels and on their uniforms. It was with this event that the First World War came to an end in Hungary.

In 1956, no newspaper dared to use the word *revolution* or to print a poem about an approaching uprising. The newspapers could only go as far as to attack the shortcomings of communism, but none of them dared to attack the system, to question the validity of the regime. Yet everyone felt that something was in the air.

The 1956 uprising brought the first phase of my life to a close. The twenty-third of October began as an ordinary day. I headed to the Alföldi Restaurant (Plains Restaurant) to meet my mother for lunch. She had a momentary lull in assignments at the graphic artists co-operative, a rest before another onslaught of deadlines would have to be met.

It was a beautiful sunny afternoon, and we decided to go up into the Castle District to visit Erzsébet, or "Erzsike," Sárkány at her office in the National Archives. We planned to pick Erzsike up, walk along the Bastion promenade, and go to the Ruszwurm Konditorei for an espresso.

As we left the restaurant, we were somewhat taken aback to see that the streetcars on the boulevard had come to a halt. The streetcar drivers, the conductors, men and women stood by their empty yellow vehicles. They were on strike.

We walked along the boulevard toward Margaret Bridge in the hope of finding a streetcar or bus that would take us to Buda, to Moscow Place. But the busses had stopped running and so had the streetcars. By now, a long line of demonstrators had begun to form and to stretch out like a flood.The young demonstrators at the head of the line carried the Hungarian Tricolors, red, white, and green, in front of the procession. The demonstrators were heading toward the statue of General Bem in Buda (General Bem was a Polish volunteer who had fought on the Hungarian side against the Austrians in 1848). The end of the procession was not visible. Ordinarily, this many people would only be seen on the street on May 1 for the workers parade, when participation was organized by the party and attendance was mandatory.

At the National Archives we found Erzsike Sárkány finishing her workday, and we took her with us to the Ruszwurm pastry shop. By now the sun had set. The lights in the coffeehouse were subdued, a mellow yellow, and people were immersed in quiet conversations. Everybody had a flyer in hand and was reading "The 16 Points." The heading was an homage to the 1848 flyer that had led to the March 15 revolution against the Hapsburgs.

We ordered coffee and *szilvórium* (plum brandy). To have witnessed what we had was like a dream. After the dark years of the Rákosi regime, a torch was being lit in the darkness of communism. The new regime of Imre Nagy, the *Irodalmi Ujság* (*Literary Gazette*), the debates of the Petőfi Circle, were all forerunners of the events of the twenty-third of October 1956. We had heard about the upheaval in Poland a few days earlier, and had animatedly discussed it by the soft light of a kerosene lamp in Aunt Iza's cottage at Nyires.

At the coffee shop, I finished my pipe, we drank our coffee, and the three of us walked out to Fisherman's Bastion. There, looking toward Pest, we saw a reddish light that projected toward the clouds around the Parliament. We descended from Castle Hill, walked through the Tunnel, and crossed Chain Bridge. We walked along Sztálin Avenue to reach Lövölde Square, where Erzsébet lived.

A neighbor told us that the crowd was going to attempt to topple the statue of Stalin. My mother and I felt that we must see such a monumental and historic event. We walked across Gorkij Allée (Queen Vilma Allée) and by the trade union headquarters. By now it was pitch black outside. The large red star above the façade of the union building had been torn down and was in shreds. The allée was packed with spectators.

All eyes were glued on the statue of Stalin. Ladders were leaned up against the monstrous body. From a distance, the people climbing the ladders seemed like small figures, ants on a tree trunk. Suddenly, welding torches lit up the colossal bronze sculpture. The welding burners wrestled with the massive mass of metal. Winch vehicles wound steel ropes around the statue and tried to tug the gigantic figure off its base. The statue reared for a moment; then the wire ropes snapped. The ladders were put back into place and the welders resumed their work. This time they decided to use the blowtorches to aim at the point where Stalin's boots and breeches met. An hour might have passed, but nobody budged. We all stood there holding our breath. Military trucks occasionally passed by, packed with civilians and workers from various factories.

Once the welders had finished, the long ladders were removed and the trucks with their winches retreated into dark corners of the square. The crowd was silent, search lights lit up the gigantic figure from every angle. The wire ropes were taut, the sculpture reeled again, and then slowly it began to bend until it crashed down onto the pavement. The crowd let out a cry.

Suddenly, a line of trucks turned in from Gorkij Avenue. "The ÁVH is shooting by the Radio! Let's go to the Radio!" shouted people on the trucks.

I bade goodnight to my mother, who decided to go back to Lövölde Square and spend the night at Erzsike's apartment. I climbed up onto a truck crammed with workers, women, and youngsters. Our truck, along with a few others, proceeded back toward the center of the city. Multitudes thronged the boulevard. People listened to radios placed in the windows of ground-floor apartments. The truck slowed down before the National Theatre. I crawled over its side and jumped down. Before me, the office of the daily newspaper *Szabad Nép* (*Free People*) lay in ruins. Right and left, shreds of paper covered the sidewalk. There was no sign of policemen anywhere.

I walked across Rökk Szilárd Street, where my Farkas grand-parents had once lived. Splinters of glass, crushed shards crackled under my feet. A crowd crisscrossed *Szabad Nép*'s printing shop, gaping at the interior. The streetlamps were shot out; the street was dark. I reached Sándor Street, where people were walking single file, flattening themselves against the walls. Only the moon gave out a meager light, silhouetting people as they walked by. Two tanks were maneuvering in the center of the road. They came to a halt, threw their hatches open, and soldiers emerged.

"Why aren't you firing?" asked a man from the crowd.

"We don't have ammo," answered the soldier.

"Can't you break the wall?" asked another.

"No, we can't," answered the soldier.

They were referring to the side of the Hungarian National Radio building. One of the soldiers who had climbed out of the tank wiped his sweaty forehead with an oily hand. The noise from crackling firearms became louder. The soldiers climbed back into their tanks and slowly drove forward toward the studio. A few young boys with rifles used the tanks for cover. "Where did you get your guns?" asked a streetcar conductor. "The police gave us their guns. We told them that we needed them more than they did, but it's not enough. We can't shoot the Radio's walls with rifles. They have plenty of hand grenades," said a boy, motioning with his hand toward the Radio.

As I stood there watching, an explosion shook the air and lit up the façade of the Radio building. Sudden flashes brightened up the night as gunfire broke out on the opposite side of the wall. A few boys came running, flattening themselves against the wall and scurrying along it. Another group came back from the firing line and asked for ammunition. Two boys standing next to me exchanged ammunition as if they were swapping stamps. One of them had a Tommy gun and rifle shells that he couldn't use. After they finished trading shells, they turned around to go back to the studio.

The noise of firing abated. We heard shots from the Radio building with few return shots being fired. "Why can't someone bring us ammunition?" asked a man in the crowd.

"No vehicle is available," replied another.

"There are trucks all around," interjected somebody else.

"That's right," said a young man, "but they're all shot up."

"Let's look!" I exclaimed, as if inspired by a ghost. A small group of us walked away from the Radio building to look for a useable vehicle. At Mária Street, we found one with a flat tire. A young man, who had come with me climbed up onto the truck and found a spare inside. He dropped it down onto the street. We searched for tools and replaced the flat. Never in my life had I changed a tire on a truck, yet that night I was able to do it. We found a driver, and a few young workers armed with Tommy guns jumped onto the truck as an escort. I suggested that they head to the Lámpa (Lamp) Factory, since it was common knowledge that the factory produced armaments. Everyone called it the Lámpuska Factory, *puska* meaning gun. As the truck took its leave, I wiped my oily hand on a wall.

An ambulance appeared and medics came back bearing stretchers. On one of them, a body lay motionless, soaked in blood. On another was a man with a bloody bandaged leg who was holding onto his rifle for dear life. At the corner of Mária Street, he jumped off the stretcher, cursed in Gypsy, and hobbled back to the Radio building. The stretcher bearers looked after him dumbfounded and lit up cigarettes.

A window on the ground floor of an apartment building opened and a man in pajamas placed a radio on the windowsill. The man briefed the bystanders. "It says," he informed them, "that the government demands a ceasefire. Those who have firearms should put them down in front of building entrances." Simultaneously, a man was handing out flyers. "Imre Nagy for Prime Minister" read their headline. A worker ran over from Mária Street and called for volunteers. A group of ÁVH had been captured and needed to be put under guard, but no one had a rifle or ammunition.

I was getting cold. To warm myself up I walked over to Kálmán Mikszáth Square. A group of people were waiting there for an eventual ÁVH breakout from the radio building. "I've spent my whole night here," said a man. "I feel totally useless." I returned to Sándor Street, feeling somewhat the same way.

From the direction of Sándor Square I heard a motor. The gathering dispersed and people ducked into doorways, looking for cover. But instead of Russian tanks or the ÁVH, a truck neared with majestic slowness, brightly lighting up the road ahead. "We brought ammo!" shouted a young boy from the same truck I had put the tire on. People ran out of their hiding places. The truck turned off its headlights, reversed, and crawled into a safer spot. Crates of ammunition were unloaded. A chain formed on the street and the crates were passed from one pair of hands to another. Within about ten minutes, the whole truck had been unloaded. The rattle of machine guns could be heard from the top floor of the building opposite the Radio.

The dim light of dawn slowly began to spread over the street. By then, some people had gone home, but the more persistent stuck around. A few of us walked over to the corner of Szentkirályi Street. There was a brisk exchange of fire. The defenders of the regime were being kept engaged by Januci Thierry's brigade, which was on the opposite side of the street, drawing the defenders' attention from what was going on right below them.

At daybreak, the size of the crowd increased. The Radio, under siege, had stopped broadcasting the previous night. Now announcements had begun anew from Csepel Island where its large antenna stood.

The side of the Radio building had scaffolding on it, since there had been some construction work under way the previous week. A few young men carrying pickaxes, machine guns hanging from their necks, climbed the scaffold. At the height of the top floor they began to chisel an opening into the wall. By, then the ÁVH had withdrawn to the other side of the courtyard and the exchange of fire on the street front slowly abated.

Suddenly a long line of military trucks appeared at the end of Sándor Street. They carried infantrymen in steel helmets, armed to the teeth. Maxim guns were affixed to the roofs of the trucks and soldiers stood in their backs. The line of trucks came to a halt. The crowd surrounded the vehicles and women tried to pull the soldiers off the trucks. Most of the soldiers were poker-faced. A few showed nervousness or had devious smirks on their faces. Some of them looked on at the crowd stunned. "What are they thinking?" wondered a woman standing close by. "The soldiers should help the young men," said one of the medics. Another woman urged the soldiers to join the fighters against the ÁVH. "You could take the Radio in no time," she shouted.

The gunsmoke and dust were suffocating. The young men on the scaffold were moving ahead. The captain of the truck column ordered the trucks to park on Szentkirályi Street. As soon as the trucks stopped, the soldiers jumped down, leaving their weapons and haversacks on the trucks, and were ordered "at ease" (they were cadets from the Officer's Training Corps of Tatabánya). Soon, the soldiers were surrounded by women and children urging them to join the fight on our side. Nevertheless these young cadets stood stoically by their vehicles. The commander kept them under control.

Now we, the bystanders, were only a few steps from the main entrance of the Radio. Most of my companions were armed. There was sporadic shooting to and fro. When the firing stopped, about fifty of us emitted some sort of a war cry and ran through the dark and cool entrance into the courtyard. Even though I was scared, I was swept away by the fervor of the moment, and kept on running across, underneath the archway. For a moment, the thought occurred to me that if someone were to drop a hand grenade into the midst of us from above, it would be a massacre. But this was only a fleeting thought.

The glass roof of the courtyard had been shot to pieces. Shattered glass covered the ground ankle-high. On the left of the courtyard stood a burned-out truck loaded with ammunition crates. I took a detour around it. We noticed bloodstains mixed with mud. We came upon bodies of fallen ÁVH officers. I bypassed a young lieutenant lying on his back, his blue eyes open, looking up at the sky. A streak of blood seeped out of his mouth; his hat lay a few feet farther away.

Another group of young men ran into the stairwell. A middle-aged man climbed on top of the burned-out truck and shouted to the men, "Gather up all guns and ammunition. We will need them!" On the righthand side of the courtyard, a group of people emerged from the stairwell. Most of them were civilian employees of the Radio; among them was Szepesi, a radio announcer. At the head of the group was an ÁVH captain wearing the green epaulettes of the border guards. He was an outright evil-faced man. One of the young men approached him and requested, "Comrade, captain, please remove the red star from your hat!" Even though the words were polite, they were uttered in a firm voice. I didn't hear the officer's reply, but I saw the young man's face turn red with anger, and the next thing I knew he gave the captain a tremendous slap. The officer's hat and glasses flew off.

At that very same moment, all hell broke loose. We were being fired on from the roof and attic, so we ran for cover. I wound up near the entrance door, and ran into a room facing the street. Two other boys ducked behind the door and a chest of drawers. I recognized one of the youths as the son of the eminent poet Lőrinc Szabó. The windows had iron bars. The entrance was blocked. We were in a mousetrap. The other fellow tried to load a flare gun, with great effort hammering a shell into it. I was scared to death. I didn't want to become a victim of "friendly fire." The three of us waited, listening for the noise to abate.

Slowly, we ventured out. As we filed out, I realized that I had been hiding in the very office that had at one time been my father's. I had visited him there frequently as a young boy and as a teenager. Gizi Flóra had been my father's secretary and Mr. Kovács his accountant. The last time I had been here we were chased down into the air raid shelter by sirens. Standing by my father's former desk, in my mind's eye I could see him behind it, holding up a sheet of paper, scrutinizing crowded columns of figures.

The shooting stopped. The stairwell became an anthill. Wounded ÁVH men were carried down from the top floor on stretchers. Following the stretchers, the able, unharmed ÁVH personnel were ushered outside. The crowd surrounding them shook their fists at the bewildered captives. The little group had a hard time passing through the teeming crowd. In the meantime, a young man removed the flag with the red star from the façade of the Radio and replaced it with one from which the communist emblem had been cut out.

Sleepiness overtook me, and I craved a warm cup of tea, so I decided to go home.

On Sándor Street, I passed a line of burned-out vehicles. On Museum Boulevard, the yellow streetcars stood motionless, some of them lying on their sides. As I turned left onto the boulevard, I caught sight of Russian soldiers standing by a long line of armored cars extending into Kálvin Square. A few steps ahead of me two

Russians were moving a wounded comrade. His knee had been shot straight through and was bandaged. They lifted him up, grabbing him by his arms and legs, and placed him into their armored car.

Just then a civilian walked by. In an apparent effort to "even the score," one of the officers turned around and shot the unarmed civilian in the temple. The man collapsed and rolled around for a few moments. Close to the corner of Museum Street, he stood up, covered his ears with his hands, and began to run. Blood spurted out of his head. He had barely run more than five yards when he fell headlong onto the ground.

Having witnessed this bloody scene, I speedily crossed over to the other side of the boulevard, heading toward Kecskeméti Street. There a stern-faced group of civilians and Hungarian soldiers formed a crowd, watching the Russians on the other side. At the corner of Magyar Street was a group of Hungarian artillerymen, equipped with light mortars, radio trucks, and field guns.

I turned into Váci Street, which was only a short distance from Dimitrov Square where I lived. I reached my apartment a few minutes later. The building was quiet. Its tenants must have gone elsewhere to listen to a foreign broadcast. Radio Budapest was telling its listeners that the uprising had been crushed and urging those still fighting to promptly lay down their arms.

I tried to mentally recapture the events of the previous twenty-four hours. Exhausted, at around nine in the morning I dozed off.

When I awoke, it was dark and an eerie silence enveloped the night. I found a note on my desk left there by my landlady, Mariska Szanyi. It said, "Your mother called, and said that you should go to Mrs. Sárkány's." As Mishi the concierge shuffled out with his keys to let me out of the building, he shook his head disapprovingly and said, "You should not go out tonight."

I walked down Váci Street. The streets felt like a medieval town where everyone had died of the plague. Some of the shop windows were illuminated, there was merchandise on display, but people were nowhere to be seen. As I left Váci Street, the road ahead of me was dark. It might have been as late as 11. There was a curfew, but nobody was patrolling the streets. I was scared and on the verge of turning around and going back, but since I was already at Erzsébet Square, about halfway to my destination, I decided to forge ahead. From the arches of the borough council building stepped out a steel-helmeted soldier. He called out to me, "Comrade, there is a curfew on. Don't you know?" I mumbled something about a sick mother. I tried to avoid Andrássy Avenue in favor of smaller side streets. It was a cloudy, overcast night with no sign of the moon. I headed toward Gorkij Allée, wrapped in the eerie silence. A railroad man walked by me.

"Is it safe to go to the center of the city?" he asked.

"There are Hungarian soldiers at Erzsébet Square," I replied.

"Do you know anything about City Park?"

"Where do you want to go?"

"To Lövölde Square," I said.

"Russian tanks are lining up on Gorkij Allée all the way to György Dózsa Avenue," he said. "You better make a detour."

Since I was almost there, it wouldn't have made much sense to turn around here either. All the streetlights were off here too. I scurried along in the pitch dark in my crepe shoes, staying close to the walls like a rat. The last part of my walk was on Felsőerdősor (Upper Forest Allée), where the Soviet Embassy was located.

The fine mist, the fog, and the darkness became my protectors and travel companions. I stopped at the intersection of Gorkij Allée and Lövölde Square. Along the length of the allée, Russian tanks were lined up like a sleeping herd of elephants. I counted five on the right and five on the left. Their motors were off, but the small red directional lights were on. I took aim between two tanks; the space between them was just enough for me to pass through. While scuttling through the gap, an unpleasant sensation overcame me. Mentally I prepared myself for a soldier to suddenly emerge from the turret and shoot me down. Finally, I reached the other side of the square and the building where Erzsébet lived. I rang the bell for some time, until at last the super came to let me in.

I went to Erzsébet's apartment and knocked on her door, which she promptly opened even though she wasn't expecting any visitors. My mother had already left. She had gone to Aunt Margaret's in Buda.

Erzsébet offered me some tea and we began a long discussion of the events of the day, starting with the toppling of the statue of Stalin. A gentle, subdued yellow light enveloped us, but the stillness of the night was soon disrupted by the sounds of artillery fire coming from the direction of the Károly Róbert Barracks. From the window we could see the muzzle fire of the guns. A steady rattling overtook the silence.

I was awakened from a deep sleep by Erzsébet. Her voice was urgent: "You had better get up. Someone shot at the Russians and the concierge said that the Russians may search our house. You are not a resident here and with the two-day stubble on your face, you look like a revolutionary." I left the house unobserved. The Russian tank soldiers were strolling between their vehicles and the embassy, and nervously gesticulating toward the roofline. Others leaned against their tanks and lit up cigarettes.

On Király Street, the shops were closed. There were no signs of any buses or streetcars, but the boulevards were crowded with people. Now and then a truck would wind its way through the crowd of demonstrators. At the corner of the Astoria Hotel, I bumped into the young man with whom I had sat in the store window earlier that night at the Radio building. We talked about the previous night. "The Radio is still broadcasting," I remarked. "It is," he said, "but they are broadcasting from an unknown location. Allegedly they're at the Cave Hospital on Gellért Mountain" "There are search parties looking for ÁVH troops out there," interjected someone else.

There were continuous discussions going on between complete strangers. Somehow, the idea of a stranger had evaporated. From time to time, Russian tanks crossed the heart of the city, but people didn't let themselves be inconvenienced in their conversations. People gave detailed accounts of what they had witnessed the previous day, surrounded by attentive listeners. All work had stopped; a general strike was announced. The noise of gunfire could be heard from several different directions.

I climbed up onto a slow-moving Russian tank crowded with young Hungarians. Atop the tank, flapping from the turret was our red, white, and green flag. From the others, I learned that the tank was headed for the Parliament. I held onto somebody's shoulder and onto the side of the turret, but as we got closer to the square I grew uneasy. A feeling of captivity came over me, similar to the one I had had in 1945 when I jumped out of the moving Russian truck and saved my wristwatch. When the road turned toward the Parliament I jumped off and continued on foot.

Suddenly, sirens screamed; ambulances sped by on the boulevard. A group of people approached from the direction I was heading. They were promptly surrounded by crowds of people pressing them for news. "It's dreadful," said a woman. "We are just coming from the Parliament."

Then came a recounting of what I would have been a part of had I not jumped off the tank. "As soon as the Russian tanks, bedecked with red, white, and green Hungarian flags thanks to the revolutionaries, arrived at the square, the firing began. The ÁVH was shooting from the attics of the buildings around the square. The people had no way to take cover. The square was full of dead and wounded. Medics didn't dare venture into the midst of the firefight to pick up the wounded who were calling for help. A few people dove down onto the grassy knoll where a subway depot was under construction. They had been gunned down from the houses behind them. Children and women were gunned down too."

It was hard to believe that among these were the very same youngsters who rode to the square on the tanks, and I was almost one of them. A man cut in, "Luckily the Russians shot first at the rooftops, thinking that the ÁVH were revolutionaries, so the ÁVH were the first victims. After that, the ÁVH fired into the crowd."

"How did you get away?" asked a woman.

"We hid behind the tanks. Some people crawled through the basement windows of the Ministry of Agriculture."

The crowd was outraged.

"They're murderers!" a hoarse voice cried out.

I ventured closer to the Parliament, across Nádor Street. Ambulances whizzed by. At the corner of Vécsey Street, a large group of people were looking at the Parliament and the tanks lined up in front of it. The square was stained with blood. The tricolor flags no longer flapped from the Russian tank turrets. The events of the day were later described as the "Massacre at the Parliament." About 150 people had died there.

At the small boulevard on Madács Square, armed students stopped the ambulances. They were rewarded for their suspicion. Instead of wounded, these ambulettes were carrying ammunition and ÁVH officers masquerading as doctors in white coats. At the same time, trucks marked with the flag of the Red Cross hurried by with young doctors and medical students. Doctors worked at first aid stations as if they were on a front line.

I returned home to my room at Dimitrov Square and conversed with the other tenants about these new developments. Most were of the opinion that events had overtaken any controlled design. There was no way to turn back the clock. It had become obvious that the regime had collapsed. No window dressing could rescue or camouflage it. The majority of the people were overcome with joy that this had finally happened, that the uprising they had fervently hoped for for so many years had finally occurred.

The insurgents lay low and slept during the day, and emerged when darkness fell. Under the cover of night, the housetops, the sewers, construction depots, the Corvin Cinema, the Technical University, the Killian Barracks, swarmed with armed young men. In the confusion, the Russians again ended up shooting at one another on Üllői Street and on Gellért Mountain. Hand grenades were tossed from the windows of apartment buildings. Opening the turret of a tank was suicide. As soon as it was opened, a cushion soaked in gasoline would be thrown at it, while from the opposite side of the building a round of machine gun fire would turn the pillows into flaming torches. As these pillows fell into the armored cars they created an instant inferno.

The students of the technical university injected nitroglycerine into raw potatoes, which then became hand grenades. At Széna Square, two young men tied a bunch of hand grenades onto the center of a rope and then positioned themselves on opposite sides of the plaza. As soon as a Russian tank rolled toward them, they pulled the rope in one direction, dropping the bundle of hand grenades dead center in front of the tank.

At Pasarét, two boys used a slingshot. They aimed for a Russian truck driver's eyes as he was coming down a steep slope. He was hit, lost control, and crashed into a wall. At Zsigmond Móricz Circle (formerly Miklós Horthy Circle), children smeared plum jelly onto the windows of tanks, blinding them. Other boys short-circuited the antennas of tanks by tying them together, thus breaking down Soviet communications. Another method of incapacitating the tanks was to wedge iron bars into their treads. As a tank started to move, the tread would fall off the tank, and the tank would end up rotating in place.

A column of Russian tanks set out on Chain Bridge to proceed up to the Castle District. Here, the freedom fighters had another unique method of holding back the onslaught. They poured barrels of liquid soap over the steep incline. As the tanks tried to approach they slid backward into each other. In another street fight, a young girl girdled herself up with a garland of hand grenades and threw herself under a tank. On yet another street, a girl jumped onto a trolley and drove it into a tank.

At Soroksári Road, a night watchman threw a wire up onto the high tension electric line, held onto it with insulated rubber gloves, and lowered the wire onto the turret of the first Russian tank that passed by. The entire tank crew was incinerated. Most of the time, it was enough to disable the first and last tank in a column. The rest would be unable to extricate themselves, at which time young men would be ready for them with Molotov cocktails. At gas stations, long lines of people formed, waiting to fill up empty bottles that were sealed with a cork and covered by a piece of cloth to serve as a fuse. Then off the people went to the nearest fighting. There were burned-out tanks and armored cars all over the streets. Budapest once again looked like a city under siege.

50

Escape to the West

By the time the calendar turned to October 30, the Communist regime had collapsed like the Spanish Armada in 1588. "*Afflavit Deus et dissipati sunt.*" "God blew at them and dispersed them" (at least according to the British). The Radio was no longer transmitting martial messages. The capital breathed freely and waited. Russian troops standing beside their tanks on Lajos Kossuth Street meekly endured the outbursts of Hungarians who shook their fists at them menacingly. A young Russian stood on a truck and offered his rifle to the bystanders. "Leave me alone," he said. "Take my gun. I don't want to fight you." Close by, a tanker was smoking and conversing with people who spoke Russian (at the time studying Russian in school was mandatory). He said, "Last night half our unit switched sides and joined the uprising." Then he added that he was not a communist and that he liked Hungarians. "When our commanding officer ordered us to fire at the 'reactionary bandits,' we told him that the whole city is made up of reactionary bandits." Peering into his tank, we saw the body of one of his comrades.

At the end of the week, a new government had formed under Prime Minister Imre Nagy. The cabinet consisted of representatives of the democratic parties of the last freely elected parliament in 1947. The Russians went about removing their burned-out tanks and armored cars and began to leave Hungary, sending their families away on ships and trains.

On the fourth of November, early in the morning, a proclamation by Imre Nagy was broadcast from Parliament. Nagy informed the nation that a newly arrived Soviet army was on the attack and that he was turning to the free world, the United Nations, to come to Hungary's rescue. This dramatic announcement brought home the realization that the Soviet Union was not about to let Hungary escape its clutches. The glorious short interlude of the Hungarian revolution had come to an end, and another bloodbath would follow.

By Thursday, new Soviet tanks had broken through the cobblestone barricade on the grand boulevard, and by the end of the week the Russians had the upper hand. The ensuing days were filled with heroic, but hopeless, resistance. As a last melancholy act, a man conjured up a *Panzerfaust* (bazooka) he had kept hidden in his pantry since 1945. He went to Margaret Bridge and tried his hand. Lo and behold, the *Panzerfaust* worked and another Russian tank burst into flames.

One evening, my landlady, Aunt Mariska, knocked on my door and told me that the invasion of Hungary by new Russian units had begun at Záhony, the border station with the Soviet Union. This disheartening news gave me the impetus to go and say farewell to my mother in case my decision to leave the country became final.

I called her up and we arranged a rendezvous at the Vörösmarty Square Espresso. We each had a double espresso. Then my mother ordered an apricot brandy and I a *Szatmári szilva* (plum brandy from Szatmár).

As we sat in the cafe sipping our brandy, our minds raced through the past, the present, and the possible future. We didn't say much. There was no need to; we could read each other's thoughts. We weren't sentimental, and we didn't show our feelings. I had no exact date for my departure or plan for how I would achieve it. We both suspected that this would be our last meeting and that perhaps we would never see each other again.

I called up Lali, who was still lodging in the city (since there was no transportation out to Veresegyház), and told him that there was no time to waste—it was time to leave and that he should meet me right away. Lali showed up an hour later in a snazzy new leather coat. While waiting for him, I had run down to the butcher shop on Irányi Street and bought three pounds of lamb chops. There was nothing else there. I changed my shoes, leaving behind my beautiful French shoes from Paris, a gift from Gyuri Sághy. I put on my faithful crepe-soled fellow travelers. I felt that it was essential to have worn-in, comfortable shoes.

As soon as Lali arrived, I pulled off his new leather overcoat. I convinced him that the coat made him look precisely like an ÁVH in civilian clothes. In exchange, I gave him a blue loden winter coat, a gift from Uncle Béla Hilberth in New York. In the back of my mind, I also had the thought that Lali's wife Greti could sell the leather overcoat for a nice sum.

I put on a fur hat instead of my usual Tiroler. Lali also wore a fur hat. I pocketed my new leather-covered Longchamps pipe, another gift from Gyuri, and one monogrammed handkerchief. Then I picked a photograph of Veresegyház up off my desk and put it in my pocket. On leaving, I called out to Aunt Mariska that I was going out to Veresegyház.

I later learned that as soon as we had left, Aunt Mariska had gone into my room and glanced around. Looking at my desk, she realized that the photo of Veresegyház was missing. With her infallible logic, she correctly deduced that I was about to flee the country. Had I been going to Veresegyház, I wouldn't have taken a photo of it along with me.

The previous night, I had looked for Ditta to bid a heartrending goodbye to her, but she hadn't been at home. Before I left, I told her parents that I planned to escape. I asked them to convey my love to their daughter. At that point I was certain that I would

Photo of Veresegyház that I took with me when I left Hungary

never see Ditta again, which only showed that I still didn't know her well enough.

∾

Lali and I walked down the great boulevard toward Nyugati (Western) Railway Station without the slightest notion which direction we should take. We kept walking, guided by our instincts, as if some invisible hand directed our steps. We stopped at Marx Square, formerly Berlin Square (now Nyugati, or Western, Square). We stood before the Tejvendéglő (Milk Bar) and took note of the trucks parked by the curb. The word Tata was written on the side of one of them. That town was a good distance from the capital and lay in the direction of Hungary's western border with Austria. We asked the driver whether he was heading for Tata, and if he would be willing to take us with him. He agreed to give us a ride, instructing us to climb up into the back of the truck, which was covered by a tarp, and to wait for him while he ate his lunch at the Tejvendéglő.

Before we climbed into the truck we went to a liquor store, where we bought one bottle of rum and one bottle of plum brandy. We needed these liquors badly to keep our nerves at bay and to protect us from the chilly weather. (Lali later told everyone that I threw up along the full length of the Austro-Hungarian border, but this I don't recall.)

We climbed into the truck, and within minutes we were on our way. We crossed the Danube over the Margaret Bridge and rode on to Transdanubia on the turnpike leading to Vienna. Before we reached the vicinity of Szentendre, the driver told us to lie flat on the bed of the truck, cover ourselves with rush mats, and remain motionless. At Szentendre, the truck stopped at a checkpoint. Our driver said a few words in Russian, and the truck's canvas coverings flapped up and down while we lay low under the mats. Soon, the motor roared and we sped off, only to stop again a short while later. As we crawled out from under our mats we saw a small group rushing toward the truck. The truck was suddenly jam-packed. A couple took their place to my immediate left. The man carefully covered his wife with a blanket. These people were aware of the roadblock, so they had gone ahead on foot until they felt it was safe to catch a ride. Our whole journey was a spontaneous, disorganized, yet effective, adventure.

It was the fifteenth of November; the days were getting shorter. At Tatabánya, the truck came to a halt. The driver informed us that he was not going any farther and that we had to leave his truck, but another truck would arrive within a half an hour that would take us to Győr. Some of the travelers took off on their own; the majority of us decided to wait. About thirty minutes later, another truck did indeed show up. We boarded the empty truck, again with a tarp over the back, and headed for Győr. By the time we got there, it was pitch dark.

Lali was somehow able to cajole the driver into giving the two of us shelter in his home for the night. He and his wife lived in a tiny cottage and turned their only bed over to us while they settled down in the kitchen and spent the night there on kitchen stools. It was the same arrangement as the one Gyuri and I had had when we made our bicycle tour of Transylvania in the summer of 1943. Then too, we had slept in the teacher's bed while he and his wife spent the night sitting on kitchen stools.

The last days and hours drained us so much that we did not have time to reflect on the events that were occurring in our lives. We were obsessed with the idea of moving on and could think of nothing else.

Our host awoke us before daybreak. A sizable group was now waiting for a ride, and we joined them. At daybreak, a truck rolled into the courtyard. The driver told us to board his open flatbed truck, and said that near the border there would be guides who could walk us over to Austria. We did bump into Russians one more time, but luckily they let the truck go after the chauffer exchanged a few words with them. As it turned out, these Russians had only been interested in a young woman sitting in our midst. The Russians tried to persuade her to get off the truck and join them, but the girl didn't have the slightest inclination of socializing with these sleazy-looking loitering Russians.

We continued on our way for about half an hour, and then the truck stopped. The driver told us that we were in the last village on the Hungarian side of the border and that he couldn't take us any farther. His was a voluntary mission, and none of us thought to offer him any money. There on the spot was a young son of a farmer who quickly made a deal with us. In exchange for guiding the group to Austria, we would give him a bundle of banknotes.

It was a bright day; the sun was shining. We trudged across plowed land on the edge of a forest. We trusted our fate to this young boy, who seemingly didn't do anything else these days other than guide refugees to Austria. On our way, we were enveloped by the colors and smells of fall. It was a reinvigorating walk in the fresh air. We kept a brisk pace and were in good spirits. Here and there, rabbits would run and jump next to us, while crows cawed above.

We reached the canal running along the frontier by the bridge at Andau. Gone were the landmines that had been placed there by the Communists. The barbed wire had been rolled up into large bales. There was no sign of any vicious dogs or border guards. A few Hungarian soldiers sat on the rails of the bridge. They paid no attention to our escape; they only wanted our remaining cash. They told us that we wouldn't have any use for our forints in Austria anyhow (this in fact turned out to be false since there was a lively black market in the Europa coffee house in Vienna). Most of us gave all our money to them. One man even took off his wristwatch and handed it to one of the soldiers.

Lali and I crossed the bridge and glanced at our watches. It was 11:23 in the morning on the sixteenth of November when our feet touched Austrian soil. There had been rumors that the border markers, the flags, had been shifted from their proper places by Hungarian soldiers in order to mislead and trap escapees. I wanted to make sure that we were indeed in Austria, so I approached an Austrian border guard and asked him whether the flags were in the right spots. Laughing, he pointed at the ground behind me and said, *"Dort ist Ungarn"* ("There is Hungary"). Then, pointing at the spot where he stood, he said, *"Und es ist hier schon Oesterreich"* ("And this is already Austria"). On that day the flags were right where they were supposed to be.

Close to the border crossing was the village of Andau. The Red Cross had set up a kitchen for refugees there. Cheerful Austrian damsels cooked sauerkraut mixed with rosy pink dices of pork in large bubbling cauldrons. I stepped into the kitchen, put my bag of three pounds of lamb chops on the table, and proudly announced in German: "I have brought lamb chops from Budapest for the poor starving Austrians." The ladies broke out in uproarious laughter. We ate a so-called *Eintopfgericht,* meaning a one-plate meal—but not the type that the Nazis served during the war. (At the beginning of the Second World War they would make it once a week, but soon this starvation diet became a daily occurrence.) Our *Eintopfgericht* at Andau was a concoction of sauerkraut, vegetable broth, beans, potatoes, and beautiful pink pork.

Shortly after we finished our meal, a group of tractors arrived, and we clambered up onto them in a makeshift arrangement. The tractors took us into the town of Neusiedl, where a school had been set up to shelter the ever-enlarging crowd of *ungarische Flüchtlinge* (Hungarian refugees). Straw was spread out on the classroom floors as our sleeping accommodations. We spent a night there. The next morning school buses took us to Eisenstadt (Kismarton), and then finally to Traiskirchen, a large complex of military barracks. These were old remnants of the Austro-Hungarian Empire, reopened for the large number of Hungarian, Czech, and other refugees.

By now, Lali and I had had enough of these makeshift lagers, or camps. Knowing that my mother's cousin János Lauringer (whom we called Janika, or Little John) was working at Radio Free Europe in Vienna, I went to the camp office and asked for permission to call Janika. I let Janika know that I was here, and asked him to have RFE broadcast the message, "The bicycle-rickshaw driver has arrived." RFE was constantly broadcasting the newly arrived refugees' messages, frequently in a disguised manner. Those who had stayed behind in Hungary could listen and be reassured that their loved ones had made it across the border once they heard the message they were waiting for on the radio.

An hour later, Janika arrived at the camp in an RFE car, checked out Lali and me, and drove us to his nice cozy apartment at 10 Peter Jordan Strasse. There, sipping Orange Pekoe tea and dining on smoked bacon and toast spread with marmalade, we felt as if we were in Abraham's bosom.

At ten in the evening, there was a knock on the door. Annelise, Janika's landlady and a friend of Aunt Blanka's, let two Sághy boys in. There he was—my best friend since high school, Gyuri, and his younger brother Lajos. We had an extremely joyous reunion.

My stay in Vienna was unforgettable. The first half of our Viennese jaunt was defined by Gyuri Sághy's presence. We tried to catch up on events in our lives over the eight years since we had last seen one another.

On November 26, to celebrate my thirty-first birthday, Gyuri took me to the Rondo restaurant under the Opern Passage, the subterranean crossing under the opera. He treated me to Wiener Schnitzel and red wine.

While I was in Vienna musing about my future, I was unaware that my father had written these words in his diary during the siege: "Károly should go to the United States. There, with his pluck, diligence, and guts he could go far." In the end, I followed the path that my father had envisioned for me.

On Christmas Eve, Janika and I went to midnight mass at St. Stephen's Cathedral. Lali stayed home, allegedly to practice his German—but knowing Lali it was more likely to give him a chance to flirt with Annelise. Annelise was a long-time widow and quite good looking. Before we went to church, she had invited all of us over to light her Christmas tree. There we had stood: Annelise, her two young daughters, her brother Wolfgang, Janika, Lali, and I. It felt strange to be in the midst of a carefree and joyful Christmas with an Austrian family. As I watched them celebrate, I couldn't help but think, "What kind of a Christmas are my mother and Blanka having? How could they possibly feel joy while thinking that we might never see each other again?" My only solace was that my mother knew that by escaping I had gained a chance to live a life of purpose. Had I remained in Hungary, I would have almost certainly been thrown into prison on account of my presence at the storming of the Radio.

The script of life choreographed yet another surprise for me. A few days after the Sághy brothers returned to Paris, Lali and I went to the Viennese police headquarters to obtain the so-called Grey Card. This card enabled *ungarische Flüchtlinge* (Hungarian refugees) to use public transportation without charge and to apply for a weekly sum of schillings from the *Fürsorgeamt* (Office for the Needy). Since the number of escapees was growing day by day, there was a long line of Hungarians snaking around the building.

When we were fairly close to the entrance, we suddenly caught sight of Ditta. She was strolling nonchalantly toward us in an elegant Swedish fur coat and a new dress, neatly perked up and coiffed. We were all overjoyed to see one another (Lali also knew Ditta well from her visits to Veresegyház). Hurriedly, we created a spot for her in front of us, which generated a loud outburst of indignation from our countrymen. We responded that we had been holding this spot for the lady. But our problems had just begun. Each person in the section of the line where we were standing, close to the entrance, had already received a number. Now we were there with two numbers for three people. We ended up juggling the two numbers between the three of us. As Lali went into one room, one of us gave the number to him. Then when he came out to go to the next room, he handed his number over to me or to Ditta. The three of us ran between the rooms alternately handing over or reclaiming one of the two numbers. Luckily, we weren't caught, and all three of us were able to get our cherished Grey Cards at the same time. With the cards, we trudged over to the *Fürsorgeamt*, where we received a decent amount of cash for the week.

I listened in total disbelief to Ditta's account of her decision to escape. She told me that once she had heard that I had left Hungary, she told her parents, "If Károly left, then one must follow suit." She reasoned that if I, who was so attached to our land in Veresegyház, was not going to stay, I must deem the situation completely hopeless. She found a group of people with whom to cross the border. At one of the camps for refugees, a well-to-do Austrian businessman picked her out and took her to his home.

Lali, Ditta, and I took the opportunity one day to make a lively jaunt to Salzburg to visit Aunt Hansi, Uncle Rory's widow. Soon, Ditta would leave for New Zealand and Lali and I for New York. Ditta had received a free airline ticket to Auckland from one of her mother's former suitors, a rich New Zealander.

Before her final farewell, all of us set out for a last dinner, at the *Rathauskeller*, behind St. Stephen's Cathedral, which had a cozy ambiance. A small *schrammli*, orchestra or tavern band, played in the background. As usual, we were treated to dinner by Janika.

It was a bittersweet evening, filled with joy and quiet misgivings. After dinner, Lali walked over to the little *schrammel* trio, a tavern band comprising a cymbalist, an accordion player, and a violinist. He took the fiddle out of the violinist's hands and began to play, quite respectfully and with great feeling, "*Csak Egy Kislány Van a Világon*" ("There Is Only One Girl in the World"). Without missing a beat, the cymbalist and accordion player began to follow him. This was the first time in my life (and the last) that I heard Lali play the violin. I was touched on a number of levels. In those days we were full of emotions. The previous weeks, the escape, the impressions of a new world, expectations of a new life, weighed heavily on our shoulders. It was a great emotional load. Without being sentimental, we were full of sentiment. When it came time for Ditta to go to the airport, we embraced each other, suppressing our tears.

Then, Lali and I went to the U.S. Embassy to follow up on our visa and travel requirements. On December 31, the last day of 1956, we boarded a long train and set out from Austria for Germany. We stopped over in Ulm, where two boys and a girl got off the train to quickly visit the cathedral. On their way back, they were late and missed our train, but a few hours later we were overtaken by a locomotive carrying the three lost travelers.

During our train ride, Éva and Peter Weszely became our traveling companions and from then on friends for a lifetime. Éva Weszely was an extremely pretty, intelligent lady and a close friend of Kata Nadasdy Szabó.

At certain stations, the train would stop and Red Cross volunteers would serve us hot chocolate and *Kaisersemmels*, or Emperor Rolls.

An uneventful journey on the night of New Year's Eve took us closer to the New World, which we were sure would be full of promise. We finally arrived at Bremerhaven on the sea.

51

Journey to the New World on the U.S.N.S. *Marine Carp*

A round the turn of the twentieth century, when Horace Greeley was urging young Americans, "Go West, young man," young Hungarians were being urged to go to sea. This was during the time of the Austro-Hungarian Empire, when Hungary had a seaport in Fiume (presently Rijeka) on the Adriatic Sea. Now it was our generation's turn to go to sea.

On January 1, our train arrived at Bremerhaven. Two ships were waiting there for Hungarian refugees. One was the U.S.N.S. *Marine Carp*, a troop carrier for the U.S. Navy. It was a fourteen-thousand ton ship that had last served during the Korean War (We later learned that this ship had been earmarked for target practice; that's the kind of shape it was in). This faithful old man-of-war became home for 1,725 of us for the next two weeks. We left the train and boarded the ship. Families were broken up. Women and children were given a separate section in the center of the ship. Péter Weszely, Pali Szabó, Lali, the Teleki boys, and I were assigned to the hull of the ship, F4. My future brother-in-law András Németh was also in F4.

Shortly after we settled into our assigned places, military discipline took the upper hand. Loudspeakers informed us of the rules. We learned that it was forbidden to fly-fish for seagulls (trying to catch seagulls with fishhooks) or to organize impromptu concerts in the staircase. Before we set out to sea, a young couple was caught lovemaking. Since they were not married, the American military officers sent them back to Vienna.

Next, a military orchestra arrived at the pier in Bremerhaven. All of its members were black, a novelty for us. As our ship pulled

U.S.N.S. *Marine Carp*

up its anchors, the musicians took out their sheet music and began to play the Hungarian anthem in a somewhat bluesy fashion. Once the travelers recognized the tune they ran to the starboard side facing the harbor, climbed up on every elevated point, and waved toward the dry land with tears in their eyes. The salt from our tears mixed with the salty mist of the sea. We must have been quite a sight to see. As we stood there teary-eyed, a strange voice came over the loudspeakers and instructed us to disperse evenly, lest the ship capsize right there in the harbor.

I left the side of the ship and went to the forecastle, where I began to accustom myself to the gentle swinging of the sea. This section of the boat was the most exposed to extreme buffeting. I looked upon this as the best training against seasickness. The weather was gorgeous; the mood among us swung from somber to elated. The Navy's Military Police was in charge. Captain Mortensen, of Norwegian descent, invited the ladies to his table for dinner. As the last chords of the Hungarian anthem faded into the distance, we left Europe behind and inched away toward the "New World."

Hungarians are by and large "land rats;" they are not seafaring people. The Columbus-like maritime emigration knocked out the majority of the travelers. Previous shiploads of Hungarians had arrived in abysmal shape, with many passengers carried off boats on stretchers. Consequently, a telegram had been sent from Washington to Captain Mortensen, instructing him to sail toward the Azores islands and from there to turn toward New York, in order to avoid as many as possible of the devastating cyclones that raged in the sea in January. Thus, our voyage had two phases. The first was a beautiful cruise in bright sunshine with a relatively calm sea; the second was a journey through the zone of cyclones.

One morning János Vámossy saw an elderly Hungarian standing by the ship's railing looking down at the sea with a forlorn, sorrowful expression. He approached the gloomy gent and said, "Don't be so sad. In a few months the homesickness will pass." "Ach," answered the man, "I'm not worried about being homesick. I'm sad because I just threw up my teeth into the sea. I came up on deck, hoping that some fresh air would do me good, but the smell of bacon and eggs billowing through the funnel only amplified my seasickness."

I figured out that it was wisest to eat but not to overfill my stomach. Some youngsters still had good appetites in spite of the risk involved. They scouted out the kosher kitchen, which allegedly served a better variety of food, and began to frequent that mess hall. But there was a problem; they needed a hat to enter. They went to János Vámossy to borrow his hat, a rare possession among the refugees. His hat thus ended up in constant circulation around mealtimes.

We were entertained with movies in the hull of the ship. Once, I was watching a war movie with Pali Szabó and he became outraged (in a tongue-in-cheek way) that the storm scene in the movie was not synchronized with the live storm that we were experiencing. It was a war movie that took place in the Pacific Ocean.

After the movies, Pali played the piano upstairs in the "recreation room." János Vámossy and the Hankovszky brothers played bridge. The guitar players organized impromptu concerts. Lali, the Teleki boys, and I practiced English. As we strolled up and down the deck, we practiced American idioms, sprinkled with expressions like "as usual," which we tried to insert into every sentence. I had bought a small paperback for eight schillings in Vienna entitled *English through Pictures*. It contained stick-figure drawings with phrases beside them, like, "May I please have a cup of tea." I thought it was the most ingenious tool for learning English. I used it so much that it eventually fell to pieces. Janika had advised us to read the war memoirs of Winston Churchill and the novels of Somerset Maugham. In his view, they were the greatest cultivators of the English language.

At the time, both of these giants were still alive. I followed Janika's advice, especially since I had previously read in Hungarian practically everything that Somerset Maugham had written, so the stories were familiar to me.

The Daily Barnacle, the ship's journal, made its first appearance on January 6, the Day of Epiphany. Its name derived from the little sea snails that attached themselves to the hull of the ship and got a free ride. They had to be removed periodically to prevent damage to the body of the ship. I read in the book of a French astrologer that the most advantageous time to scrape off these little pests was when the moon was waning.

Our dear *Marine Carp* brought us safely to the New World, and served her country well. Not long after fulfilling her final day of transporting thousands of Hungarian refugees, she went to sleep in an everlasting dream with her sister ships at the bottom of the sea.

While we were sailing over by ship, refugees were also being airlifted, mostly women and children. The planes took a route from Salzburg to Munich, and then on to the Azores islands for refueling. From there, they flew to Newfoundland, and finally to New York. These U.S. Air Force airplanes were also on the last legs of their useful lives. One of them started out with all four engines functioning, but by the time it reached New York it was down to two. Another landed in New York with one of its engines in flames.

While the airlift droned away above the ocean, our faithful old *Marine Carp* sliced the waves, gobbling up the miles. As we approached the Azores islands, the sky was blue; the January air was brisk and invigorating. Our ship had a following of about a dozen dolphins, who eagerly awaited various delicacies thrown overboard by the sailors. Between the ship's two funnels, on a small platform, an impromptu choir formed and sang in rounds, in canon. There, the choir was sheltered against the wind and kept somewhat warm by the heat from the funnels. Our religious escorts of various denominations and a lady representative of the Red Cross were delighted to hear the performance. They had never before heard a Hungarian folk song in three-part harmony. The translation of it in English would be:

> I caught a mosquito.
> It was bigger than a horse.
> I fried its fat.
> It weighed more than a ton.

Whoever believes this
is a greater ass
than a horse.

The first half of our journey was relatively smooth sailing,
though it was not like cruising on the Danube. By the second half
of our trip, however, we were constantly on the lookout for squalls.
During our meals in the mess hall, we were amused by how in a
split second a pewter water pitcher or a milk container could slide
back and forth on the table. We almost never had to ask someone to
pass it. While shaving, we had to coordinate the movements of our
hands with the waves. Even going to the bathroom required some
skill. One had to move along with the toilet seat in order to stay put.

While our group took a constitutional stroll on the deck and
practiced speaking English, Kata Szabó received lessons from the
military police on how to conjure a bottle of Coke out of a vending
machine. By the railing, an elderly man in a streetcar driver's uniform and a young lady were having a chat. They had both been born
in Cleveland, so they were U.S. citizens. Somehow they had gotten
stuck in Hungary, and had had to wait years before they could see
the United States again.

It took our ship about a week to reach the Azores islands. The
weather was still beautiful. At midday one could sunbathe on the
deck.

Among the multitude of refugees, I bumped into a father of
four, a jeweler by profession. I learned that he had also been deported
to Hunya, where he had befriended Berti Roediger. The two of them
had lengthy discussions about war, history, and politics. This man
had been doubly persecuted. First, as a Jew in 1944, he was deported
to Mauthausen. After surviving that, under the Communist regime
in 1951, he and his family had been deported to Hunya. These two
involuntary journeys were enough to make him leave Hungary the
first chance he could. As he sarcastically remarked, "The last thing
I need is a third forced relocation."

As we left the Azores, we spotted another ship, not just any ship
but one with the hammer and sickle painted in red on its funnel.
In all likelihood, its cargo was an import of grain, even though the
Soviet Union was supposedly self-sufficient in everything. Now the
ship, with its hated emblem, made us see red. In an instant, a "Revolutionary Council" was formed. The council elected a directorate

of three that was sent as a delegation to Captain Mortensen. They asked the captain for nothing less than to turn himself, the military police, and his ship over to the protective custody of the newly formed "Revolutionary Council.." He was also to grant permission to activate the ship's guns and to fire on the Russian vessel. Captain Mortensen's response was that while he was completely sympathetic to our feelings, his instructions would not allow him to be party to a diplomatic incident.

We were bowed but not beaten. Since we weren't satisfied with Captain Mortensen's reply, the committee decided to organize a "peaceful" demonstration. We decided that when our ship came alongside the Russian freighter, all of the passengers would move to the side of the ship facing the Soviets, lean over the guard rails, and yell, "*Job tvoju maty!*" an obscenity (telling them to have sexual intercourse with their mothers) that we had learned from the Russians. We would have to be satisfied with a verbal onslaught instead of a physical exchange.

Once we had the spiritual satisfaction of accomplishing our mission, we turned our attention to the weather. There were rumors of an approaching storm. Pali Szabó went to Captain Mortensen to inquire how likely it was that we would get caught in a cyclone. He was not only gathering information but also practicing his English on the sly. With a sublime air, Captain Mortensen answered, "There's not even a breeze." Hardly had he finished his sentence when he lurched forward and slid full-length across the twenty-foot-long deck in front of a perplexed Pali. After this episode, all of the doors were locked from the outside so that no one would be swept overboard. Fortunately, we were already rapidly approaching our destination: Brooklyn, New York.

Our group in F4 kept hearing the rumbling play of the waves next to our heads. Our nerves were on edge. An empty Coca-Cola bottle rolled up and down and from one side to the other until a few outraged voices shouted, "Catch that damn bottle for heaven's sake!" A volunteer then climbed under the beds and arrested the culprit. Before we had been ordered inside, we could see the ship's propeller spinning in the air every time a tidal wave lifted the boat's stern. The deck had become unsafe. Even a young freedom fighter we had dubbed "Captain Nemo," who had been so seasick that he had remained on deck between the two funnels even overnight, was now forced to leave his favorite spot and join us down below. He was wrapped in blankets and covered from head to toe with soot that belched out of the funnels. He resembled the statue "Anonymous" in Budapest's City Park of King Bela IV's notary, a huddled-over, hooded man. In his case, the statue would have been called "Seasick Man."

Darkness fell as our ship arrived at the navy shipyard in Brooklyn. With feelings of sadness and nostalgia, we said goodbye to the *Marine Carp*. We were offered employment on the ship as cooks, dishwashers, or stokers for four hundred dollars a month along with room and board, but since my friends didn't take the offer, I declined as well. I was reluctant to be separated from my little gang and from Lali.

Camp Kilmer, New Jersey, was my launching pad in the United States. It promised a new beginning. We arrived at the camp on the sixteenth of January, 1957, were assigned to barracks, and then taken to the mess hall.

For the first few days, our group stayed together. János Bacsák, a friend of the Nádasdy family, visited us. He was the first person to give us a realistic, intelligent, and gloomy briefing regarding what we would face in the United States.

"Every taste, every smell, every sound, every color is going to be an attack on your nervous system. It will take you some time to get used to it. When you do, you will also finally be able to put your hand in your pocket and distinguish whether you have a penny, a dime, a nickel, or a quarter in your hand."

We spent a couple of nights at Camp Kilmer's refugee barracks, and afterward countless others in New York.

Epilogue

My loyal reader may rightfully have asked, "And what happened next?" I became part of a new Hungarian diaspora. The new life I began after docking in Brooklyn was entirely different from the previous one in all respects. For each of us, it was an existential endeavor, an emotional trauma, and carried with it different ambitions, careers, and luck (karma!). Our steady wonderment was mixed with utter disbelief.

Many of the refugees wanted to return—not to Communist Hungary, but to a country that now existed only in our imaginations. We had been picked up by a tornado, dropped down, met with the Wizard, and dreamed about going back. I yearned for a vineyard, a winery in Burgenland, Austria (close to Hungary, but on the other side of the Iron Curtain). Others plunged passionately into forging new careers. We all wanted to learn to speak English as quickly as possible.

The cognoscenti wrote that this Hungarian exodus surpassed any that had come before. As Harrison Salisbury wrote in the *New York Times*, never in the history of the United States had so many people from one ethnic group, with such high intellectual status and education—not to mention enterprising spirit, stamina, and dedication—arrived at the same time. We were all willing to jump into the melting pot without knowing whether there was any liquid in the cauldron.

At the outset, we looked to our fellow landsmen for company. In those early days, we liked to practice American clichés. On the weekends, we went to Long Pond Inn in Putnam County, New York. We fondly called the body of water there "Hungarian Lake," thereby glorifying the duck pond. We swam, flirted, threw darts, and drank.

In the evenings, we crowded into Old John's tavern (John, the owner, looked like the Big Bad Wolf). Here, Pali Szabó, half-naked with a towel on his head, hit the piano and we gyrated like wild dervishes to the tune of "Sweet Georgia Brown."

The more we drank, the more lively things became. The more Pali drank, the better he played. We were a rowdy bunch. Some of us slunk out into the parking lot to take a swig of Gallo's Light Dry Muscat from the trunks of our cars. Others stuck with the ten-year-old applejack served at the bar.

Old John (who was a secret bookie; he once showed me his telephones and radios with which he practiced his bookmaking activities) shared with me his puzzlement about us: "You are such interesting people, intelligent characters with strange rituals. I notice that every evening you drink a lot, laugh boisterously, sing, and dance. The mood is highly elevated, the music is wild; you folks are partying it up. Then suddenly the place becomes eerily quiet. Without any sign, everyone clams up, stops talking, stops laughing. Pali doesn't hit the keys anymore and everyone leaves."

Our lives began to unfold in different directions. After a while, some observed that we were not entirely Hungarian any longer; we were slowly becoming American.

~

The rest is yet to come.